THE EPISTEMOLOGICAL SIGNIFICANCE OF THE INTERROGATIVE

ASHGATE NEW CRITICAL THINKING IN PHILOSOPHY

The *Ashgate New Critical Thinking in Philosophy* series aims to bring high quality research monograph publishing back into focus for authors, the international library market, and student, academic and research readers. Headed by an international editorial advisory board of acclaimed scholars from across the philosophical spectrum, this new monograph series presents cutting-edge research from established as well as exciting new authors in the field; spans the breadth of philosophy and related disciplinary and interdisciplinary perspectives; and takes contemporary philosophical research into new directions and debate.

Other Titles in the Series:

Matter, Imagination and Geometry
Dmitri Nikulin
Textual Narratives and a New Metaphysics
Raymond T. Shorthouse
Hume's Scepticism and the Science of Human Nature
Paul Stanistreet
Communities of Individuals
Michael J. R. Cross
Hegel's Metaphysics of God
Patricia Marie Calton

The Epistemological Significance of the Interrogative

JAMES SOMERVILLE
Department of Philosophy, The University of Hull

Routledge
Taylor & Francis Group
LONDON AND NEW YORK

First published 2002 by Ashgate Publishing

Reissued 2018 by Routledge
2 Park Square, Milton Park, Abingdon, Oxon OX14 4RN
711 Third Avenue, New York, NY 10017, USA

Routledge is an imprint of the Taylor & Francis Group, an informa business

A Library of Congress record exists under LC control number: 2002022508

ISBN 13: 978-1-138-72759-5 (hbk)
ISBN 13: 978-1-138-72757-1 (pbk)
ISBN 13: 978-1-315-19028-0 (ebk)

Contents

Preface

The epistemological significance of the interrogative is revealed in the interrogative clauses following *know* and other verbs attributing knowledge to their subjects — knowing *who*, *what*, *where*, *whether*, and so forth. The problem of how to account for such clauses is posed in the first section of Chapter 1.

The book divides broadly into three. The first three chapters are concerned with scene setting, presenting some of the crucial arguments and justifying the approach adopted. The next four chapters each deal with specific areas in need of clarification because of prevalent views about questions. The last two chapters analyse the logical form of questions and logical relationships between types of question.

From the perspective of so-called theories of questions the approach is unorthodox. What may be called the Aristotelian approach is followed. In general it has regard to the context thoughts are expressed in but specifically gives primacy to conceiving things interrogatively. Such a conceptual approach to logic rivals the Fregean tradition later theorists of questions are reliant on — even if they do not always acknowledge their debt. But a broader approach to the interrogative than a symbolic or formal one is required to draw out the lessons for epistemology.

The Introduction (Chapter 1) begins with the argument that the occurrence of interrogative clauses after *know* shows that knowledge in particular and thought in general can be interrogative in form. Reid's suggestion is then taken up that questions, while hitherto neglected by philosophers, are as suitable objects for logical study as propositions are. It is noted that Reid nevertheless confines questions to a social use of language — what may be called the speech-act fallacy. The third section outlines the general features of propositional, as distinct from interrogative, forms of thought. The three main types of question are then described and their manner of formation in language reviewed. The final section briefly comments on stock philosophical approaches to questions.

Chapter 2 is concerned to highlight some remarkable features of interrogative clauses. First a list of the kinds of interrogative clause and of the verbs and phrases governing them is given. The second section draws attention to the unique feature of what is dubbed the opaqueness of questions and interrogative clauses, their inability to say anything at all. Building on the finding of the previous chapter that interrogative clauses utilise an interrogative form of thought in abstraction from people actually asking or answering questions, the third section moves towards the concept of what answers a question — what people aim to elicit in asking a question, but also what interrogative clauses following *know* succeed in doing. It is argued in the fourth section that a consequence of thought taking interrogative form is that concepts too can be interrogative in form, and a sketch is given of how interrogative concepts structure thought generally. A final section briefly surveys non-indicative grammatical forms other than interrogative.

The aim of Chapter 3 is to challenge the feeling that questions must have something to do with knowledge — more particularly, the acquisition of knowledge in enquiry. The overall argument of the book is that things are the other way round: it is not that questions are concerned with knowledge; instead, knowledge can be thought of in relation to a notional question. The characteristics of enquiry in general are approached, with the help of a famous passage from Plato's *Meno*, through consideration of the peculiarities of philosophical enquiry. The first section considers the philosopher's question, *What is a question?* The second argues against a questing model for questions, insisting on the distinction between asking questions in the course of enquiry and asking questions as such. Two further models, each of which aims to abstract questions as objects of logical attention from the asking of questions whether or not during enquiry, are found in the next two sections to fail: the first, the *quæsitum* model, because confusion between finding what is to be sought and finding out returns to the idea of enquiry; the second, the matching model, because it requires a direct as distinct from a relative notion of what answers a question so as to judge that it matches the question, contrary to the opaqueness of a question's specification of what is required to answer it.

Chapter 4 starts by reviewing Reid's doctrine that asking questions is a social intellectual operation. The distinction between the asking of a question and the question asked is reinforced by the denial that a question must be addressed to somebody, even if only oneself. It is argued that as an object of logical attention a question can be abstracted from any acts of asking it. Accordingly, the view of idealist philosophers like Collingwood that questions are tied to acts of asking is rejected, as also the more recent assumption that asking a question is necessarily to perform a speech-act. While questions must be capable of formulation in language, there is no requirement that questions be put to anybody.

Chapter 5 prepares the way for the chapter on interrogation, the putting of questions to others. Austin's doctrine of explicit performatives is subsumed under Reid's four social intellectual operations. The notion of a presumption is then introduced, and the presumption underlying the answering of questions, as also the making of statements generally, is stated. The presumption, which also governs the giving of testimony, is that one is in a position to know to be so what one tells others.

Chapter 6 begins by considering the part played in conversational interchange by interrogation. The presumption underlying interrogation is then stated and dubbed (after Reichenbach) the cognitive correlate of interrogation. The third section considers more specific enquiries interrogators may pursue: enquiries involving the corroboration or refutation of previously given testimony, enquiries into the extent of others' knowledge or the authenticity of their opinions, and tests of their knowledge and understanding. The next section exposes confusions in accounts which attempt to reduce interrogative to imperative sentences. The final section explains some idioms as resulting from the cognitive correlate of interrogation.

The analysis in Chapter 7 of the neglected notion of a request is modelled on Hume's distinction of a promise from either a resolution, a desire or an act of will (*Treatise*, III ii 5: third paragraph). The function of requests is seen to differentiate them from commands. The distinction from invitations is also noted. It is argued that since requests can be conveyed to third parties, requests cannot always be expressed by imperative sentences. Their genuine interrogative character is accordingly defended. The last two sections reveal the confusions, and also circularity, involved in the definition of a question as a request for information.

The analysis of interrogative form required to account for the interrogative clauses following *know* is presented in Chapter 8. The first section concedes that questions have sometimes been accorded the status of objects of logical attention distinct from the asking of them; but counters that the 'question' referred to in talk of asking a question simply reserves a place for some interrogative clause following *ask*, just as the 'proposition' in talk of asserting propositions reserves a place for either a clause introduced by *that* or a complete declarative sentence standing alone. It is then argued that a question always asks something, so there is no interrogative counterpart to an unasserted proposition. The notion that questions are suppositions and therefore unasserted is an old-fashioned view which might not be suspected to lie behind Frege's account of yes-no questions. The third section of the chapter aims to show otherwise. Frege declined to analyse word questions; but his brief comment on them as being incomplete has given rise to the quantification analysis, which is rejected in the second section. The fourth section contains the analysis of interrogative form, and articulates the principle of interrogative opaqueness. When applied to questions, the principle amounts to a denial that a question can contain its conformable answers. The application of the principle to interrogative clauses which answer questions is made in the final section.

A chance to follow up some previous remarks about questions — in other words, to tie up some loose ends — is taken in Chapter 9. Topics covered include: - Hare's view that multiple-choice reformulations of questions provide an analysis of interrogative form; the distinction between *what* and *which* questions; an explanation how yes-no questions can be worded as alternative questions and both as *which* questions; questions that require identification of their subjects; and focused questions. But the chapter serves a deeper purpose. It aims to exemplify the Aristotelian approach to logic and to develop it so as to apply to the conception of questions themselves. Hence the attention given to Whately and Cook Wilson. It is concluded that notwithstanding the logical differences between the main types of question, questions have an overall unity in their interrogative form.

What was originally intended to be a final section on logical issues more conventionally treated is placed in an appendix. The logical study of questions themselves is distinguished from erotetic logic, the logic of the asking of questions, part of the applied logic of debate and enquiry. The term *erotetic* is thus returned to the sense employed by Whately rather than serving as the arch variant introduced by the Priors for the plain *interrogative.*

The Epilogue reviews some of the salient findings of the book and looks forward to the development of an interrogative approach to epistemology.

The method of exposition of interrogative form employed is mainly analytical, the method of enquiry. A brief account employing the synthetical method is contained in the first part of 'Time and Interrogative Logical Form', *Philosophy*, Vol. 76 (2001), pp. 55-75. What in the notes to the article is referred to as section iv of Chapter 9 of this book is now the Appendix.

From the above description of contents it will be apparent that there is a lot on questions. The philosopher of logic will find in Chapter 2 a description of the logical features of interrogative clauses; in Chapter 8 an analysis, not hitherto given, of the unique logical form of questions; in Chapters 1, 8 and 9 criticism of standard analyses of yes-no, alternative and word questions; in Chapter 3 an attack on the very enterprise of devising a theory of questions; and in Chapters 1, 2, 3, 8 and 9 criticism of the whole approach of theorists to questions. But the conceptual approach to logic employed throughout (and especially in Chapters 2 and 9) has implications beyond questions. For the propositional is being conceived in relation to a notional question, and such a notional context for a proposition suggests, as is mentioned in Chapter 9, that not all logical distinctions may be capable of being captured — or at least easily — by logical symbolism.

There is not only something for the philosopher of logic. The philosopher of language will find in Chapters 1, 2 and 4 in the rejection of the speech-act fallacy in logic an account of the relationship of logic to the philosophy of language; in Chapters 1, 4 and 5 an account of the relationship of Reid's doctrine of social intellectual acts to Austin's doctrines of performative utterances and explicit performatives; in Chapters 4, 5, 6 and 7 other observations on the social uses of language; and throughout several points about idiomatic usage.

The epistemologist will find in Chapters 1 and 2 warnings against intellectualism, the error of supposing that only those who articulate their knowledge in propositions that are the contents of beliefs can be held truly to know — parallel to the error in logic of supposing that propositions concern truth or falsity rather than states of affairs (including states of affairs of being true or false). But also in Chapter 3 an account of the conditions of enquiry; in Chapters 5 and 6 of the connection between making statements and knowledge; and in Chapters 4, 5 and 6 several observations about testimony. In the end it must be admitted that the work is a mere prolegomenon to a more thorough exploration of an interrogative approach to epistemology that is argued for.

Since abridged versions of some sections of the first eight chapters were submitted as a PhD thesis in August, 1998 under the same title, acknowledgments are due to Mr David Murray, appointed first as University of London adviser for the thesis, and to his successor, Dr Keith G. Hossack; and to the examiners, Dr Gabriel M. A. Segal of King's College London and Mr Bede Rundle of Trinity College, Oxford, whose vigorous probing during the examination, and report, proved helpful in identifying areas needing more consideration during the final revision of the complete book from October, 2000 to February, 2001.

Chapter 1

Introduction

Interrogative Clauses Following *Know*

When Austin condemned as 'barbarous' the expression *He knows his pain in a way we can't*, he argued that *I know what he is feeling* means *I know the answer to the question 'What is he feeling?'* The *what*, he pointed out, is not a relative but 'an interrogative (Latin *quid*, not *quod*)' pronoun.[1] 'No one before Austin, it is fair to say', John Passmore observes, 'has ever illuminated such a topic by means of so nice a grammatical point'.[2] The failure in the main of epistemologists previously to take note of the interrogative clauses following *know* is more astonishing than the paucity of those who have subsequently taken at least some notice of them. One exception is Ryle, who, a few months earlier, had complained that philosophers 'have not done justice to the distinction which is quite familiar to all of us between knowing that something is the case and knowing how to do things'.[3]

Although Ryle's paper aroused some interest in the interrogative clauses taken by *know* — it may, indeed, have prompted Austin's remarks — his notion of 'knowing how' is narrower in two respects. First, the interrogative construction with *how* selected by Ryle is only one among others: one can also speak of knowing *what* to do, besides knowing *where*, *when*, *to whom*, *whether*, and so forth, to do it. Second, these constructions are not simply interrogative but also infinitive in accordance with Ryle's evident concern with what may be called practical knowledge, knowledge bearing on action. At the end of his paper Ryle indeed suggests some link between knowledge generally and the answering of questions when he argues that even knowing *that* should encompass knowing 'how to answer particular questions' since it 'involves knowing how to use that knowledge'. Yet in his book, in his desire to 'correct' what he calls 'the intellectualist doctrine' — which misconstrues exercises of the intellect as 'the apprehension of truths' — he takes 'finding the answers to questions' to 'constitute theorizing', 'the knowledge of true propositions or facts' or 'knowledge of truths'.[4] He noted, however, that besides *know*, other verbs such as *learn* and *find out* take the same *how to* construction, whereas *believe* cannot.[5]

It looks as if Ryle were distinguishing between, on the one hand, knowing how to answer particular questions, which might be thought generally to comprise a piece of practical knowledge, or knowing how to solve problems,[6] which clearly comprises specific pieces of practical knowledge, and, on the other, finding the answers to questions, the aim of 'theorizing' whose successful outcome is the knowledge of truths. There would thus be some difference for Ryle between Austin's 'knowing the answer to the question' and his own 'knowing how to answer' the question. Both phrases, however, employ interrogative constructions. For 'knowing the answer to the question' is to be construed as being elliptical for knowing what — occasionally which — the answer to the question is.

Somebody might know how to answer a particular question without being asked that question and thus without being put to the test of having to say what the answer to it is. But somebody who knows what the answer to the question is should be able to say what the answer to it is when called upon to do so. Now, the answer to a question is supplied by a word or phrase. If one knows how to answer a question, one will know what to say in answer to it — know what word or phrase to give in answer to it, which is to know what word or phrase supplies the answer to it. But to know what word or phrase supplies the answer to a question is to know what the answer to it is. Any contrast between a piece of practical knowledge and the knowledge of truths, the aim of 'theorizing', then, cannot turn on any difference between knowing how to answer a question and knowing what the answer to it is, for there is no difference.

Yet when one knows how to answer a question, or — what amounts to the same thing — knows what the answer to it is, one knows that what some word or phrase, taken in the light of the question, says is so is true, which is the knowledge of a truth falling, in Ryle's view, within the province of the aim of 'theorizing'. Thus, although people might often know generally what others are feeling, or know how to do something, without necessarily knowing that some word or phrase when given in answer to a question says truly that something is so, they could not know what the answer to a question is without thereby knowing that some word or phrase when given in answer to the question says truly that something is so. If intellectualism is taken — admittedly more narrowly than it is by Ryle — as the position that all knowledge is 'the apprehension of truths', then knowing what the answer to a question is in requiring such a knowledge of truths bears out intellectualism. For knowing what the answer to a question is requires being able to say what the answer to it is, which requires knowing what word or phrase supplies the answer, which in turn involves knowing that what the word or phrase, taken in the context of the question, says is so is true. What promised to be a fresh start in epistemology has only led back to intellectualism, taken for granted by most epistemologists — namely, that all knowledge is the knowledge of truths.[7]

The objection to intellectualism that arises here is illustrated by the knowledge possessed by non-human animals. Cows and sheep undeniably see, smell and hear what or where things around them are; but to see, smell or hear what or where things are is to know what or where they are. A cat knows when it is usually fed, a dog knows who is at the door; they are thus certainly capable of factual knowledge, if not the knowledge of truths. Even an account restricted to human knowledge has to accommodate such rudimentary instances of knowing, since human beings are not constantly exercising their intellectual powers but share many of their life-depending accomplishments with their non-human fellow animals. Like the cat, I unthinkingly and unerringly home in on the 'fridge door when I feel need of sustenance.

What has gone wrong with Ryle's talk of knowing how to answer particular questions? Though intended to deflate some kind of intellectualist doctrine, it has unwittingly only reinforced it. Some exercise of the intellect is needed for both asking and answering questions: in particular, the ability to understand and speak a language. It might be open to doubt whether persons really did know how to answer a question if they never actually said what the answer to it is. Ryle, indeed, appears to qualify his previous position that knowing *that* requires knowing how to answer various questions when he later observes: 'Not all knowing is knowing what to say.'[8] Cats and dogs do not give the slightest indication of knowing how to answer any questions, because since they cannot speak they cannot say what the answer to any question is, or even understand what an answer says. But they do know where things are, when regular occurrences take place, whether their human keepers are pleased or displeased with them, and so forth. Some other account of the interrogative clauses taken by *know* is required: the gloss on them as knowing how to answer questions, or knowing what the answers to questions are, must be flawed.

The flaw involved can easily be seen by considering again Austin's formulation. It contains a reduplication of interrogative clauses, disguised by the partial ellipsis of one of them. *Knowing what he is feeling* is presented as being equivalent to *knowing the answer to the question 'What is he feeling?'* — an ellipsis for *knowing what the answer to the question 'What is he feeling?' is*. The *what* now occurs twice in the formulation; which is accordingly open to the challenge that, if it were adequate, *knowing what the answer to the question ' ... ?' is* ought to be expandable as *knowing what the answer to the question 'What is the answer to the question " ... ?"' is*. And so on. The interrogative clause can be no more eliminated than the allusion to the question. The accounts offered by Austin and Ryle only presuppose rather than explain the interrogative clauses taken by *know*.

Austin's general point was that the verb *know* only exceptionally takes a direct object. It is more usually followed by a clause; and he draws attention to the interrogative clauses that often follow it. His point is not invalidated by the convenient way of speaking of knowing, believing or doubting 'a thing'. Somebody might respond to another's remark that something is so with *I doubt it*. The 'thing' here that is known, believed or doubted, is only a stand-in for some clause. Similarly, to ask a question, to ask 'something', is to ask what is expressed by an interrogative clause. Hence the rather contrived examples philosophers come up with of *know* followed by a relative *what* as distinct from an interrogative *what* tend to obfuscate the point Austin was making.[9]

To take an earlier instance, Reid speaks of a child's act of asking a question presupposing 'a desire to know what he asks'.[10] Unless he has forgotten, the child will know what he asks (the interrogative *what*); but Reid evidently means the *what* to be a relative — that is, desires to know 'the thing which' he asks. The 'thing' here is a proxy for an interrogative clause, such as asking where the cat is; so what the child desires to know here, Reid supposes, is where the cat is. The formulation 'a desire to know what he asks' on either interpretation of the *what* presupposes rather than explains the interrogative clauses taken by *know*: the first directly, the second because the relative *what* only stands in for some interrogative clause which complements the verb *ask*.

It was seen that those credited with knowledge characterised by an interrogative clause need not in virtue of exhibiting their knowledge, let alone in virtue of possessing it, answer a question. Indeed, if they have not the use of language they will be quite incapable of saying what the answer to any question is. It follows that there need not have been any question put to them or even asked by anybody. Consequently, interrogative clauses taken by verbs conveying knowledge need not express a question either actually asked by anybody or actually answered by those credited with the knowledge. How, then, is the allusion by these clauses to a question to be accounted for? Although speakers readily avail themselves of this facility afforded by language without feeling any disquiet, having had one's attention drawn to it one might on reflection find it puzzling: how does knowing come to be associated with questions? The exact nature of the association requires examination.

If the actual asking or answering of a question in some language by some person must be excluded in accounting for these interrogative clauses, the only explanation is that the question alluded to by such clauses somehow serves as a way of conceiving the knowledge. For when the asking and the answering of questions by persons are put to one side, all that remains is the thought expressed by the clause — a thought abstracted from the thought of anybody's asking or answering the question alluded to in the clause. When knowledge is characterised by an interrogative clause it is being conceived through an allusion to a question, even although no question may have been asked or answered by anybody so that no words need have been uttered by anybody. Accordingly, the wider term *interrogative* is appropriate for this way of conceiving knowledge: the knowledge is being conceived by means of the interrogative.

The epistemological significance of the interrogative lies in the interrogative clauses, ignored by most epistemologists, taken by *know* and other verbs conveying knowledge. An adequate account of these clauses will establish the general relevance of the interrogative to epistemology. They invoke an interrogative, not a propositional, conception of knowledge.

Now, there is a minimal and a non-minimal way of taking both propositional and interrogative characterisations of knowledge. The knowledge credited to non-human animals no more consists in an ability of theirs to judge that what various propositions say is true than it consists in an ability of theirs to answer various questions; for lacking the use of language, they possess neither ability. Yet their knowledge can be conceived by others crediting the knowledge — that is, by human beings generally, including epistemologists — both propositionally and interrogatively. Knowledge can be characterised in a minimal way as propositional or interrogative merely in the conception of others and not necessarily also by those in possession of it. For one can know without forming a conception of one's knowledge; without reflecting that one knows, on one's knowing, or on one's knowledge. Knowledge characterisable in a non-minimal way as propositional or interrogative, by contrast, requires in addition that those who are held to know conceive it thus too; and accordingly, to have the use of language. For it is either knowing that what some proposition says is so is true or else knowing what the answer to some question is. But knowing what the answer to some question is, it was seen, comes down to knowing a truth, knowing that what some proposition says is true.

The error in what Austin says about knowing the answer to a question and Ryle about knowing how to answer a question, consists simply in their taking all interrogative characterisations of knowledge in a non-minimal way. Identifying their error, however, still leaves the allusion to a question by interrogative clauses governed by verbs conveying knowledge to be accounted for.

Now, both the thought expressed in a question and the thought expressed by these interrogative clauses have an obvious affinity. Indeed, the thoughts share the same form. But such clauses show that this interrogative form is not confined to the asking or answering of questions; they show that thought itself must be capable of taking an interrogative form. Hence the interrogative is foremost a form of thought, a way of conceiving things. The key, then, to accounting for the interrogative clauses taken by *know* is the interrogative, the form of thought expressed equally in questions and by interrogative clauses generally. But the form taken by thought is a matter of logic; for the logical form taken by an expression of a thought expresses the form of that thought. So, the logical form of questions and of interrogative clauses generally reflects the form of the thought they express. Thought must be capable of being expressed interrogatively as well as propositionally.

A full explanation of how interrogative clauses following verbs conveying knowledge utilise interrogative logical form will not emerge until the end of Chapter 8. An account of the logical features of interrogative form generally, besides criticism of traditional misconceptions of it, will be presented in the same chapter. But in view of more pervasive misconceptions about questions what needs to be argued before then is that the interrogative indeed constitutes a form of thought having application beyond the asking or answering of questions; more especially, that the interrogative does not pertain solely to the asking questions of others — that is, to interrogation — but falls within the province of logic, not just the more specialised domain of the philosophy of language.

What makes it difficult often to think of the interrogative as extending beyond a merely social use of language is that questions and their answers have to be expressed in language. But the same applies to the propositional. Logic as a whole concerns highly general features of and relationships between thoughts, which must then be expressed in some language in order to display their features and relationships. Not having language, non-human animals are equally incapable of understanding logic. But if the features of and relationships between thoughts, which are the concern of logic, are to be laid bare, they must be abstracted from the more specific thoughts exhibiting them. The difficulty experienced by many philosophers with questions seems to be in judging the level of abstraction appropriate: they seem unable to conceive the interrogative in abstraction from the thought of somebody asking or answering some question on some occasion. But the interrogative clauses taken by *know* require them to do so.

The Traditional Neglect of Questions

Because the predominant philosophical accounts of knowledge have been exclusively propositional, the significance for epistemology of the availability of interrogative characterisations of knowledge remains virtually unexplored. Whereas some philosophers, notably Plato, have set knowledge in stark opposition to belief, others have barely been able to conceive that there could be knowledge without any accompanying belief. But whenever knowledge is compared with, or indeed opposed to, belief it is being confined to knowing *that*; for the verb *believe* cannot take interrogative constructions, and direct object constructions after *believe* and *know* are too unrelated in sense to bear comparison.

Little regard has been paid to the interrogative clauses taken by *know* not simply because the whole field of questions has also tended to be neglected. What accounts of questions have been offered fail to recognise their distinctive interrogative logical form. A satisfactory account of these interrogative clauses will therefore also provide the basis of a satisfactory account of questions, since both exhibit interrogative logical form.

In view of the frequent occurrence of the very word *question* in the writings of philosophers — as well as other terms bearing interrogative import, such as *issue*, *problem*, *difficulty*, *puzzle* and *enquiry* — their omission to explore the field expressly is surprising; especially since in the twentieth century they have reflected on their own experience of the practice of philosophy, insisting on, in Moore's words, 'clearness as to the meaning of the question asked',[11] and so have recognised the peculiarity of philosophical questions. Their silence is the more remiss in so far as a variety of questions and problems can be thought to comprise the very subject-matter of philosophy.

The lack of interest by philosophers in the notion of a question was observed long ago by Reid. After distinguishing between what he calls the social and the solitary intellectual operations of the mind, Reid writes: -

> In every language, a question, a command, a promise, which are social acts, can be expressed as easily and as properly as judgment, which is a solitary act. The expression of the last has been honoured with a particular name; it is called a proposition; it has been an object of great attention to philosophers; … . The expression of a question, of a command, or a promise, is as capable of being analysed as a proposition is; but we do not find that this has been attempted; we have not so much as given them a name different from the operations which they express.[12]

Elsewhere Reid took Aristotle to task for neglecting non-propositional forms of speech: -

> He observes justly, that, besides that kind of speech called a *proposition*, which is always either true or false, there are other kinds which are neither true nor false; such as, a prayer, or wish; to which we may add, a question, a command, a promise, a contract, and many others. These Aristotle pronounces to have nothing to do with his subject, and remits them to oratory, or poetry; and so they have remained banished from the regions of philosophy to this day: yet I apprehend, that an analysis of such speeches, and of the operations of mind which they express, would be of real use, and perhaps would discover how imperfect an enumeration the logicians have given of the powers of human understanding, when they reduce them to simple apprehension, judgment, and reasoning.[13]

As an illustration of the attitude deplored by Reid, when Hobbes comes to discuss propositions in his treatment of logic, he introduces the subject thus: -

> In philosophy, there is but one kind of speech useful, which some call in Latin *dictum*, others *enunciatum et pronunciatum*; but most men call it *proposition*, and is the speech of those that affirm or deny, and expresseth truth or falsity.[14]

Reid adds that a problem, though called a proposition in mathematics, in logic 'is not a proposition: it is one of those speeches which are not enunciative, and which Aristotle remits to oratory or poetry'.[15] The remark reveals that Reid recognised that a problem is conceived interrogatively, not propositionally. A problem is a task expressed in relation to a question: *how*, *what*, *when*, and so forth *to* … . Thus, there are hints in Reid that the interrogative comprises a distinctive logical form. 'Not all problems are questions,' Ryle declares;[16] but while not all problems may happen to be posed by anybody or set for anybody, all problems are conceived in relation to a question. The statement of what a problem, or indeed, a question is may be accurate or otherwise; but the problem or question itself is not capable of stating anything.

Reid may have been made aware of the logical importance of questions owing to the influence of his mathematician uncle, James Gregory, who, as Reid relates, published a thesis printed at Edinburgh in 1690 containing the argument that 'there neither are nor can be more than two categories, viz. Data and Quæsita'.[17] The objection to such a scheme, it might be thought, is that the classification is superficial, being merely relative to what happened to be given or what was still to be sought for by a particular investigator. Reid's scorn, however, is directed on the claim that such a division is exhaustive. Ryle in a similar vein condemns 'the belief in some decalogue of categories' as 'Scholasticism'.[18] Reid further takes the thesis as exemplifying Bacon's *idola specus*, 'prejudices which have their origin ... from something peculiar to the individual' — here what is of interest only to a mathematical frame of mind. The so-called theories of questions devised in the twentieth century usually exhibit the same tendency. But Gregory's division suggests a distinction between what can be taken as being so and what can only be a subject for investigation; and in turn, between the type of thought expressed in a proposition and the type of thought expressed in a question. So although *data* and *quæsita* are implausible candidates for categories of being, the proposal that they mark fundamental abstract logical forms, and so categories of thought, merits more serious consideration.

Reid is maintaining, then, that a question, a command or a promise is each as worthy of the attention of philosophers as a proposition is. One indication, he adds, of the failure to provide analyses of questions, commands and promises is that whereas philosophers have given the name *proposition* for the expression of judgment, no special names have been introduced for the expression of the social intellectual operations of asking questions, issuing commands and making promises.

Here the main inadequacy in Reid's conception of a question is betrayed. For while it is plausible to think that the implication of his view that 'promises cannot exist without being expressed' accords with Austin's performative account of promising,[19] and something similar might be said of issuing commands too, there is nothing intrinsically social about asking a question. Admittedly, questions are frequently, even usually, put to others; but questions can also simply occur in thought. Philosophical questions typically have no addressee. So once the distinction between social and solitary intellectual acts of mind is seen to be unconnected with the difference between asking questions and passing judgments, it can further be seen that what philosophers have failed to attend to is not the social act of asking others questions but what, in accordance with his talk of mental acts, Reid regards as the objects of this type of act — that is, questions themselves.

That Reid himself really thinks that the contrast is between a question and a proposition, rather than an act of asking a question and an act of judging, is seen from his writing the 'expression of a question, of a command, or of a promise', not the 'expression of an act of asking a question, of the act of issuing a command, or of the act of making a promise'. He even writes 'a question, a command, a promise, which are social acts can be expressed as easily and as properly as judgment, which is a solitary act'. It is he himself, oddly, who has 'not so much given them a name different from the operations they express'. For while his argument suggests that a question is as distinguishable from the asking of a question as a proposition is from the judging that something is (or is not) so, the noun *question*, unlike *judgment*, is not constantly but only rarely also used in a verbal sense for the asking of questions;[20] instead the word *questioning* is available. If one is to begin to be clear about questions, one must first distinguish the asking of a question from the question asked.

Questions for Reid are essentially bound up with a social use of language and cannot be considered in isolation from the addressing of words to others. Such a view implies, contrary to what Reid apparently intended, that questions are appropriately dealt with by the philosopher of language alone rather than primarily requiring the attention of the logician. For Reid's notion of a social intellectual operation of the mind is virtually the notion of what has come to be known as a speech-act. Speakers usually, though not invariably, address their words to others; and when they do, they perform what Austin called a speech-act. Writers too sometimes address their words to others, though often the words they write simply constitute a record for their own purposes. But since the written merely does duty for the spoken word, the term *speaker* when used of the authors of speech-acts should be understood to include on occasions some writers as well.

The assumption that questions must always be put to others will be called the speech-act fallacy about questions, part of a wider misconception of what logic studies. It assumes that one cannot ask a question without thereby asking somebody the question. Such an approach to questions is incapable of providing any account of the interrogative clauses taken by verbs attributing knowledge, and so cannot serve to establish the epistemological significance of the interrogative. For although these clauses allude to a question, there is no implication that any question has been put to anybody. Admittedly, the term *interrogative*, deriving from the verb *interrogate*, originally pertained to the putting of questions to others. But by metonymy the term has come mainly to connote what pertains to questions themselves, whether put to others or those one asks, as the idiom goes, only of 'oneself'. Now, interrogative characterisations of knowledge require that thought be interrogative in form. But the form taken by thought is a matter of logic; not merely of a social use of language, which introduces extra-logical considerations. What lies outside logic, regardless of its intrinsic interest, is thus irrelevant to the examination of the form of thought exhibited by interrogative clauses following *know*.

The Propositional and the Interrogative

The propositional needs to be delineated before the interrogative can be distinguished from it.

A proposition is traditionally defined as what is capable of being either true or false. Hobbes observed: '*True* and *False* are attributes of Speech, not of Things;' but his addition that 'where Speech is not, there is neither *Truth* nor *Falshood*' is misleading — as also his previous remarks that 'truth, and a true proposition, is all one' and that 'falsity and a false proposition being the same thing'.[21] While truth and the truth are what true propositions set forth, it is only a truth which could be assimilated to a true proposition. And although a falsehood may be said to be a false proposition, falsity, like truth or the truth, is rather to do with what propositions express. Moreover, the concept of the truth is distinct from the concept of truth: there is no parallel in any talk of 'the falsity'; one tells the truth or else one tells a falsehood.

The notion of a proposition is a mere abstraction from the notion of people's thinking, supposing, judging, believing, asserting, stating, and so forth, *that* ... ;[22] the proposition being what completes the clause introduced by *that*. An abstraction is something purely notional, conceived apart from the thoughts of other things it is in reality inseparable from. Besides being expressible by a clause introduced by *that* or a clause equivalent in meaning, such as the accusative and infinitive construction permissible after some verbs, a proposition is also expressed by a complete declarative sentence. For the utterance or composition of a declarative sentence standardly carries with it the implication that its author asserts that what it expresses is so — that is, in the absence of any device, such as quotation marks, indicating, as R. M. Hare puts it, 'non-subscription'.[23] Propositions, then, cannot be conceived apart from the possibility of their expression in language, and to this extent Hobbes is right to link being true or false to speech and not things, states of affairs or facts.

Care must be taken if unintended implications of talking about propositions are to be circumvented. There is a suspicion that those who protest that propositions are not objects are simply confusing the notion of an object, which is a relative notion, with the notion of a thing, which is not. Nevertheless, at its clearest the notion of an object is derived from grammar, what is a direct object of a verb. Yet whether whatever a verb governs, including a clause, is best thought of as an object is debatable. More debatable still is whether the *what* some mental or linguistic act or mental state is directed to is best described as an object. Talk of objects of knowledge may be sanctioned by philosophical tradition, but is clarity served by speaking of what is expressed by a clause as an object?

As will become apparent in the first section of Chapter 8, logicians speak of a proposition as being asserted, by contrast with being merely supposed or entertained, rather than the *that* ... which is asserted, supposed or entertained. But this talk of propositions has to be understood as referring to nothing more than the *that* ... asserted, stated, judged or supposed; not to something, 'the proposition', over and above the *that* ... , which just is the assertion, statement, judgment or supposition. A proposition is a thinkable or a sayable, what is expressible by the *that* ... whenever anybody actually thinks (whether judges or merely supposes) or says *that* ... . There is no 'object' of the thinking or saying other than in the sense of the clause introduced by *that* formulating the thought or saying. Again, to speak of believing, or the belief, *that* ... or, as Ryle has it, 'the knowledge of true propositions', is to refer only to the *that* ... believed or the *that* ... known to be true; there is no additional thing, 'the proposition', accompanying the belief or the piece of knowledge.[24] Finally, it should not be supposed that (as in the last example) propositions as such say that something is true — though some propositions may happen to do so if they say that some other proposition is true. Instead, propositions as such concern states of affairs, and say that such states of affairs do or do not obtain; that is, say that something is or is not so.

The characterisation of knowledge as knowing *that* involves the wider notion of the propositional as distinct from that of a proposition *tout court*. The notion of the propositional extends the notion of a proposition as the *that* ... thought or said in two ways.

First, while only persons can undoubtedly be said to think *that* ... , words, sentences, clauses and propositions, besides persons, can in a derivative sense be said to say *that* ... . When a belief or a piece of knowledge is specified as the belief or the knowledge *that* ... , the clause which follows can, by an abstraction of thought, be conceived as itself saying *that* ... . The clause may thus be described as propositional in form. To characterise knowledge as knowing *that* is to conceive it propositionally. That is, the form of the thought whereby the knowledge is conceived is propositional; just as a clause introduced by *that* is propositional in form, the grammatical structure of language mirroring the logical structure of thought. Remarkably, it has been seen, knowledge can be conceived propositionally as knowing *that* even though some of those credited with knowing *that*, such as non-human animals, have neither thought nor said *that* ... .

Secondly, not just clauses introduced by *that* but many other clauses, besides phrases and single terms — falling within the class of what linguists call 'nominalisations' — can also be construed as saying *that* ... , even if only implicitly or elliptically. They too may be classed as propositional in form. *His death was sudden* says that he died suddenly. *The man who was at the door laughed* says that there was a man at the door and that he laughed. Sometimes what would be said by a paraphrasing sentence is not that something is, was or will be so — that is, said indicatively — but another mood of the verb or a modal auxiliary verb would be used instead. *Precautions against fraud will be taken* says that action will be taken lest fraud occur. *The elimination of poverty is desirable but impossible* says that it is desirable but impossible that poverty should be eliminated. All such sayings by such sentences can, despite the modal uses of their verbs, be construed as sayings *that* ... , and thus are propositional in form.

Knowledge can be conceived propositionally, and sentences or clauses which say things are propositional in form, because the form of thought employed in such a conception of knowledge, and expressed by such sentences or clauses, is propositional. Thought here refers not to the taking or giving of thought — minding or 'the activity of reflecting'[25] — but to thoughts either thought or thought of. Now, logic has to do with the form and structure of thoughts, not of the thinking of these thoughts. Thoughts are often thought during the course of pondering or reflecting, besides daydreaming or idle musing, but also while engaged in actions or activities demanding thought in the sense of giving mind or paying heed to actions, things, events, processes, situations, and so forth. People, things, events, processes, states of affairs, facts, truths, numbers, and so forth are obviously not themselves thoughts; rather they are what people's thoughts are about or of. But then people, things, events, processes, states of affairs, facts, truths and numbers, cannot themselves be thought, only thought of.

Since a proposition expresses the thought *that* ... , it can itself be thought as distinct from thought of. It is thus a thinkable besides a sayable. Thoughts are propositional in form when they are thoughts *that* ... . Henry Hiz denies that a question expresses thought, 'because it is an expression of suspended thought, of lack of judgment'.[26] But not all thoughts are judgments *that* ... , or even thoughts *that* ... . One thinks: *Where is the minister?* besides: *The minister is over there*. So thought can also be interrogative in form and not just propositional. It will emerge that people, things, events, facts, and so forth can also be thought of interrogatively besides propositionally.

Thinking a thought — as distinct from thinking of something, having a thought of it — requires having thoughts of what are usually not themselves thoughts: thoughts of people, things, events, facts, and so forth; what the thought is about, its subject. Thoughts themselves may even occasionally be thought of; here they themselves are made the subject of thought, the thought being about lower-level thoughts. But usually thinking thoughts involves structuring thoughts of what are not themselves thought *tout court* into a thought which is thought *tout court*, not simply thought of. The resultant thought is propositional or interrogative in form depending on the way the thoughts of things are structured into a whole which is thought as distinct from thought of.

Knowledge, whether characterised propositionally or interrogatively, can frequently be safely attributed to non-human animals. In general knowledge can be attributed minimally, solely on the basis of competent performance, besides non-minimally on the basis of intelligent discourse too. Thoughts, whether propositional or interrogative in form, can be unquestionably attributed only to those who have the use of language. In so far as it is conceivable to attribute thoughts to non-human animals, albeit with much anthropomorphism, it is rather when their behaviour evidences their failures as yet to learn. The dog barking up the wrong tree might be imagined as entertaining a false thought; and still more fancifully, hesitation or an inability to initiate any responsive action might be supposed to give expression to interrogative thoughts of doubt or perplexity. But a mistaken dog does not judge, not even wrongly; nor does a nonplussed cat think: *What to do next?* Just as the dog cannot articulate any belief, so the cat cannot specify what is required to answer a question.

Essential to interrogative form, it will emerge, is the facility of specifying in some way what has yet to be further specified. But while striving or seeking activity by a person might be sufficient evidence of the occurrence of such interrogative thoughts — as *How to do such-and-such?* or *Where is it?* — the asking of questions, even in thought, can scarcely be ascribed to non-human animals, which have no use of language.

Now, a question cannot sensibly be said to be either true or false. Hence it follows from the definition of a proposition that the thought expressed in a question cannot be propositional in form. So a question cannot be conceived propositionally, nor can any interrogative clause taken by itself. Accordingly, unlike what is propositional in form, questions and interrogative clauses cannot themselves say that anything is so. Instead, they exhibit interrogative form. When people utter an interrogative sentence they doubtless in one sense say something — that is, utter words; but the interrogative sentence they utter cannot itself say *that* ... . Indeed, the distinctiveness of interrogative forms of thought, it will emerge, just lies in their complete incapacity to say anything at all: whereas a proposition is a thinkable by being a sayable, a question is instead a thinkable by being an askable; and an interrogative clause in general is a thinkable by being either an askable or an answerable.

Types of Questions and their Formation

There are three main types of question. The distinctions will be considered at greater length in Chapters 8 and 9.

First, there are what are nowadays called 'yes-or-no questions', commonly abbreviated to 'yes-no questions', which, as the label indicates, usually admit *Yes* or *No* as answers to them. Sometimes a slightly fuller, often more emphatic, answer may be given, whether with or without *Yes* or *No*: as *(Yes,) She is* or *(No,) He isn't*. Answers can also sometimes be qualified: as *Probably* or *Certainly not*; *(Yes,) Very much* or *(No,) Not at all*.[27] In answer to a question *Yes* indicates affirmation and *No* denial, what is being affirmed or denied being gathered from the question. The yes-no question, *Are whales fishes?* is distinct from the (false) proposition, *Whales are fishes*, since no question is capable of being true or false; but to answer the question by *Yes* is to affirm that whales are fishes, and by *No* to deny that whales are fishes. In answering a yes-no question one is normally committing oneself to an assertion — that is, either an affirmation or a denial. Those who answer *Yes* (or *They are*) to the question, *Are whales fishes?* have not expressly asserted that whales are fishes. Yet they can fairly be reported as having done so and are held to that assertion; for this answer, taken with the question, yields the proposition, *Whales are fishes*. Thus, while answers to yes-no questions are not themselves propositions, or indeed assertions, nor ellipses of any proposition or assertion taken in isolation from the question, to give them in earnest is normally to be held to assert that something is or is not so.

Secondly, there are questions making use of specific interrogative words, such as *who*, *what*, *which*, *how*, *why*, and so forth, called by Frege 'word questions' (*Wortfragen*) and by linguistic theorists *wh*-questions, the Old English consonant *hw*, the origin of the smoother modern English consonant *wh*, being the counterpart to the Latin consonant *qv* (*qu*).[28]

These labels are more perspicuous than the terms *general* and *special* or *content* which have also been used for the distinction between these two main types of question. Of course, *how* does not have the *wh* consonant, and is not pronounced even like *who*, let alone like *what* or *where*; nor do all the interrogative words in Latin start with *qu*. More seriously, to speak of *wh*-questions would let in the interrogative conjunction *whether*, which, because in its interrogative use it is used to introduce interrogative clauses alluding to yes-no questions, should not be classified along with *who*, *what*, *why*, and so forth. The same objection might be brought against the description, 'word question'; since the description is vague enough to apply to the interrogative conjunctions *if* and *whether*. Though obviously based on the question, one might instead apply the classification to the sort of answers admissible, thus bringing it into line with the first label, 'yes-no questions'. That is, answers admissible to the second type of question are supplied by a word or phrase — strictly, one of the terms of the proposition which can, when taken with the question, be constructed from the answer. The answer *The milkman* offered in answer to the question *Who is at the door?* is a term of the proposition *The milkman is at the door*.

In answering any question, it should be noted, respondents do not normally explicitly state the *that* ... they commit themselves to; though they might if what they said the first time round was not heard properly. They are nevertheless held to such an assertion. Respondents generally state expressly and in full the assertion they are held to in answering a question only when it is important that there be no misunderstanding, as in the formal examination of the testimony of witnesses, or where there is some risk of mishearing as when speaking on a poor radio link. And even here the full statement serves merely to clarify the way answering would normally be done.

This feature of ordinary language, that all questions are normally answered by a single word (*Yes* or *No*) or an abbreviation which is only intelligible when taken in the context of the question it is in answer to (*Yes, they are*; *They are not*) or a term (*The milkman*), is not merely a result of streamlining of conversational interchange. It reflects a logical feature of interrogative form: answers to questions borrow their form from the form (type) of question they are given in answer to, so that they cannot be fully understood in isolation from the questions they are answers to. In short, questions determine the form of any answers to them; it is not, as theorists of questions suppose, that answers to questions determine the form of a question. So, while to give an answer to a question is normally to be held to an assertion, an answer to a question, as abstracted from an answer given by somebody, is usually supplied by a word, phrase or term, not as such by a proposition.[29]

It is misleading to say, as Ferenc Kiefer does, that 'an answer turns a question into a proposition'.[30] As questions cannot be either true or false, whereas propositions are defined as what are capable of being either true or false, neither can be 'turned into' the other. Rather, a question enables an answer to it to be turned — or rather, expanded — into a proposition. That is, a question determines how an answer to it can be expanded to yield a proposition, which might then, and only then, be considered in isolation from the question — by contrast with such an answer itself, which must always be understood in the light of the question it is an answer to.

Renford Bambrough speaks of 'cases where the answer to a question takes a different form ... from what the form of' the 'question seems to require', adding that 'an unexpected form of answer is still an answer'.[31] It is more fruitful, however, to distinguish answers people give to questions from some reply or response in general they may make. That is, to restrict the term *answer* to what bears some logical relation to the question — namely, to the notion of something that conforms to the form of a question, the form of answer admissible by the question. For while a question itself is incapable of saying anything, let alone saying anything true or false, it presupposes that something is so — or not so, sometimes — which is the presupposition of the question. Now, the presupposition of a question is determined by the form of the question in that for the question to ask what it asks, what the presupposition says has to be understood — even although it has not (usually) been expressly asserted. Change the form of the question, and its presupposition changes; but the converse is beside the point because the presupposition of a question, being merely a presupposition and not as such an independent assertion, is never considered in isolation from the question. So conceived, interrogative presupposition is a purely logical notion turning on the form of the question, distinct from what is suggested or implied by the meaning of the terms comprising the subject of a question, still more from what is suggested or implied by speakers in any speech situation. But further, interrogative presupposition is distinct from logical implication or entailment; since the *relata* in those relationships have to be capable of being either true or false; whereas with interrogative presupposition a question, which has no truth-value, stands in a logical relation to a proposition which is its presupposition.

The presupposition of a question in turn determines the form of what answers it can admit, though without determining any particular answer to it. In this way there is a logical relationship between question and answer generally; whereas the relationship between a question and any particular answer to it is governed by considerations lying outside the question itself, such as the truth, the facts of the case and states of affairs generally. There is a distinction, then, between an answer given by somebody to a question, from which a conformable or an admissible answer to the question can be abstracted, and some reply or response in general to a question — which might instead challenge the justification for asking the question on the grounds that its presupposition is false or doubtful; or be a confession of ignorance of the answer.

The third main type of question comprises what are often called alternative questions like *Is she coming or going?* There can, indeed, be more than just two items listed in the question as in *Was he wearing the white shirt, the blue shirt or the green shirt?* Conformable answers are supplied by an item; that is, respondents in mentioning an item are held to be asserting that the item obtains. The presupposition of such questions, as determined by their form, standardly dictates that just one of the items listed obtains, so that the *or* in the question has to be taken as exclusive. Such a presupposition justifies, where there are more than two items listed in the question, the use of the term *alternative* rather than *possibility*; for if one item does not obtain, it is standardly presupposed by an alternative question that one other item from the list obtains instead. Respondents who show that they do not accept this presupposition by making the reply, *Both* or *The white and the green one*, are, as distinct from giving a conformable answer, challenging the appropriateness of asking the question[32] — as they also do by replying *Neither* or *None (of them)*. But sometimes, which explains the qualification 'standardly' above, admissibility of taking the disjunction as inclusive is made explicit as an alternative in its own right,[33] as in *Is the vehicle used for business or social purposes, or both?*

A conformable answer to an alternative question may incidentally be given by a proposition, as when the alternatives itemised in the question are states of affairs, including events or actions, so that answering that one of them obtains happens to yield a proposition, as in *Was the pilot flying the aircraft or was the autopilot engaged?* But even then a respondent might well answer *The former* or *The latter*. Such an answer is actually the name of a state of affairs, event or action, not as such a proposition. Yes-no questions likewise usually concern states of affairs, events, actions and the like, and only sometimes concern the truth or falsity as such of a proposition, as when the question is specifically whether some proposition expressly mentioned is true or false.

It is often held that yes-no questions are to be taken as special cases of alternative questions. Theorists often lump the two types of question together under some such title as *whether* questions.[34] Thus, *Did she go?* is taken to be elliptical for *Did she go or did she not go?* making it resemble in form *Is she coming or going?* Now, a yes-no question can indeed occasionally be rephrased as an alternative question; that is, contradictories can be explicitly itemised in a question for potential respondents to mention one of them in giving their answer, rather than, as in a yes-no question proper, as alternatives only presupposed by the question as being logically exclusive. A yes-no question proper mentions only one of the contradictory alternatives, even although the presupposition of the question is that either this alternative or its contradictory obtains — in the example, that either she went or she did not go. So since only one of the pair of contradictories is mentioned in a yes-no question proper, yes-no questions are not simply a species of alternative questions. And since the presupposition of a yes-no question is true in virtue of its logical form alone, whereas the presupposition of an alternative question, if indeed true, need not be true even in virtue of the meaning of the terms alone — she might be standing still rather than either coming or going — yes-no questions are clearly more fundamental logically than alternative questions in always having a logical truth as their presupposition. By contrast, some alternative questions might have quite contentious, perhaps false, presuppositions.

Dwight Bolinger has argued that yes-no questions, as distinct from alternative questions, serve to elicit a respondent's confirmation of the one alternative mentioned rather than being neutral between contradictories, and moreover, show a preference for *if* over *whether* in the introduction of interrogative clauses in indirect constructions.[35] To ask *Did she go or did she not go?* rather than simply *Did she go?* would be to hector; still more to ask *Did she go: Yes or No?* And asking whether or not she went is, it appears, a more detached, speculative question than simply asking if she went — a much more everyday question. Now, the presupposition of a yes-no question is that one of a pair of contradictories obtains; the presupposition of an alternative question, by contrast, is that one of two or more mutually exclusive — not necessarily logically exclusive — alternatives obtains. Therein lies the logical difference between them. So there is no logical requirement to dress up a plain yes-no question as an alternative question: instead, there is only some extra-logical reason why in some conversational situations one might mention both of the contradictories.

Language has various subtle distinctions for the different purposes speakers may have in asking questions — especially of others — and for the different expectations they may entertain about how these questions should be answered; but these distinctions are irrelevant from a logical perspective. For instance, negative yes-no questions tend the speaker's expectation on the side of a negative answer; they are, as linguists say, 'conducive' as distinct from neutral between an affirmative and a negative answer. Such factors have no logical significance, however, since an affirmative or a negative answer are equally admissible logically as unqualified answers to negative yes-no questions.

English used to distinguish *Yea* and *Nay* as answers to the positive question from *Yes* and *No*, which were originally confined to the negative version of the question; but *Yes* being also an emphatic alternative to *Yea* eventually supplanted it. That such a distinction is logically dispensable is shown by modern speakers of the language not feeling any need of, and usually being quite ignorant of, any such distinction, though other languages still observe a parallel distinction. By contrast, in modern English *Yes* indicates simply an affirmation and *No* a denial, regardless of whether the question was positive or whether the negative, conducive version of the question was used instead. For while like all answers to questions they must be understood in the light of the question, *Yes* and *No* do not look back specifically to the polarity of the question but rather look forward to the polarity of the answer.[36] To suppose, as Michael Dummett does, that it is 'more logical' to juxtapose *Yes*, the sign of affirmation, with a denial, as in *Yes, we have no bananas* (in answer to *Have you no bananas?*) is to be in the grip of a particular theory about yes-no questions.[37] The use of *Yes* and *No* is a matter of usage, having to do with answering yes-no questions, not with the logical character of yes-no questions themselves. ('Yes-no' is merely a more or less apt label.) Indeed, *Yes* and *No* need not be said in answer to a question but can signal agreement or disagreement, assent or dissent, from another's statement or proposal of a course of action. It is still misleading to say that *Yes* always goes with agreement, *No* disagreement, rather than (in modern English) the affirmative, or the negative, that follows. For *Yes* signals disagreement or dissent, *No* agreement or assent, if either is in response to what is negative.[38]

What are known as tag questions, abbreviated questions tagged on to the end of sentences, are simply shortened, conducive yes-no questions, and do not themselves form a distinct logical type.

While the insistent *Did she go: Yes or No?* itemises admissible answers explicitly, the supposedly non-elliptical, alternative recastings of yes-no questions — as: *Did she go or did she not go?* — do not in fact admit the one-word answers *Yes* or *No*. True, saying *Yes* or *No* in addition to stating one of the contradictories is also admissible; but then the accompanying statement of one of these contradictories renders *Yes* or *No* logically superfluous. Answers admitted by alternative questions therefore set them apart from yes-no questions proper; for even when yes-no questions are recast as alternative questions — and there is no requirement in logic to recast them thus — they no longer admit *Yes* or *No* alone as answers.[39]

It is easy to see how alternative questions come out as co-ordinate, disjoined yes-no questions: *Was he wearing the white shirt, the blue one or the green one?* co-ordinates the disjunction of three yes-no questions: *Was he wearing the white shirt? or Was he wearing the blue shirt? or Was he wearing the green shirt?* So alternative questions turn out to be rather species of yes-no questions, not the other way round.[40] But although co-ordinate yes-no questions, *Yes* and *No* alone are not admissible answers to alternative questions, it was seen; otherwise it would be unclear which of the two or more disjoined yes-no questions was being answered by *Yes* or *No*. Instead, admissible answers to alternative questions are given by mentioning one of the alternatives listed — which makes them resemble the admissible answers to word questions.

Indeed, an alternative question can always be rephrased as a particular sort of word question, the relevant interrogative word here being the interrogative pronoun *which*, or the interrogative adjective *which* together with a category noun readily supplied from the sense of the original alternative question. In the previous examples, *Which was he wearing?* — that is, *shirt of which colour?* and *Which direction is she heading for? Which* contrasts with *what*, as will be seen in Chapter 9. The Latin *utrum*, which can introduce alternative questions in direct speech as well as the interrogative clauses alluding to them in indirect speech, means literally 'which of two?'. In English, indeed, the context sometimes implies that *which* offers only alternatives — including sometimes even contradictories — as distinct from various possibilities; so that *which* then in effect alludes to an alternative question — or a yes-no question — introduced in indirect speech normally by *whether* rather than *which*.

But unlike alternative questions, *which* questions as such do not presuppose that only one of the listed items obtains. They allow for more than one possibility obtaining. Asked which of a number of novels listed has been awarded a prize, one could equally answer *All*, name just one, or more than one, without challenging the propriety of asking the question as answering *None of them* would be to do so.[41] If 'making a nil return' is intended to be admissible, the question should rather be preceded by the question *Have any of these novels been awarded a prize?* And if the requirement is that respondents list all those that have won a prize, as distinct from giving only some instances, it should be made explicit. There is no way to do so (in English) by simply asking a *which* question; instead the question has to be preceded by the questions *Have any of these novels won a prize?* and *How many of them have?* and *Which of these have?* in turn. Sometimes, indeed, the subject of the question precludes more than one possibility obtaining, as when the question is which age was a person at death; for one can die only once. And sometimes when the pronoun *which* governs a singular verb or the corresponding adjective also governs a singular noun, or when the definite article occurs in a following description, there is a suggestion, of varying strengths, that only one answer can be correctly given, as with alternative questions.

It is to misunderstand the logic of alternative questions to suppose that they can be as open as *which* questions as such are about whether or not they presuppose that there is only one correct answer; and, consequently, whether a complete set or only a sample of correct answers is required. Admittedly, any alternative question — and even a yes-no question occasionally — can be rephrased as a *which* question; but such a way of framing alternative and yes-no questions does not provide any argument for applying the less stringent presuppositions of *which* questions as such to alternative questions, let alone to yes-no questions. Much confusion results from attempting to apply the threefold classification of complete set, one or more examples, and sole correct answer to alternative besides *which* questions.[42] Consistency requires that the threefold classification be applied to yes-no questions too, although it is clear that the three classes collapse into each other in their case.

The mistake here stems from the more general assumption that a conformable answer to a question is as such a proposition. It is held that giving the answer *The white one* has to be construed not just as *He was wearing the white shirt* but rather as *He was wearing the white shirt but neither the blue shirt nor the green shirt* if the alternative question *Was he wearing the white shirt, the blue shirt or the green shirt?* is to have, as it is wrongly thought that it might sometimes not have, the presupposition it actually does have — as if the presupposition of a question were to be determined by conformable answers to the question rather than conformable answers to a question being determined by the presupposition of the question.[43] For the form of the question determines its presupposition, which in turn determines its conformable answers. The conformable answers to a question, not being fully comprehensible in isolation from the question, can determine neither the presupposition of a question nor the form of a question. As a mere presupposition, the presupposition of a question equally does not stand apart from the question; nor is it stated as an answer is, but is only presupposed by the question. In short, the presupposition of a question cannot be determined by answers statable in answer to the question; it can be determined only by the form of the question it is the presupposition of.

An account in English of the interrogative form exhibited in questions may be expected to pay most attention to the way questions are expressed in English. To attempt to embark on a survey of the differences between languages in the formation of questions (or, indeed, the giving of answers) might risk losing sight of the fundamental logical points to be advanced. But the main devices languages deploy to form questions can be briefly reviewed at a high level of generality, lest it be thought that there is some danger of being misled by features peculiar to English grammar and idiom into dubious generalisations about the interrogative as a form of thought. The review will also serve as a reminder of how questions are formed specifically in English. Six main ways can be distinguished, though most are not employed for all types of question.

First, a distinctive interrogative intonation in the spoken language clearly marking off questions in direct speech from statements, besides other types of utterance, is usually reserved for yes-no questions, as also a modified version of it for alternative questions. In several languages — French for instance, besides Russian and Japanese,[44] but not really in English — a yes-no question as such may even be asked standardly in informal speech simply by intonation, there being no other difference between the interrogative sentence expressing the yes-no question and the counterpart declarative sentence. Notwithstanding differences between languages generally in their intonation patterns, interrogative intonation serves within particular languages as a distinctive mark of yes-no and alternative questions.

Second, inversion of subject and (auxiliary) verb can be one mark of a yes-no or an alternative question in direct speech. In English, since such inversion also occurs widely elsewhere — after *neither* and *nor*, for instance — word order is insufficient by itself, just as interrogative intonation is insufficient by itself, to indicate a question; so that both interrogative intonation and subject and verb inversion are required in the spoken language to express yes-no and alternative questions in direct speech.

Third, an affirmation simply juxtaposed without any conjunction with its contradictory can be used — though not in English, of course — to express yes-no questions both in direct speech and as alluded to by interrogative clauses in indirect constructions. In Chinese *Did she go?* can be expressed as what would literally in English run 'She went she did not go?' or with some truncation of the negative clause.[45]

Fourth, specific interrogative words, such as *who*, *what*, *where*, and so forth are used, both in direct speech and in indirect constructions, to form word questions and the interrogative clauses which allude to them. Languages differ in their restrictiveness in the placing of the interrogative word within the sentence or clause and in whether any markedly distinctive intonation is additionally employed in the spoken language.

Fifth, interrogative particles can serve to mark questions of all types both in direct speech and in indirect constructions. The main differences between languages turn on how widespread or restrictive is the use of such interrogative particles. In modern English they are used only for introducing interrogative clauses in indirect constructions alluding to yes-no and alternative questions, where they serve as interrogative conjunctions attaching the interrogative clause to the main clause. To this extent it is a little misleading to regard *if* and *whether* as interrogative particles proper, since they cannot in modern English mark a question at all in direct speech, nor allude to a word question in an indirect construction. In many languages an interrogative particle can be used to indicate yes-no and alternative questions in direct speech besides in interrogative clauses alluding to such questions in indirect constructions. Latin has *-ne* and *utrum ... an ...* . In Chinese the interrogative particle can be used only in direct speech. In some languages, such as Japanese, they can even be used with word questions both in direct speech and in interrogative clauses alluding to word questions in indirect constructions.[46]

Sixth, some languages form questions quite normally by employing an impersonal construction with a relative clause, what linguists refer to as a cleft construction. Thus, French has *Est-ce que ... ?* and *Qu' est-ce que ... ?* but only in direct speech. In principle the device is employable in indirect constructions, as can be seen from how a literal translation in English might go: 'He asked what it was that ... '. In other languages, including English, the cleft construction is not the standard way of forming a question but, as will be seen in Chapter 9, is reserved for questions having a distinctive focus — that is, implying some contrast. *Was it you who did it?* differs from the plain *Did you do it?* in that it is focused on the *you*, implying a contrast with other persons. Again, *Where was it that you went?* — or the simple *Where did you go?* with the emphasis on the interrogative word — focuses on the identity of the location, suggesting the possibility of a previous misidentification.

A principle of economy dictates that what might appear to be redundancy in different ways used to form questions may often serve to make subtle distinctions between types of uses of language — colloquial, say, as distinct from formal, literary or polite. It would be rash, further, to assume that a device employed in one language is equivalent in usage to its (would-be) counterpart in another language. The juxtaposition of an affirmation with its contradictory to form yes-no questions in Chinese lends no support in itself to the view that yes-no questions in English must contain a suppressed contradictory alternative; that there is a contradictory alternative is an inference resting on the Law of the Excluded Middle rather than something that needs to be explicitly itemised within the question by language. And it cannot be assumed that in English there is no difference in usage between *You were there?* uttered with interrogative intonation, and *Were you there?* simply because many other languages can form, quite normally, yes-no questions by interrogative intonation alone.

The question mark, it would seem, was originally intended as a written sign for interrogative intonation but was extended by analogy to all questions in direct speech, even those such as word questions where there is (in English) usually no interrogative intonation. As a question in direct speech is indicated by the occurrence of an interrogative word or particle, or, in English, by inversion for yes-no and alternative questions, the use of question marks is often redundant. They would not be missed, since by not tolerating any following punctuation, they interfere with the overall punctuation of a sentence when interrogative sentences are being quoted. Occasionally, though, a question mark serves to differentiate an interrogative from a relative pronoun. Authors like to give such titles as 'What is wrong with … ' to articles. The absence of a question mark indicates that they are telling, not asking, their readers what is wrong with such-and-such an ism.

Stock Accounts of Questions

Since a question determines, through its presupposition, the form of what would answer it, there is a logical relationship between a question, which is interrogative in form, and what would answer it, which, when actually stated, is propositional in form. But since the presupposition of a question is a proposition, the interrogative also presupposes the propositional. Having a different logical form, a question cannot be the same as its presupposition;[47] but then presuppositions generally are not to be identified with what they are presuppositions of. Thus, the interrogative both stems from and points towards, both glances back at and looks forward to, the propositional. The relationship between the two requires, indeed, some distinction between them. The interrogative is not a species of the propositional, even though it cannot function without the propositional.

The conception of the interrogative argued for here contrasts with the theories of questions dominating the sparse treatment given to the field hitherto in philosophy. As will be seen in the first section of Chapter 3, implicit in the project of coming up with a theory of questions is almost invariably an attempt to equate a question with something other than a question, such as the set of its conformable answers or the presupposition of the question — though it is seldom baldly stated that questions can just be 'analysed away'.[48]

To the extent that the interrogative logical form exhibited by questions has not hitherto been recognised, all theories of questions are reductive in that they misconstrue this logical form propositionally. A question may happen to have some propositional content if it happens to have a proposition as its subject, as when it asks if, how or why something is true; but questions as such do not contain propositions or anything propositional in form.

Most stock accounts, however, do not equate questions directly with the propositional but employ some mediating notion. Writing in 1949, Hare acknowledges that 'the question ... has assumed great importance in the thought of some philosophers, for example Cook Wilson and Collingwood'; but, he continues, 'it seems not to be so basic as' statements and commands. Arguing summarily 'that questions can be translated without loss of meaning into commands', Hare concludes: 'we need say no more about questions'.[49] His position appears moderate in comparison to the proclamation of David and Stephanie Lewis: 'Questions and other imperatives ... differ only in the superficial grammatical flags they fly. Therefore it seems eminently reasonable to treat them alike in formal semantics.'[50]

The major objection to such accounts is that whereas a command — and the term is used throughout here in its generic, grammatical sense — is always addressed to somebody,[51] a question can also occur in thought only. Undeterred by this shortcoming of the speech-act fallacy about questions, Hare does later say a little more about questions. His 'general thesis' is 'that it is sometimes possible to explain meaning in terms of speech acts', in particular 'the meanings of the interrogative sentence form', as 'an invitation or request, or perhaps on occasions even an order'. Cases of wondering or asking oneself, he says, 'present no extra difficulties beyond those associated with all cases of *oratio obliqua*'.[52] What would it be to proffer an invitation to oneself or request oneself to do an action? While accounts like Hare's might initially appear plausible when a question is put to another — though such accounts are confused even here, it will be shown in Chapters 6 and 7 — they are totally inadequate for the asking of questions as such, let alone the questions asked themselves.

Happily, Hare has been well brought up philosophically and has not escaped the influence of Cook Wilson and Collingwood. For it is possible to trace in Aristotelian commentary, grammar, rhetoric and traditional logic something approaching an alternative tradition to conceiving thought in exclusively propositional ways, where it is argued that the import of a proposition itself can be determined by the question it can be conceived as answering.[53] Even Frege, whose interest in questions was slight, found it instructive to consider questions when giving an account of what it is to grasp the sense of a thought.[54] The Aristotelian approach, as it may be conveniently called, is as yet still propositional in outlook: the reference to a question is intended solely to fix the proposition more determinately by providing a context for its assertion. Moreover, it is wrongly assumed that answers to questions constitute propositions as such. And the notion that things, events and states of affairs can be conceived interrogatively as well as propositionally has barely been broached. Nevertheless, it will be found that this approach can be developed so as to highlight the distinctive form of the interrogative.

Now, Hare shows some recognition of the significance of questions in his very distinction of statements and commands from each other. By adopting the Aristotelian approach he takes the distinction to amount to what would supply answers to different kinds of question: -

> A statement, however loosely it is bound to the facts, cannot answer a question of the form 'What shall I do?'; only a command can do this.[55]

When he contrasts the kind of question which 'presupposes that there is some unalterable fact to be stated', and the kind which 'presupposes that there is a choice … between alternative courses of action', he seems to have forgotten about any reduction of questions to commands. 'To ask the second sort of question', he rightly says, 'is to deliberate'. But on the account he has just proposed all questions whatsoever would involve deliberating — between alternative ways of acting in accordance with the supposed command by answering in one way rather than another.[56] In typical philosophical fashion, Hare speaks as if his 'translation' of questions is inoperative once he returns to using ordinary language. There is thus a disparity between Hare's traditional Aristotelian background and a different approach derived from Frege.

The presumed commonplaces of the stock accounts of questions have been repeated uncritically by successive generations of authors as if what they have to say had never been said before.[57] Jaakko Hintikka 'registers' his 'disappointment with' both the 'respectable-sized body of work on the logic of questions ("erotetic logic") among logicians' and the 'fair number of papers by linguists on the grammar of interrogatives'. He continues that, notwithstanding his 'somewhat gloomy view of the current scene', he believes that

> the key to the logic of questions is fairly straightforward. In a way, nothing could be simpler. If there is anything here that virtually all parties agree on, it is the idea that a question is a request for information. The questioner asks his listener to supply a certain item of information, to make him know a certain thing. Thus all that there is to the logic of questions is a combination of the logic of knowledge with the logic of requests (optatives, imperatives).[58]

The near unanimity among contributors to the field that questions are 'requests for information' (whatever that expression is supposed to mean) is responsible for its unsatisfactory state. The assumption that 'nothing could be simpler' is hardly conducive to an enquiring mind. And if one approaches a topic already convinced that one knows 'all that there is to' it, one is unlikely to learn much from it oneself or have anything to teach others.

Martin Bell remarks similarly: 'on all sides there is agreement that to ask a question is to issue a command of some sort, a request for example, and this is surely correct'.[59] What is correct rather is that there is agreement among theorists; but it is due to the word *request* being seized on without much thought. Another author confides: 'Questions, I want to say, are requests for information.'[60] The obvious, even trite, air is explained by requests being, not commands, as Hare, Bell and many others have assumed, but instead by requests being themselves a kind of question, as etymology indicates. A further author goes so far as to declare: 'It is, in fact, probably tautological that questions are requests for information.'[61] The account is certainly unenlightening; for no attempt has been made to examine what 'a request for information' is. These constant equatings of questions with requests not only betray a lack of interest in requests but also, it will be seen in Chapter 7, confusion about questions. Linguistic theorists have fallen into a jargon of their own; but philosophers might have been expected to know better and to have offered some diagnosis, based on an analysis of the notion of a request, of the confusions in such accounts. Instead, obvious counterexamples to them are stigmatised dogmatically as 'non-standard' questions.[62]

The assertion that an interrogative sentence (*Fragesatz*) contains a request (*Aufforderung*) is also to be found in Frege.[63] His authority has thus bolstered the assimilation of questions as such to requests. There is no reason to think that he was doing anything other than mouth what he took to be a truism about a field he was less interested in than his chosen topic of the pivotal place in logic of the notion of truth, which he recognised could not apply to questions.[64] His unsuccessful struggle to accommodate questions within his scheme is nevertheless instructive, it will be seen in Chapter 8. What amount to no more than *orbiter dicta* has furnished several subsequent philosophers with the fundamentals of their accounts of questions, besides having a more discernible influence on specific authors, a line of descent passing through Frege's pupil, Carnap, to Ryle and Hare.[65] It is this Fregean tradition, competing with the Aristotelian approach also detectable in Hare, that Hare doubtless had in mind when he declared later that he was 'not conscious of being original' in his 1949 article; but he is — at least here — too modest, since his proposal to reformulate questions in ordinary language in the manner they are framed in some questionnaires and so-called multiple-choice examinations is new.[66] This proposal will be examined in Chapter 9.

Nuel Belnap, who in previous contributions to the field has likewise simply assumed that questions contain requests,[67] now holds that 'interrogatives and imperatives are not just marked differently from declaratives, but possess fundamentally different underlying content structures' — though his account is not really non-propositional, since he takes 'the content of an interrogative to be — put circularly — the property of being an answer to the interrogative'.[68]

The temptation to prefix such words as *I ask* or *I wish to know* to interrogative sentences has proved irresistible to many philosophers, who imagine they have thereby given a propositional analysis of interrogative sentences. Since the words are clearly being used performatively here, the resulting sentence cannot express anything either true or false; hence, despite appearances, it does not express a proposition. Besides, since the question asked or alluded to has then to be expressed by an interrogative clause following the verbs *ask* or *know*, no analysis of questions has in fact been given. While genuine reports of the questions people ask are propositions, the interrogative clauses contained within such reports constitute ineliminable interrogative, and thus non-propositional, components of these propositions.

An argument in an apparently contrary direction, that the propositional is to be understood as constituting what might be offered in answer to various questions, constitutes the Aristotelian approach. But the method of construing propositions by conceiving them as being given in answer to a question still accords, rightly, overall primacy to the propositional. A more revolutionary approach would be to accord primacy to the interrogative. Collingwood's doctrine that '*Every statement that anybody ever makes is made in answer to a question*'[69] is best regarded as merely giving exaggerated expression to the Aristotelian approach. *Question* and *answer* are correlatives. It does not follow, however, that everything that can be said, as opposed to asked, must actually be said in answer to some question — which is what Collingwood apparently holds. As Hume observed, it does not follow that 'because every husband must have a wife, that therefore every man must be marry'd'.[70]

A language having no means at all of expressing questions can be imagined. Such a language would be more primitive than existing human languages — like the artificial formal languages invented by philosophers and logicians. A supposed language that could express questions but nothing else would not qualify as a language. For what could its sentences be used to say, as distinct from ask? And what sense could its sentences even have if they could be used only to ask, not say, things? Questions cannot be conceived without conceiving the possibility of answers to them, just as answers cannot be conceived without conceiving the questions they are in answer to. But answers, unlike questions, say things. What Wittgenstein imagines is crucially different: 'a language consisting only of questions and expressions for affirmative answering and denial'.[71] In such a language it is not impossible to affirm or deny things.

Notes

1 Austin (1946), pp. 97 and 96; cf. pp. 90-91. See also Woozley (1953), pp. 161, 166-7, 172.
2 Passmore (1957), p. 449. The sentence is omitted in the second edition — cf. (1966), pp. 450-51, 454.
3 Ryle (1945b), p. 215.
4 Ryle (1945b), p. 225. Ryle (1963), II (2); p. 27.
5 Ryle (1963), II (3); p. 29.
6 Ryle (1951), p. 258.
7 Cf. Pendlebury (1986), pp. 365-6.
8 Ryle (1951), p. 258.
9 See, for example, Vendler (1975), p. 99 and Hintikka (1976), pp. 15-16.
10 Reid (1785), II viii; pp. 244-5.
11 Moore (1903), p. 24; cf. p. vii. Cf. also Waismann (1965), p. 4.
12 Reid (1785), I viii; p. 245; cf. p. 244b.

13 Reid (1774), II v; pp. 34-5/692a. cf. I iv; p. 13/685b and Correspondence in (1983), p. 72a. See: Aristotle (1928a), 4; 17a1-7 and (1924), 19; 1456b8-19.
14 Hobbes (1656), I iii 1; p. 26.
15 Reid (1774), II vi; p. 35/692a.
16 Ryle (1951), p. 258.
17 Reid (1983), p. 68b; cf. pp. 70a, 72b. Cf. also: Reid (1785), VI viii; p. 473b and (1774), II ii; p. 23/688b.
18 Reid (1774), II iii; pp. 23-5/688b-9a and (1785), VI viii; p. 473b. Ryle (1938), p. 179.
19 Vesey (1991), p. 3. Cf. Reid (1764), IV ii; p. 118a.
20 Cf. Cohen (1929), p. 353; contrast Bell (1975), pp. 198, 200.
21 Hobbes (1991), iv; p. 27 and (1889), I v 10; pp. 21-2. Cf. Ryle (1930), pp. 37, 38.
22 Cf. Ryle (1945a), p. 208.
23 Hare (1989), p. 26.
24 Ryle (1963), II (2); p. 27; cf. (1930), p. 26.
25 Ryle (1958), p. 392.
26 Hiz (1978a), p. IX.
27 See *OED*, xx, p. 732d. Cf. also Hiz (1978a), pp. XI-XII; Bolinger (1978), p. 103; Rundle (1990), pp. 129-30.
28 Frege (1918), p. 346/355; cf. Carnap (1937), p. 296. And see, for example, Chomsky (1957), p. 90; cf. *OED*, xii, p. 950a and xx, pp. 179c-80a.
29 Cf. Tichy (1978), pp. 278-9, 280. But contrast Aristotle (1928a), 5; 17a19.
30 Kiefer (1983a), p. 2. Cf. Wunderlich (1981), p. 136.
31 Bambrough (1966), p. 170.
32 Cf. Belnap (1963), pp. 27-8. Contrast Hintikka (1976), pp. 75-9.
33 Cf. Belnap (1963), pp. 50, 87; Belnap and Steel (1976), p. 58.
34 See, for example, Belnap (1963), pp. 15, 39, 79 and cf. p. 100; Belnap and Steel (1976), pp. 18, 20.
35 See Bolinger (1978), pp. 91, 92, 95-7, 102 and 104.
36 See *OED*, x, p. 261c; xx, pp. 708b and 732b, c. Cf. Kiefer (1980), pp. 98-9, 106-7; Hoepelman (1983), pp. 19-35, 198-200, 202-5, 208.
37 Dummett (1981), pp. 306-7; cf. Kiefer (1983a), pp. 3-4.
38 Cf. Wunderlich (1981), pp. 137-9.
39 Cf. Hoepelman (1983), pp. 210, 213-14, 226-7.
40 See Bolinger (1978), p. 103.
41 See Belnap (1963), pp. 16-18, 23-7; 28-34.
42 See Belnap (1963), pp. 50, 77, 86-9, 93-4, 95-7, 102-6; Harrah (1963), p. 32 and cf. p. 37; Åqvist (1965), pp. 60, 63-5, 67, note 2, 77, 124, note 8, 126, 156; Bell (1975), pp. 195-7, 204; Belnap and Steel (1976), pp. 46-7, 57-62; and Hintikka (1976), pp. 75-9.
43 See Belnap (1963), pp. 127, 129; Belnap and Steel (1976), pp. 109, 113-14, 121.
44 See Comrie (1984), pp. 18-19; Hinds (1984), pp. 162, 177-80.
45 See Li and Thompson (1984), pp. 52-4.
46 See Li and Thompson (1984), p. 55; Hinds (1984), pp. 159-61.
47 *Pace* Harrah (1961), pp. 40-43; (1963), pp. 28-9. Cf. Prior (1971), p. 77.
48 Llewelyn (1964), p. 70.
49 Hare (1949), pp. 4-5.
50 David and Stephanie Lewis (1975), p. 47.
51 See Hare (1952), p. 177.
52 Hare (1970), pp. 85, 80-81.

53 See for instance: Kahn (1978), p. 227 and p. 267, note 2; Campbell (1823), II iv, pp. 232-4; Whately (1913), II iv § 1, pp. 65-6; Cook Wilson (1926), i, II iv §§ 57-9, pp. 119-26; Ryle (1929), pp. 3-8.
54 See Frege (1919), pp. 362-6/373-7.
55 Hare (1952), p. 46. Cf. (1949), p. 6; (1952) pp. 1, 15, 43, 60, 74; (1963), pp. 54-62; (1981), pp. 87-8, 214-16.
56 Hare (1949), p. 6. Cf. Wheatley (1955), pp. 51-2 and 60, note 1.
57 See the historical survey by Struyker Boudier (1988); especially p. 22 and cf. p. 26.
58 Hintikka (1974), pp. 103, 104; cf. Åqvist (1965), pp. 8-9.
59 Bell (1975), p. 205.
60 Nesbitt, (1973), p. 256.
61 Schiffer (1972), p. 85.
62 See, for instance, Åqvist (1965), pp. 8, 48; Bell (1975), p. 209; Hintikka (1976), pp. 23-4.
63 See Frege (1918), p. 346/355 and (1919), p. 362/373. Cf. Waismann (1965), p. 407.
64 See Frege (1918), pp. 342-6/351-5 and (1919), p. 364/375.
65 See Carnap (1937), p. 296; Ryle (1938), pp. 172-6; Hare (1950), pp. 22-4 and (1970), pp. 77-86. Cf. Mary and Arthur Prior (1955), pp. 48-9.
66 Hare (1970), p. 81, note 2; cf. pp. 80-81 and (1949), p. 5.
67 Belnap (1963), pp. 13, 22, 28, 43, 46, 63, 64, 67, 70, 77, 94, 95; Belnap and Steel (1976), pp. 3-4, 18, 20, 31, 35, 49, 58.
68 Belnap (1990), pp. 5 and 14-15.
69 Collingwood (1940), p. 23; cf. (1939), pp. 31-9.
70 Hume (1978), I iii 3; p. 82.
71 Wittgenstein (1958), I § 19, p. 8[e]; cf. I § 22, pp. 10[e]-11[e].

Chapter 2

The Interrogative

A thought is interrogative in form when it takes the form of a question. Any sentence containing an interrogative clause expresses a thought which contains a component thought. As the expression of a component thought, an interrogative clause is interrogative in form because it alludes to a question. A sentence containing an interrogative clause may, of course, be propositional in form. But if the whole sentence expresses a question, the sentence is interrogative. If the whole sentence expresses a performative utterance, the thought expressed cannot be propositional in form: in being the performing of a speech-act, the utterance cannot itself be true or false since the doing of anything cannot be true or false.

The task of this chapter is to explore the logical characteristics of interrogative clauses. While all interrogative clauses share the feature of what will be called interrogative opaqueness, clauses governed by verbs like *ask* serve a function incompatible to that served by clauses governed by verbs like *know*. What is common, it will emerge, to interrogative clauses is the exercise of the concept of what answers a question, which underlies interrogative form generally.

Interrogative Clauses

There are interrogative clauses corresponding to, on the one hand, yes-no and alternative questions and, on the other, word questions. That is, there are those clauses introduced by *if* or *whether* — when these words are used as interrogative conjunctions, for they have other uses. Then there are clauses introduced by the interrogative pronouns *what* and *which*, *who* and its other cases *whom* and *whose*; the interrogative adjectives *what* and *which*; and finally, the interrogative adverbs *when*, *where*, *how* and *why*. These are the interrogative words in constant use in modern English — *whithers* and *whences* being archaic.

Most verbs and verb phrases governing interrogative clauses take the full range. But Lauri Karttunen notes: 'So-called "emotive factives", such as *be amazing*, *be surprising*, and *bother* ... do not allow whether-questions.'[1] More significantly, *doubt* and *question* usually govern only the first type of interrogative clause; though they can also take a clause introduced by *which* if the clause alludes in effect to an alternative or a yes-no question so that *which* has to be understood as *whether*. But when used in the negative or in questions *doubt* and *question* can govern other interrogative clauses, and even take a propositional construction.

Those verbs taking either type of clause fall into various groups. First, verbs of enquiry, such as *ask*, *wonder*, *investigate*, *consider*, *examine*, *study*, *conjecture*, *speculate*; verbs of debate, such as *debate*, *discuss* and *query* (in a loose sense of asking questions about); and, with an infinitive construction, verbs of deliberation, such as *consider*, *contemplate when*, *how*, *whether*, etc. to do something. Verbs of decision express the making up of one's mind, such as *choose*, *determine*, *resolve when*, *how*, *whether*, etc. to do something. A large group is formed by verbs conveying knowledge headed by *know* itself. Various subgroups fall within: perceptual verbs, such as *see*, *hear*, *taste*, *smell*, *feel* (but not *touch*), *observe*, *notice*, *watch*, *witness*; verbs of discrimination, such as *discern*, *distinguish*, *tell*, *recognise*, *appreciate*; verbs of comprehension, such as *conceive*, *grasp*, *understand*, *think*, *judge*, *imagine*; verbs of discovery, such as *find out*, *learn*, *diagnose*, *ascertain*, *establish*, *verify*, *prove*, *infer*, *calculate*, *estimate*; verbs implying the previous acquisition of knowledge, such as *have learnt*, *recognise*, *remember*, *recollect*, *forget*; finally, verbs conveying the communication of knowledge from one person to another, whether specifically verbally, such as *say*, *state*, *tell*, *inform*, *report*, *testify*, *mention*, or non-verbally, such as *show*, *reveal*, *point to* or *out*; and, with an infinitive construction, the communication and acquisition of practical knowledge, such as *teach*, *instruct*, *learn when*, *where*, *how*, *whether*, etc. to do something. There are also some verbs that are foremost saying verbs and when governing interrogative clauses convey saying correctly, but where an attribution of knowledge would usually be withheld, such as *bet*, *guess*, *predict*, *suggest*. These might be called verbs of mere saying. Also contrasted with knowledge are negative phrases marking impairment or the falling short of knowledge: *not being certain*, *sure* or *clear*, *being uncertain*, *unsure* or *unclear*. Then there is a group of verbs and verb phrases which might be called verbs of concern, such as *care (about)*, *have*, *pay regard to*, *be interested in*, *mind*, *worry about*. Lastly, while all the verbs listed so far have persons as their subjects, there is a group of phrases expressing connections or the lack of connections that occur in sentences where the subject is not a person. Examples are: *to be affected by*, *to depend on*, *to be important (for)*, *to matter (to)*, *to make a difference (to)*, *to be (ir)relevant to*, *regardless of*, *irrespective of*.

In this rough classification there appears to be an overall distinction between groups of verbs which simply raise a question and those which, in differing ways, relate instead to the answer to a question. Verbs of enquiry, debate and deliberation obviously simply raise a question. Verbs of decision have to do with settling the question: the answer either has been or is to be decided on. Verbs attributing knowledge, those of mere saying and those marking impairment of knowledge bear on the answer to the question. Verbs of concern convey that people are affected by the answer to the question. And the connection or the lack of it expressed by the last group of phrases is between the subject of the verb and the answer, whatever it might be, to the question. This general distinction, however, is too crude. When decisions have yet to be taken, the question what to do remains to be settled, so it still arises. And people have interests in future contingencies; but in caring about what is going to happen it would seem that they can be exercised only about the question (*What is going to happen?*) — for how can they be exercised in the present about its answer when they do not yet have its answer?

The Opaqueness of the Interrogative

Since interrogative clauses following verbs of enquiry, debate and deliberation raise a question, they can be construed as either reporting a question that has been asked by somebody or, in general, as expressing a question that arises whether or not somebody has actually raised it. They are accordingly called indirect questions by grammarians. Clauses following the verbs in other groups, especially those following verbs conveying knowledge, although traditionally also classified by grammarians as 'indirect questions', are not, in the main, adequately thought of as simply expressing a question.[2] Instead these clauses usually allude to not just a question but also the answer to it, using the very words used in other contexts simply for the raising of the question. But since such clauses do not say what the answer to the question is, they may be described as opaque in contrast with the transparency of propositional constructions. There is no connection, incidentally, with so-called referential opacity, which has instead to do with relationships solely between propositions. Interrogative opaqueness — and the different form of the word is deliberately chosen to avoid confusion — has to do instead with the relationship between interrogative and propositional forms of thought.[3]

In contrast with the *that* clause in the sentence *He remembers that the king was deposed*, the interrogative clause in the sentence *He remembers what happened* does not say what happened — though it says that whatever it was, he remembers it. That is, the clause does not reveal what the answer is to the question *What happened?* Yet the whole sentence conveys that what he remembers constitutes the answer to this question whatever the answer to it is. Note that the sentence does not convey that he remembers (what) the answer (is) to the question *What happened?* — only that what he remembers amounts to the answer to the question whatever it may be. A way of avoiding the intellectualism Ryle unwittingly committed himself to by his talk of knowing how to answer questions is thus suggested: for it is perfectly possible for one to have knowledge of some fact without being able to say anything about what one knows.

Admittedly, with verbs of mere saying, as distinct from verbs attributing knowledge, the person usually does also actually say something; but the interrogative clause does not itself say anything — nor, indeed, what the person said. If I guessed who won, I either actually said, or was prepared to say, who the winner was — that is, my guess can be specified as saying correctly that some particular person I named as the winner was indeed the winner; but the clause *who won* does not reveal what this saying *that* ... of mine was, nor indeed who won.

Whether what thus constitutes the answer to a question is conveyed by the sentence as also being known depends on the sense of the verb and whether the sentence is in the negative or is itself interrogative, besides what is said of the clause. Thus: *He guessed what happened* or *I forgot what happened* and *What happened is debatable* or *It is not certain what happened*, all allude to the answer to the question *What happened?* but convey that the subject or the world at large does, or may, not know what happened. The same obviously applies to negations of *know*: *I don't, he doesn't, know what happened.* And the interrogative sentence *Does he know what happened?* only asks a question about, and does not say, what happened.

Clauses following verbs of decision, when the context implies that the decision has already been taken, likewise do not say what has been decided: *They decided whom to appoint* does not say who the successful applicant was. Clauses following verbs of concern and phrases expressing connections or a lack of them usually convey a person's interest in, or the connection or the lack of it with, the answer to a question; but they do not say what the answer is. Sentences containing clauses expressing a lack of connection with the answer to a question alluded to, indeed, say what they say regardless or irrespective of what the answer may be.

Clauses following verbs of enquiry, debate and deliberation are equally opaque in that they do not say anything at all but only ask a question. If I ask who went, the clause *who went* does not say who went; for I have only asked who went.[4] Indeed, it is obvious, and hence unremarkable, that questions or reports of questions do not themselves reveal what the answers to them are. Likewise, the clause in *They have to decide whom to appoint* expresses a question without saying what the answer to it will be. So all clauses that only raise a question are opaque since they cannot themselves reveal what the answer is to the question they raise.

What is distinctive about the clauses after verbs in the remaining groups is that these clauses do not in the main raise a question but instead allude to the answer to a question in the very words of the question alluded to in the clause: the answer is alluded to obliquely, since it is alluded to only through or by means of the question. Whereas clauses belonging to the first class are opaque because they merely raise a question without saying what the answer to it is, clauses in this class are opaque because although they allude to the answer to a question alluded to, they equally do not say what the answer to it is but allude to the answer obliquely only through the question. The term *interrogative* as applicable to logical form can be understood, then, as pertaining to not only the simple expression of a question but also the oblique allusion to the answer to a question through the allusion to a question.

It might be objected that the distinction between those interrogative clauses that only express a question and those that allude to its answer obliquely is arbitrary because the verbs like *ask* and *know* involve 'essentially parallel constructions'.[5]

An argument could be developed along the intellectualist line previously rejected. Not only is knowing or remembering who went, it might be argued, knowing or remembering (what) the answer (is) to the question *Who went?* but asking or wondering who went is asking or wondering what the answer is to the question *Who went?* All these interrogative constructions, it might be concluded, allude to the answer to the question whatever verb governs them.[6]

The import of the objection that interrogative clauses, taken in themselves, do not have different senses depending on which verb governs them is sound. Yet expressing a question is clearly not the same as — indeed, is incompatible with — alluding obliquely to the answer to a question. True, the specific verb governing the clause usually determines whether the clause simply expresses a question or obliquely alludes to its answer,[7] or, indeed, whether an interrogative clause, as distinct from, say, a *that* clause, is permissible at all. What has to be explained, though, is how the same set of words can at one time express or report a question, and at another time instead allude obliquely to the answer to a question.

No elucidation of the sense of interrogative clauses is provided by arguing that the sentence *He asked what he is feeling* means *He asked what the answer is to the question 'What he is feeling?'* since, as was seen, the interrogative clause containing the words *the answer* remains uneliminated. Besides, saying *asking what the answer is to a question* is no more than an elaborate way of saying *asking a question*. Granted, to ask what the answer is to a question is, strictly, to ask a different question from the original question; but the more elaborate question could not be asked without thereby asking the original question. Since the more elaborate question contains the original question, the elaboration is superfluous. On the one hand, then, if intellectualism is to be avoided, *knowing what he is feeling* need not be *knowing what the answer is to the question 'What he is feeling?'* and on the other, *asking what he is feeling* is not to be explicated as *asking what the answer is to the question 'What he is feeling?'* without logical pleonasm. In either case the insistence on including the words *(what is) the answer to the question* leads to an infinite regress.

There is still the difficulty to be met of how interrogative clauses as a whole can, without any shift in their sense, serve the two incompatible functions of simply expressing a question and of alluding to its answer obliquely. How can the use of interrogative clauses after both *ask* and *know* be given a uniform account? If talk here about either asking or knowing what the answer is to the question has to be rejected as having no explanatory value, the alternative is to conceive the question as only raised in the clause when governed by some verbs or in some contexts, but as answered in the clause when governed by other verbs or in other contexts.

In clauses after *ask* and similar verbs the question is plainly conceived merely as asked. The clauses after *know* and kindred verbs can also be said to allude to a question; but not conceived as asked — or as 'unasked', either;[8] such clauses allude to a question conceived rather as answered, and so not as either asked or unasked. They allude to the answer to a question interrogatively, and hence obliquely, in the very words of the question alluded to. Since they do not themselves say anything, they are not propositional in form. They do not perforce say what the answer is to the question — either as it would be stated by a respondent in response to the question or as contained within the complete proposition whose assertion a respondent is held to in answering the question. Thus, in those interrogative clauses that allude obliquely to the answer to a question by alluding to the question, the allusion to the answer is not propositional but interrogative.

But all interrogative clauses, it will be argued, in giving expression univocally to a thought that is interrogative in form thereby invoke the specific relationship holding between the answer to the particular question they allude to and that question itself, yet without specifying what the answer to it actually is. Herein lies the opaqueness of all interrogative clauses: this specific relationship is expressed only interrogatively, not propositionally. Interrogative form therefore explains how the same set of words can in one context simply express a question yet in another allude obliquely to the answer to a question: for the answer to a question can be alluded to interrogatively in the very words of the question. So an interrogative clause following a verb like *know* does not have a different sense from the same clause following the verb *ask*.

Failure to appreciate the flexibility of interrogative form in accommodating both the expression of questions and non-propositional allusions to their answers leads to attempts to skate over this difference in function. The misguidedness of construing asking a question as asking what the answer to it is was earlier laid bare. Variations on this unoriginal theme with *tell* or *request* will be met in Chapters 6 and 7. Such accounts misconceive the asking of a question as somehow covertly referring to its answer, which is conceived as contained in the question itself, and thus conceived propositionally.

Another kind of attempt to dissolve the difference in function between interrogative clauses taken by *ask* and *know* is found in Hintikka's confidence that *ask* 'can, and must, be analyzed in terms of the absence of knowledge (among other features)'.[9] Instead of taking the interrogative clauses governed by *know* as alluding to a question, an attempt is made to explicate questions and the interrogative clauses governed by verbs like *ask* and *wonder* by means of the clauses governed by *know*. But asking what happened is no more analysable as not knowing what happened than not knowing what happened is analysable as asking what happened. Not knowing what happened has to do exclusively with being ignorant of what is merely conceived as the answer to the question *What happened?* and has nothing at all to do with the actual asking of that question. So likewise, asking what happened concerns the question solely and makes no direct allusion to either its answer or the epistemic state of the questioner.

The Concept of What Answers a Question

The notion of the answer to a question now needs to be considered, since it has not only been employed in accounting for some, though not all, interrogative clauses — namely, those governed by *know* besides several other verbs, by contrast with those governed by *ask*; the notion also figures in the explication yet to be given of the univocality of interrogative clauses: all interrogative clauses, it was said in outline, invoke a specific relationship holding between the answer to the particular question they allude to and the question itself.

An answer to a question is distinct from the answer to a question. Here *an answer* must be understood throughout not as some reply or response in general people might make to a question but as what bears some logical relation to the question, a conformable answer. As was seen in the previous chapter, a conformable answer to a question can be understood only in the light of the question; so that while the question dictates the form of its conformable answers, the relationship is asymmetrical:[10] if one did not hear or is ignorant of the question, one can at best only guess what the question was from a conformable answer to it.

The topic preoccupying theorists, of categorising different sorts of answers, direct, complete, partial, and so forth, seems to stem from an assumption that the relationship of any proposition to a question can be studied so that a proposition which follows from another proposition can be viewed as providing some sort of answer to a question.[11] But even if propositions as such were conformable answers to questions, they obviously could not be begun to be understood as qualifying as candidates for conformable answers to a question in isolation from the question. Sometimes people do not give a straight answer, as it is said: they only drop hints which can serve as material for constructing an answer. But such respondents are clearly not giving a conformable answer to the question, so that such cases are irrelevant to consideration of the logical relationship between question and answer.

When people answer questions what they say in answer to them is said to be either correct or incorrect, right or wrong. The terms *correct* or *incorrect* are to be preferred; because sometimes people speak of asking the right questions or of some question being the wrong question to ask about something. This way of appraising questions will be mentioned briefly in the Appendix. What should be noted is that the terms *correct* and *incorrect* could not be applied to the asking of questions — unless a speaker's command of grammar is being appraised. Being more widely applicable, the terms *right* and *wrong* do not isolate the kind of appraisal appropriate to answering questions.

As was seen, a conformable answer to a question usually consists in a word, a phrase or a term and is not as such a proposition. It follows that the use of the terms *true* or *false*, which apply to propositions, is not appropriate for answers people give to questions; even although the assertions respondents are normally held to when answering questions are either true or false, and even although respondents are presumed to take these assertions to be true. Answers people give to questions are not, *qua* answers, true or false but instead correct or incorrect; for since the word, phrase or term constituting a conformable answer to a question has to be taken in the context of the question, given answers to questions are to be appraised by reference to the question, where truth or falsity cannot apply. By contrast, the terms *correct* or *incorrect* apply strictly to something done — to wit, the giving of an answer; then by extension to conformable answers themselves, which are abstractions from people's answerings of questions.

Ordinarily, then, both an answer and the answer to a question are spoken of. Talk of an answer to a question does not preclude that such a given answer may be incorrect. Talk of the answer to a question, on the contrary, implies that to give it would be to answer correctly.

A remarkable consequence of the correctness built into the notion of the answer to a question is that those interrogative clauses governed by a verb which conveys that its subject does something that can be done either correctly or incorrectly imply that what was done was done only correctly; for these clauses allude to the answer to a question. Of course, interrogative clauses taken by *know* and other verbs conveying knowledge might be said to imply correctness, since one cannot be said to know if one is, or does something, wrong. But knowing itself is hardly something that is done; so a rather different account will have to be given to accommodate interrogative clauses following *know* and kindred verbs. The point here rather is that interrogative clauses following verbs such as *tell* and even *guess* imply correctness, for they allude to not just an answer but the answer to a question. If I guessed who won my guess must have been correct; but if I guessed that the Conservatives won, it cannot be inferred from that alone whether my guess was correct or incorrect. There is no proof against irony, however, where what is said should not be understood literally. Rather as *know* can sometimes be used ironically for what is merely taken to be knowledge, so it is not impossible that interrogative clauses following *tell* occur occasionally filtered through an ironic gauze.[12]

One awkwardness of the established way of speaking of the answer to a question is that with word questions — especially those loosely or vaguely worded — more than one correct answer to the question may be capable of being given, and this possibility should not be excluded simply by the mode of expression chosen. But the implication of uniqueness often borne by the use of the definite article is not invariable, and may only be a consequence of some implicit limitation on the domain of discourse. Thus, when a questioner knows only that the giving of one particular answer would be correct, 'the answer' referred to by the questioner is just this answer. If the giving of another answer would be equally correct, the questioner could well concede after the fact had been pointed out, 'That too is the answer to the question.' And when a questioner, or a respondent, does not know any answer to a question — that is, does not know what (or which) answer or answers it would be correct to give — 'the answer' simply refers to whatever they aim to elicit or give regardless of whether distinct but equally correct answers may be capable of being given.

Theorists do not like the ordinary talk of the answer to a question because they would wish answers to questions to be either true or false, as propositions are.[13] They also have a tendency to speak of 'the possible answers' to a question, meaning thereby answers, 'true' or 'false', that one could give in answer to the question if one did not dispute the propriety of asking the question; in other words, the type of answers provided for by the question. Answers conforming to the form laid down by the form of the question are better described as admissible or conformable answers. For such theorists do not mean by 'a possible answer', what the expression ordinarily means, an answer that when given might happen to be correct, what is possibly the answer to the question. A question whose presupposition is false has no answer, has no possible answer or answers to it, in the ordinary sense; that is, there is nothing that is the answer to it. But on the usage of theorists, by contrast, such a question would have 'possible answers' to it in that its conformable answers could be derived from the question through its (false) presupposition.

By an unanswerable question is meant, not a question that has no possible answer in either the ordinary or the theorist's sense, but simply a question whose answer cannot be given — often owing to the answer to it being unknown rather than to there being no answer to it to give.[14]

Despite ordinary talk of the answer to a question, ordinary usage might appear to incline towards the usage of theorists to the extent that it allows that answers people give to questions may be incorrect. An incorrect answer, it might be urged, is still an answer. By apparent contrast, an erroneous fact would be a contradiction in terms, for it would not be a fact at all; and an observation, as distinct from a purported or an alleged observation, could likewise not be incorrect. But by an answer here can be meant only somebody's answer, at least an answer somebody might give; for strictly it is only people's answerings which can be said to be either correct or incorrect. So the absence of any correctness built into the notion of a given answer is hardly surprising: what is given as an answer to a question need not in fact be the answer to it, any more than what is offered or presented as an argument or evidence for something need actually be an argument or evidence for it, as distinct from some person's supposed argument or purported evidence for it. It will be seen in Chapters 5 and 6 that when in earnest, conscientious respondents purport to give what they honestly take to be the answer to the question.

Although it is as old as the verb, the noun *answer* evidently derives from the verb:[15] an answer, or the answer, to a question is what is or may be given when people answer the question. When its subject is a person, the verb does not preclude answering incorrectly. The obviousness of this point may inhibit notice of a further point having the same explanation in answers people give to questions being only what they present as the answer to the question. The further point is that while the verb *answer* takes a clause introduced by *that* which states what answer was given by the person, the verb does not take an interrogative clause. For if the verb *answer* took an interrogative clause there would be an implication (as with *guess*, *say*, *state* or *tell* followed by an interrogative clause) that any answer presented was in fact correct — as distinct from merely being presented as being the answer to the question. So if one wants to refer back to a question that somebody has just answered, one does not do so by employing an interrogative clause after the verb *answer*; instead, one mentions the question specifically as *the question*, ... This construction precludes any implication that the person has answered correctly. For not only is the question mentioned after *answer* conceived simply as asked, what answer was given is not even specified — by contrast with the *that* construction. The answer the person gave is specified in *He answered that she had gone out*; but not in *He answered the question, 'What did she do?'* For while it incorporates a report of the question asked, it does not say what answer the respondent gave.

Accusations levelled at politicians and examination candidates of failing to answer the question might suggest that the verb is used less freely than the noun. But failing to answer the question here means presenting as an answer what is evasive or irrelevant, serving only to conceal, say, guilty knowledge or culpable ignorance, and not giving an answer of the form provided for by the question. As the voguish idiom has it, it is failing to 'address' the question. A similar usage can occur with the noun: an interviewer may reprimand a slippery politician with 'That's no answer.' Such talk bears out that answering a question is not to be determined solely by a respondent but is also subject to logical constraints.

Three kinds of case have to be distinguished. First, where what is presented as an answer conforms to the question. Here the politician or candidate did answer the question and may have answered it correctly or incorrectly. Second, where what is offered in answer to the question does not conform to the question. Here although the respondent may claim to have answered the question, the charge is that the question remains to be answered as it was undoubtedly answered in the first kind of case. Third, silence or a blank script; or an explicit refusal to answer the question. The quibble that the question has been answered in the second kind of case because it is distinct from the third kind of case overlooks the crucial, though obvious, point that what is presented in answer to a question should at least relate to the question — but, further, should also conform to the question if an answer as distinct from a reply is to be given.

Those who insist that examination rubrics instruct candidates to 'attempt' rather than simply answer questions perhaps have in mind that only honest attempts to give conformable answers — whether or not correct — should be countenanced, even though such attempts may turn out unhappily to be just as failures as answers as flagrant evasions are. But it is not less reasonable to tell somebody to do something than to try to do it, for a driving instructor to tell a learner to engage reverse than to try to engage reverse. This talk of attempting, however, carries a faint suggestion of a stronger, what Ryle would call an achievement, sense of the verb *answer* whereby the meeting of some standard is achieved. Scientists in saying that some question is as yet unanswered are not necessarily denying that they or their colleagues have attempted, unsuccessfully, to come up with answers to it. Perhaps 'answered' here has to be understood as answered satisfactorily.

While ordinary talk of failing to answer the question points to the logical relationship between question and answer, ordinary usage does not sanction an achievement sense of either noun or verb such that answers people give to a question can only constitute the answer to it and answering it can only be to give the answer to it. For while ordinary usage cannily distinguishes between the answer to a question, and various people's answers to a question, it does not really have an established place for any answering other than people's. But if one is a bit uncertain quite what the question put to one is, one might ask after one has attempted to deal with it, *Does that answer your question?* Significantly, what is doing or not doing the answering here are the words one has said. Such a way of speaking of words, as distinct from people, as answering a question is required to account for the specific relationship between the answer to a question and the question itself; for such a relationship can be uncovered only by abstracting the language used from people's use of language. Hence a broader application of this use of the verb *answer* will help to elucidate the relationship underpinning interrogative form.

It was seen in the previous chapter that it is established practice to extend, by an abstraction of thought, the usage of verbs relating to the use of language beyond persons and apply them derivatively to sentences or clauses. As well as talking about people saying, stating, things, asking questions, and telling others of things or to do various actions, one can also speak of sentences or clauses themselves as saying, stating, things, asking questions, and telling one of things or to do various actions. Reading from a newspaper I may introduce what I report to another with 'It says (states) here that ... '. A notice may be said to tell or warn one to do or not to do something. And a written interrogative sentence, such as on an official form, may be said to ask the reader some question.

Philosophers have long spoken of propositions as asserting things; and questions may be said to ask things. This type of usage was slipped into earlier when it was said that some interrogative clauses raise questions and others allude to the answer to a question but do not say what the answer is. But sentences or clauses could not be said to say, state, assert, ask or tell things unless people could; the performances of sentences and clauses are abstractions merely conceived apart from the linguistic performances of people. If 'speakers can say that the earth moves by uttering' the sentence *The earth moves*,[16] it is only because that sentence can be taken as a possible saying of some person. By contrast, people are said only derivatively to imply something — that is, only because something else, such as their words, bodily disposition, tone of voice or gestures, imply it.[17]

The verb *answer* is sometimes similarly extended so as to be used impersonally. Instead, therefore, of speaking of *the answer to a question*, which while implying the desired correctness in the giving of it also unfortunately tends to suggest that only one answer can be correctly given, the somewhat artificial phrase *what answers the question* may be introduced. The subject of the verb *answer* here is not a person but what is meant by words, a thought. The phrase thus serves to evade connotations of ordinary talk of people answering questions that are irrelevant to interrogative form. Since the subject of the verb is not a person, answering here cannot be done incorrectly. But the phrase has other advantages. Equally, since words or clauses are not actual agents, when they answer a question they do not exactly answer it correctly either. Yet the verb acquires an achievement sense so that for an interrogative clause to answer a question is for it to measure up to some standard set by the question.

If you remember what happened, you need not have actually answered the question *What happened?* correctly; for there may be nothing that you do — either correctly or incorrectly. Certainly, remembering is not quite something you do, even correctly. Instead, the interrogative clause, *what happened* itself answers the question *What happened?* — though not correctly, still less incorrectly. It does so in the sense that it measures up to the standard set by the question by alluding obliquely — that is, interrogatively — to what answers this question quite independently of your remembering (though what answers this question is not independent of what you remember).

The verb *answer* when used impersonally can even govern an interrogative clause, and so thereby preclude anything but the answer to the question. Hearing what you pronounce on somebody's character, I may observe, *Well, that answers the question what sort of a person she is*. In idiomatic language the impersonal use of the verb *answer* is often figurative, so any implication of success is somewhat diminished: a train service may answer a need, but not very well, a quite innocent man may answer the description of an offender.

Talk here of *the answer to a question*, it was seen, led to intellectualism. In construing knowledge characterised interrogatively as knowing what the answer is to a question its interrogative character is equated with the knowledge of a truth, knowledge that what some proposition says is true. Thus, an interrogative conception of knowledge is being misconceived propositionally. For the answer to a question is what is given when somebody answers the question correctly, so that knowing what the answer is to a question presupposes the capacity to answer questions and to formulate and have knowledge of truths. Instead, a hint of Aristotle's might be adopted by construing interrogative clauses following *know* as conceiving a piece of knowledge rather as what answers some question.[18] The piece of knowledge is thus characterised as knowledge of what answers the question, not as knowledge of what the answer is to the question. The concept of what answers a question applies to what is expressed by some words, a thought; the possessor of the piece of knowledge is not what here answers the question. Thus, conceiving the clause itself as answering the question explains how interrogative characterisations of knowledge can be attributed to non-human animals, how they can be credited with knowledge and understanding as manifested by what they do, though they have no use of language and so no knowledge of truths.

Moreover, use of the artificial phrase *what answers the question* in place of the ordinary phrase *the answer to a question* can do justice to the clear univocality of interrogative clauses after both *know* and *ask* and also avoid the infinite regress engendered by the phrase *knowing (asking) what the answer is to the question ' ... ?'*. For to know *what*, *where*, etc. is to know what answers the question alluded to by the interrogative clause that follows; and the object of asking *what*, *where*, etc. is, in general, to elicit what answers the question alluded to by the interrogative clause that follows. These two incompatible functions of interrogative clauses each invoke the concept of what answers the question, something already available in some contexts but not yet available in others. The concept expresses — but in interrogative form, and hence opaquely — the specific relationship between what it is that answers a question and the question itself.

The artificial phrase will be used solely in the exploration of interrogative form; not when the answer to a question is being conceived propositionally.

Interrogative Concepts

The phrase, *knowing what answers the question* itself contains an interrogative clause, the question alluded to being *What answers the question?* It takes an interrogative clause to account for interrogative clauses. But when the clause occurs where a noun or noun phrase is required, after such verbs or verb phrases as *elicit*, *obtain* or *seek (after)*, *find*, *come into possession of*, it is a relative clause, the *what* being a compound relative pronoun understood as *that which* or 'the thing(s) which'.

This differentiation between interrogative and relative clauses might seem a fickle consequence of some verbs being unable by themselves directly to govern clauses — as opposed to taking nouns or nouns phrases, including relative clauses, as direct objects, or with a preposition. The impression of arbitrariness is reinforced by the compound relative pronoun, adjective or adverb being in English and several other languages, unlike Latin, the same word in many cases as its interrogative counterpart. But if the ability or inability of a verb to govern interrogative clauses is of more than grammatical significance, so might its inability to govern any clauses. Moreover, unlike its interrogative counterpart, a clause introduced by a compound relative pronoun can be the subject of a predication — that is, something can be said to be true of it. But neither an interrogative sentence nor an interrogative clause can (by itself) say anything.

There is an explanation, derived from what in the previous chapter was called the Aristotelian approach, why not just the compound relative words *what*, *when*, *where* and *how* (together with the obsolete *which*, *who*, *whom*, *whose* and *why* for the modern English *the one which*, *the one who*, *the one whom*, *the one whose* and *the reason why*) but also the simple relative pronouns *which*, *who*, *whom* and *whose* mimic their interrogative parents.

A relative clause with its antecedent can be conceived as citing what answers the word question alluded to by its parent interrogative clause by means of a term of the proposition that can be constructed from a conformable answer understood in the light of the question. Simple antecedents of relative clauses may be more or less specific: *The twenty-eight year old futures dealer who ...* contrasts with the more general description, *The man who ...* . But any relative clause with its antecedent functions as a single yet compound term. Such a term is not, indeed, one of Mill's supposed 'many-worded names'. For since, as will emerge shortly, the term itself contains a proposition, it cannot be a name. Yet antecedent with clause serves, as a name also serves, as a single term of the whole sentence (declarative or interrogative) which functions therein as one item mentioned. For a list might be compiled of not only names but also descriptions consisting of relative clauses with their antecedents.

The complete (declarative) sentence beginning with the relative clause and its simple antecedent, *The twenty-eight year old futures dealer who broke Barings Bank* ... says, whatever else it goes on to say about him, that this twenty-eight year old futures dealer broke the bank. Thus, relative clauses with their antecedents contain propositions — indicated by clauses introduced by the conjunction *that.* Indeed, *that* itself can also be a relative pronoun, thus bearing out that the relative clause that follows is propositional. Now, the relative clause with its antecedent can be seen to cite by a single term what answers the question *Who broke Barings Bank?* — namely, *A twenty-eight year old futures dealer.* Moreover, *knowing who broke Barings Bank* is knowing what, as expressed by the interrogative clause, can be conceived as answering, in interrogative form, this question. The words *who broke Barings Bank* occur not only in the direct question and the interrogative clause but also in the coupling of relative clause to antecedent.

Clauses introduced by a compound relative pronoun or adverb might be said to be as virtually opaque as their interrogative parents in that the suppressed antecedent is always highly general, such as 'the thing', 'the time', 'the place', 'the way'. The sentence *What she did was shameful* in principle cites by a term what answers the question *What did she do?* But the sentence does not reveal exactly what she did, though it says that she did 'a thing'. In this respect the relative clause may seem not far removed from its interrogative parent in *He knows what she did.* Of course, the thing she did can be stated precisely, as in the sentence *What she did was steal a coat.* But the relative clause here reveals only in the most general terms what answers the question — namely, that she did a thing. Yet while quite uninformative, the relative clause is still propositional, and so does not actually have the feature of interrogative opaqueness; that is, the clause does actually say something, albeit highly general.

Clauses introduced by the compound relative pronouns or adjectives *whatever, whichever, whoever,* and adverbs *whenever, wherever, however* are even more uninformative. Here what is said about what answers the question is maintained even in ignorance of what it is, it being dismissed as irrelevant to what the sentence says.[19]

Even clauses introduced by simple relative pronouns are comparatively uninformative when conceived, according to the Aristotelian approach, as citing the single (though compound) term constituting what answers the parent word question. The description, *the person who broke Barings Bank* only nominally answers the question *Who broke Barings Bank?* For it does not identify the culprit independently of the question; and all that the question reveals, through its presupposition, is that somebody broke the bank. But the description does identify some individual through (the presupposition of) the question to the extent that, whoever that person was, it was the person who broke the bank. However uninformative, something is said about that person. Beyond that no further identification is given by the description.

In summary: the difference in function between the interrogative and the relative clause both introduced by *what* is that only the latter actually says anything. Since it says that she did a thing, the relative clause is propositional in form. Yet it can be construed as citing by a term of this proposition what answers the question *What did she do?* The direct question instead only asks what she did. And the interrogative clause after verbs attributing knowledge only alludes obliquely to what answers the question *What did she do?* without actually either saying what she did or citing the term that answers this question. What the interrogative clause expresses is expressed interrogatively only through an allusion to a question, not propositionally in the way a relative clause cites by a term what answers some question.

The object of asking a question, it was said earlier, is to elicit what answers the question. But here the *what* is a compound relative pronoun, meaning the thing, whatever it is, that answers the question. Somewhat like the parent interrogative clause, it is not revealed here what it is that answers the question — other than that what is to be elicited is a thing which does succeed in answering the question. The concept of what answers a question might accordingly be thought to be exercised whether given interrogative expression by means of an interrogative clause or propositional expression by means of the corresponding relative clause; for both express what is ultimately conceived by allusion to the same question — namely, *What answers the question?* But the matter is more complicated.

A consequence of thought taking interrogative besides propositional form is that concepts too can be either interrogative or propositional in form. A concept should not be equated with what a term means regardless of the context of its occurrence. Even the meaning of words within a sentence or clause is determined by the thought expressed — what is thought, as distinct from thought of. Concepts are not, therefore, simply elements out of which thoughts are constructed; for here the character of a part is determined by the whole, not the other way round. Accordingly, the concept of what answers a question when the phrase *what answers the question* occurs in an interrogative clause is an interrogative concept —

meaning thereby a concept of what either raises, or answers in interrogative form, a question; but when the phrase occurs in the corresponding relative clause it is a propositional concept — meaning thereby a concept of what does not raise but instead answers a question, though in propositional form by expressly stating and not merely by alluding interrogatively to what answers it. For *what* is ambiguous.

Concepts are exercised when a thought is thought but are not themselves thought — though they can sometimes be thought of, by philosophers. Instead, concepts are thoughts of something or other, what constitute parts of what is thought *tout court*. Now, the opaqueness of interrogative concepts exercised in interrogative clauses and sentences parallels the comparative uninformativeness of the propositional concepts exercised in relative clauses conceived according to the Aristotelian approach as citing what answers some question, even though the latter's citing is propositional. Thus, the ambiguity of *what* can strike one as only an arcane distinction of grammar in the face of the great affinity there appears to be between interrogative concepts exercised in interrogative clauses and their propositional counterparts in relative clauses.

This affinity is explained by the propositional concept being what Reid calls a relative conception: 'it gives us no conception of what the thing is, but only what relation it bears to something else'. Reid has in mind the notions of secondary qualities and of substance, where any notion of them is only relative, and hence obscure.[20] (The use of the term *relative* here is unconnected with relative clauses.) What Reid later calls the 'direct' conception of a thing can, however, lead to the notion of the relationship it bears to other things: -

> when, by attention, to one of the related objects, we ... judge that it must, from its nature, have a certain relation to something else, ... and thus our attention to one of the related objects produces the notion of a correlate, and of a certain relation between them.

Thus, a relative conception can be quite distinct, while the direct conception can indeed sometimes be obscure.[21] The propositional concept of what answers a question is essentially relative — relative, that is, to its parent interrogative concept, which is direct; but once what answers a question has been stated as being such-and-such, as the answer to any question is stated propositionally, a direct notion of what answers the question is obtained — that is, a notion of what answers the question as being such-and-such becomes available.

The interrogative concept of what answers a question is the highest genus of all interrogative concepts. Wherever questions and interrogative clauses occur the general interrogative concept is being exercised of what answers, in interrogative form, a question raised or alluded to; and any other interrogative concepts also being exercised fall under this general concept. That is, other, more specific interrogative concepts are concepts of things answering specific types of question. And wherever what answers a question is expressly stated the counterpart general propositional concept is being exercised of what answers, in propositional form, a question; and any other, more specific propositional concepts also being exercised, the counterparts to interrogative concepts, fall under this general concept. Since questions determine their conformable answers, interrogative concepts structure their counterpart propositional concepts exercised in stating conformable answers to them.

While the Aristotelian approach has traditionally been propositional in outlook and has not expressly given recognition to interrogative concepts, it can nevertheless be developed into a doctrine of interrogative concepts. Conceiving what is propositional in form as answering some question is to have a propositional concept; yet one that is merely relative to its parent interrogative concept, not a direct one. So although interrogative concepts are exercised only where some interrogative sentence or clause occurs, or can be understood, their counterpart propositional concepts, which are exercised far more widely in the stating of answers to questions, point to the organising work of their interrogative parents.

Interrogative concepts figure in thought more than might be suspected owing to the interrogative clauses giving them expression often being concealed: *knowing the answer to a question* is elliptical for *knowing what the answer to a question is.* So even the ordinary expression *the answer to a question* can signal the exercise of an interrogative concept. When it is elliptical for an interrogative clause it expresses in interrogative form the interrogative concept of what the answer to a question is. The words *the answer*, accordingly, lead a double life: being elliptical for sometimes an interrogative, sometimes a relative, clause. That is, *the answer* can also be elliptical for the clause, *what the answer is*, introduced by a compound relative pronoun. A teacher may announce to her class: *The answer to question 4 is 1815.* Her announcement may be construed as: *What the answer is* (*The 'thing' which is the answer*) *to question 4 is 1815.* The relative clause in stating what the answer to a question is — namely, that it is a 'thing' — echoes the original question, *What is the answer?* Hence the propositional concept of the answer to a question, in being essentially relative, invokes its parent interrogative concept. If the question was *In what year was the Battle of Waterloo fought?* then *1815* states what the answer to the question is, so enabling a direct notion of the answer as being *1815* to be formed.

The *what* after the verb *state* can introduce an interrogative clause just as much as the verb *know*; but the *what* can sometimes be a compound relative pronoun. *He stated what was incorrect* could perhaps be read as saying that he stated (correctly) what pieces of information (given by others) were in fact incorrect; but it is more readily readable as saying that the thing he himself stated was incorrect — brought out better by *What he stated was incorrect.*

The solution Ryle once proposed to the problem that false propositions could scarcely be subsistent entities — namely, that 'when I state what I know, the fact that I know, and the meaning of my statement are not two things but one', so that even when I state what is not a fact, I state what would be the case if it were a known fact[22] — derives what force it has from the ability of the verb *state* to take interrogative constructions, together with the correctly doing so thereby implied. His solution will not do, since there is an equivocation between an interrogative and a relative reading of the *what*: stating what are a series of facts does not differ as far as the statements themselves go from stating what are a series of falsehoods, and is quite distinct from stating what the facts are.

There are many instances of ellipses concealing interrogative concepts. Austin noted that '"knowing the winner of the Derby" means "knowing *what won* the Derby"'. Seeing or noticing the colour of the wallpaper is seeing or noticing what colour the wallpaper was.[23] By contrast, a newspaper report begins: *The winner of the Derby is* ... . The phrase *The winner of the Derby* as it occurs here is to be construed as being elliptical for a relative clause. While the concept of a winner being exercised here is therefore propositional, being essentially relative it still invokes its parent interrogative concept, the concept of what answers in interrogative form the question *What won?*

Abstract nouns used for physical dimensions and quantities capable of being given numerical values can, when governed by the appropriate verb, conceal interrogative clauses too, and thus express interrogative concepts, as in the examples given by Bede Rundle: 'weight, height, length, strength, distance, volume, speed, density, shape'. Other examples of terms that often conceal interrogative clauses are: *price*, *name*, *age*, *occupation*, *marital status*;[24] in short the sort of terms making up field names in a database. All these terms, when used to state what answers the question alluded to in the concealed interrogative clause, also express the counterpart propositional concepts. To say truthfully *I am six foot tall* or *You are 47* is to state that something is so of myself or you. Yet the concepts of height and age are primarily interrogative because the terms *height* and *age* can often be used to either raise a question about somebody's height or age, or allude interrogatively to what answers it; that is, to state what my height or what your age is.

It would be a mistake to suppose that such concealed interrogative clauses are invariably introduced by *what* followed by a noun, so that 'the noun indicates the *identity* of what is known'.[25] Sometimes, indeed, the concealed clause simply retains the noun, as in the instances of *the colour* and *the answer*. Here, though, the phrase offered in explication, 'the *identity* of what is known' has rather to be explicated as knowing what the colour or the answer is, for identity is itself foremost an interrogative concept. Often, though, the noun can be replaced by an adjective or a verb, so that even if there is a *what*, the clause is different.[26] Knowing what the temperature is means knowing how hot it is; a thing's weight, how heavy it is or what it weighs; its price, how much, or what, it costs; my height, how tall I am; your age, how old you are; your marital status, whether you are married, separated, divorced or widowed; your name, what you are called; his address, where he lives; the cause of the accident, what caused it; the result of the trial, what happened at the end. Rundle has also argued that knowing the meaning of a word is knowing what the word means, that *meaning* used in such contexts 'is best understood in clausal terms'.[27]

Many fundamental logical and metaphysical concepts are primarily interrogative in form. They are not predicative concepts. The predicative falls exclusively within the propositional: terms expressing predicative concepts are those that can be predicated of the logical subject of a proposition, so are capable of being true of that subject. Since it can be true of Socrates that he was a philosopher — in other words, the proposition expressed by the declarative sentence *Socrates was a philosopher*, is either true or false — the concept of a philosopher is a predicative concept. Interrogative concepts, by contrast, are of what either raises or answers interrogatively types of question. Thus, *calling* or *profession*, by contrast with *philosopher*, can express an interrogative concept.

The terms expressing counterpart propositional concepts to their parent interrogative concepts cannot be predicated of the logical subject of a proposition; they can only be logical subjects of propositions. *You are 47* does not, despite the appearance conveyed by this idiom, predicate *47* of the subject *you*. The logical subject of the sentence is rather *your age*, and *47* is predicated of the years you have lived up to now. In being used to state what your age is the term *your age* expresses a propositional concept. Yet the concept invokes its parent interrogative concept of age; for the sentence cites by a term — namely *47* — what answers the question *How old are you?* In the sentence *His age is advanced*, by contrast, the term *age* does express an interrogative concept; since the term means here how old he is. Neither interrogative concepts nor their propositional counterparts, then, are predicative concepts.

Aristotle's categories were so named by him because, he held, they constitute the main types of predication. His categories themselves, though, are primarily interrogative concepts — namely, those of *identity* (that is, *substance*), *quantity*, *quality*, *relation*, *location*, *time*, *position*, *state*, *action* and *affection*.[28] These concepts allude to questions of the type *Who* (or *What* or *Which*) *is it?* or *What, which kind* (or *sort*) *of? How much* (or *many*)*? What is it like? What is the connection between* (or *with*)*?* or *How is it connected to? When? Where? How is he disposed? How is he dressed? What did he do? What was done to him?* Thus: *The identity of the deceased is unknown* means that *who* (*what kind of person* or perhaps *which person*) *the deceased was* is unknown; that it *is unknown* what answers the question *Who was the deceased?* which is the sort of question implicitly alluded to by the term *identity*. Likewise, concepts such as those of explanation, method and reason allude to such questions as *How did it come about* (or *to be*)*? How is it to be done?* and *Why should it be?* or *Why should I do it?*

Only what cites by a term what answers the implicit question belongs to a type of predication. In belonging to a type of predication what is stated in answer falls under an Aristotelian category, but is not itself one. *The deceased was a police officer* or *was a Belgian*, *was tall and thin* or *was slumped over a table* contain different types of predicables, which each fall within different categories; but the categories of *identity*, *quality* and *position* are not themselves predicative concepts. The implicit question, or rather the interrogative concept, 'collects', in Ryle's word, the relevant predicates.[29] Hence through the exercise of interrogative concepts questions are able to 'structure' pieces of 'information' expressed in propositions.[30] So Aristotle was not wrong to regard his categories as grouping types of predication, even though his categories are not themselves predicative concepts.

Since many of the fundamental concepts exercised in thought — such as the Aristotelian categories — are primarily interrogative, the interrogative is not only a form of thought but also organises all thought, whether interrogative or propositional in form. It can do so because of the asymmetry of the relationship between question and answer: whereas a question determines the form of what answers it, a conformable answer to a question cannot determine the question whose form it conforms to.

The distinctiveness of interrogative concepts may be missed because the terms for them also have propositional uses. First, terms expressing concepts like Aristotle's categories lead a double life, sometimes expressing an interrogative concept, sometimes the counterpart propositional concept, depending on whether they can be explicated by means of an interrogative or a relative clause. Since the sentence *The detective studied the position of the body* can be construed as *The detective studied how the body was positioned*, the term *position* expresses an interrogative concept. But in *The position of the body had led to great loss of blood* the term conceals a relative clause, and so expresses the counterpart propositional concept; so also, *The identities of the two patients were confused.* Again, *He found out the price of the computer* and *The price was high* conceal respectively an interrogative and a relative clause. But secondly and differently, *The price depressed him* conceals a clause like *that the price was so high* or *that the price was so low*, depending on whether the consumer's or producer's perspective is adopted. Since these last clauses are introduced by *that* they are obviously not interrogative but propositional in form.

Again, one of Aristotle's categories is time. The category can readily be conceived as alluding to *when* questions. But it would be wrong to think that all uses of the word *time* give expression to an interrogative concept. First, the words *the time* in *The time is half past four* conceals a relative clause — although the propositional concept here invokes its parent interrogative concept, for it cites by a term what answers the question *What time is it?* Second, *Time flies* invokes no interrogative concept; for any conceivable question being answered here would be *What flies?* and so would not ask *When? Time* here means instead the passing of time. Another of Aristotle's categories is action, which can be construed as alluding to the question *What was done?* In *Actions speak louder than words* the sense is that whether or not people act and how they act is more important than anything they say. *His action was careless*, it might be argued, states what answers the question how he acted; but the word *carelessly* would do so. Here, as also in

Action was required immediately, no question about what was done or whether it was done has been answered. *Action* in these instances means no more than acting.

Other Grammatical Forms

Thought takes at least two fundamental forms, the interrogative and the propositional. Grammar suggests other forms thought might take, such as exclamatory, optative or imperatival. It would be to stray too far afield to explore whether such grammatical forms mark irreducible forms of thought. But as philosophers tend to take the grammatical imperative as a paradigm of the non-declarative while either ignoring the interrogative or attempting to reduce it to either the imperatival or the propositional, a few remarks about imperative sentences are in order.

Philosophers often speak blithely of 'imperatives' as if these comprised a class co-ordinate with propositions, questions, exclamations or wishes. Sometimes, as in Kant, it seems that the term is not simply an abbreviation for 'imperative sentence'. Only two of the Ten Commandments are in fact expressed in the imperative mood: *Remember the sabbath day* and *Honour thy father and thy mother*. Now, just as a person's asking of a question can be reported by the verb *ask*, so a person's addressing of an imperative sentence to another can often be reported not merely by *said*, but more specifically by *tell*. But whereas a report that a person asked a question is never in need of further explanation since a question belongs to a clear-cut logical category, a report that a person told another to do something often requires to be construed more specifically still. For as yet what *tell* at most refers to is the addressing of an imperative sentence to another, which cannot simply be taken as expressing 'an imperative' — whatever that may be — as an interrogative sentence can simply be taken in its standard occurrences as expressing a question.[31] Unlike declarative, interrogative, exclamatory and optative sentences, imperative sentences stand in need of some interpretation. Does the sentence on this occasion express an order, a directive, an injunction, a demand, a warning, a threat? Or is it perhaps part of a set of instructions, a piece of advice, a methodological rule, a principle of action? And since requests and invitations are sometimes expressed informally by imperative sentences, the sentence may not tell at all, but instead ask, the addressee to do something. Thus, theorists who hope to reduce questions to commands of some sort are seeking to explain the quite straightforward by the relatively indeterminate.

Terms can be coined for whatever it may be that is expressed in the imperative mood. Hare at one time decided to 'follow the grammarians and use the single term "command" to cover all these sorts of thing that sentences in the imperative mood express'; but later, speaking of 'the genus of speech-acts typically expressed in the imperative mood', introduced 'the word "imperation" for the genus of "tellings to", meaning, roughly, "speech-act for which an imperative is a natural form"'.[32] Even if care is taken not to confuse the generic, and artificial, sense of *command* with its specific, mainly military, sense, the amorphousness of imperative sentences in comparison to the relative determinateness of declarative, interrogative, exclamatory and optative sentences cannot be concealed by terminological fiat. For if nothing essentially, but only typically, is expressed in the imperative mood, then, as G. J. Warnock observes, 'imperatives' will comprise 'a class whose bond of union is nothing more than grammatical'.[33]

It follows from this heterogeneity that the imperatival, however conceived, is not necessarily expressed by what is grammatically imperative, as C. L. Hamblin recognises in what could be viewed as a riposte to Warnock: -

> the test of what is or is not a command, or any sort of imperative, is ultimately functional, not grammatical. (How else would we even be able to make the *grammatical* distinction?)[34]

But Warnock is quite aware that there is a 'large and heterogeneous class of utterances that could be said to function in an imperative way'. The issue arising from this heterogeneity is whether there is anything further to go on once 'the grammatically identifiable class of actual sentences in the imperative mood' is forsaken as the criterion of the imperatival. Even Warnock seems to think there is: -

> That one speaker is addressing another person, or other persons, or just conceivably himself, seems in this case somehow to get into the sense of the sentence itself; ... imperatives seem 'practical'.[35]

This characteristic reference to the doing by an addressee, whether literal or figurative, of what the verb of the sentence conveys is precisely the reason for doubting whether the imperatival could be as fundamental as the interrogative. The imperatival by virtue of its sense requires some — at least understood — addressee, even if in marginal instances the only candidates are figuratively oneself, some person one imagines present, or even an inanimate thing. Paradoxically, those languages like English, where the subject of the verb in the imperative mood in the second person is normally suppressed, still require it to be understood. Perhaps the subject is suppressed simply because there is no need to mention it explicitly when it is required by the sense — rather as a diarist similarly truncates first-person singular subjects from verbs. Imperative sentences are thus typically but not invariably — a qualification constantly needed with such an amorphous category — confined to the sphere of action in social settings; an area which, though of great generality, is yet more limited in scope than the form of thought as such. For the form of thought about action can be only a part of the form of thought as such.

The assumption that the interrogative is likewise confined to language used to address others, and so falls specifically within the purview of the philosopher of language as distinct from the philosopher of logic, carries with it the implication that the interrogative derives solely from social interactions between speakers and so fails to mark a form of thought as such. However inappropriate such a view of the interrogative is, it seems only the appropriate one to take of the imperatival.

Thought, it can safely be taken for granted, must be structured logically if it is to be — as thought sometimes is not — intelligible, of determinable and unequivocal content, communicable and coherent; and if thought is to have any logical structure, it must also be capable of formulation in language, it further seems reasonable to insist. But it by no means follows that all structural features of language reflect forms of thought. A thinker may feel surprise, admiration, frustration, and so forth; may feel longing or repugnance; may draw up principles of action or lay down *desiderata*. So a thinker may think in language employing exclamatory, optative and imperative grammatical forms. Even if such forms are employed in thinking less rarely than might initially seem, their standard employment is when words are addressed to others. Since words in silent soliloquy borrow grammatical forms employed when the words are addressed out loud to others, the employment in thought of forms which are grammatically exclamatory, optative or imperative provides no reliable indication that such forms reflect logical features of thought as such. To do so they must be capable of abstraction from all notion of interaction between different speakers and thus become free of any social or merely conventional determinant; and so have no built-in requirement for an addressee, whether literal or figurative. Whereas the interrogative, the exclamatory and the optative all pass this test, the imperatival, whether or not expressed in the imperative mood, fails it.

In the strict sense mood is a distinctive form taken by the verb — say, by inflexion; but in a broader sense mood concerns distinctive uses of the verb which may be determined by parsing regardless of whether a specific language marks a mood by a distinctive form of the verb.[36] Some languages, not English, have a distinctive form of the verb for the optative mood; yet the English sentences *God save the Queen* and *May you burn in hell* can be seen to express wishes, and so to employ their verb optatively. But the existence of a mood — even in the broader sense — is insufficient evidence of some irreducible form of thought. Grammarians also recognise conditional, subjunctive and conjunctive moods, as distinct from the indicative mood, without logicians being compelled to reconsider whether either the antecedent or the consequent of an *if ... then* sentence is propositional in form. And the infinitive mood fulfils a variety of purely grammatical functions where the verb is not finite — that is, has no subject of its own. Thus the existence of the imperative mood need have no logical significance.

It is only philosophers, and linguistic theorists misled by them, who speak of the interrogative as a mood.[37] If they do not suppose any distinctive use — as opposed to distinctive form, like inflexion — of the verb makes a sentence interrogative, it is incumbent on them to explain what they mean by 'mood'. One account is that 'verbal mood' should be distinguished from 'syntactic mood'; the former is supposed to concern the differences between 'indicative, subjunctive, optative, etc.'; the latter between 'declarative, imperative and interrogative'.[38] The imperative clearly belongs on the first list, indeed is a prime instance of 'verbal' mood; and no explanation has been given why it should occur on the second list. Is it just fortuitous that the grammatical imperative coincides with a 'syntactic' mood? The heterogeneity of its possible interpretations makes that improbable. The notion that there is such a thing as 'syntactic' mood, with its juxtaposing of the imperative and the interrogative along with the declarative, betrays the dubious assumption that the interrogative differs from the declarative in a way comparable to the way imperative sentences differ from indicative sentences — thus apparently also conflating the declarative, which is not a mood either, with being in the indicative mood.[39] There is the further suspicion that the interrogative is spoken of by philosophers as a mood only because they tend to regard it as not just analogous but actually reducible to the grammatical imperative.

Why is there no coincidence between the two supposed types of mood in the case of the interrogative? Because the interrogative, unlike the imperative but like the declarative, is not concerned with a type of use of the verb. In his discussion of verbal inflexions in Latin, Varro lists six categories: tense, person, interrogative, responsive, optative and imperative. It is evident that his list is of types of inflexions of the verb, since tense and person cut across the distinctive uses of the verb described as mood in the broader sense.[40] Besides, only yes-no and alternative questions can be formed in Latin by adding the suffix *-ne* to a word, which need not even be a verb; thus in Latin inflexion of the verb does not as such mark the interrogative. And although in modern English subject and verb are inverted for yes-no and alternative questions in direct speech, inversion also occurs widely elsewhere;[41] in conditional sentences, for instance. *Should auld acquaintance be forgot* makes a good question but was not meant as such.

There is no reason to think that the verb in an interrogative sentence is used in any way different to its use in a declarative sentence. That is, if the verb in a declarative sentence is in the indicative, subjunctive or infinitive mood, so likewise is it in any counterpart interrogative sentence. The verb of a sentence, granted, cannot be in two moods within the same sentence.[42] But the reason why the verb of an interrogative sentence cannot be, say, in the optative mood is not that the interrogative is a mood too; rather, the optative mood gives voice to the speaker's wish, which cannot then within the same utterance be made the subject of a question: I cannot pray that God bless the Pope and at the same time be asking something about the wish I am thereby giving voice to. Admittedly, in English the verb of an interrogative sentence likewise resists the imperative mood.[43] Resort has to be made to either an infinitive construction or a modal verb: *Am I to shut the door? When is she to serve tea?* or *Should I shut the door? When should she serve tea?* Latin would use a jussive subjunctive here. Indeed, the argument about a verb being in only one mood at a time works rather the other way: the use in German, noted by Frege, of the conjunctive mood for interrogative clauses reporting direct questions and similar uses of non-indicative moods in other languages, tells against regarding the interrogative as a mood in its own right.[44] And while a few languages, such as West Greenlandic, rich in moods in the strict sense express questions by a distinctive inflexion of the verb,[45] most languages are perfectly able to express questions without having any interrogative mood in this sense of mood.

Philosophers have taken imperative sentences as furnishing a paradigm of the non-declarative chiefly because imperative sentences do not say anything that could be said to be either true or false. *Shut the door* does not 'declare' that anything is so, and thus is not itself either true or false. The point of issuing an imperative sentence is rather to achieve the doing of the enjoined action by one's addressee. Setting aside devious or figurative uses, a speaker in issuing an imperative sentence is presumed to intend that the addressee do the enjoined action. Optative sentences give voice to the speaker's wishes for a broader range of items, including past actions and by other agents, as well as things and states of affairs.[46] It is argued, quite correctly, that what an imperative sentence says cannot, even in standard situations, simply be identified with the proposition that the speaker wants the action to be done by the addressee, such as *I want you to shut the door* — what Reichenbach calls the 'cognitive correlate' of the imperative sentence. Rather, when a speaker utters the sentence *Shut the door* the proposition *I want you to shut the door* is usually true but the speaker never actually says that anything is so when issuing an imperative sentence.[47] A parallel argument might be deployed in connection with the optative mood. A roughly parallel argument, in any case, certainly applies to interrogative sentences.

The distinction between, on the one hand, the proposition that a speaker who issues an utterance with a certain grammatical form has certain beliefs, intentions, purposes, desires, wishes or attitudes and, on the other, what the utterance itself says, is quite secure irrespective of whether what the utterance says has ultimately to be interpreted propositionally. The issue is whether what the speaker's words say is expressible by a proposition that does not itself contain some non-propositional form of thought.

Now, a speaker in addressing an imperative sentence to another can always be reported as having told the other to do some action. The verb *tell* almost fits, but not quite, when the sort of thing an imperative sentence says needs to be communicated to a third party who is being enjoined to do the action. *He told you to lie low* could simply report the words he addressed to you previously. *He tells you to lie low*, by contrast, has no implication that he spoke to you at all; instead, it communicates to you that he said that you are to or should lie low. The verb *say* is less accommodating: *He says to lie low* is ambiguous: who is to or should lie low, the speaker, the addressee or both? To remove any ambiguity it has to be expanded to: *He says that I am to, should, lie low*, or *He says that you are to, should, lie low* or *He says that we are to, should, lie low.*[48]

Thus, it is plausible to argue, in outline, that imperative sentences can be analysed as saying something which is indeed propositional — namely, that the addressee is to, or alternatively, should, do some action; and that they say this irrespective of what intentions, purposes, desires or wishes the speaker may happen to have, or not have. Such an account receives additional confirmation from what was previously noted, that the verb in an interrogative sentence cannot be in the imperative mood: instead, as in indirect speech, the verb *to be* followed by an infinitive construction or the modal verb *should* have to be used if one is to ask a question about what an imperative sentence says. The onus, then, is on those who would deny that the imperatival is propositional to show that to say that an action either is to, or should, be done by somebody cannot be to say anything that is either true or false.

The non-declarative, then, is not necessarily non-propositional. But since interrogative sentences only ask something and do not say anything at all, they are clearly both non-declarative and non-propositional. Moreover, an interrogative, and hence non-propositional, residue is ineliminable from reports of people's askings of questions. And sometimes, as will be seen in Chapter 7, an imperative sentence has to be taken as a request or an invitation; in which case it has interpreted interrogatively rather than propositionally.

Imperative sentences often demand some interpretation; other non-declaratives do not. But whether the optative and the exclamatory mark distinctive forms of thought again depends on whether a report of what the speaker said contains any non-propositional residue. As the function of the optative is to voice the speaker's wishes, grammatically optative sentences can be reported — much more readily than imperative sentences — by *I*, *You*, *He*, etc. *wished that* ... . Yet uttering of the words in the first-person, present, non-continuous tense *I wish that* ... would actually be to give voice to a wish, just as the original optative sentence did; for these are performative utterances, not reports on oneself. Likewise, the words *My wish is that* ... may also sometimes function performatively. Reports of optative sentences, however, are not to be thought as translations of the original sentences; merely substitutable for them as reported speech in general is substitutable for direct speech. The reports are clearly not equivalent in meaning to the original sentences; for what these said, unlike what is reported as being said, is not capable of being either true or false. In fact the reports say something more than the original sentences, which simply give voice to speakers' wishes without saying that they have these wishes. But convenience and economy provided by such non-declarative grammatical forms is no argument for irreducibility.

Utterances may be exclamatory in tone yet declarative, interrogative or imperatival in form, as in: *You're a dreadful cynic*, *Why did he have to go?* and *Get out of my way*. The issue, again, is whether the grammatical form — as in *How wonderful you are!* and *What a mess you've made!* — signals a distinct logical form. The use of interrogative words in what are grammatically exclamations affords another illustration of the exercise of the propositional counterparts to interrogative concepts. *So* and *such* are strictly exclamatory in form only, as they commonly are, in ellipsis as fragments of sentences. Not being elliptical, *You're so wonderful!* and *It's such a pity that he had to go!* are arguably exclamatory merely in tone. The optative, though usually sanctioning an exclamation mark — as do *so* and *such* — likewise falls within what is exclamatory in tone.

Anscombe's translation has Wittgenstein say: 'we do in fact call "Isn't the weather glorious to-day?" a question, although it is used as a statement'. In Wittgenstein's German the question is positive, not negative. Whichever version of the question is employed — and a tag question, as in *The weather is glorious today, isn't it?* would serve equally well — the utterance is primarily exclamatory, not assertoric. But the added feature of anticipation of the concurrence of an addressee makes it a question addressed to another and not simply an exclamation — in effect, *The weather is glorious today, don't you agree?*[49]

The exclamatory, whether as a grammatical form or purely in tone, evidently gives voice to the speaker's attitudes to states of affairs presupposed or previously acknowledged. Again, the availability of the propositional paraphrase that the speaker has the attitude given voice to shows that the exclamatory does not constitute a distinctive form of thought.

Notes

1 Karttunen (1978), p. 167. Cf. Hintikka (1976), p. 71; Kiefer (1981), pp. 166, 174, note 15 and 175, note 17.
2 Contrast Woozley (1953), p. 161.
3 Stampe (1974), pp. 160, 164-6 and Woozley (1953), p. 161.
4 Cf. Stampe (1974), p. 164.
5 See Brown (1971), p. 225; cf. Stampe (1974), p. 164, note. 3.
6 Cf. Prior (1971), pp. 75-6.
7 Cf. *OED*, xx, p. 187c.
8 Contrast Bell (1975), pp. 199, 201-3.
9 Hintikka (1976), p. 70; cf. pp. 7, 16-17, 22-3, 24, 69-70. Contrast Kiefer (1981), pp. 171-2.
10 Cf. Welbourne (1989), p. 181.
11 See Harrah (1961), p. 43; (1963), pp. 27, 39; Belnap (1963), pp. 18-21, 137-48 and contrast p. 61; Stahl (1969), p. 212; Hintikka (1974), pp. 136-7; Belnap and Steel (1976), pp. 36, 125-30; Harrah (1984), pp. 715, 720.
12 Cf. Welbourne (1986a), pp. 36, 92, 96, note 16.
13 See Belnap (1963), pp. 5, 19; Åqvist (1965), p. 142.
14 Cf. Belnap (1963), p. 134; Belnap and Steel (1976), p. 116.
15 See *OED* i, pp. 497b-9c.
16 Segal (1991), p. 107.
17 *OED*, vii, p. 725c.
18 Aristotle (1928b), II i and ii; 89b21-2 and 89b36-7.
19 Cf. Stampe (1974), pp. 162, 170.
20 Reid (1785), II xvii; p. 314a; cf. xix; pp. 322-3; III vii; p. 359b and (1788), I i; pp. 513-14.
21 Reid (1785), VI i; pp. 420-21 and (1788), I i; p. 514a.

22 Cf. Ryle (1930), p. 27; cf. pp. 32-8.
23 Austin (1946), p. 96. Rundle (1972), pp. 165, 171.
24 Rundle (1979), p. 233; (1990), p. 175. Stampe (1974), p. 163 and p. 167, note 7.
25 White (1982), p. 30; cf. Stampe (1974), pp. 166-9. Contrast Vendler (1967), p. 96 and Rundle (1979), pp. 239, 242; (1990), p. 172.
26 Cf. Rundle (1979), pp. 238-40, 378; (1990), p. 175.
27 Rundle (1990), p. 171; cf. p. 177 and (1979), p. 378. Cf. also Stampe (1974), p. 167, note 7.
28 Aristotle (1928a), 4; 1b25-2a4. See also Kahn (1978), pp. 239-41, 243, 248-50, 261-3; Ryle (1938), pp. 170-71, 172-3; Whately (1913), II v § 3; p. 85 and IV ii § 1; pp. 159-60.
29 Ryle (1938), p. 171; cf. Rundle (1979), p. 244.
30 Hookway (1996), pp. 10-11.
31 Contrast Wilson and Sperber (1988), pp. 96-8.
32 Hare (1952), p. 4; (1968), p. 56.
33 Warnock (1976), p. 137. Cf. Austin (1962), pp. 32, 73-4, 76-7.
34 Hamblin (1987), p. 6; cf. Mitchell (1957), pp. 180-81.
35 Warnock (1976), p. 126; cf. Hare (1952), p. 177.
36 See Whately (1913), Appendix I iii; p. 195, note 5.
37 See, for instance, Reichenbach (1947), p. 340; Ross (1968), p. 77, note 1.
38 Hausser (1980), p. 93, note 1; cf. Hausser (1983), p. 100.
39 Cf. Rundle (1990), pp. 84-5 and 145. Cf. also Wilson and Sperber (1988), p. 99; but contrast pp. 78-9, 91, 94, 95 and 98.
40 Varro (1951), X 31, 32; ii, p. 559; cf. IX 32; ii, p. 461-3.
41 Cf. Rundle (1990), p. 91.
42 *Pace* Wilson and Sperber (1988), pp. 99-100.
43 Contrast Rundle (1990), p. 145 and cf. Wilson and Sperber (1988), pp. 99-100.
44 See Frege (1892), p. 153/167. Cf. Rundle (1979), p. 307.
45 See Sadock (1984), pp. 197-9.
46 Cf. Hare (1949), p. 7; Gandhi (1976), p. 41; Rundle (1990), pp. 97-8.
47 Reichenbach (1947), p. 342; cf. pp. 19-20 and 340. Cf. also Hare (1949), pp. 19-20; (1952), pp. 5-6.
48 Contrast Bolinger (1977), pp. 171-2 and p. 181, note 18.
49 Wittgenstein (1958), I § 21; p. 10e. Cf. Hudson (1975), pp. 8-12, 19.

Chapter 3

Questions and Enquiry

Since the interrogative clauses taken by *know* have no bearing on the asking of questions, still less the putting of questions to anybody, the significance of the interrogative for epistemology lies in what pertains to questions themselves, conceived as abstracted from anybody's actually asking them or putting them to anybody else; but also, if intellectualism is to be avoided, as abstracted from anybody actually answering them. Many philosophers have apparently found difficulty in thinking of questions, thus abstracted, as objects of logical attention having a distinct yet parallel status to propositions. But as will be seen at the end of the chapter, if questions themselves are thought of as divorced from all notion of asking, instead of being conceived interrogatively they will be misconceived as being propositional in form. Even when conceived as abstracted from anybody's asking of them, questions still ask something: they themselves are quite incapable of saying anything.

In this chapter the widespread assumption that questions are to be understood as essentially relating to enquiry is challenged. Its task is to disentangle questions as objects of logical attention from the pursuing of enquiries. As etymology suggests, an enquiry is articulated and guided through the questions that arise during its course about its subject,[1] though often these questions are only implicit. Now, philosophers usually start from the wrong end, trying to account for questions by relating them to enquiry without realising that the notion of enquiry itself involves the notion of asking questions. Even although *ask* is paradigmatically a verb of enquiry when its subject is a person, it will become clear that questions need not be asked solely in the course of an ongoing enquiry. Still less can questions themselves, as abstracted from people's askings of them, be defined as related to enquiry. So throughout three items will have to be distinguished: asking questions in the course of an enquiry; asking questions as such; and questions themselves.

Since enquiry has as its aim the acquisition of knowledge, to tie questions conceptually to enquiry is in effect to define questions by reference to knowledge. It might therefore be anticipated that the epistemological significance of the interrogative is a familiar theme: namely, that questions are essentially connected to enquiry. But to take enquiry rather than the interrogative as the more primitive notion would instead be to argue for the different, commoner view that the epistemological has significance for the interrogative. The contention argued for here is the reverse: the interrogative has instead significance for epistemology — which is owing, not to any raising of questions in enquiry, but to the interrogative constructions taken by *know*. It is not that questions have anything necessarily to do with knowledge; instead a piece of knowledge can sometimes be conceived as having to do with some question.

The account of enquiry is initially approached, somewhat deviously, by considering the specific philosophical enquiry into, as it is said, 'the nature of a question'. The peculiarities of philosophical enquiry will serve to bring out forcibly a feature of all enquiry.

The Question *What Is A Question?*

The interrogative is already implicated in the notion of not only enquiry but also the nature of something. The concept of the nature of a thing is interrogative to the extent that it is the concept of what answers questions of the type *What sort of thing is it?* Now, one can only refer to the nature of something when one knows at least something about that sort of thing beforehand: how to pick out some of its instances, what category it falls under, often how to specify some of its salient features or manifestations. In enquiring into the nature of human beings, of water, or of the treasury, one is asking what sort of animal a human being is, what sort of stuff water is, what sort of institution the treasury is. Enquiries into the nature of things, as with all enquiries, cannot start from a state of total ignorance about their subjects. Generally such enquiries have the aim of obtaining further, usually more fundamental, knowledge about their subjects.

The peculiarity of the *What is ... ?* questions, or questions about 'the nature of' something, typically posed by philosophers in their enquiries, as distinct from the questions posed by other enquirers such as scientists and historians, is that the elementary categorisation allowing specification of the subject, usually taken for granted in other enquiries, is lacking. At first such philosophical questions appear to be like the questions asked by young children who know virtually nothing of the thing being enquired about, not even what rudimentary classification to give it. Often what produces satisfaction is some explanation of the meaning of an unfamiliar word; and in giving an explanation one also by the way tells the child something about things, the world, life or categories of thought. If a boy asks what divorce is, one might begin by saying what the word *divorce* means, thus enabling him to determine what category divorce falls under — a mixed mode Locke would say; a legal dispensation, to be more exact. Philosophical *What is ... ?* questions seem similarly indeterminate between a regard for the meaning of words and for things, the world, life or categories of thought. The difference is that philosophers, like most adults, already know a fair deal about not only the meaning and usage of the words involved but also the world, life and categories of thought. If they avow ignorance, as Socrates did, the suspicion is that their professed ignorance is mere pretence; more charitably, in claiming not to know they may be deceiving themselves, be simply confused about the actual extent of their current knowledge or else perplexed about what they do know.

Such apparently ignorant posing of questions recalls the questions Plato makes Meno ask Socrates on the subject of the definition of virtue: -

> And how will you enquire, Socrates, into that which you do not know? What will you put forth as the subject of enquiry? And if you find what you want, how will you ever know that this is what you did not know?[2]

If one knows nothing at all about a subject, as Socrates earlier protested that he knew 'literally nothing about virtue',[3] how is one even to begin to know what questions to ask about it in order to start one's enquiry into it in the hope of remedying one's ignorance? Even supposing one comes across the answers to the questions one did not know to ask, how will one ever recognise that they are the answers to these questions if one did not know to ask the questions to begin with? Plato's general intention seems to have been to show how Socratic ignorance can deal with this difficulty: one must first come to know one's ignorance.[4] That is, in an enquiry one has to know what one currently does not know about a subject in order to raise questions about it in striving to remedy one's ignorance; but further, in order to be able to recognise that any knowledge one has obtained somehow about a subject provides the answers to these questions, one again has to know what one previously did not know about it.

If Socrates really knew nothing at all, as he professes, about the subject under investigation, his attempt at investigation would not be possible. The difficulty raised by Meno establishes that despite his profession of total ignorance Socrates must already know at least something about the subject if he is even to attempt to enquire into it: that at the very least he knows one thing about the subject, that he knows nothing (else) about it. More specifically, Plato seeks to argue, what Socrates unwittingly knows about the subject is recoverable through recollection. If it seems that Plato intended the irony that Socrates, who, in Whately's words, adopted 'that interrogatory method of disputation' furnished from Zeno's '*erotetic* method of disputation', should be confronted with a supposed difficulty about the asking of questions, it should be recalled that the argument in the *Meno* is that the spontaneous recovery of knowledge in others can be facilitated through the putting to them of questions.[5]

Awkwardly for Plato's doctrine of recollection, Reid raises a parallel difficulty about trying to recollect itself. If one is to try to remember something one must surely have some notion of what one is trying to remember; but if so, it would seem that one remembers it already. Reid's solution to the difficulty is that 'we must remember something relating to it, which gives us a relative conception of it'. A common experience with short-term memory presents the difficulty more acutely than Reid's example of trying to remember what a friend had commissioned one to do: one remembers that something has just slipped one's mind but one has no other idea what it could be.[6] But still, it can be said, one knows what one is trying to remember: namely, what one has just forgotten, whatever it was. So what one is trying to remember is specifiable at least relatively as what one has just forgotten.

Regardless of Plato's specific solution, Meno's difficulty serves to confirm that any enquiry whatsoever — not just philosophical enquiries and those into the natures of things — can only proceed from pre-existing knowledge about its subject. The lesson has wider application beyond enquiry: it is a condition of the framing of any question, whether or not in the course of an enquiry, that there be some way of specifying what the question is about, its subject. Even the boy who asks *What is divorce?* has to pronounce the word whose meaning he is ignorant of. This condition of framing any question in any circumstances about any subject may well be 'a platitude', as Michael Welbourne calls it; but what he also calls 'the underlying logic' will prove to be crucial for the understanding of interrogative form.[7]

The condition assuredly applies, embarrassingly, to the enquiry into 'the nature' of a question; in other words, to the question, posed by Felix S. Cohen, *What is a question?* Those unaware of Cohen's article might well exclaim, *What a question!* on being informed of it, since the posing of such a question demands explanation itself. For ignorance of what a question is can hardly be admitted when the posing of that very question only betrays knowledge of what a question is. The answers to all other, including philosophical, questions do not await the answer to this question: that philosophers, like others, can ask and answer questions generally only shows that they already know what questions are, how to spot and deal with them when they encounter them. If theorists often seem to betray grave misunderstanding of questions, it is such as paradoxically also coexists — perhaps only in their off-duty hours — with much unreflective understanding of them.

As Ryle says of philosophers who go about asking of expressions of a certain type 'what they really mean': -

> But the whole procedure is very odd. For, if the expressions under consideration are intelligently used, their employers must already know what they mean and do not need the aid or admonition of philosophers before they can understand what they are saying. ... And, at least, the philosopher himself must know what the expressions mean, since otherwise he could not know what it was he was analysing.[8]

So what does the enquiring philosopher need to know?

If Plato's solution to the difficulty raised by Meno establishes that Socrates is not really in the position he affects to be in, of total ignorance about the subject under investigation, it has nothing to say on the need for enquiry, which instead is raised only in the first half of the eristic dilemma Socrates immediately goes on to present: -

> You argue that a man cannot enquire either about that which he knows, or about that which he does not know; for if he knows he has no need to enquire; and if not, he cannot; for he does not know the very subject about which he is to enquire.[9]

The art of wrangling, or eristics, comprises in Whately's view 'sportive disputations', 'much in the same way as men amuse themselves with propounding and guessing riddles'.[10] This dilemma is such an instance.

Now, the horns of the dilemma are of different orders. According to its letter, the first horn argues that one cannot enquire about what one knows because then one has no need to engage in enquiry. Superficially it denies the possibility of enquiring about what one knows; but the argument is actually based on the superfluousness of enquiry given one's state of knowledge, not on its sheer impossibility. The second horn, by contrast, argues for the sheer impossibility of enquiry and simply urges that one cannot enquire about what one does not know. The first horn is thus not strictly comparable to the second. Its gist, that one has no need to enquire about what one already knows, misstates a quite legitimate point, it will be seen in the next section.

Part, then, of what seems odd about posing a question like *What is a question?* is that no explanation as yet has been offered for posing it when the questioner so evidently knows what a question is, and accordingly — or so it might initially seem — knows what the answer to the question *What is a question?* is already. But if some satisfactory explanation is available, posing it may yet be in order.

First, though, something should be said about the question itself. Cohen says that if his question 'does, in its claim to significance, presuppose a solution', 'so too does the answer to' 'the more common inquiry into the nature of propositions, assertions, or judgments'. Elaborating, he continues: 'in order to answer the former question we must assume that it is a question, just as we must assume that any real definition of a proposition is a proposition', adding: 'In neither case, however, does this consideration involve a vicious regress.'[11] These remarks appear to mean that just as it must be assumed that the answer to the question *What is a proposition?* comprises the proposition that results from completing the schema *A proposition is ...* , so it must be assumed that if the question *What is a question?* is itself a significant question, then it presupposes a 'solution'. Further on Cohen expressly states: 'By a significant question, I mean a question to which some proposition is *the* true answer.'[12] The business about no 'vicious regress' being involved in these assumptions seems intended to counter the arguments that because the definition of a proposition itself constitutes a proposition, a proposition has first to be defined before the definition of a proposition can be given; and because the question *What is a question?* is itself a question, the answer — 'solution' is Cohen's gratuitous variant — to the question *What is a question?* has first to be given before this question can be asked.

The assumptions Cohen makes would be unexceptionable if they merely provided a basis for the argument that no more circularity is involved in asking a question about a question than in asserting a proposition about a proposition; for provided the two are kept distinct, the one in the object language, the other in the meta-language, no infinite regress will result. But what Cohen assumes is that the propositional schema *A proposition is ...* supplies the form of a definition of a proposition and that filling in the blank in the propositional schema *A question is a* —— would supply 'the true answer to' the question *What is a question?* So he assumes that a 'real' definition of a proposition must itself be a proposition; and that there is one, and only one, proposition which is the 'true' answer to his question *What is a question?* (An answer to any question, it was pointed out in Chapter 1, is not as such a proposition; instead, a conformable answer to a word question is one of the terms of the proposition that can be constructed from the conformable answer with the help of the question.)

What is wrong with posing the question *What is a question?* is that the question presupposes that it is answerable by a term or terms which could fill in the blank in the propositional schema *A question is a* —— . Now, it might be thought that the question is answerable in the requisite way if one gave what Moore describes as the sort of 'very disappointing' answer he gives to the question *What is good?* — namely: 'my answer is that good is good, and that is the end of the matter'. But this sort of answer is not of the requisite form: both Cohen's and Moore's question require the blank to be filled in by a term or terms differing from the term to be defined and applying exclusively to the subject defined. Moore tacitly acknowledges that this is the sort of answer required when he goes on to urge that good 'cannot be defined'.[13] Note that it is a logical requirement that the requisite answer be given by a term or terms not already occurring in the question, not any epistemic considerations about informativeness.[14]

As the interrogative marks a fundamental form of thought, the notion of a question is ultimate, and so indefinable without circularity — and certainly not definable by means of a propositional schema. In desperation Hume wrote about the concept of belief: -

> I confess, that 'tis impossible to explain perfectly this feeling or manner of conception. We may make use of words, that express something near it. But its true and proper name is *belief*, which is a term that every one sufficiently understands in common life. And in philosophy we can go no farther, than assert, that it is something *felt* by the mind, which distinguishes the ideas of judgment from the fictions of the imagination.[15]

Everybody too understands sufficiently what a question is, though it cannot be defined in a single proposition. The presupposition of Cohen's question, that it can be answered by a term or terms which complete the blank in the propositional schema *A question is a* —— , is thus false.

It is not, strictly, a defect of a question itself that its presupposition lacks justification, even that it is false. If what it presupposes were true, the question posed by Cohen would be in order. Something is wrong, however, with the asking of a question whose presupposition there is no good reason to think true; even if, strictly, the question itself cannot be faulted — say, on grounds of lack of coherence or intelligibility. But even if such philosophical questions were answerable in the requisite way, it might still be in order to ask them though their answers were already known to all. The point here is that any need for asking a question should be disentangled from matters more of logic, such as the status of the presupposition of the question asked. So, since the first horn of the eristic dilemma concerns the need specifically for enquiry, it provides no broader lesson about questions — unlike the difficulty raised by Meno. Even so, some explanation is required why philosophers in their enquiries ask the questions they do.

In speaking of philosophers' *What is ... ?* questions as 'pseudo-questions', Collingwood was pandering to the coiners of a once fashionable phrase; but his account is suggestive. The 'vague formula', he says, 'is only a vague portmanteau-phrase covering a multitude of possible questions but not precisely expressing any of them'.[16] His account suggests that the very airing of such questions in philosophical thinking is to be viewed itself as symptomatic of a concern to comprehend in some unspecified manner, which some of the concealed 'multitude of possible questions' might serve better to bring out. Waismann points to a resemblance between how questions and exclamations can be used to express feelings of astonishment or wonder. Rather as the questions children ask can often express no more than petulance, disappointment or the desire to be the centre of attention, so philosophical questions are often likewise not to be taken literally as the form of the question indicates.[17] The contrast with taking a question literally shows that it is an exaggeration to say that all questions people ask express 'a need for understanding, knowledge, explanation or puzzlement or perplexity'.[18] What is typical of philosophical questions is not typical of questions as such, since philosophical questions are not typical questions. Yet sometimes some questions asked by people seem primarily to be a way of giving vent to such emotions as 'despair, frustration, or bewilderment'; and rhetorical questions often serve to arouse, if not evince, emotion.[19]

The danger of taking philosophical *What is ... ?* questions literally is twofold. The first, obvious, risk is that the subject under investigation will be changed, subtly or blatantly, by an arbitrary redefining of terms. Cohen supposes that the attitude of Lewis Carroll's Humpty Dumpty to words, rather than being patently ridiculous, gives 'voice to a methodological postulate of all advanced scientific thought'.[20] Theories of questions constitute proposed answers to Cohen's question *What is a question?* By contrast with genuinely explanatory theories in the sciences, the theories of philosophers are in constant danger of ending up as futile exercises in attempts to argue, contrary to Butler and Moore, that everything is not in fact what it is but strangely turns out to be another thing instead.[21] Leaving aside truly dotty accounts — and there are plenty of them — such a way of proceeding usually ends up in the much less heroic position of equivocation between the newly promulgated official use of a term and an inevitable reversion by the philosopher to its use in what Hume calls common life — a type of equivocation pervasive in Hume's own philosophy and detected by Moore in 'naturalistic' definitions of *good*.

A second, less obvious, danger lies in the too ready assumption that supplying what is presupposed by such *What is ... ?* questions — namely, some definition statable in propositional form of the subject being enquired into — would be the only means to cure any ignorance of or resolve any doubts that supposedly exist about its identity. In general one can identify what a sort of thing is by producing instances of it; and to be able to do so one has first to know what it is. Now, knowledge of what something is characterised interrogatively; and attribution of such knowledge, it has been seen, can be minimal: the possessors of such knowledge need not be able to state in a proposition that the thing is such-and-such.

Asking what something is invokes a sense of *identify* dubbed by Austin as 'cap-fitting': it presupposes that the thing or a specimen of it is given, and requires that one find a description that fits. He opposed this 'cap-fitting' sense of *identify* to what he dubbed the 'bill-filling' sense, where one is given instead a description and required to pick out the thing or a specimen of a sort of thing. Here the question asked is *Which is it?*[22] Philosophers' *What is ... ?* questions seem oddly to fall between the two: a description is supplied, as with *which* questions, but no specimen is given, unlike ordinary *what* questions. Thus, while *What is a question?* is odd, *What is the question?* is not. More will be said in Chapter 9 about questions that require identification of their subjects.

The first danger, misidentification of the subject, arises because the posing of a question of the *What is ... ?* form falsely suggests that the identity of what is being enquired into must actually be unknown or at least doubtful. Accordingly, it is sometimes imagined that there can be scope for perhaps startling discovery in philosophical investigation. Philosophical investigation does exist, but it is not the sort detectives or journalists, or even research scientists, engage in, where it might not be possible to rule out in advance entirely novel findings. Socratic ignorance, coming to realise how much one does not know, is more beneficial in scientific than philosophical enquiries. For there are no specifically philosophical facts to be uncovered. Instead, philosophy works on the plain facts of common experience together with those discovered by the various sciences. Philosophy may surprise by breaking down ingrained habits of thought and stimulating closed minds to engage in thought; but then it does so by bringing people to a recognition of what they already know. When philosophers innovate it is frequently a sign that they have gone astray.

Further, the absence of any answer to a philosophical *What is ... ?* question statable in a definition does not prove that there must be any actual ignorance of or doubt about the identity of the subject of the enquiry. On the contrary, philosophers know as well as others what, say, a question or knowledge is. More fundamentally, if there were complete ignorance or genuine doubt about the identity of the subject of the enquiry the question could scarcely be asked; that was the point

Meno's difficulty served to bring out. So rather than answers in the requisite propositional form, what philosophers seem to be aiming for when they pose such questions is a better understanding of their existing knowledge of the subject. Any ignorance or doubt, while about the subject of the enquiry, cannot, then, be about the identity as such of the subject of the enquiry.

So philosophers ask a question like *What is a question?* during their enquiries because although they know, in this instance, what a question is, they do not fully understand what a question is. Praising Socrates for having 'set the example of the true philosophic method for all times', Schlick argues that philosophers' *What is ... ?* questions embody attempts 'to clarify thought by analyzing the meaning of our expressions and the real sense of our propositions'. He concludes that 'philosophy was misunderstood when it was thought that philosophical results could be expressed in propositions ... It must be defined as *the activity of finding meaning.*'[23] Schlick is right that philosophical results are not exclusively to be reported as matters of knowing *that*, consisting of propositional knowledge, but rather of understanding *what*, *how* and *why*, consisting of knowledge characterised interrogatively; but he overlooks the sort of objection Ryle brought, that philosophers must at least know what they are attempting to clarify.[24]

Philosophical *What is ... ?* questions thus form a special case of the difficulty Meno raised. Meno's difficulty shows how in one way all questioners, whether or not they are also enquirers, must already know at least something about the subjects of their questions, although in another way when they are also enquirers, they do not know something about them.[25] Likewise, philosophers in posing their typical questions in their enquiries both already know something about and yet apparently seek new knowledge about the subjects of their investigations. The difference is that these philosophical *What is ... ?* questions, posed as they are in pursuance of a philosophical enquiry, are misleadingly framed. Such questions can never be taken literally, not even outside the conduct of an ongoing philosophical enquiry. Philosophers are not really ignorant of the identities of the subjects of their enquiries but on the contrary are quite familiar with them. And the knowledge they actually possess here does not constitute knowledge that the things various propositions say supply the answers to their questions. For their knowledge, which they share with others, is not to be characterised propositionally as the form of their questions misleadingly requires. What is already known by them does not constitute the answers to their questions because there are no actual answers to questions with false presuppositions. Somewhat as a dog knows where its bone is buried without knowing what the answer is to the question *Where is the bone buried?* so philosophers know what a question is without knowing what the answer is to the question *What is a question?* But the difference is that whereas there is often in fact some answer to the former question, there is never any actual answer to the latter.

Thus, if philosophers are tempted to take their questions literally, they will misconceive the new knowledge sought by them as statable in a single definition.

Since any answer of this form is not forthcoming, the puzzle still to be resolved which distinctively arises from the posing of these philosophical questions is what sort of ignorance or doubt do philosophers hope to remedy or remove in their enquiries? It is not obvious at first that there can be any ignorance or doubt that the provision of even answers of other than the requisite form would cure or remove. There is certainly none about the identity as such of the subjects of their enquiries. Nor are these *What is ... ?* questions to be taken as being about words. While a word such as *proposition* is a term of art, having a definition, the terms in these philosophical questions are often ones whose meaning the philosopher has usually been well acquainted with since childhood.

The contrast between, on the one hand, grasping the difference between a question and, say, an exclamation, or between knowing and guessing, and on the other, being able to put into words what will convey perspicuously what the difference is, points to a distinction between implicit, unreflective knowledge and articulated, reflective knowledge; between the way everybody, including the enquiring philosopher, has knowledge of, and the way some genuine ignorance or doubt can be felt about, such subjects. The philosopher aims to give an account of questions or knowledge, to explain what a question or knowledge is, something not every one who knows perfectly well what a question or knowledge is can do. Hence the need for philosophical enquiry.

Philosophers aim in their elucidations to clarify what the difference is between the notion under investigation and both apparently similar and contrasting neighbouring notions. But philosophical understanding does not consist merely in adequately grasping how various associated concepts are interrelated, for those with sufficient intelligence who are not philosophers can do that. It requires in addition being able to capture in words what the connections and differences are between the concepts.[26] The explications philosophers give will be made up of a series of remarks some of which may well constitute propositions; though typically philosophers will also press into service questions and exclamations, puzzles and jokes. But no single remark in isolation will be sufficient to the task, as a single propositional definition was assumed to be. It will be a matter of, not literally showing and pointing out, but of showing and pointing out with words; of drawing people's attention to and reminding them of what they are implicitly already quite familiar with. The aim of philosophical elucidations is thus to communicate understanding of how the concepts interconnect through the communication of interrogatively characterised knowledge; not primarily to state that the such-and-such relations obtain between the concepts, a matter of communicating *that*.

Wittgenstein perceptively lists some of the main contenders for an account of questions that somebody starting to think about the field might fasten on: -

> If you do not keep the multiplicity of language-games in view you will perhaps be inclined to ask questions like: 'What is a question?' — Is it the statement that I do not

> know such-and-such, or the statement that I wish the other person would tell me … ? Or is it the description of my mental state of uncertainty?

Unfortunately, many philosophers do not get beyond these crude proposals. Wittgenstein himself seems not only to be rightly suspicious of Cohen's question, for it misleadingly tempts philosophers to fix on just a single type of instance; but also to imply that no general account of questions can be given.[27] He is premature if the latter is his contention. For a contrasting notion can often orientate philosophical understanding of a subject by helping to determine what category the subject falls into. The lack of any immediately obvious identifying category, it was seen, is the peculiar mark of philosophical *What is ... ?* questions.

Now, just as Hume, despite his difficulty in saying what belief is, had no doubt that there is a clear difference between belief or judgment, on the one hand, and conception or imagination, on the other, so it has become apparent that a philosophical account of questions must be guided by the contrast between the notions of a question and of a proposition. Not indeed in a misconceived attempt to argue that a question is somehow essentially propositional; but in taking the undeniable difference between questions and propositions to be indicative of some basic commonality between them, thus enabling identification of the category both belong to. What both Reid and Cohen hint at, that an account of questions must run parallel to that of propositions, points the way forward. Questions, like propositions, are objects of logical attention.

Wittgenstein seems to be making a further point, though it has been misunderstood:[28] while one can imagine different ways questions might have been formed grammatically from the way they are in fact — say, by a distinctive use of assertoric or imperatival expressions — these devices would still only serve to express questions because of the function they have in the language; so that questions are not reduced to assertions or commands merely because the use of grammatically non-interrogative forms to express questions is conceivable. So Wittgenstein continues: -

> Of course it is possible to substitute the form of statement or description for the usual form of question: 'I want to know whether … ' or 'I am in doubt whether … ' — but this does not bring the different language-games any closer together.[29]

Earlier he had remarked: -

> We could imagine a language in which *all* statements had the form and tone of rhetorical questions; or every command the form of the question 'Would you like to … ?'. Perhaps it will then be said: 'What he says has the form of a question but is really a command', — that is, has the function of a command in the technique of using the language.

And: -

> We might very well also write every statement in the form of a question followed by a 'Yes'; for instance 'Is it raining? Yes!' Would this shew that every statement contained a question?[30]

The answer to this rhetorical question is clearly *No*. Wittgenstein is arguing that questions cannot be eliminated from language by rephrasing them in grammatically non-interrogative ways. Far from endorsing, he is mocking the proposed reductions he mentioned at the beginning of § 24.

The reason for treading over well-trodden ground again is not to highlight the paradoxical character of philosophical enquiry; nor to reject philosophical *What is ... ?* questions as meaningless or 'pseudo-questions': only if taken literally rather than as expressions of philosophical perplexity is it inappropriate to ask such questions. Instead, the object has been to demonstrate the futility of the enterprise of devising a theory of questions. So failure to devise any alternative to those on offer should not be taken as any deficiency. A theory-free account is aimed at. Besides, philosophy progresses largely through negative criticism, which should not be lightly dismissed. As Locke saw ''tis Ambition enough to be employed as an Under-Labourer in clearing the Ground a little, and removing some of the Rubbish, that lies in the way to Knowledge'.[31]

The Questing Model

The word *question* seems to be connected to the idea of a quest; and this impression receives some confirmation from Varro, who observes that the Latin noun *quæstio* is derived from the verb *quærere*, 'to seek'.[32] These slightly different primitive models, to adopt Austin's notion,[33] may appear to be good starting points for an account of questions; but they will turn out to be misleading. Asking a question is not a kind of questing for something, nor seeking to do something. Besides, people's askings of questions must not be confused with questions themselves. These models, however, are less inappropriate for enquiry.

The first horn of the eristic dilemma of Plato's *Meno* can be brought into line with its second horn if the dilemma is interpreted as invoking a crude model of a quest for enquiry. It would thus be arguing that one cannot search for what is already in one's possession, that one cannot find what one never lost. It would then turn on the sheer impossibility of enquiry, as does the second horn; not on its mere superfluousness. Of course, one might not realise that one already had a thing in one's possession or that one had not lost it, as when I look for spectacles already on my nose. So the model becomes strained: the things 'searched for' in enquiry are not physical but pieces of knowledge.

The slightly different model of seeking — that is, to do something — can take over. The argument now becomes: one cannot seek to know what one already knows. Again, one might not know that one is already in possession of a piece of knowledge, as Socrates apparently does not realise how much he already knows about virtue. But 'to seek to know' can only mean to seek to come to know; so that the argument has to be that one cannot seek to come to know, discover, learn or find out what one already knows. This, surely, is the argument required, since the aim of enquiry is to obtain knowledge; but obtaining knowledge is coming to know what one previously did not know. The argument thus turns on the impossibility of striving to do what one has already achieved: more particularly, of seeking to come to know what one has already come to know; in other words, reverting temporarily to the cruder model, of searching for what one has already found.

There is one exception, which would explain the position Socrates is in: one may have come to know something but have forgotten it, made a discovery but be unable to recall it; or, on the cruder, searching model, found something only to mislay it. And so one 'searches for', seeks to retrieve, one's previous knowledge. Here one is seeking to come to know again what one previously came to know, to rediscover or relearn it; to find again what one previously found. Hence the story Socrates relates of how 'all enquiry and all learning is but recollection' serves as Plato's refutation of 'this sophistical argument about the impossibility of enquiry'.[34] Plato seems in effect to be arguing that the eristic dilemma is false: it is not true that one either knows about or does not know about the subject of one's enquiry, for one can both know something about it and also not know something (else) about it. Plato's explanation of how one can know what one knows about it is that one can know it through recollection. It was left to Wordsworth to spell out what Plato only implies, how it is that one can come not to know something about the subject: 'Our birth is but a sleep and a forgetting: ... Not in entire forgetfulness, ... do we come ... .'[35]

Yet forgetting what one once knew and mislaying what one previously found do not actually furnish counterexamples to the eristic dilemma. For if one has forgotten, one no longer knows now — which clearly entails not knowing; and the second horn disposes of the case of not knowing. The difficulty Meno raised, rather, points to the falsity of the dilemma. What has been emphasised up to now — by Plato also, but somewhat differently — is that all enquiry must start from pre-existing knowledge, so that one knows some things about a subject but not others;[36] not, as in the argument suggested by the seeking model for enquiry, that one cannot enquire into what one already knows. The first horn of the dilemma in its original form seemed to deny, contrary to what the difficulty Meno raised helps to bring out, that one must already have some knowledge about the subject of an enquiry. For the first horn originally argued, with a deceptive air of plausibility, that one has no need to enquire about what one knows. The inference therefore would be that one enquires only about what one does not know; but this conclusion is blocked by the second horn, which argues that one cannot enquire about what one does not know since one does not know what one is enquiring about.

In Jowett's translation there is a move from the phrase 'enquire into', used in the presentation of the difficulty raised by Meno, to the vaguer 'enquire about', used in the presentation of the eristic dilemma. But now, the dilemma can be dismissed as false in the light of what Meno's difficulty establishes. For his difficulty establishes that one both knows something about and also does not know something (else) about a subject of enquiry. The vagueness of the *about* saves the dilemma from triviality; for its second horn hints at without actually raising the apparently vexing question whether it is possible to enquire into what one does not know. By contrast, as originally worded, the argument of the second horn, that it is impossible to enquire about — rather than into — what one does not know since one does not know what one is enquiring about, is unconvincing. One must surely know how to specify the subject of the enquiry and so know at least something about what one is enquiring about, is the obvious objection — as also what the difficulty raised by Meno serves to show. On the other hand, the revised and more precise version of the argument of the first horn suggested by the seeking model for enquiry, that one cannot enquire into — rather than about — what one knows and has not forgotten, has greater force than the original version, that one has no need to enquire about what one knows. Again, the objection to the original argument is that surely one can have need to enquire about what one knows, as when there are aspects or parts of the subject one is still ignorant about.[37]

Thus when the dilemma is refined, it collapses: the second horn has to be rejected and the first horn embraced. For if the argument of the second horn is refined into 'one cannot enquire into what one does not know', it becomes just silly on reflection rather than raising a vexing question. Admittedly, one does not know (yet) what it is hoped enquiry might eventually reveal; but is not the aim of enquiry to make what is presently unknown known? Enquiry by its very character is directed to the unknown; which in effect is what the refined version of the argument of the first horn urges. For now its argument is that it is impossible to enquire into what one knows and has not forgotten, which was what the seeking model for enquiry also suggested. Any purported enquiry into what is already known and has not been forgotten could only be a sham. So far from there being merely no need to enquire into what one knows and has not forgotten, as a more precise formulation of the apparently plausible argument of the original first horn would run, it is quite impossible to engage in genuine enquiry into what one already knows and has not forgotten: those conducting the investigation Nixon instigated into the Watergate burglary were only going through the motions, since they already knew who had commissioned the crime.

The difficulty Meno raised seizes the philosophical imagination because its lesson has application beyond enquiry: it concerns the possibility of framing questions about any subject; and as any answer to a question takes its form from the question, the possibility also of setting out criteria for what counts as answers to the questions framed. By contrast, for the first horn of the eristic dilemma to apply beyond enquiry to the asking of questions as such, a reversion would be required to something like its original version: it will then deny any need, not for enquiry, but to ask a question when one knows what the answer to it is. Yet despite much received philosophical opinion to the contrary, people do sometimes have a need to ask questions they already know how to answer. The peculiarity of the philosopher's *What is ... ?* questions, though, lies not in the questioner's already knowing what the answer is to the question, because such questions have no literal answer; instead it lies in the form of the pre-existing knowledge possessed by the questioner being at odds with the form of answer required by the question.

The eristic dilemma is thus concerned solely with the epistemic position of an enquirer. It is not concerned with the asking of questions as such, still less with questions themselves. It indicates, indeed, some difference between asking questions during an enquiry and asking questions as such. For if there were no difference, the revised version of its first horn, that it is impossible to enquire into what one knows and has not forgotten, would entail that it is impossible to ask questions whose answers one already knows.

But why would anybody ask a question whose answer is already known? Well, there is no single motive for asking questions, such as the one favoured by many philosophers: namely, the obtaining of knowledge about the subject of the question from an addressee. Just as assertions or statements need not express judgments currently passed but can recite previously reached conclusions or relate discoveries already made, so included among expository and some didactic uses of language is the raising of questions about to be answered by the person asking the question — as is suggested by the occurrence of both *ask* and *answer* on Austin's list of 'expositives'.[38] The rehearsal of such questions may sometimes indeed be faithful to questions actually posed during previous enquiries, but more often (as in the first sentence of this paragraph) makes use of the interrogative concept exercised simply in order to specify a topic and indicate how it is going to be treated. Journalists are taught to write their reports with answers to questions introduced by *who? what? where? when? how?* and *why?* in mind. In this way interrogative concepts can structure not only the conduct of an investigation but also reports of its outcome, besides the presentation of an argument, even the ordering of a narrative.

Bell supposes that in such cases the 'question is *raised*, though not put'; where no answer is provided he says that the question is left for an 'audience to consider'. He compares such uses of questions to their use in books, where 'the question is, as it were, in quotation'.[39] But while Cohen's question was previously considered and was, as it were, in quotation, it was definitely not raised. And questions raised in expository and some didactic discourse are genuinely asked and not merely considered, despite not being put to anybody either singularly or collectively and regardless of whether an answer to them is subsequently provided by the person raising the question. Such instances show, as against Bell's view that '*ask* carries the sense of a command',[40] that asking questions need not be asking questions of anybody at all; whereas a command has to have an addressee, even if only figurative. In interrupting a lecturer who had just asked a question in this manner, a member of the audience by volunteering an answer would have misunderstood the function raising the question had on that occasion — though admittedly, teachers also frequently put questions to a class in the expectation or hope that somebody in the class will venture an answer.

The barrister's maxim that one should never ask a witness in court questions whose answers one does not already know shows further that it is not impossible to put to others questions about what one knows and has not forgotten. Here there is also a need to ask the witness the questions: namely, to have the witness present the evidence to the court. And Socrates himself not only knows how to answer the questions he puts to the slave boy,[41] he needs to put these questions, he supposes, if he is to reawaken the boy's pre-existing knowledge. More frequent in real life than Socratic interrogation is asking another, *Have you heard, do you know, what happened?* as a preliminary to imparting the answer to the question *What happened?* — the point being to guard against telling others what they already know. At other times asking another *Have you heard what happened?* is just a way of putting the question *What happened?* to the other irrespective of whether one knows or is ignorant of the answer to the question.[42]

Although questions asked of others are sometimes, it will be seen in the third section of Chapter 6, asked in the course of some more specific enquiry into how the other will respond,[43] as in the case of examination questions, the person asking the question may also already know how the respondent is going to answer, as in the case of questions asked by counsel who has carefully rehearsed the answers with the witness beforehand. But even these, together with questions one asks oneself, asked not out of ignorance but purely as a means of ordering one's thoughts, are parasitic on the outcome of previous enquiries. Thus, while the questions occurring in expository and didactic discourse form no part of an ongoing, unfinished enquiry, they feature in a reconstruction of a previously conducted and concluded enquiry.

Questions asked in the conduct of an enquiry may lend some support to Hintikka's view that *wondering whether* entails *not knowing whether*; but scarcely his conclusion that there are 'good reasons for analysing "wonders" semantically in terms of "doesn't know" (among other elements)'. His view that the same applies to *asking whether* only indicates the difference between the asking of questions as such and enquiry.[44] Asking a question cannot as such be equated with enquiring. For if in asking questions one were always thereby seeking knowledge, one could not, as in purely expository discourse, ask questions about the subject of an enquiry after it had been concluded. Yet *ask* remains a verb of enquiry when its subject is a person, despite not all askings of questions occurring during the actual conduct of an enquiry; for if a question is not asked during an enquiry it at least relates to some previously conducted enquiry.

What, then, is one seeking in asking a question as such if it is not necessarily knowledge? The general object of asking a question, it was said in Chapter 2, is to elicit what answers the question: from either an addressee or one's own resources. If the latter, either by engaging in enquiry or relying on the outcome of a previous enquiry. Instances involving devious interrogators who seek to trick their respondents into refusing to answer are not exceptions to the former, any more than a kindly uncle who lets a precocious nephew beat him at chess shows that the object of the game is sometimes to lose; for one can perform an act in defiance of its object, which defines the intention people are presumed to have in performing them.

Hobbes declares: 'But of the Desire to know, there is a peculiar expression, called *Interrogative*.' Hume tacitly invokes a similar model when, in discussing curiosity, which he equates with the 'love of truth', he draws parallels between philosophy and both hunting and gaming; but Hume is explaining 'the pleasure of study', evidently a psychological project concerning the motive for enquiry, not distinguishing 'formes of Speech' as Hobbes is.[45]

Hobbes would be right to think that curiosity is often expressed, in the sense of manifested, by a tendency to ask questions; and also that a desire to know is often the motive for engaging in enquiries. But he has made two errors. First, his term *expression* clearly refers to linguistic expression. So it seems his view ought to be that it is as if a speaker in asking a question were saying *I desire to know* ... — which is on the pattern of Reichenbach's 'cognitive correlate'. But Hobbes is not so unsophisticated: he himself allows that while

> generally all Passions may be expressed *Indicatively* ... some of them have particular expressions by themselves, which neverthelesse are not affirmations, ...

and among these latter he includes the interrogative. As Reichenbach puts it: 'The question itself, however, merely expresses this desire but does not say it.'[46] Secondly, whereas the object of enquiry is to obtain knowledge, even those engaged in the pursuit of knowledge may have no ardent desire to learn, as their teachers throughout the ages have themselves learnt from experience with regret. As Cook Wilson noted, wondering is not 'identical with' 'the desire for knowledge'.[47] Curiosity is idle to the extent that a question occurring in thought does not prompt any desire to know what the answer to it is, or at least any strong enough to initiate an enquiry if the answer is not immediately apparent. Admittedly, if one loses interest in the answer to a question one asks oneself one will usually cease to ask the question — unlike questions put to others, where other considerations, such as politeness or duty may override any lack of interest in the subject.

Thus Hobbes has not only confused the function of a type of linguistic expression (the sign *for*) with what its employment often provides evidence of (a sign *of*),[48] he has also confused the object of enquiry with a motive people may or may not have for engaging in it. Enquiry has as its object the acquisition of knowledge, but the object of enquiry is not necessarily what moves people to seek to attain knowledge; any more than the cultivation of plants, which is the object of gardening, need be the motive for engaging in gardening, which may be, say, to earn a living. Hobbes has psychologised his accounts of both the linguistic form of the interrogative and the goal-directed character of pursuits such as enquiry.

The Hobbesian *dictum* also reflects the all too common failure to distinguish carefully enough a question from somebody's asking of a question, besides asking questions as such from enquiry. The seeking model seems tailored to enquiry; but seeking or looking for something is rather a form of enquiry, so the model explains nothing. It may be wondered in particular whether it illuminates the goal-directedness of enquiry;[49] for is not seeking itself goal-directed? The model's constituent ideas of either striving or searching both presuppose the having of some end in view. Instead, such ideas are apt to mislead. For the ideas of seeking and hunting suggest a particular conception of the quarry in enquiry. What is sought in enquiry, it has been seen, is not a physical thing or an animal but a piece of knowledge.

In any case, the seeking model will have to be modified if it is to be made to work for the asking of questions as such, even more so for questions themselves. Like enquiry, asking a question is also directed to an end; but asking a question, as distinct from asking a series of questions or asking a series of people the same question, is not an activity. And enquiries are conducted, engaged in and pursued, can be protracted and thorough; but none of these things could be said of asking a single question.

Collingwood speaks oddly of a 'three-minute long question' perhaps because he has confused asking a single question (whether a particular sparking plug is working) within a more general enquiry (into why my car won't go) with that enquiry itself. Elsewhere he says that the 'act of asking' a question 'continues for the whole duration' 'before the act of answering it begins'.[50] Just as I can hold life-long beliefs I only occasionally think of, so I can ask a question not only on particular occasions but also continue to ask that question until — at least — I get an answer that satisfies me. Whereas talk of an act is appropriate when a question is asked on a particular occasion, when a question continues to be asked the person asking the question may rather be said to be in an inquisitive state.[51] And in asking others the question I need not, as in cases of straightforward enquiry, be ignorant of any answer that satisfies me: I may be waiting to hear if my respondents repeat a particular answer I myself came up with previously, as is the habit of bores, who eventually reveal their preferred answer, as also the job of examiners.

What one is seeking in asking a question as such, as distinct from during an enquiry, is not knowledge but what answers one's question. Philosophers who subscribe to the Hobbesian *dictum* offer no explanation of the link they presume between such an object in asking a question and the object of enquiry; that is, between eliciting what answers a question and the attainment of knowledge. Thus they have not demonstrated that questions have essentially something to do with knowledge. The usual motive for asking questions during an enquiry, wanting to know, serves the object of enquiry, which is the acquisition of knowledge. But such philosophers suppose that this object — or rather, usual motive — characterises asking questions as such, and even somehow questions themselves. Welbourne provides an instructive case, since he is not defending a theory.[52] In trying to account for questions by reference to the object of or usual motive for enquiry, such philosophers have inverted the logical order between knowledge and questions: the pursuit of knowledge in enquiry requires instead to be explicated by means of the concept of what answers some question. In short, instead of the stock epistemological conception of the interrogative what is required is a new interrogative conception of knowledge.

Questions as *Quæsita*

The seeking model for asking of questions as such takes the end in view, eliciting what answers the question, as the provision of something sought. It accordingly suggests a modified model for questions themselves, which, unlike people's askings of questions, cannot be said to have an end. As the form of a question determines what would answer it, a question is viewed by this further model as the specification of what is to be sought when the question is asked; the setting out of a *quæsitum*. On this model the idea of questing, more appropriate to enquiry, and the idea of seeking, more appropriate to an act of asking a question on a particular occasion, both fade away. The governing idea is that the question itself specifies what is to be sought, regardless of whether anybody engages in any enquiry or actually asks the question on any occasion.

If, then, the idea of a quest is to be of any service in an account of questions themselves, as distinct from either people's askings of questions generally or during the course of an enquiry, one idea suggested by etymology, seeking, will have to be passed over to give way to another: namely, the idea of what is to be sought. Since the verb *question* means to ask (another) questions, it is parasitic on the noun. The noun, indeed, standardly refers not, as its ending might suggest, to the action of asking but rather to what is asked: not to a *quæstio* but to a *quæsitum*. Admittedly, the noun also has a few verbal senses, mostly obsolete; those which survive occurring only in phrases of negative import — with the exception of *in question* — such as those cited in *The Oxford English Dictionary*: '*beyond (all) question, ... past, without question*'.[53] The term as it occurs in Prichard's expression 'thinking without question' is not being used, as it usually is in modern English, in the mainly parenthetical phrase *without question*, meaning *unquestionably*. Prichard, indeed, introduces his expression with: 'an unquestioning frame of mind … one in which it did not occur to us to doubt something'.[54] What he evidently means is *unquestioningly*.

On the *quæsitum* model the idea of seeking to do something will be equally out of place. Seeking to attain or achieve something is distinct from the seeking involved in a search, because success does not consist in anything being found. When seeking is striving to do some action, what is sought is not something one hopes to find but rather an effect, outcome or a result of action. If seeking in the sense connected to searching is to be regarded as seeking to do something it can only be seeking to find something; but there is no need to force the verb into this construction: it makes perfect sense to speak of seeking things as well as seeking to do things. Enquiry may appear to override this dichotomy between seeking what can be found and seeking to do something, because on the cruder quest model of enquiry the acquisition of knowledge is viewed as finding something. One inadequacy of this model, that it misrepresents the nature of the quarry, has already been noted; another will shortly be pointed out. Besides, to return to enquiry would be to refocus on the idea of seeking to do something, acquiring knowledge, rather than on what is to be sought as the model for questions themselves.

The idea of what is literally sought must now be explored. What is sought — in the sense of what can be found by searching — may be either what one has already come across, as when I have misplaced some possession, or it may be what one has not yet encountered but is able to specify in general terms, as when I am looking for a reliable plumber. In the second sort of case what one is seeking may not in fact exist to be found; whereas in the first sort of case, it must have existed if one actually encountered it previously, though it may no longer exist. The character of what is sought, the quarry, will dictate the appropriate method of search, should the effort be made to conduct one. Hobbes contrasts 'a man's casting his eye upon the ground, to look about for some small thing lost', which he classifies as 'ranging', with 'hunting or tracing, as dogs trace the beast by the smell, and men hunt them by their footsteps';[55] and later, with a more methodical search 'as one would sweep a room, to find a jewell'.[56]

The interrogative concept of location governs the concept of what is sought in the sense of what can be found. The power of the *quæsitum* model is revealed by the readiness of people to pick examples of *where* questions when they think of questions. What one searches for, or merely seeks, in this plain, literal sense must be — if it still exists — at some place; and to find it is thereby to find it at a certain place, to locate it. Hence only physical things and their qualities, properties and relations can be sought in the literal sense. Smells, sounds and tastes are locatable to the extent that the bodies which are their sources are.[57] To trace a smell or sound to its source, or track a series of footsteps or a trail of litter, is to follow through space a path that it is hoped will lead to what is sought, the source or agent responsible. And to trace the source, say, of a river is to seek the spring it begins from. Less literally, to search for evidence at the scene of a crime is to seek in the vicinity indications of the circumstances of its perpetration.

The literal notion of what is sought is readily extended: one may be said to seek initially not the thing itself but its location. But surely, it might be objected, to seek a thing is to seek to find it at the place it happens to be, and this in turn is to seek the place it happens to be at, its location; so to seek a thing is thereby to seek its location. Not so: seeking the location of a thing is neither seeking the thing at the place it happens to be; nor, still less, seeking the place the thing happens to be at, unless one were to strive to sweep the whole of space for the place just as in Hobbes's example one sweeps a room for a lost jewel. Instead, seeking the location of a thing is seeking where it is.

The interrogative form of the concept of location comes into play here. True, the place a thing happens to be at is its location in the sense that a reference to that particular place supplies what answers, in propositional form, a *where* question. But in seeking the location of the thing one is not seeking that particular place, or any place at all. Until one finds what one is seeking, the location of the thing, one does not know that this place, or some other place, is the place where the thing is. The clause following *seek* introduced by a compound relative pronoun, like all such clauses, is virtually opaque. What one is seeking in seeking the location of a thing is whatever it is, the 'thing', that answers the question *Where is it?* — something quite abstract; not something physical, as things and the space they occupy are. Hence on the *quæsitum* model for questions themselves what is to be sought is what answers a question — in this paradigmatic case of location, a *where* question. And to find what answers this question, one does not always have to find the actual thing at its place or find, go to, the actual place it is at: one can instead be told where it is. So I may find my plumber in a trade directory.

The *quæsitum* model thus extends the notion of something sought beyond the realm of physical things. What are to be sought, *quæsita*, turn out to be such 'things' as locations, times, identities, natures, quantities (including measurements and prices), methods, reasons and explanations, qualities, alternatives and the truth. These *quæsita* relate to the interrogative concepts exercised in, respectively, questions introduced by *where*, *when*, *what* (or *who*, *whom*, *whose*), *what kind of*, *how much* (or *how big*), *how*, *why*, *which*, questions of the type *What is it like?* and (in indirect speech) *whether* or *if*.

Nevertheless, the model confuses literally finding or encountering, on the one hand, and finding out or coming to know, on the other. I do not literally come across plumbers in a directory as I might at the race track; rather, I find out where they live, learn of their addresses. Finding the location of something, and so being able to locate it, is not literally finding or coming across something but rather finding out or coming to know something: namely, what answers a *where* question. But now, the idea of what is to be sought, the *quæsitum*, has turned out only to return to the cruder quest model for enquiry, which misleadingly describes successful enquiry as 'finding' or 'meeting up with' a piece of knowledge, the 'quarry' — rather than as finding out or discovery. Talk of 'finding' pieces of knowledge or information is figurative for coming to know or learning through being informed. Likewise talk of 'finding' the answer to a question.

So the *quæsitum* model, while designed for questions themselves, as opposed to either enquiry or the asking of questions as such, has only reverted to enquiry. The explanation is that literally finding a thing is thereby finding where it is, which in turn is finding out where it is, finding out its location; it is finding out what answers a *where* question. Literally finding a thing is necessarily finding something out — namely, where the thing is, its location. But the converse does not hold: finding something out need not be literally finding or coming across a thing at some place.

It might be argued that the *quæsitum* model for questions just proves philosophers like Hobbes right: questions are to be defined by reference to enquiry, where knowledge is sought; so that the notion of a question is to be explicated by reference to knowledge. The model certainly helps to explain the enduring attraction of such a stock view of questions. But quite apart from the confusion between literally finding a thing, a quarry, and finding something out, no explanation, it was noted earlier, has been given of the supposed link, through enquiry, between questions and knowledge. For it needs to be explained why being able to give the answer to a question (when it has an answer, that is) is thereby to be in possession of a piece of knowledge about the subject of the question — though it was seen that the knowledge possessed by non-human animals shows that the converse is false. In assuming that eliciting what is to be sought — namely, what answers the question — is a matter of finding something out — that is, coming to know something — the Hobbesian view compounds the deficiencies in the quest model for enquiry with an inadequate conception of the interrogative as parasitic on the concept of knowledge.

The confusion between finding out and literally finding arose because to find a thing at a place is thereby to find where it is, to find out where it is. The obvious way to try to salvage the *quæsitum* model is to restrict the *quæsitum* to what can be said to be found only in some exclusively figurative way without thereby finding anything out. Before considering whether sense can be made of such a notion, the exploration of the spatial model of finding must be completed with an account of how it is readily further extended figuratively to accommodate knowledge acquired from others and also conclusions based on material supplied by others.

Many cases of finding out or learning are the result of having been informed or taught rather than finding out for oneself. In this way it becomes possible to talk not just of 'finding' information but in a less obviously figurative sense of 'finding' it, say, in a reference book. What one can find out or come to know extends beyond information in the strict sense of what one person informs another of to cover what is the product of the work of others; such as stories, reports, accounts, judgments, verdicts, official results, explanations, arguments, criticisms, objections, justifications and interpretations.

So the concept of location is extended figuratively to, first, the 'location' of information about the literal location of what is sought, so that one is said to find plumbers in trade directories; next, the 'location' of information generally, so that one is said to find facts (or, indeed, myths) in encyclopaedias, people's addresses in the telephone directory, words in dictionaries, or references to books in bibliographies; then, the 'location' of the products of others, so that one is said to find accounts of historical events in contemporary newspapers or arguments for providence in theological tracts.[58] Finally, one may find what forms the basis of conclusions one draws for oneself as when one finds evidence or sources for, or influences of, something: so I may be said to find evidence of embezzlement in the accounts, or trace sources of and influences on authors back to their predecessors' works.

Clearly, finding such 'things' is different from finding stray dogs. It is not literally finding anything but rather finding out or coming to know things. In the final stage, indeed, it is not just learning or coming to know merely by being informed by others; for first-hand discoveries can be made among archive material.

If there is to be any finding without necessarily finding anything out it will have to be finding without finding the thing at some place, either literally or figuratively.

The Matching Model

Another, more specific, idea suggested by the *quæsitum* model is that what is to be sought, which the question specifies, is what fits or matches the question. Spatial ideas still govern what literally fits or matches: a key fits or fails to fit a lock due to its shape, clothes fit or fail to fit due to their size and the size of the would-be wearer, and two triangles match due to their congruence. But matching especially has more figurative uses: colours may be said to match if their juxtaposition is not visually displeasing. Although the phrases *correspond to* and *answer to* have no spatial connotations, they are too obviously derived from the relationship between a question and what answers it to be explanatory.

When the idea of what is to be sought is taken as being what fits or matches, a move is made away from the idea of finding a thing literally at some place and so from the idea of finding anything out. Undeniably, if what is to be sought is to fit spatially, it has to be somewhere. Yet where one finds it is often irrelevant to the attainment of the end, and one can often take the thing to where it is required. If I find a key that will fit, admittedly, I must have found it somewhere; furthermore, I must have found out whether or not it does fit the lock. But taking these prior conditions for granted, the model concentrates on the idea of the relation of fitting between key and lock; and then abstracting from all spatial ideas, views the relationship between the determination by the question of what is to be sought and the thing sought, what answers the question, as a relationship of fitting or matching.[59]

Another way of viewing this model is to take the idea of what is to be sought as implying that something is missing that needs to be supplied. The idea of finding then becomes just the idea of supplying what is now at hand, the missing piece to be fitted into the whole — where it was found being irrelevant to the model. So now what answers a question according to this model fills a gap in a propositional schema, rather as the last piece in a jigsaw snaps into its right place or a spare part takes the place vacated by a worn-out component. An even simpler model, designed for yes-no questions, is that what answers the question is just what fits the facts.

The idea of finding has virtually dropped away from these models; which is to their credit, since this idea confines the concept of what answers a question to what has come to be known through enquiry. It can be argued that rather as a proposition is conceived as being either true or false regardless of whether anybody knows or has come to know whether what it says is the case, so a question may be conceived regardless of whether it has been actually asked by anybody; and likewise, what answers it may be conceived regardless of whether anybody knows or has come to know what answers it. Thus, the two items, the question and what answers it, are conceived on these models as matching one another in abstraction from anybody either asking the question or knowing, or coming to know, what answers it. The models have finally freed questions from their customarily supposed restriction to enquiry. For both questions and what answers them are rightly treated as subjects for logical study conceived in abstraction from all notion of people's asking or answering of questions. Yet the models are unsatisfactory.

Apart from the simple model which equates what answers a question with what fits the facts, the notion of meeting the standard set by the question built into the notion of what answers a question has been overlooked. For several different, and incompatible, things may happen to fit, match or meet a mere specification. The analogy of the final piece of the jigsaw is apt precisely because the piece has its right place which no other has. The example of keys is also instructive in that keys are made to fit particular locks. One can therefore speak of the right key or keys for a lock, the key or keys made for that lock; though it may sometimes happen that some other key, made for another lock, will fit well enough to open and lock a lock. By contrast, the physical features of a suspect may fit or 'answer to', as it is said, the descriptions given by witnesses to a crime, yet the police may have apprehended an innocent person; an explanation or hypothesis may fit what has been observed but turn out to be incorrect; and a new account of an obscure event may fit what little was hitherto known of it but could still be wrong. The notion of a 'possible answer' has loomed large in writings of philosophers who 'theorise' questions. But what merely happens to fit is not good enough for what answers a question. What is to be sought is not anything that would or might answer but what actually succeeds in answering the question; since the object of asking a question is to elicit not just an or any answer to it, but, as it would be ordinarily said, the answer to it.

The notion of a standard to be met is not only built into the relationship between a question and what answers it; it is also, of course, implicit in the concept of knowledge. Nevertheless, if questions are to be taken as objects of logical attention, they cannot be conceptually linked to knowledge, as the Hobbesian view urges. First, the presupposition of a question, that there is something that answers it, may be false; so what might have answered the question if its presupposition had been true would not in fact exist to be known. That interrogative clauses taken by *know* share the same presupposition as the question they allude to[60] shows indeed that knowledge characterised interrogatively has to be understood by reference to questions, and not questions by reference to interrogative characterisations of knowledge. Second, what answers a question may not actually be known by anybody. Here, though, there is potential knowledge — provided that what answers the question exists to be known. Third, even if what answers a question were actually known, the question may never have occurred to anybody, so that such knowledge would not be conceived by those who possessed it in relation to the question. Non-human animals are necessarily in this situation, for no questions ever occur to them.

Only by proceeding in the opposite direction, by characterising knowledge interrogatively, can some link be forged between a piece of knowledge and a question. The link cannot be made the other way, from a question to a piece of knowledge. For the relationship between a question and what answers it is logically independent of any person's state of knowledge or ignorance. In short, questions themselves are not to be explicated by reference to knowledge; nor yet knowledge by reference to questions — or at least not directly. Rather, both a question and a piece of knowledge are to be explicated by reference to the notion of the same standard they both set.

The priority of the relationships here also explains why asking questions is not restricted to enquiry. Enquiry gives point to the asking of questions by aiming to meet the same standards invoked by questions asked as such on its subject. That is, the object of enquiry is the attainment of knowledge, which attainment meets the standard set by the piece of knowledge involved. But the object of asking a question is to elicit what answers it; and if there is indeed something that answers the question, this answering (by the words constituting a conformable answer to the question) meets the standard set by the question — a standard also applied to any knowledge characterised interrogatively which alludes to that question. So, the explanation why being able to give the answer to the question *Where is the cat?* is thereby to be in possession of a piece of knowledge is that the standard set by this question for what answers it is the very standard set by the piece of knowledge characterised interrogatively as *knowing where the cat is*.

The same standards, then, which guide questions asked as such also guide enquiry, the pursuit of knowledge. But since what answers a question whose presupposition is false does not exist to be known, and since a question can be asked even when the answer to it is already known, the notion of asking questions is wider in scope than the notion of enquiry. Thus, the received view that the epistemological has significance for the interrogative mistakenly gives logical priority to the standards set by pieces of knowledge over the standards set by questions.

The matching model could be repaired if the fit is made tight enough — as it is on the simple model of fitting the facts — to exclude what might have answered but does not actually answer the question: such as what is merely not inconsistent with a description, a reasonable but false hypothesis, or plausible but inaccurate accounts. Even when repaired, the model is unsatisfactory. For while its merit lies in abstracting the notion of a question from situations where people ask questions, the notion as such of what actually meets a specification is just the notion of a description — more generally, a predicate — being true of a thing, of what falls within some class. The notion could just as well apply to what makes a proposition true, other than an existential proposition. And on the simple model that what answers a question is what fits the facts, any true proposition would do. This much too broad notion of meeting a mere specification fails to capture the peculiar interrogative form of thought questions employ to characterise their relationship to what answers them. On the matching model questions are conceived propositionally, not interrogatively. The model has given almost exclusive attention to the conformable answers to a question;[61] and as repaired, to what answers a question — hardly surprising when the fundamental idea of the *quæsitum* model as such is that a question sets out what is to be sought. This type of model has strangely bypassed questions themselves, a common failing of philosophers' accounts.

The failure of the matching model to capture the interrogative form of thought expressed in a question stems from the assumption that since a question — once abstracted from the thought of anybody's asking of it — is conceived as not asked by any person, it cannot itself ask anything. Admittedly, a question specifies the form of what would answer it; but it does so without specifying what actually answers it, if there is such a thing. So if the question were conceived as not itself asking anything, what would be conceived would be just a specification of its conformable answers; a specification taking propositional form only and contained within the question itself. That is, the specification of the form of what would answer the question would be explicitly set out in or stated by the question as what any conformable answer to it must meet;[62] instead of merely being presupposed, without being stated, by the form of the question, as is an interrogative specification of the form of what would answer a question.

In other words, the question instead of asking something would say what the specification is: say either indicatively that conformable answers are of a certain form or say imperativally that they are to be of a certain form. But a question does not say anything at all; it asks something. A question determines the form of what would answer it, not by saying anything, but simply by asking in the way that it asks — that is, by its asking presupposing that something is so. Thus, the specification of what would answer the question is made through the presupposition of the question. A question has no need of any propositional element contained within it to take on its task of asking; nor could this task be accomplished by any purely propositional element.

On the matching model the specification by a question of the form of what answers it is misconceived propositionally. What is overlooked is that this specification is achieved interrogatively by means of interrogative concepts. For instance, a *where* question specifies that whatever answers it should be the location of the thing in question. As the concept of location here is an interrogative concept, the specification of the form of what answers the question is itself interrogative in form. So what would answer the question is conceived in the question interrogatively as where the thing is. By contrast, a set of possible grid references specify what might answer the question, the possible location of the thing, only propositionally.

The deficiency of the matching model can also be seen by considering that in order to find a match between two items one first has to have what Reid calls a direct notion of each item; but the notion of the thing to be sought, the thing that answers the question, can only be a relative notion — relative, that is, to the question it answers.

Notes

1 Cf. Hookway (1996), p. 7.
2 Plato (1892), ii, p. 39; 80d.
3 Plato (1892), ii, p. 28; 71b. Cf. Welbourne (1986b), pp. 234-8.
4 Plato (1892), ii, p. 44; 84b-c.
5 Whately (1913), Introduction, § 2; p. 3. Plato (1892), ii, pp. 45 and 46-7; 84c-d and 85c-6b.
6 Reid (1785), III viii; p. 359b; cf. Waismann (1965), pp. 390-91. Cf. also Whately (1913), IV ii § 1; p. 162 and White (1974), pp. 306-10.
7 Welbourne (1986b), p. 235; cf. pp. 236, 240-41. Cf. also (1989), pp. 180-81.
8 Ryle (1932), p. 39. Cf. Cook Wilson (1926), i, §§ 11 and 62; pp. 41 and 132.
9 Plato (1892), ii, pp. 39-40; 80e.
10 Whately (1913), Introduction, § 2; p. 3.
11 Cohen (1929), p. 350.
12 Cohen (1929), p. 359.
13 Moore (1903), p. 6.
14 Contrast Hintikka (1974), pp. 153-4.
15 Hume (1978), Appendix, p. 629.
16 Collingwood (1939), p. 122. Cf. Cook Wilson (1926), i, § 9; p. 36.
17 See Waismann (1965), pp. 5-9, 41, 405, 407, 411-12, 416. Cf. Presley (1959), p. 65.
18 Bambrough (1966), p. 170; cf. Rhees (1966), p. 173.
19 Rundle (1990), p. 91; cf. p. 92. Cf. also Wheatley (1955), p. 54.
20 Cohen (1959), p. 9. Cf. Lewis Carroll (1970), VI, p. 269.
21 Cf. Moore (1903), p. 206.
22 Austin (1953), pp. 142-3. Cf. Welbourne (1986b), pp. 242-3; cf. also pp. 236-7, 239-40.
23 Schlick (1931), pp. 217 and 220.
24 Ryle (1932), p. 39.
25 Cf. Cook Wilson (1926), especially i, § 12; pp. 44-5 but also i, §§ 1, 9, 10, 56, 57, 58; pp. 25, 36, 37, 118, 120-21, 122.
26 Cf. Welbourne (1986b), p. 243.
27 Wittgenstein (1958), I § 24; p. 12[e].
28 See Hamblin (1958), pp. 160-61; Llewelyn (1964), p. 70, note 7 but contrast p. 85.
29 Wittgenstein (1958), I § 24; p. 12[e] and cf. (1956), I, Appendix I; p. 49[e].
30 Wittgenstein (1958), I §§ 21-2; pp. 10[e]-11[e].
31 Locke (1975), The Epistle to the Reader, p. 10.
32 Varro (1951), I, 79; i, p. 247.
33 Austin (1956a), p. 202.
34 Plato (1892), ii, p. 40; 81d.

35 William Wordsworth, *Intimations of Immortality from Recollections of Early Childhood.*
36 See references to Cook Wilson cited above.
37 Cf. Cook Wilson (1926), i, § 9; p. 36.
38 Austin (1962), p. 161; cf. p. 88 and Wilson and Sperber (1988), p. 93. Cf. also Ryle (1963), chapter IX.
39 Bell (1975), p. 209. See also Ajdukiewicz (1974), pp. 92-4 and (1978), pp. 162-3.
40 Bell (1975), p. 206.
41 Cf. Ryle (1979), p. 72.
42 Cf. Dummett (1981), p. 331.
43 Cf. Welbourne (1986a), p. 9; cf. (1980), p. 319.
44 Hintikka (1976), p. 70.
45 Hobbes (1991), vi; p. 45; cf. p. 42. Cf. Hobbes (1889), I xiii 6; p. 67 and I ix 18; p. 45; (1656), I iii 1; p. 25. Hume (1978), II iii 10; pp. 451-3.
46 Hobbes (1991), vi; p. 45; Reichenbach (1947), p. 340.
47 Cook Wilson (1926), i, § 10; p. 37.
48 Cf. Austin (1950), pp. 125-6.
49 Cf. Hobbes (1991), iii; p. 21 and vii; p. 47.
50 Collingwood (1939), p. 32; (1940), p. 24.
51 See Vendler (1972), p. 32.
52 See Welbourne (1979), pp. 2, 9; (1980), p. 319; (1986a), p. 8. Cf. (1986a), pp. 76-9; (1986b), pp. 229-30; (1989), pp. 180-82.
53 *OED*, xiii, p. 7a-b: senses 1b, 1d and 2a. Contrast Cohen (1929), p. 353 and Hausser (1980), p. 94, note 8.
54 Prichard (1950), p. 97. Cf. Ryle (1937), p. 154 and *OED*, xiii, p. 7a, sense 1a.
55 Hobbes (1889), I iv 3, 4; p. 14.
56 Hobbes (1991), iii; p. 22. Cf. Waismann (1965), p. 387.
57 See Waismann (1965), pp. 388-9.
58 Cf. Carlson (1988), p. 178.
59 See Harrah (1961), pp. 41, 42; (1963), p. 28; Belnap and Steel (1976), p. 68.
60 Cf. Hintikka (1976), pp. 83-4.
61 Cf. Åqvist (1965), pp. 11-12, 141.
62 Cf. Ryle (1950), pp. 245-6.

Chapter 4

Asking Questions

As subjects for logical consideration questions are abstracted from all notion of people's askings of questions, whether or not during the course of an enquiry. This chapter argues against the view, often merely suggested by what some philosophers have said, that questions are conceptually bound to acts of asking them, so that questions cannot be conceived without also conceiving these acts of asking. Often a further view is implicated, which several philosophers and most linguistic theorists take for granted: that asking a question is necessarily the putting of the question to — that is, the interrogating of — another. The term *interrogation* will be used throughout simply for the putting of a question to others, even although it is commonly used in a narrower sense for the insistent and often hostile manner of putting a series of questions to others.

The assimilation of asking a question as such to interrogation is just the speech-act fallacy about questions, which when taken with the first view results in tying questions asked of others to the speech-acts of the askings of these questions. The element of truth in the speech-act approach is that questions, like propositions, must always be formulated in language. But it does not follow that the prior performance of a linguistic act is required, as with commands and promises, in order to form any notion of a question. It does not follow, that is, that questions can only be conceived as asked during interrogation, any more than that propositions can only be conceived when assertions or statements are made. At other times when the first view alone is held, even a question occurring in thought or expository discourse is thought incapable of being considered apart from the act of thinking or asking.

The Social Intellectual Acts

A common misapprehension is that a question must always be asked of somebody. Thus Ryle: 'if no one is being asked anything, no question is occurring'.[1] Had he said 'nothing is being asked (*tout court*)' his remark would have been unexceptionable.

Reid, it was seen, classed asking a question along with giving a command and making a promise as social intellectual acts of mind.[2] Later philosophers have generally similarly supposed that a question, like a command, always has an intrinsic reference to some addressee. Accordingly, they have assumed that asking a question is essentially putting a question to an addressee. But the putting of questions to others, it will be seen in Chapter 6, carries with it a presumption which is completely absent when questions are simply asked. Such philosophers tend to confine the verb *question* to its specific sense of interrogating a person; despite the verb also being used in the different sense — where in the positive it governs only an interrogative clause introduced by *if* or *whether* — of raising queries or doubts without any accompanying expectation that anybody will answer any questions.[3] The artificial use of the verb *question* by linguistic theorists in the sense of generating a question about what a term of a proposition expresses is different again.[4]

As was pointed out in Chapter 1, Reid oddly contrasts acts of judgment, which, he holds, are 'expressed' by propositions, with questions, commands and promises themselves rather than with acts of asking questions, giving commands or making promises. As his point is, apparently, that questions, commands and promises are counterparts to propositions, the reference to acts of mind seems uncalled-for. If commands and promises cannot be conceived apart from acts of commanding or promising, that only serves to distinguish their status as social acts from the status of propositions and questions as objects of logical consideration.

Reid seems to have run his distinction between the solitary and the social into the distinction between the propositional and the non-propositional. C. A. J. Coady notes that 'the opposition of the social operations to the expression of propositions' is invalidated by 'such social operations as accusations, warnings, and reports', which 'certainly do' 'express propositions'.[5] Reid himself in speculating about the origin of the term *judgment* tacitly acknowledges that judgment is a social besides a solitary act when he speaks of a judge passing 'sentence in a cause' in 'tribunals of justice'.[6] Equally, it is not essential to the non-propositional that it be addressed to another. Reid gave an example in his account of Aristotle of a wish, which need not be voiced in public;[7] but a wish, even when voiced in public, does not engage others. In short, the social involves more than merely the non-solitary. A question, too, can just cross one's mind, be asked only in thought. Even speaking is not essential to asking a question, any more than it is to judging that something is so; for although one may think one's thoughts formulated in words and even think 'aloud', as it is said, thinking is not as such speaking. Reid's distinction, then, should have been between what are exclusively social acts, as issuing a command, making a promise and giving testimony are, and what can sometimes be solitary besides social, as passing judgment and asking a question can be.

What is to be made of Reid's odd talk of the 'expression' of mental acts by their objects? One of his concerns is to account for the difference between the social intercourse among human beings that relies mainly on communication by language — whether by actual words or non-verbal signs doing duty for words — and the non-linguistic social intercourse that also exists among non-human animals and sometimes between human beings and non-human animals. Brutes cannot give testimony or make promises, he points out;[8] neither can they ask each other questions. For these social intellectual acts require the use of language. The purposeful use of even gestures to communicate with others constitutes language, made up of non-verbal signs; for these signs are to be understood as substitutes for words. Thus, a question may be put to another by the raising of an eyebrow and doubts communicated to another by the pursing of the lips. Such gestures would have no communicative function if they merely accompanied one's private queries or doubts without any intention of conveying something to others. Reid thus needs to explain how the 'expression' of the social intellectual acts of mind bears on communication specifically by language.

'Judgment can be expressed by a proposition only,' Reid declares — evidently using 'express' differently from Coady.[9] But in what sense can propositions be said to 'express' acts of judging — or questions, commands and promises 'express' acts of asking others questions, issuing them commands and making promises to them? One sense might be that a proposition presupposes somebody's act of judgment, that the objects of mental acts provide evidence for, confirm the existence of, these acts and their agents.[10] What is 'expressed' here, then, is an act of mind; not something that is part of language, even if the manner of its 'expression' is through language. Elsewhere Reid uses *express* in the more familiar linguistic sense: 'a particular judgment can only be expressed by a sentence, and by that kind of sentence which logicians call a *proposition*'.[11]

But in fact Reid uses *express* in a sense going beyond that of simply providing evidence for the existence of something; to wit, the sense of 'being known to' another. This slightly richer sense, however, is still insufficient to secure the essentially linguistic character of the objects of the social intellectual operations; or, on the other hand, to render language inessential to those of the solitary intellectual operations. He says of the social 'the expression is essential', they 'cannot exist without being expressed by words or signs, and known to the other party'. If they are to be social, they must be expressed in the sense at least of being capable of becoming known through their products to others; but it does not follow from their being social, as distinct from intellectual, that these operations can be 'expressed' — assuming it makes sense to speak of operations being expressed — only by words or signs, if 'signs' here refers solely to what does duty for words. And it follows trivially that the solitary 'may exist, and be complete, without being expressed, without being known to any other person'. But it is false that 'in the solitary, the expression of them by words, or any other sensible signs, is accidental'.[12] On Reid's own showing, what he supposes one solitarily judges, a proposition, is part of language. The capacity to be given expression in language is as essential to the objects of the solitary as it is to those of the social intellectual acts.

Reid has evidently equivocated between a sense of *expressed* meaning 'being known to the other party' — whether through words or by 'other sensible signs' that do not constitute language — and the sense of requiring formulation in language. In short, he has failed to distinguish *signs of* from *signs for*. Bodily posture, popularly misconceived as 'body language', usually not being intentional, does not amount to signs for attitudes or moods but instead provides merely signs of them: it is neither language nor a language. Even swearing, in a secular age, may be only a sign of exasperation, notwithstanding its once being a sign for an oath. And something merely becoming known to others is not the same as making it known to others, which is what linguistic communication involves.

Despite the promise held out by his strictures on Aristotle that the interrogative would be treated as a non-propositional form of speech parallel to the propositional and equally deserving the attention of the logician, what little Reid says about questions seldom strays beyond some presumed commonplaces. True, he holds that asking a question is an irreducible act of mind, distinct from either judgment or reasoning; but he goes on to say in Hobbesian fashion that it 'supposes ... a desire to know'.[13] Oddly, the distinction between asking a question and the question asked, parallel to the distinction between an act of judgment and a proposition, seems never to have been as clear to him as might have been expected. While he recognises the essentially linguistic character of propositions, questions, commands and promises, his distinction between the solitary and the social intellectual operations casts little light on that character. And by classifying asking questions as an exclusively social operation, he restricts asking questions to the putting of questions to others. As with so many philosophers and linguistic theorists, he has conflated questions as subjects for logical consideration with their function in social intercourse.

It may seem surprising that the customary restriction of questions to enquiry is not inevitably accompanied by such a common misconception. For it may seem obvious that when one 'makes enquiries', as it is said, one usually does so by asking others questions. But the quest and seeking models need not be taken as requiring the putting of questions to others. As the examples given by Hobbes illustrate, searching or seeking can be entirely solitary besides collaborative: the man searches alone for the lost jewel, but is in the company of his fellows and dogs when out hunting. Philosophers have tended to think of enquiry — especially their own philosophical enquiries[14] — as pursued individually, often being loath to concede that enquiry can even be collaborative let alone dependent on assistance from others. If Socratic interrogation appears to be an exception, it is because, it will be seen, it is in aid of a quite distinctive enquiry.

Philosophers, then, have usually felt no qualms about conceiving researches as such, and not just their own, as mainly self-sufficient enterprises. For they have been apt to think of enquiry as the pursuit of knowledge, and have not specifically related enquiry to the asking of questions. Instead, as has been seen, they have usually proceeded in the opposite direction, binding questions to enquiry; with the result that they have viewed questions as merely subservient to, rather than structuring, enquiry. But once enquiry is conceived not simply as the pursuit of knowledge but more specifically as involving asking questions 'for information' — in Reid's words,[15] which were to become hackneyed — it begins to be appreciated that enquiry is typically pursued by asking questions and so can also be conducted by asking others questions.

There thus arises a curious contrast between, on the one hand, the traditional suspicion by philosophers of testimony — though not shared by Reid — together with its almost total neglect by most twentieth-century epistemologists, and, on the other, the widespread insistence on the supposed truism that a question is a request for information, by which is apparently meant a request to be informed. In view of this stock account of questions, philosophers might have been expected to take testimony more seriously than they have latterly. Perhaps their frequent undervaluing of testimony is thought to justify their reductive view of and hence dismissive attitude to questions. A more probable explanation is that the conceptual link between information and testimony has escaped theorists, who give no inkling that they appreciate that to conceive knowledge as constituting information is to model it on the giving of testimony. Conversely, those who rightly regard the testimony of others as a major source of knowledge tend to take questions seriously.

Asking Oneself Questions

To Hobbes's credit, he does not relate the desire to know, curiosity, to asking questions specifically of others. The context of his remarks suggests more Aristotelian wonder than Socratic interrogation.[16] As the latter is the means offered by Plato of solving the difficulty raised by Meno, and as the seeking model would not preclude joint enquiry between Socrates and his interlocutor, it is unsurprising that, if Welbourne is right, the Greek for *ask* cannot be used where questions are not asked of others.[17] Fortunately, English is more flexible: the reflexive pronoun in *I asked myself* ... does not refer to an addressee, either actual or figurative, in oneself; on the contrary, it serves to rule out that the question is asked of anybody at all. French uses the same sort of dummy reflexive pronoun in *se demander*, its word for *wonder* — as noted by John Llewelyn.[18] Doubting can involve asking questions without putting them to anybody, not even oneself — questioning without questioning anybody; and queries likewise can occur merely in thought when nobody else happens to be present to put them to.

Whereas the reflexive pronoun in *I washed myself* implicitly contrasts a part of one's body, face or hands, with what is not, say, clothes or a car, a dummy reflexive pronoun meets the purely grammatical requirement of some verbs in some contexts for an indirect object without implying that anything corresponds in reality to the indirect object. The same sort of dummy reflexive pronoun occurs in talk of people talking 'to themselves'. To be said to be 'talking to oneself' can, but need not, imply that one mistakenly believes there is (still) somebody there whom one is addressing; as when one mistakes a shadow for an intruder or is unaware while continuing speaking that the person one was speaking to is no longer there, say, when one has been cut off on the telephone. Still less need it imply that one is subject to an hallucination of an addressee, as when one thinks one sees a ghost, or the delusion that what are in fact some of one's own thoughts are thought or spoken by somebody else who is answering one back. Instead, the reflexive pronoun can simply be a dummy: one is talking, no doubt about that; but one is not supposing that one is addressing one's words to anybody, not even figuratively to oneself.

What makes a use of language social in the sense required by Reid as opposed to asocial, 'solitary' in his sense, is the intention of the speaker to engage another in what is said; not whether the words are publicly expressed, nor indeed whether any other person happens to be present. The lack of clarity in Reid's account is due largely to his failure specifically to cite intention in place of his vague talk of social acts 'being known' to others. If I am in the habit of, as it is said, 'thinking aloud', of speaking 'to myself', to use the dummy reflexive pronoun, my being overheard does not turn what I say, the proposition expressed by the clause introduced by *that*, into a statement of mine made to others. For I do not intend to tell anything to anybody; nor indeed, to address anybody, let alone myself. One may also wonder 'aloud', air in public the doubts or raise the queries that have crossed one's mind; for such instances constitute 'thinking aloud' too.

In the requisite sense the 'solitary' asking of questions can extend beyond even spoken soliloquy. Questions raised in the presence of others without being put to them include expository questions such as a lecturer poses as a way of organising material being presented to an audience. Besides sporadic doubts, queries, wonderings and puzzles, questions asked in the course of some specific enquiry can likewise often be aired publicly while not being put to anybody, either in particular or at large: one is not asking others, still less putting the question to oneself; for one is not expecting others or oneself to come up with some answer. Instead, one is specifying, in interrogative form, what is required to answer the question; that is, indicating a *quæsitum*. So while the speaker's words are addressed to others, the question itself is not put to anybody. Questions posed in philosophical enquiries and scientific discussions are usually of this character, and they may also feature in moral, political, literary, or religious debates. These 'speculative questions', as they have been dubbed, continue to be asked, while not being put to anybody, in the absence of any satisfactory answer being available.[19]

Questions occurring merely in thought are plainly not put to others; for thoughts are not literally addressed to anybody, not even the thinker.[20] G. C. Field objects to Hare's reduction of questions to commands, arguing that 'we quite normally and naturally put questions to ourselves', adding that this habit constitutes 'a stage in the process of thinking'.[21] If the questions are 'put to ourselves', they are so only in the sense that they are asked 'of ourselves', where in this idiom the reflexive pronoun is a dummy. It will be argued that such questions are not actually put to or asked of anybody, not even oneself. Questions occurring in thought may be said to arise, to be raised, posed or asked by the thinker; but they are not put to or asked of anybody at all.

Questions occurring in thought may be of several kinds. As was seen, one may frame expository questions 'to oneself', to use the dummy reflexive again, as a way of ordering an argument, an explanation or even a narrative; or one may be thinking up questions suitable to set for an examination paper. But the commonest kind is when one has not yet come up with the answer to the question. Now, it has been widely assumed that just as questions featuring in enquiries dependent on others' testimony are put to them, so the questions featuring in enquiries conducted without the aid of others can only be put to oneself.

Bosanquet denies that questions one asks oneself when one is ignorant of the answer 'can be genuine questions', because the 'essence' of a question 'is to be addressed to a moral agent, not ourselves except by mere metaphor'.[22] Whereas this is true of a command, his ruling on 'genuine' questions is gratuitous. In making enquiries one can often obtain the knowledge sought through putting questions to others; but it does not follow that when one is without the assistance of others one must be putting the questions one raises to oneself, even in only some figurative sense. The only alternative is not that the question is put, albeit metaphorically, to oneself; instead, there is the possibility that the question is not put at all — either literally or metaphorically.

Sometimes it is purely incidental that the question is not put to another: 'Because there is no one to ask I have to find out on my own,' Welbourne observes:[23] one would ask somebody else if one could. At other times, as when one is trying to remember what one was dreaming, one is perforce thrown back on one's own resources in any attempt to answer the question; for there is no one else who could be in a position to know. When one wonders what to do, cases of what have been styled 'deliberative questions',[24] one has to make up one's own mind, decide for oneself, what is going to be one's answer to one's question — even if one resolves to follow the advice or go along with proposals of others,[25] as when you do not dissent from my answer *Let's go for a drink* to your question *What shall we do now?* Deliberative questions, of course, are not asked in the course of enquiry. But as with trying to remember what one was thinking yesterday, while others may be able to help with suggestions or promptings, coming up with the answer to the question is a task unassignable to anybody else — unlike, say, trying to remember, find out, where one put one's keys. When one scrutinises one's own motives, feelings or desires, such self-examination does not constitute the interrogating of oneself but rather an enquiry into oneself, which, without the assistance of others such as therapists or counsellors, is self-conducted. That these various kinds of questions sometimes are not, or intrinsically cannot be, put to another is no proof that they must be put to oneself.

Nevertheless, the enquiries where only one's own resources can yield knowledge are singular. When Plato has Socrates temporarily reduced in the *Gorgias* by an uncooperative interlocutor to answering his own questions, the unwelcome implication that the whole enquiry could just as well have been conducted by one individual is concealed by the monologue Socrates is forced into being restricted to a recapitulation of the argument. Socrates did not give birth himself to the answers to his own questions, not because his questions were of a kind that to do so would be beyond the capacity of any individual person, but merely because to do so would undermine his analogy of a midwife with its consequent division of labour between interrogator and respondent.[26]

Usually, to obtain the answers to one's questions one has to 'make enquiries'; and often these have to be pursued by putting one's questions to others. This truism is denied by implication by Collingwood. 'To ask questions which you see no prospect of answering is the fundamental sin in science,' he declares. As he makes clear: -

> These questions are not put by one man to another man, in the hope that the second man will enlighten the first man's ignorance by answering them. They are put, like all scientific questions, to the scientist by himself.

Scornful of 'scissors-and-paste history', which 'has to do with ready-made statements' which 'other people have made', Collingwood seems to imagine that 'a scientific historian' somehow breaks free from any reliance on testimony.[27]

Admittedly, Socrates in enabling his interlocutors to give birth to the answers to his questions was not, despite any professions to the contrary, relying on their testimony; he was after all pursuing a philosophical argument, not engaged in scientific or historical research.[28] For philosophical questions, in marked distinction from scientific and historical questions, are to be answered, if they can be answered at all, from the questioner's own resources without resort to interrogating others. Rather than being in pursuit of what others were prepared to testify to, Socrates was hoping to get their assent to what he himself was already prepared to assert.

Collingwood's characteristic traditional philosophical suspicion of testimony rules out any suggestion that he supposed that in asking a question one is necessarily seeking testimony so that when a question occurs in thought one must be seeking testimony from oneself. But in the absence of this traditional suspicion of testimony, the assumption that every question one asks oneself can only be answered solely from one's own resources likewise results in supposing that all such questions must be put to oneself.

Questions asked in thought are no more self-addressed than judgments are statements made to oneself, what one literally tells oneself.[29] The contrary supposition arises from importing features of language peculiar to its use in addressing others into its use for the expression of thought. Even if the use of language to express thought were reliant on its use to address others — though arguably the two uses are interdependent — language used to express thought clearly cannot be used in exactly the same way as language used to address others simply because there can at best be only a figurative addressee in thought. So the distinction between speaker and addressee required for speech addressed to others, marked by *I* (or *we*) and *you*, can have only figurative counterparts in thought. As writing sometimes has no need either for this distinction, it can sometimes be closer to thought than speech.

Bernard Mayo writes: 'We do not ask for information we already have;' and goes on to say that 'in the case of factual enquiry' asking oneself questions

> is not common or standard because it is on the whole not a successful method of enquiry. It does not yield information. It performs only the function of 'reminding ourselves' of what we already know, or of 'consulting our memory'.

'A person very seldom asks himself for information,' he adds. But why might asking oneself a question be imagined as such to yield information? And why is it then inferred that asking oneself a question performs a function only when one already knows what the answer is to the question? Only because it has been assumed that just as in asking another a question the object is to elicit the answer to the question from one's addressee, so in asking oneself a question the object must be to elicit the answer to the question solely from oneself, that one is seeking to answer oneself back. Yet if I ask myself whether the post has arrived, my posing this question does not by itself serve to elicit the answer; I have to investigate — even if the answers to some other questions, such as where I put my keys, can often be had without further investigation, say, from memory or through inference. Mayo thus implicitly takes asking oneself a question as requiring, when one already knows what the answer is to the question, that one literally tell oneself something — that is, testify to oneself; and when one does not, that one inform oneself of something. The reason is that he has simply assumed that the questions one asks oneself can only be put to oneself. No wonder he has difficulty with the notion: one would have to play in turn both the part of teller or informant and of the person told or informed.

Mayo's assumption also explains the difficulty he has in conceiving how 'a first-person locution can figure as an answer to a first-person question', as when I adopt the resolution, *I shall* (*will*) ... as my answer to the deliberative question which occurs to me only in thought, *What shall I do?* As Reid pointed out, the second person is used for addressing others, whether literally or figuratively.[30] Had the question actually been put to somebody, as when one asks another for one's orders or advice, a conformable answer would have been supplied by the term filling the blank in sentences of the form *You will* (*should*) ... .

Mayo's assumption is made explicit in Llewelyn's expression 'self-interrogation'. Like Mayo, Llewelyn also gets side-tracked by the epistemic position of a questioner, arguing, with a version of the eristic dilemma, that self-interrogation is otiose.[31] Like Mayo, Llewelyn has conflated being a questioner with being an interrogator; but the restriction of asking questions to enquiry adds to the confusion. First, being unable to answer a question one asks oneself does not preclude making enquiries — by either trying to find out the answer for oneself or asking others. Second, one's already knowing what the answer is to one's question does not preclude one's having reasons for asking it, as when one is ordering one's thoughts.

The same sort of error occurs in Ramchandra Gandhi's account, that 'in thinking, in what appears to be a case of asking myself questions' there is involved the '*imagining* that the questions are addressed to me', notwithstanding his denial — surely correct — that it makes 'literal sense' to ask oneself a question.[32] If I imagine I am being questioned by somebody, I can also imagine answering the question on the spot from my present resources without making further enquiries; but if the person whom I imagine is questioning me is myself, I ought to be able to imagine answering myself back. But there is no possibility of one's actually answering oneself back — any more than there is of literally telling oneself something or of self-informing. Having doubts or queries occurring to one is not at all as if somebody else were quizzing one.

Collingwood, it has been seen, tries to model enquiry on the mainly self-sufficient character of philosophical enquiry. His view derives from Cook Wilson's account of thought: -

> When we ... are wondering what is true and putting questions to ourselves about it, we should be said to be *thinking*. This is certainly the ordinary view, and it seems natural enough when we reflect that this wonder is the force which brings into play that thinking which is the investigation of a given problem.

There is an echo of such a view behind Field's talk of needing 'to discover what are the right questions to ask before we can expect to get an answer'.[33] In contrast with Mayo's talk of question-and-answer being 'a colloquy, not a monologue', asking oneself a question and then coming up with an answer are viewed here as stages in what Hobbes originally called 'discursion', and later '*Mentall Discourse*'.[34]

One may sometimes in such a train of thought give verbal expression to one's thoughts by making use of forms of words standardly employed only in addressing others; that is, one refers in silent soliloquy to oneself figuratively as if one — or rather, a part of oneself — were a separate person. Silent soliloquy affords a yet further way of taking the expression *talking to oneself*, where the dummy reflexive crops up again. In this figurative way one may speak of telling or urging oneself to do something — to get out of bed, though obedience cannot be guaranteed; or telling, but only in the sense of reminding, oneself that something is so. What such expressions mean is that one has decided or is determined to do some action or is reflecting or has borne in mind that something is so. For although one can tell others both what they already know besides what they do not yet know, one can tell oneself — though merely figuratively — only what one already knows; otherwise one would be capable of self-informing.

Both imperative and emphatically or concessionary assertive declarative modes of speech may occur figuratively in thought. And as Llewelyn insists, in asking oneself a question when the question concerns oneself, one may even refer to oneself in the second person, as in *What are you going to do now?* Here the question concerns what I, the person who has the thought, am going to do next.[35] But one cannot put a question to oneself, either literally or figuratively; because there is no possibility of one's actual answering oneself back. So it is the use rather of the second person for oneself that is figurative here. The words *What are you going to do now?* figuratively express a thought involved in deliberating. Besides, questions about oneself are scarcely the only questions one can ask in thought; so only some, not all, questions asked in thought can make figurative use of the second person for oneself. And only where an actual addressee is logically required, as with commands and promises, can there be any scope at all for any notion of addressing, albeit merely figurative self-addressing.

Literal self-addressing is not possible. One cannot really answer oneself back or respond to one's own thoughts or remarks. One can only, when insane, mistakenly believe that one is responding to another's thoughts or remarks when these thoughts and remarks are in fact one's own; and so mistakenly believe that some of one's thoughts are not one's own thoughts but the thoughts of the presumed other who is in fact nobody other than oneself. But if one does not seriously suppose that one is addressing another, one can sometimes still figuratively address oneself. Here one is treating different stages of one's train of thought as if they were contributions from separate thinkers or speakers without seriously believing that they are. So only by a metaphor is there any 'interior dialogue' of the soul.[36] A later thought is not actually an answer or even a response, to a previous thought; for neither is the earlier nor the subsequent thought, *qua* thoughts, addressed to anybody. And if the first thought takes the form of a question, it cannot be put even figuratively to oneself.

Mayo's difficulty about correspondence in person between question and answer disappears once it is understood that when one asks oneself a question about oneself, there are not literally two persons, speaker and addressee. When put to another, as in asking for instructions or guidance, the question in the first person *What shall I do?* requires an answer in the second person; for the respondent is now addressing the interrogator. But when occurring only in thought as a deliberative question, a question in the first person requires an answer in the first person too; just as any question in the third person, regardless of whether or not it is put to anybody, requires an answer in the third person. That a question in thought about oneself may sometimes be framed in the second person does not go to show, as Llewelyn imagines, that it, or the version of the same question in the first person, must be self-addressed.[37] Seeing that in either version both question and answer actually concern just the one person, an answer in the second person would be as appropriate as an answer in the first person to the version of the question in the second person, just as either would be to the version of the question in the first person.

To put a question to another is to go beyond merely asking the question; just as to make a statement to another is to go beyond merely judging that something is so. Suppose I have some complicated instructions to be carried out by a subordinate. I may think them out carefully. When I have finished, I have still to issue them to somebody. Until then I cannot be said to have told anybody to do anything; so far I have only thought about or considered what instructions I should issue.[38] Note that another person must enter into the very conception of telling another to do something. By contrast, I may think up the questions I require answers to in pursuance of some enquiry. If I need some help, I shall hope to put these questions to somebody whenever the opportunity arises. Until then I have not put my questions to anybody; but I have already asked my questions in thinking them up, not merely considered asking them. Thus, questions asked of others are questions one asks oneself, as the idiom with the dummy reflexive pronoun has it, with the additional factor of being put to another. Similarly, before telling others of some incident I may think carefully, trying to be sure in my own mind what happened. I have judged what I take to be the truth; I have yet to make a statement to anybody, to tell others what happened.

Abstracting from Mental Acts

A question need not be put to anybody; but neither need it be actually asked, posed or raised by anybody. In abstracting the notion of the question asked from the notion of asking a question there is a parallelism with the abstraction of the notion of a proposition from the notion of judging, believing or stating that something is or is not so. Cohen declares that 'a question, like a proposition, ... is a logical entity'.[39] The phrase may be a stock-in-trade, but questions and propositions are hardly things that exist. Rather, both are objects of logical attention; in other words, subjects for logical study. Questions do not exist apart from the possibility of people asking them — that is, asking *whether*, *when*, *why*, etc.; nor propositions apart from the possibility of people judging or stating that things are or are not so.

One can attend to, conceive, consider or think of an aspect, element or feature of something apart from — that is, independently of thinking of — its other, constantly accompanying aspects, elements or features without thereby committing oneself to the independent existence of that aspect, element or feature. Moreover, an object of consideration need not itself be an object of some previous act of some kind, let alone a thing; it is merely what is being considered. A pain may not only be felt but also attended to. Although it is an object of attention, it is not an object of feeling, still less a thing; merely the way one feels some part of one's body. Philosophers have also attempted to make acts of mind themselves become objects of their attention.

Questions, then, no more exist apart from possible acts of asking or putting them to others than propositions exist apart from possible acts of judging or stating that something is or is not so. Both can be conceived, however, in abstraction from any actual acts of asking, judging, putting questions or making statements. Now, the status shared by questions and propositions, of being abstractions from people's askings or judgings respectively, is liable to attack from those who would tie questions or propositions so tightly to the acts of asking or judging them as to make them inconceivable in isolation from these acts.

Reid's talk of propositions 'expressing' acts of judgment can probably be taken as no more than a way of denying any independent existence to propositions. But instead of implying that propositions generally can be conceived only by relating them to possible acts of judging, this talk might perhaps be taken rather as binding each particular proposition to an actual act of judgment so that the proposition could not be conceived apart from the act of judging it. This interpretation, indeed, seems to jar with Reid's insistence on an overall distinction between mental operations and their objects, coupled with his declaration that the 'object of judgment must be expressed by a proposition'.[40] For although he does not suppose that an object of judgment has independent existence as the objects of sense-perception have, he would seem to require that it be at least distinguishable from the act if it is to be the genuine object of the act: it cannot be like the walk that I walked on a particular occasion, which is only a grammatical object of the verb and not distinguishable from my then having walked thus. Even so, there is a hint of the view that the object, though distinguishable in thought from its act, might not be conceivable without also thereby conceiving the particular act whose object it is. If propositions were such objects of judgment, no two persons could be said to affirm or deny the same thing and thus there would be logical relationships between, not propositions, but acts of judgment. Any such binding of propositions to acts of mind would stymie propositional logic; just as taking a person's asking of a question to be somehow part of the question asked has the consequence that 'no two persons could ask the same question'.[41]

Commands and promises, by contrast, require to be conceived as the objects — or rather, products — of particular acts of commanding and promising. While a command or a promise can be considered to some extent apart from the acts which occasioned them, abstraction in thought is more limited for them. Can I be said to have issued the same command or made the same promise on two separate occasions to two different persons? In one sense, yes; the same kind of action may have been commanded or promised, and the very same words used, on both occasions. In another sense, no; the circumstances of my issuing the utterance, my situation at the time, the status of my addressee, may all materially affect the character of what is purportedly commanded or promised.

This limitation may appear to apply to statements also. 'Statements always belong', Zeno Vendler says, 'to a person: they are somebody's statements'.[42] Although words themselves can in a derivative sense be said to state things, when people make statements, they always — even if only implicitly — make them to others. Statements are always conceived as actually stated by somebody to somebody else, though often it is immaterial who makes the statement to whom. Yet statements can readily be conceived in abstraction from their actual addressees. Questions put to others can similarly be conceived without always conceiving the addressees. In this way the identities of statements and of questions put to others are more easily determinable than those of commands or promises. For with the former the identity of the utterance can often be preserved if the same person issues it. So I can often be said to have made the same statement or put the same question on two separate occasions to two different persons. With commands and promises, however, it may be that on the one occasion I did give a command or make a promise, but that on the other occasion, though I used the very same words, some defeating factor in the situation voided my act of commanding or promising.

That commands and promises essentially relate to actions, unlike questions put to others and statements, is one evident reason for the complications in deciding whether the same command or promise can be given or made on two different occasions by contrast with the relative ease of determining that the same question was put or the same proposition stated on two different occasions to two different people. Contrary to prevalent philosophical opinion, putting a question to another is no more telling or asking one's addressee to do some action than making a statement to another is. However, the fundamental difference between propositions and questions, on the one hand, and commands and promises, on the other, is not the latter's concern with action.

Rather, commands and promises have an intrinsic reference to another person: they cannot be conceived without the distinction between commander and commanded, promiser and promisee. The notions of act, agent and addressee are all built into them; so these notions are at work even when a command or promise is merely contemplated as distinct from actually issued or made. By contrast, the notions of a question and a proposition have at most only the notion of a possible act, of asking or judging, implicit in them. There can be no act without an agent, though there can be an agent without an addressee. But if the object of the act can be abstracted in thought from the act, so too can the act be abstracted from the agent. Questions and propositions might be said to have, to adopt a phrase of Locke's, 'a secret reference' to possible acts of asking and judging; but the possible agent of such possible acts is conceived merely as anybody.

The Speech-Act Fallacy in Logic

Since making statements and putting questions to others require language addressed to others, they are appropriate subjects for specifically the philosopher of language as distinct from the philosopher of logic. So too, issuing commands and making promises. But since commands and promises also relate to the structure of society, the study of them impinges on political organisation and law. Austin originally opposed to 'descriptive language' a mixture of various types of utterances issued in special situations;[43] which may explain how he came oddly to lump what, from the standpoint of the philosopher of language, not to mention the philosopher of logic, are peripheral uses of language — as in betting or rituals and ceremonies, such as the marriage service or the naming of ships — together with more fundamental and less conventional — in short, non-institutional — uses of language involving what Austin later came to call 'speech-acts'.[44] Thus, the philosophy of logic came to be muddied with matters of social convention, ritual and custom, which are quite foreign to logic.

Since propositions and questions can occur in thought only, which is not addressed to anybody nor as such speaking, any expression they have in language lacks the special features of language used in speaking to others. In particular, language used in the expression of thought is not subject to what Austin called 'infelicities' — especially the kind he classified as 'insincerities' — which social uses of language may be subject to. Austin indeed lumps propositions (and questions, by implication) having false presuppositions together with his other infelicities;[45] but although such 'unhappiness' may often flow over into social uses of language, it is properly a defect of thinking: of judging or asking under some misapprehension. To the extent that philosophers of language consider propositions and questions themselves, they transcend mere speech and reach thought.

Locke typically breaks with logical tradition in distinguishing between mental and verbal propositions. For 'a bare consideration of the *Ideas*, as they are in our Minds stripp'd of Names', which is his description of mental proposition, is at odds with the traditional account of a proposition as a sentence in the indicative mood.[46] The basis of his distinction is the difference between 'the two sorts of Signs commonly made use of, *viz. Ideas* and Words'. But he characteristically reveals a keener understanding than his official stance commits him to when he remarks tritely 'they lose the Nature of purely *mental Propositions*, as soon as they are put into Words'. He omits to explain why 'it is unavoidable, in treating of mental Propositions, to make use of Words'.[47] The point is surely that propositions and questions are part of language — even although a particular language need not be employed to think or express them. Now, if they are always expressible in some particular language (such as English or German) they must be so expressed when specifically mentioned in that language. Thus in practice, Locke's deviation from tradition is slight.

Reid's declaration that 'mental affirmation or denial … indeed is only another name for judgment', for 'there may be judgment which is not expressed', simply again betrays his equivocating use of *express*.[48] Propositions and questions need not be expressed in the sense of communicated to others; but even when merely thought, they require to be expressed, in the sense of formulated, in language.

That propositions must always be capable of being expressed in words without being identifiable with any particular verbal formulation would remove the sort of objection made to the logician's notion of a proposition perhaps suggested by Collingwood's criticism of propositional logic: -

> The logician's proposition seemed to me a kind of ghostly double of the grammarian's sentence, ... logicians have almost always tried to conceive ... that which is either true or false, as a kind of logical 'soul' whose linguistic 'body' is the indicative sentence.[49]

One might retort by arguing that a proposition or a question is no more to be identified with any of its particular verbal formulations than a piece of music is with any of its performances. But the retort misses the point of Collingwood's objection. It is not that propositions, though supposedly distinct from indicative sentences, turn out to be remarkably similar to them.[50] Instead, Collingwood's objection is that indicative sentences are quite inadequate expressions of propositions as he understands propositions. To this extent his declaration that he is using the term *proposition* to 'denote a logical, not a linguistic, entity' is misleading. For he is refusing to conceive propositions as abstracted from people's thinking *that* .... His conception of propositions, indeed, is more psychological than logical. And his 'logic of question and answer' is not a counterpart to but a replacement for propositional logic.[51]

Elsewhere Collingwood declares: 'Whenever anybody states a thought in words, there are a great many thoughts in his mind than are expressed in his statement.' He then dismisses

> the so-called 'propositions' of the fashionable modern logic, which are called propositions even when nobody in fact propounds them, and would on that account be more accurately called 'proponibles'.[52]

Citing Cook Wilson, he had a couple of years earlier argued that 'even the logical structure of a proposition is not always clear from its written or printed form', rejecting the logicians' conception of the proposition as 'a fictitious entity'.[53] Although in his *Autobiography* Collingwood is loath to acknowledge any debt to Cook Wilson, there can be little doubt about his direct source for the doctrine of the Aristotelian approach that 'you cannot tell what a proposition means unless you know what question it is meant to answer'. Collingwood proclaims: -

> Meaning, agreement, and contradiction, truth and falsehood, none of these belonged to propositions in their own right, propositions by themselves; they belonged only to propositions as the answers to questions: each proposition answering a question strictly correlative to itself.

But what question a proposition was meant to answer is, he insists, 'an historical question'. So the implication of his phrases 'a process of question and answer' and 'the questioning activity' is not just the Cook Wilsonian doctrine that asking a question is to be engaged in thinking, but that the question asked cannot be studied apart from the historical circumstances of the asking of it.[54] So Collingwoodian propositions are as bound as Collingwoodian questions are to people's askings of questions in the course of their thinking.

The torch Collingwood inherited from Cook Wilson passed to Austin. Even although Cook Wilson was a realist and repudiated the term *judgment*, the implicit psychologism of his logic is akin to Collingwood's avowed idealism. The speech-act fallacy about propositions and questions might appear remote from the psychologism and idealism of a less fashionable period. Yet there is an affinity. While Collingwood binds propositions and questions to people's acts of thinking, Austin binds uttering the words that express propositions and questions to the situations such utterances are issued in.

Pursuing the argument that 'stating, and by the same token describing and reporting, ... are speech-acts no less than all these other speech-acts that we have been mentioning and talking about as performative', Austin looks ahead in his lectures: -

> we see that in order to explain what can go wrong with statements we cannot just concentrate on the proposition involved (whatever that is) as has been done traditionally. We must consider the total situation in which the utterance is issued — the total speech-act — if we are to see the parallel between statements and performative utterances, and how each can go wrong.

The conclusion anticipated is: -

> Once we realise that what we have to study is *not* the sentence but the issuing of an utterance in a speech situation, there can hardly be any longer a possibility of not seeing that stating is performing an act.

The need for a general theory of speech-acts, he says 'arises simply because the traditional "statement" is an abstraction, an ideal'.[55]

Although philosophers at Oxford, owing to the influence of Cook Wilson, have chosen to speak of 'statements' in place of the traditional term *proposition*,[56] a statement is ordinarily understood as the product of the social act of stating, of telling others that something is so; whose 'normal or standard ... employment ... is in the expression of *knowledge*'.[57] So if one is disinclined generally to see any parallel between the sort of infelicities Austin mentions which may be present in the examples he gives of performative utterances and the way 'statements' may go wrong, the specific argument likely to persuade will be that 'there are very many things which having no knowledge of, not being in a position to pronounce about, you just can't state'. Austin's example is: 'You *cannot* now state how many people there are in the next room.'[58] An explanation is readily at hand: the interrogative clause introduce by *how many*, together with the required formulation in words conveyed by *state*, implies knowledge of what the answer is to the question alluded to. In effect Austin is legitimately pointing out that a guess or prediction does not count as making a statement to another, since in making a statement to another one purports to be in a position to know to be so what one tells others. But then a statement in the ordinary sense of what one tells others is so is not what Austin presumes is the 'traditional' abstraction of philosophers. The term *proposition* has been traditionally reserved for that; and a proposition, it has been seen, though always a part of language, is not to be identified with any particular verbal formulation.

The same applies to questions. Ryle, whose treatment of logical topics resembles some features of Cook Wilson's, concedes too readily that asking — evidently another — a question 'is doing a specific conversational job'.[59]

Propositions and questions are indeed abstractions, conceived as removed from any actual issuing of utterances in any actual speech situation. A question must be distinguished from the situation it is, or might be, asked in; for a question can at most be only the product of a speech-act, it cannot itself be a speech-act. As Hamblin objects, mistaking a point of Wittgenstein's for proposals to reduce questions to something else: 'The proposed reductions aren't accounts of the content of the question itself; they are accounts of the situation in which the question is asked.'[60] In insisting that an utterance cannot be abstracted from the situation it is issued in, Austin blurs the distinction between this situation and the product of the speech-act — that is, the content of the utterance issued and performed in the situation. In particular, the distinction between the act of issuing a statement and the statement issued.[61]

The speech-act fallacy in logic rests specifically on the confusion of the requirement that propositions and questions be expressed in language with their often in fact being expressed in a particular language employed on a specific occasion by an individual speaker in a specific situation addressing specifiable others. It is assumed that the proposition or question involved when people judge that something is so or ask *whether*, *what*, *why*, etc. must, not just may, be stated or put to others.

Reid's equivocating use of *express* betrays a similar confusion. Expression in the sense of communication is essential to the social acts in that the intention to address others must be conveyed to others if the act is to be effected. More particularly, the speaker must make known to others what piece of testimony is being given, what question is being put, what command is being issued, what promise is being made. This obvious requirement is met through the resources of a particular language — not necessarily verbal, for there are gestures and sign languages as well. In a roughly parallel way, thinkers must know what proposition or question they think, must be able to formulate the propositions and questions they think. They are enabled to do so too through the resources of some particular language. It does not follow, however, that whatever requires expression in the sense of linguistic formulation also requires to be actually conveyed to others;

although by being expressed in language a thing becomes capable of communication to others, as when the thoughts expressed in my diaries become accessible to an historian two hundred years hence.

What gives rise to confusion is that asking oneself questions and judging or believing that something is so, whether in thought or out loud, can be expressed in the same language as that used in putting questions to others and giving testimony — or what is superficially the same language; for it is a mistake to think that all features of language used to speak to others carry over to language used to express thought: that there can be any literal use for the distinction between speaker and addressee, the *I* and the *you*, when a particular language originally designed for speaking to others is employed for the expression of thought. Reid observes: 'I believe, in all languages, testimony and judgment are expressed by the same form of speech;' adding: 'To distinguish them by the form of speech, it would be necessary that verbs should have two indicative moods, one for testimony, and another to express judgment.'[62]

Neither a mental act nor a speech-act differentiates a proposition from a question or either from a command. Rather, the form of speech — what was described above as the resources of some particular language — determines not only what are propositions and what are questions but also what are statements made and what are questions put to others. While the objects of the solitary acts may be conjectured to have originated from those of the social during the prehistory of language, logically the products of the latter may be viewed as the objects of the solitary acts supplemented by being addressed to another: a statement is just a proposition judged to be so but also communicated to another; and a question put to another is just a question asked in thought that is then put to another.

Where the tradition Locke deviated from goes astray is in identifying the form of speech used to give linguistic formulation to a proposition with the indicative mood.[63] As subordinate clauses in a compound proposition may be rather in the subjunctive or conditional mood, the form of speech employed to give verbal formulation to a proposition is more properly declarative, as distinct from interrogative. Austin is right to hold that the sentence is not what the philosopher (of either language or logic) has to study; but once the qualification *declarative* or *interrogative* is added, the object of study becomes not the mere words which go to make up the sentence but what the sentence says or asks, since these qualifications refer to the logical function served by the sentence.

One reason perhaps why the speech-act fallacy has been more prevalent with respect to questions is that the insistence by philosophers on some distinction between a proposition or a judgment, on the one hand, and its expression by a declarative sentence, on the other, has had no parallel with questions. In ordinary parlance 'a question' refers as often to an interrogative sentence — especially spoken — in some language or other as to what that sentence means.[64] People do not naturally speak of interrogative sentences as distinct from questions. By contrast, *proposition* is a term of art introduced for the object of logical as opposed to grammatical or philological attention.

Certainly, if, like the logical positivists, one wants to condemn what philosophers write as meaningless, the distinction between an interrogative sentence and the question, if any, it expresses must be held to. Cohen begins cautiously: 'many apparent questions lack significance'. Although he later laments the indiscriminate use of *question*, he slips: 'for want of recognizable criteria of interrogative significance much philosophical discussion consists of a useless attempt to answer meaningless questions'.[65] For Schlick there is no such thing as a meaningless question: 'It would not be a genuine question at all, but a mere row of words with a question-mark at the end;' then he slips: 'We must say that a question is meaningful, if we can *understand* it, … .'[66]

Such lack of scrupulousness in distinguishing questions from the interrogative sentences standardly giving them expression helps to explain the tendency to assume that questions must always be put to others, or if not that, then addressed to oneself. For it is difficult to think of questions as objects of logical attention conceived as abstracted from their being asked by anybody if they are taken to be identifiable with utterances spoken to others in specific situations. Even the philosopher of language must abstract, both what is said and what is meant, from its expression in a particular language; and perhaps also from its expression in a particular verbal way within a particular language.

Thus, the term *question* is often used imprecisely. Hamblin opposes questions to statements, and connects his contrast to 'the difference between … an act of question-asking and an act of statement-making'.[67] Admittedly, sometimes others ask one *Is that a question or a statement?* or *Are you asking me or telling me?* when they are unsure whether what one has said is to be taken as a question put to them, and so requiring some response from them, or simply a statement made to them, which might require no comment from them. Rumours can start when people wrongly suppose that others are telling them that something is so when they are only asking them something. The contrast here, then, is between a question put to and a statement made to another. The contrast between questions as such and statements is therefore false. The contrast should be between questions and propositions. Awkwardly, there is no single term for a question put to another parallel to *statement*, which, when used strictly, is a proposition one judges to be so and relates to another. A suitable coinage might have been *an interrogation* had not Cohen used it instead for 'the act of questioning'[68] — a use which merely perpetuates the failure to distinguish a question asked as such from a question asked of others. Of course, a question itself can be stated. In philosophy, as elsewhere, a clear and unambiguous statement of the question to be discussed is an essential first step. Here the statement takes a form like, *The question is …* .

Notes

1 Ryle (1950), p. 245. Cf. Dummett (1981), p. 353 but contrast p. 311.
2 See also Reid (1788), V vi; p. 664a.
3 See *OED*, xiii, p. 8b-c: senses 1a and 4a; cf. 3a and b. Cf. Searle (1969), p. 67, note 1; Bell (1975), pp. 193, 200, 202, 205-9, 211. Contrast Austin (1962), pp. 61, 88.
4 See, for example, Hiz (1962), pp. 256-9.
5 Coady (1992), p. 56.
6 Reid (1785), VI i; p. 413b. Cf. Coady (1992), pp. 56-7 and Reid (1785), VI i; p. 415b.
7 Compare Reid (1774), II v; pp. 34-5/692a with Aristotle (1928a), 4; 17a1-7.
8 See Reid (1785), I viii; p. 245a; (1788), V vi; p. 665b. Cf. (1764), IV ii; p. 118a.
9 Reid (1785), VI i; p. 414a. Cf. I vii; p. 243a.
10 Cf. Ryle (1930), pp. 15, 19.
11 Reid (1788), V vii; p. 671b. Cf. Whately (1913), II ii § 1; p. 41.
12 Reid (1788), V vi; p. 664a.
13 Reid (1785), I viii; pp. 244-5.
14 Cf. Welbourne (1986a), p. 11 and (1986b), p. 229.
15 Reid (1788), V vi; p. 664a. Cf. (1785), I viii; p. 244b.
16 See Aristotle (1928d), I ii; 982b11-24 and 983a14-21. Cf. Hobbes (1889), I ix 18; pp. 45-6 and (1991), xi; pp. 74-5.
17 See Welbourne (1986b), p. 229; cf. p. 238. See also Hiz (1978b), p. 213 on Polish.
18 Llewelyn (1964), p. 77.
19 Cf. Wilson and Sperber (1988), p. 93.
20 Cf. Vendler (1972), pp. 66-7; Gandhi (1976), p. 33.
21 Field (1950), p. 232.
22 Bosanquet (1911) i, pp. 33-4.
23 Welbourne (1986b), p. 229.
24 See Bambrough (1951), p. 96b; Wheatley (1955), pp. 50-55. Cf. Cook Wilson (1926), i, § 9; p.37.
25 See Mayo (1956), pp. 58-60, 62-3; Llewelyn (1964), pp. 82-5.
26 Plato (1892) ii, pp. 397-401; 505-9. Cf. Collingwood (1939), p. 35 and (1946), p. 274.
27 Collingwood (1946), pp. 281, 274, 275; cf. Collingwood (1939), p. 35. Cf. also Coady (1992), pp. 241-5, 248.
28 Cf. Welbourne (1986b), pp. 241-2; Ryle (1979), p. 72.
29 Cf. Cook Wilson (1926), i, § 80; p. 197. Contrast Collingwood (1940), p. 23.
30 Mayo (1956), pp. 60, 61, 59. Reid (1785), I viii; p. 245b. Cf. Carlson (1988), pp. 145, 158-9. Cf. also Welbourne (1986b), pp. 241-2.
31 Llewelyn (1964), p. 77. Cf. Bosanquet (1911), i, pp. 33-4.
32 Gandhi (1976), p. 31.
33 Cook Wilson (1926), i, § 9; p. 36. Field (1950), p. 232. Cf. Collingwood (1946), p. 281; Hookway (1996), pp. 7 and 11.
34 Mayo (1956), p. 60. Hobbes (1889), I iv 1, 3-5; pp. 13-14 and (1991), iii; p. 20.
35 Llewelyn (1964), p. 80.
36 Llewelyn (1964), p. 77.
37 Llewelyn (1964), pp. 82-3, 85.
38 Cf. Vendler (1972), pp. 31, 36.
39 Cohen (1929), p. 352.

40 Reid (1788), V vii; p. 671b and (1785) I i 9; p. 224a; ii 6; p. 233a; II xi; p. 292b.
41 Lewis and Langford (1932), p. 334. Cf. Ryle (1930), pp. 17-18, 28.
42 Vendler (1972), p. 209; cf. pp. 72, 82, 106, 114, 137-8; contrast p. 118.
43 See Austin (1946), p. 103; cf. (1962), pp. 73-4.
44 Austin (1953), p. 150.
45 Austin (1962), pp. 48-54, 136-7; and (1970), pp. 248-9.
46 Locke (1975), IV v 3, 2; cf. 4-6; pp. 574-6. Cf. also Reid (1785), VI i; p. 413b; (1788), V vii; p. 671b; Whately (1913), II ii § 1; p. 41; Ryle (1930), p. 37.
47 Locke (1975), IV v 2 and 3; p. 574.
48 Reid (1785), VI i; p. 413a.
49 Collingwood (1939), p. 34.
50 See Somerville (1989), pp. 534-5. Cf. Ryle (1930), p. 26.
51 Collingwood (1939), pp. 31 and 36-7.
52 Collingwood (1940), pp. 21, 33.
53 Collingwood (1938), pp. 265, 266. Cf. Cook Wilson (1926), i, II iv §§ 57-9, pp. 119-26 and Whately (1913), II iv § 1, pp. 65-6.
54 Collingwood (1939), pp. 33, 39, 35.
55 Austin (1970), pp. 249-50; (1962), pp. 52, 138 and 147.
56 Cf. Collingwood (1924), p. 11.
57 Ryle (1930), p. 33.
58 See Austin (1970), p. 249 and (1962), p. 137.
59 Ryle (1950), p. 246.
60 Hamblin (1958), p. 160; cf. Llewelyn (1964), p. 70, note 7. Cf. also Wittgenstein (1958), I § 24; p. 12[e].
61 Cf. Searle (1968), pp. 422-4.
62 Reid (1785), VI i; p. 413b.
63 Cf. Dummett (1981), p. 357.
64 Cf. Cohen (1929), p. 353.
65 Cohen (1929), pp. 350 and 353.
66 Schlick (1936), p. 466.
67 Hamblin (1963), p. 63.
68 Cohen (1929), p. 353. Cf. Mary and Arthur Prior (1955), p. 56.

Chapter 5

Stating Answers

Philosophers go astray in ascribing features of interrogation to the asking of questions as such, more so to questions themselves. No presumptions attach to the posing of questions in thought or in expository discourse, still less to questions themselves. A presumption exists only within a social setting, something being presumed of a person in some situation by others — often generally, but occasionally also in some specific capacity. When a speaker puts a question to another, something is presumed not just of the speaker *qua* speaker but also, it will emerge, of the speaker with respect to the addressee.

An account, in the next chapter, of the presumption underlying interrogation will help to disentangle peculiarities attaching to the asking of others questions from logical features of questions themselves. Before that the notion of answering questions must be considered. Since to answer another's question is to state that something is the answer to it, some consideration of the presumption underlying statement-making as such is also apposite. It was seen in the last section of the previous chapter that a statement is, in Ryle's words, employed 'in the expression of *knowledge*'.[1] In this way stating that something is the answer to a question is to purport to know what the answer to it is. Accordingly, the presumption underlying statement-making in general serves to explain further how questions themselves have been mistakenly thought to have something necessarily to do with knowledge.

Answering

Questions may be asked only in thought or in the course of giving an exposition besides being put to others. So questions are not necessarily linked to the social, even when asked out loud and in company. It must now be pointed out that one may equally answer a question, even out loud and in company, without necessarily being the respondent of some interrogator; without necessarily, that is, giving one's answer to an interrogator.

Questions appear to be bound up with colloquy or dialogue, and to occur in soliloquy or monologue only to the extent that a thinker can be viewed as somehow combining the parts to be performed in turn by speaker and addressee, because the acts signified by the correlative verbs *question* and *answer* seem, when not conceived as abstracted from, respectively, interrogators' acts of questioning others and respondents' acts of answering interrogators, to be performed by necessarily distinct persons. A question, in Collingwood's words, 'looks forward to' its answer;[2] yet it does not say what the answer to it is. Questions merely ask things without saying anything. So for a person to ask a question, whether or not of another, is plainly to do something different from answering a question: somebody who asks a question is not saying anything either. But somebody who answers a question is necessarily saying something — or so it might seem.

To ask a question, even out loud, is not to say anything other than in a minimal sense of pronouncing words; the contrast between saying the words making up an interrogative sentence and asking a question being marked by Austin as that between a 'phatic' and a 'rhetic' act.[3] Since the object of asking a question is to elicit the answer to the question, the rhetic act performed by those who answer an interrogator's question is the stating of what they purport to be the answer to the question, which is the stating of their answer to the question. And they can legitimately be held to the assertion that something is so that can be yielded from the answer they state taken together with the question they have answered. Thus, only by metaphor, so it might seem, can the division of labour between questioner and answerer be united and the two jobs be done in turn by just one person: the same person cannot, so it might seem, literally both ask and answer the same question; just as, recalling the etymology of *answer*, the person who swears in answer to a charge is not the same as the person who brings the charge.

Such a conclusion is based on not only the already contested assumption that in asking a question as such one must thereby be an interrogator — that is, be putting the question to somebody, even if only metaphorically to oneself — but the further assumption that in answering a question one must thereby be a respondent — that is, be addressing words in response to an interrogator who has previously put the question to one. Yet one can come up with or across, sooner or later, one's answer to a question one has asked 'oneself', as it is said, without one thereby having literally to state to oneself what the answer to it is; that is, without having to answer oneself back — which one would attempt to do only if one were insane.

Admittedly, *answer*, in contrast with *ask*, usually implies there is some addressee, the indirect object of the verb, as in *Answer me*. But the notion of answering a question can be abstracted from the notion of answering an interrogator. Indeed, to be said to have come up with the answer to a question one has asked oneself does not imply that one has stated what the answer to it is to anybody; for in answering one's own question one need not give anybody an answer, not even oneself. Here answering is not being held by others to any assertion or statement, for one may say nothing at all; instead, it is merely to commit oneself to a judgment.

Another reason, then, why the speech-act fallacy about questions has seemed plausible is that answers to questions are usually given to interrogators, who have put the questions, by respondents, who are to answer the questions. But just as one can ask oneself a question, without thereby becoming an interrogator — without thereby putting the question to anybody, still less oneself — so too can one come across the answer to a question one previously asked oneself without thereby becoming one's own respondent. Here one is not playing the parts consecutively of interrogator and respondent. In venturing what one takes to be the answer to one's own question, one can at most be said, in the fashionable phrase, to be 'addressing' the question, not addressing oneself.

The original idea behind answering, of course, was rooted in the notion of being a respondent. Responding to an interrogator is an instance of a social intellectual act, and will serve to bring to light factors underlying such social uses of language.

Explicit Performatives of the Social Acts

Originally answering was the making of a sworn statement in rebuttal of a charge laid against one. The derivation of the verb *answer* thus explains why its central sense always implies some addressee. The Latin *respondere*, Varro says, literally means to promise in return; and a promise must always be made to somebody. Varro lists the responsive among six categories of inflexions of the verb.[4] Since his list is expressly confined to verbs, the responsive comprises only those answers given to questions supplied by a verb; perhaps also, in conformity to his unilluminating example, only in the first person. The notion of a 'responsive mood' cannot be applied generally, as it is by Roland R. Hausser, to given answers without making the notion of mood irredeemably lax.[5] Instead, what Varro barely hints at is a distinctive use of the verb in the first person when answering a question, as exemplified by Austin's prime instances of a performative utterance: namely, the responses in the marriage ceremony and an affirmative answer to a question like *Do you promise* (*swear*)?

Answers to questions are normally given in a form that reflects the logical relationship between the abstractions, question and answer. But while one can answer the question *Do you promise?* with *Yes* or *No* as with any other yes-no question, more obviously ritual responses, as in the marriage ceremony (*I will*, *I do*), are less like answers given to questions generally. The explanation seems to be that where a response signals a performative utterance it becomes desirable, sometimes essential, to make what is being done by the speaker in uttering the words explicit. Thus, answering the question *Do you promise?* by *Yes* or *I do* alone might not make explicit enough the performance of the act of promising marked by the words *I promise*. (Note that a negative answer would not constitute a performative utterance.) By contrast, *Yes* or *I will* would be quite sufficient in answer to the question *Will you promise?* since it holds respondents merely to the assertion that (in certain circumstances) they are willing to promise.[6]

The speech-act of answering, as originally conceived, could itself be made explicit by a performative utterance such as *I swear that ... (in response to the charge laid against me)*. Austin opposes what he calls 'the explicit performative' to 'the primary utterance'.[7] The explicit performative for answering, then, would be *I answer you that ...* . It should be stressed that in issuing any explicit performative neither the speaker nor the words themselves assert anything, say anything capable of being true or false. An explicit performative never states, reports or describes the performance of the deed that is done with the words; the issuing of the utterance just is the performance of the deed. Deeds themselves, unlike assertions about deeds, cannot be true or false. Here, then, although what follows the *that* ... makes explicit the assertion one is held to in giving one's answer, in making explicit one's act of answering one is not making any assertion. Similarly, the explicit performative for the putting of a question to another would be *I ask you* (*where*, *when*, *who*, *if*, etc.) ... .

Since *ask* and *answer* here take as their indirect object the second person, referring to an addressee, they are not being used as in expository discourse. Austin's inclusion of *ask* and *answer* in his list of expositives thus masks an important distinction. He includes them in a subgroup along with *inform*, *apprise*, *tell*, and *rejoin*,[8] thereby suggesting that the speaker may be not just thinking aloud in company but, further, engaging in a social intellectual operation. Indeed, his list juxtaposes purely expository uses of verbs, such as could equally occur in spoken soliloquy or monologue, with verbs which can occur only in colloquy or dialogue. As Vendler points out, the list described by Austin as being 'of "explicit performative verbs"' contains several '"thinking"' besides '"saying" verbs'.[9] But while Austin opposes *question*, 'a pure explicit performative', to *wonder* or *doubt*, his concern is not with thinking but 'the issuing of an utterance in a speech situation'. While some of the verbs on his list could still apply to their subjects even when they are not giving a running commentary on their current or previous trains of thought to others, he is not concerned, for instance, with recognising or doubting themselves, but rather with saying to others *I recognise that* or *I doubt*; which when the saying is sincere is itself to recognise or doubt.[10]

To parody Kant, it must be possible for the words, *I say to you* to accompany all my sentences addressed to others. These words could therefore explicitly introduce each of my sentences addressed to others, since each of them implies — in a special sense to be noted later — that I am saying words to somebody, performing a phatic act. *I say to you* is therefore the highest genus of explicit performatives, or of speech-acts as Austin later came to think of them.[11] An addressee is not just a hearer, who may simply be a bystander or an eavesdropper; instead, the addressee is picked out by the speaker[12] — buttonholed, if a reluctant addressee. As it is always the case that I am the speaker and you are the addressee, the explicit performative here is, strictly, redundant; yet it has rhetorical uses, and when the sentence that is to follow is in the third person, the explicit performative may help to make clear that the words are the speaker's own rather than reported or quoted from somebody else. *I say to you: ...* would contrast, then, with *I quote: ...* .

It might seem that the sentence, *I am speaking to you* need equally never actually be said. Yet teachers often have occasion to address the words to daydreaming pupils. Its virtual performative character, despite being in the present continuous tense, can be seen from its negation, far from being self-stultifying, being sometimes employed to reprove conversational gatecrashers. While saying *I am not speaking to you* in one sense belies itself, in another it serves to exclude the addressee from being the addressee of the immediately prior speech-act being made explicit. And *I am not asking you* or *I am not telling you to do it*, with the *you* stressed, have no trace of paradox about them. *I am not telling you that it is so*, however, serves not to differentiate between addressees, but rather to disclaim that what one says is to be taken as testimony. Each of these negatives contrasts with some positive explicit performative.

There is never any occasion, by contrast with explicit performatives, to add the Kantian *I think* explicitly to each of my thoughts, even although that additional thought must always be true of each of my other thoughts. For unless I am mad, I am never in danger of thinking that the thoughts which I think are not mine, of confusing my thoughts with those of anybody else's — even when I am thinking about, considering, the thoughts of others; or hear, or dream, that others speak. In pondering the thoughts of another communicated to me by speech or in writing I am having my own thoughts about the thoughts of another: the other's thoughts here do not occur detached from my own. When I talk to others, however, it is sometimes useful to guard some of my utterances with an *I think* to make clear that I am only expounding my opinion to others as distinct from making a statement to them.

The distinction needs to be marked between, on the one hand, purely expository discourse, where only the speaker's words are addressed to the addressee, and on the other, language serving to effect social intellectual operations, where the addressee is more engaged by the speaker in the interchange than simply hearing out an exposition of the speaker's thoughts or arguments. The addressee of a social intellectual operation has a specific part to play in the operation, by contrast with one to whom expository discourse is directed, who has no part to play in the exposition other than to listen attentively with an effort to understand.

And so beyond the phatic act the main types of rhetic act can be marked by an explicit performative. Rhetic acts at the most general are acts of either saying or asking; but more specifically within the class of saying things are: first, asserting, followed only by a propositional construction and stating (to somebody) or telling somebody, followed by a propositional or interrogative construction; second, telling somebody to do something.[13] Explicit performatives signal the performance of these rhetic acts by use of the present perfect (non-continuous) tense in the first person.

Questions put to others can be taken to be primary utterances whose explicit performatives start with the words *I ask you* followed by an interrogative conjunction or a particular interrogative word introducing an interrogative clause alluding to the question put to the addressee. Questions put to others can thus be marked off from those utterances containing merely expository questions, whether or not they are introduced by *I ask* (tout court), *I ask myself, I question, I doubt, I wonder.* Neither type of explicit performative — interrogation or the posing of purely expository questions — should be taken to be any part of the asking of questions as such. For when a question is asked merely in thought there is no speech-act performed at all, either a primary utterance or an explicit performative. Still less is uttering *I ask (you)* part of the meaning of an interrogative sentence or somehow contained in the notion of the question asked itself, as some philosophers and linguistic theorists have supposed.

Assertions addressed to others can likewise be taken to be primary utterances which contain a proposition and whose explicit performatives start with the words *I say to you that* ... . More specifically, statements made to others can be made explicit by being prefaced with the words *I state (to you)*, *tell you*, *testify*, *that* ... . Such more specific explicit performatives serve to differentiate the making of a statement from, to mention Austin's examples, the exposition of an argument, the making of a suggestion, betting, or the issuing of a warning or protest. The last three examples clearly go beyond the expository.

Commands can be made explicit by being prefaced with the words *I tell you to* ... or perhaps *I say to you that you are to*, *should*, ... But there is no contrast here with an expository use of imperative sentences because whatever imperative sentences are variously used to express, the intention of the speaker in uttering them is always presumed to be to engage an addressee.

The above three types of explicit performatives are distinctive and may be called 'rhetic explicit performatives'. For what follows them is itself the primary utterance. That is, when the explicit performative is deleted what remains is the primary utterance, a complete sentence. The same is not true generally of Austin's examples of explicit performatives. Nor of Reid's fourth example of a social intellectual operation, promising: only the construction with *that*, not *to*, yields a complete sentence when the words *I promise* ... are deleted.[14]

Reid's four examples of social intellectual operations each employ a distinctive form of speech in expressing their products. The fourth, promising, may be taken as representative of the form of speech employed by the whole class of performative utterances, including the three rhetic explicit performatives, besides other explicit performatives. The distinguishing mark of the performative form of speech is that although it is itself incapable of expressing what is either true or false, it is parasitic on the declarative form: *I promise* does not say anything true or false; but *I promised* does.[15] So likewise *I ask* in contrast with *I asked*. The other three forms of speech are just those employed in the primary utterances corresponding to the three rhetic explicit performatives: namely, the declarative, interrogative and imperative sentences constituting these primary utterances. The declarative and the interrogative, unlike the imperatival, in addition to being forms of speech, also express fundamental logical forms of thought. Thus, the declarative and the interrogative do not exclusively express products of their respective social intellectual acts — as is seen from their use to express thought, as also speech not addressed to anybody. But even to think what an imperative sentence expresses is to think of the — at least possible — performance by some agent of the action specified.

What is Presumed of Speakers

Speakers are presumed to believe what they say. They are also presumed to believe what is presupposed by what they say, as also by the questions they ask — whether or not these questions are put to others — and by what they tell others to do. Such general presumptions attaching to speakers engaging others in a social intellectual operation carry over to the form of speech used to effect the speech-act. For instance, it is presumed that the author of a declarative sentence believes that what the sentence says is so is true, even when the identity of the author is unknown; and the presupposition of a question asked by an interrogative sentence likewise.

In addition to such general presumptions, speakers are presumed in making statements to others, asking others questions and telling others to do actions, to intend that their addressees perform the specific part assigned to them in the social operation; for the object of the social operation, which speakers are presumed to intend to promote, is to engage addressees to play their part in the operation. The three rhetic explicit performatives, in signalling what social intellectual operation the speaker is engaging the addressee in, thus adumbrate what is specifically presumed thereby of the speaker.

Take asking others questions, to anticipate a little of the next chapter. A question in the second person when spoken in the presence of others can usually be safely taken as being put to, as engaging, an addressee. So there is generally no need to preface the question with *I am asking you*. Or to say this in addition — except when the addressee did not hear properly the first time the question was put; or, the *you* being stressed, which person the speaker is putting the question to is in doubt. Questions in the second person have the same feature of always referring to an addressee as have imperative sentences, which, either implicitly or explicitly, normally use the second person.

A question in the third person, or even first, when spoken in the presence of others is usually also being put to an addressee to answer — unless, that is, the question is purely expository. So understood is the presumption that the addressee is to tell the speaker what the answer is to such a question, even though the question is not in the second person, that the words *Now, I ask you* have come to be used in a merely exclamatory way to preface a rhetorical question where no intention is presumed that the addressee is to give any answer.[16] By contrast, the words

Now, I ask myself may preface a genuine question, as when a speaker airs doubts publicly; but not a question put to anybody.

It is seldom recognised that when a question in the third person — such as, *What is the capital of Peru?* — is put to another, the presumption that the addressee is to tell the speaker what the answer is to the question is no part of the meaning of the interrogative sentence expressing the question. For the notion of an addressee is contained in neither the meaning of an interrogative sentence nor the notion of a question as such. That the intention of a speaker in putting a question in the third person to another is that the addressee tell the speaker what the answer is to the question is only a presumption attaching to the speaker's use of the interrogative form of speech together with the speaker's (social intellectual) act of putting a question to another. A question in the third person put to another thus conveys more to the addressee than simply what is expressed in the interrogative sentence. For although there is no reference in the interrogative sentence to an addressee, as there is with a question in the second person, the addressee is nevertheless being engaged by the speaker.[17]

There are, of course, exceptions to what are only presumptions. There are several non-earnest uses of language, as with examples cited in textbooks or philosophy lectures, playacting, recital of poetry, elocution exercises, (fictitious) storytelling, guessing (in some situations), mimicry and in parlour games; also non-literal uses of language, such as joking, exaggeration, sarcasm, irony, personification, and so forth. Leaving aside such non-standard uses of language, failures of presumptions to hold constitute abuses by speakers — of either the specific social operation or, in general, the addressee.

Addressees can legitimately complain of deceit, or at least insincerity, if speakers do not abide by the requirement that they believe what they say in earnest. Addressees would also be entitled to complain that speakers were being culpably misleading if they did not at least believe what is presupposed by any of their utterances, though such abuses are more common in philosophical texts than real life.

Moore pointed out that

> even where I do not mean what I say, my words may be said to imply either that I think that A is B or that I know it, since they will commonly lead people to suppose that one or other of these two things is the case.

And elsewhere, that

> when a man asserts anything which might be true or false, he *implies* that he himself, at the time of speaking, believes or knows the thing in question — a sense in which he *implies* this, even if he is lying.[18]

Using words with the intention of leading others to suppose that something about one is so is a good way of describing presumptions underlying the addressing of words to others. What others usually suppose, what is presumed by them, is something in general about the speaker; but with the social intellectual operations the speaker is usually presumed in addition to have specific intentions with respect to the addressee which serve the object of the social operation. Of the abuses of the three rhetic speech-acts (social intellectual operations), abuses of statement-making are the most serious. Abuses of commanding and interrogating are rarer.

The notion of assertion tends to abstract from any notion of an addressee, so that the speaker's intentions towards the addressee do not ordinarily figure in the aim of assertion. In the ordinary sense to assert that something is so is to give out publicly — imply, in Moore's sense, by one's act of speaking — that one (at least) believes that what one says to be so is indeed so. It is noteworthy, however, that Moore's observation does not really fit the rhetic explicit performative for assertion — namely, *I say to you that ...* . What I imply when I assert that something is so is that I at least believe, or know, it be so. Only those who are already convinced that Austin was wrong to deny truth-value to performative utterances[19] would attempt to argue that this explicit performative implies that I either believe or know that I say something to you.

It is, of course, more than logically possible to say what is not so, for what one says not to be true. Speaking falsely comes about because either one mistakenly believes that what one says is so; or one believes (correctly) that what one says is not so, only one intends to deceive others. The aim of assertion, therefore, is to say what is true; and to believe, correctly or mistakenly, that one has intentionally done otherwise, is an abuse of assertion. (A third possibility, where one does not care whether what one says in earnest is true or false, and may accordingly not believe one way or the other, is also an abuse.)

Speakers, then, are presumed at the very least to believe what they assert. Accordingly, if a speaker baldly asserts without any qualifying *I think* what can only be a mere expression of opinion — because the area is not one where knowledge can be expected to be had, or no supporting argument or evidence has been offered — the appropriate charge, when speakers do not believe what they say in earnest, is of not so much lying as insincerity. People sometimes lack the courage of their convictions; hypocrites cloak their true sentiments under respectable commonplaces. If I voice as if they were my own opinions I do not actually hold, or expound to others arguments whose cogency I do not accept as if I did, I am not exactly a liar; but I am guilty of insincerity, just as much as — to take the sort of failure Austin had in mind by his insincerities — if I say *I congratulate you* when I feel mortified by your success.

Answering, Statement-Making and Testimony

Ryle says, much too baldly, 'an answer to a question is a statement'.[20] An answer to a question is rather an abstraction from somebody's answering the question; and in answering a question, one does not normally make an explicit assertion. Instead, a word, phrase or term supplies what one takes to be the answer to the question. Yet one is normally held to an assertion derived from one's answer taken with the question.

As with all who answer questions, respondents in giving their interrogators an answer to a question put to them are normally held at least to an assertion. (Conformable answers to questions asking what the addressee's advice or command is, as also deliberative questions, are exceptions.) But respondents of interrogators are usually held further to be making a statement to them, unless what is said in answer is avowedly offered as an expression of opinion or a mere guess. Guessing, especially as a game, is a doubtful use of language in earnest. If I am asked to say which fist conceals a coin, my pointing to your left fist scarcely constitutes making a statement to you — unless, being a cheat, I know, or suppose I know, that what I present as my guess is correct. Answers given to questions put to others in parlour games generally likewise exemplify a non-serious use of language, as do the questions asked.

Thus, in giving their interrogators an answer to a question put to them respondents are usually held to be making a statement to them. But respondents also thereby state what their answer is to the question. Since the object of asking questions is to elicit the answer to the question, respondents purport — and so are presumed — in stating what their answer is to the question to be stating what they take to be the answer to the question. They are not simply presumed to be giving merely a conformable answer.

The sense of such verbs as *state* and *tell* conveys the saying of something; so that stating or telling (when it is not *telling ... to*) is always stating or telling *that* ... — even when the stating or telling is characterised interrogatively. So in answering the question put to me *Where were you born?* I am taken to have made the statement that I was born in such-and-such a place. Now, the interrogative clauses governed by *state* and *tell* convey that the stating was done correctly. So I at the very least purport to state where I was born; but I thereby also actually state what my answer is to that question.

In summary, respondents are presumed in answering in earnest a question put to them to be stating what they take to be the answer to the question. In answering with a word, phrase or term, they can always be held to be stating *that the answer to the question is* ... — in default of its being made clear that what is being offered is only a guess or an expression of opinion. So if I state *1815* in answer to the question, *When was the Battle of Waterloo fought?* I can be held not only to the statement that the Battle of Waterloo was fought in 1815 but also to the statement that the answer to the question *When was the Battle of Waterloo fought?* is 1815. The explicit performative *I answer you that* ... can therefore be made more explicit with the words *I state (to you), tell you, in answer to the (your) question that* ... ; or even more explicitly: *I state (to you), tell you that the answer to the (your) question '... ?' is* ... .

The making of statements to others can, of course, be spontaneous and gratuitous, not solely in answer to questions put by others. Stating is more specific than assertion since it involves telling another. For in stating one is presumed, not simply to believe what one says, but to know to be so what one tells others; and so not merely to express one's opinion to them — though, of course, one can also state to others what one's opinions are. If I pronounce the president to be a fool, I can surely be taken to be making only an assertion. Since the description can rarely be taken to be known to apply, I can only be taken as expressing my opinion. So, whereas I said to you, I did not exactly tell you that the president was a fool. Giving testimony is in turn more specific. For when one presumes, as when giving what one takes to be the answer to a question during a quiz or test, that others already know to be so what one tells them and that they take it to be sufficiently established quite independently of one's telling them, one does not purport, and neither is one presumed, to be giving testimony — still less to be informing one's interrogator of the truth of what one states.

As will emerge in the next section, in making statements to others generally, and so, specifically, in giving interrogators answers to questions or in giving testimony, speakers are presumed to engage their addressees in the social intellectual act.

Reid's '*principle of veracity*', if taken in isolation from its counterpart, '*the principle of credulity*', can seem to overlook any presumption of speaker towards addressee; and so can seem more suited to assertion than statement-making. For what is commonly called veracity, which serves the aim of stating generally, is not to be taken literally as speaking the truth. Speaking falsely cannot always in practice be avoided even with the best of intentions, for mistakes are easily made. Veracity is rather refraining from stating what one knows, or thinks one knows, to be false. Reid's omission of any mention of knowledge in connection with veracity in his initial account of testimony explains why it seems more suited to assertion. Moreover, his talk of 'a propensity to speak the truth', dresses up in psychological garb what he scarcely hints is a logical feature. The principle which serves the object of assertion, in contrast with statement-making, is that one at least believe what one says — as distinct from states — to be so; what might better be called a principle of sincerity. If Reid finds 'that truth is always at the door of my lips, and goes forth spontaneously, if not held back', it is a consequence of the aim of assertion, which is to say what is true; not the work of some instinct.[21]

Hence Moore's 'think', or 'believe', is too wide for stating — despite his disjunction being with 'know'. It can be amended 'to think (believe) one knows' to accommodate cases of erroneous, as distinct from what is called 'false' — that is, dishonest — testimony.[22] For the object of giving testimony, as of stating generally, is to tell one's addressee something one knows to be so. So although what one tells one's addressee may sometimes turn out to be incorrect, as when one does not actually but only thinks one knows it, there is no abuse — unlike when one knows, or thinks one knows, that it is, or may be, not so.

In giving testimony specifically and in stating generally, then, speakers are presumed to know, or at least to think that they know, that what they testify to or state is so. A different sort of abuse arises where speakers are just guessing or only of the opinion: what is bare assertion is being passed off as if known by the speaker; though one can also testify without abuse to what is candidly offered as no more than a guess or one's opinion. A more complicated abuse arises where in addition there is an intention to deceive: the speaker does not know that what is stated to be so (either spontaneously or in answer to a question put) is or may be false but is only guessing or of the opinion.[23]

It is tempting to suppose that logicians are primarily concerned with propositions, epistemologists with statements; for in making a statement to another, one is presumed to have knowledge. But there is a tradition of regarding a proposition as the setting down of what is to be proved by argument; and while argument clearly falls within the jurisdiction of the logician, if the premise of an argument or what is adduced in support of a conclusion is claimed to be known, the epistemologist has an interest in the affair too. A proposition in the sense of what is to be proved is potentially a statement, what could be related to an addressee. Questions being non-propositional in form, the logician's interest in them beyond the use and abuse of the asking of them in debate and argument will, accordingly, be limited — as will be seen in the Appendix; while doubts, queries, puzzles and wonderings will often be of major concern for the epistemologist.

In making statements to others, even in giving them testimony, there is no presumption that they do not know what one has to tell them; though if one believed, or had not forgotten, that all of one's addressees present already knew and had not forgotten what one has to tell them, one would scarcely bother to relate it to them spontaneously — by contrast with being told by somebody to do so or being asked a question on the matter. Likewise, in answering such a question, there is no presumption that one's interrogator does not know what one has to relate. While knowledge usually gets spread around through people giving testimony, the dissemination of knowledge is strictly incidental to the object of testimony, and no part of the object of stating as such. For acquiring entirely fresh information is not the only thing of importance: receiving corroboration from others of what one already knows can be also. And while giving testimony is always telling others that something is so, not all such telling is the giving of testimony, it was seen: in giving the answer to a quiz question respondents tell their interrogators what is agreed to be common knowledge.

Hence Bell is right to contrast *tell* with *inform*; and Welbourne wrong to contrast such things as reminiscing and reminding with telling, which, he supposes, in assuming 'ignorance on the part of the audience', is to impart knowledge. Somebody may, though, intend to inform others of something thinking that they do not already know it; in which case the person only tells them it, not informs them of it.[24] What one imparts to others is usually said to be, not the truth, but knowledge and information; and what one informs others of, facts or what is so. By contrast, the ordinary phrase is *telling the truth*. For not only can the truth bear repetition, its repetition is sometimes demanded.

Since to state or tell others that something is so — or, indeed, inform them of it — is always to state, tell or inform *that* ... the knowledge thereby implied (in Moore's sense) by one's stating, telling or informing is usually characterised propositionally. Only in a report of what a speaker stated would the knowledge thereby presumed be characterised interrogatively. Even then, what was actually stated is not reported: *He stated where she lived* does not reveal what the particular statement he made was. Furthermore, such presumed knowledge has to be taken non-minimally, since those who make statements imply that they themselves are in possession of the knowledge, and so they themselves must conceive it somehow. From these two factors it follows that those who make statements are presumed not only to know to be so what they state to be so but also to believe it to be so. This conclusion will not surprise traditionally inclined epistemologists; yet it is a remarkable feature of statement-making. For knowing *that* is not invariably accompanied by belief: while non-human animals, and even human beings in some situations, are frequently safely credited with knowledge *that*, attributions of beliefs to them are far less secure.

More significantly, knowing here is not something superimposed on believing, as traditionally inclined epistemologists have it. The belief is given out to others rather as stemming from the possession of the knowledge; for the belief is expressed as an articulation of knowledge already in one's possession: in stating one gives out that one believes *that* ... by virtue of one's knowing *that* ... . With stating, then, as distinct from assertion, Moore's disjunction should be replaced by the conjunction 'believe and know': speakers are presumed to believe the things they state, tell or inform others of, or testify to; and to believe them to be so because they know them to be so.

The Addressee's Part

The intention speakers are presumed to have with respect to their addressees in making statements to them is that their addressees believe what they tell them on the basis that they know to be so what they tell them. Hence the part to be played by their addressees is to believe what they are told on that basis. The intention here rests ultimately on the object of assertion, which is to say what is true; for the truth merits belief, both speaker's and hearer's.

It might seem that as the object in stating is to tell others what one knows, the part to be played by the addressee must rather be to know what the speaker knows. There is an ambiguity here: in telling me what in fact you merely believe, I know only that you hold a certain opinion; whereas in telling me what in fact you know as well as believe, I not only now know that you have a piece of knowledge in your possession but also come into possession of it myself — that is, if I did not already know it. When the *what* after *tell* is an interrogative pronoun, I get to know the extent of your knowledge — and, by inference, your ignorance — from what you tell me. When the *what* is a relative pronoun, I either come to, or already, share some piece of knowledge with you; for the knowledge you possess implied by what you tell me, being characterised propositionally, is not hidden behind an opaque interrogative characterisation but is thereby revealed to me by what you tell me.[25] The two readings of the *what*, however, are linked: getting to know the extent of your knowledge about some subject is thereby acquiring from you some knowledge about that subject — that is, if I am not already in possession of it. However, the knowledge, either about the subject or the extent of your knowledge of it, I thus acquire from you through what you tell me becomes available to me only if I believe what you tell me.

For suppose that you tell me something you know to be so but I do not believe what you tell me. I shall think that not only do you not actually know to be so what you told me but also that I myself do not know it to be so; for had I already known it to be so, I would have believed what you told me when you told it me, my belief here being merely an articulation of knowledge I already possessed. So although I have been told about the matter and am actually in a position to know about it, the knowledge is not accessible to me because I think I do not know the thing. If I can be said in a strained sense to 'know' it, since having been told about it I am at least in a position to know it, I do not know that I 'know' it.[26] Thus, knowledge can become available to others through testimony only if others believe what the speaker states. The part to be played by the addressee in testimony, then, as with stating generally, is to believe what the speaker states on the basis that the speaker knows it to be so, just as the speaker is presumed to believe it to be so on that basis too.

The suggestion that the intention those who make statements are presumed to have with respect to their addressees is to let them know that what they state is so fails to fit situations where the addressee already knows it and so does not take what is stated as testimony, as in test situations; or where the addressee has some intelligence of it from the testimony of a third party which the testimony now being given corroborates. More importantly, any intention to bring one's addressee to a state of knowledge, 'to make him know a certain thing' in Hintikka's odd phrase,[27] could be fulfilled in the giving of testimony only if the addressee believed — already believed where the testimony is merely corroborative — what one states. For knowing that something is so can hardly be said itself to be a part to be played by somebody, as distinct from what results if one plays the part of believing what the speaker states. The verb *know* has a usable imperative, but it cannot be construed as telling one's addressees to know *that* ... ; only that they should know *that* ... , the function of the imperative here in exploiting the transparency of the *that* clause being simply thereby to inform them of, let them know, what follows it. True, the speaker's ultimate intention, even when lying, is, in Welbourne's words, that the utterance 'be received as grounded on and thus expressing knowledge';[28] but this can be done only through addressees believing what the speaker tells them.

But is believing, any more than knowing, something one can do at will? Has not Hume pointed out that belief consists 'in something, that depends not on the will, but must arise from certain determinate causes and principles, of which we are not masters'? Specifically, Reid's principle of credulity is more appropriately thought of than its counterpart, the principle of veracity, as a natural instinct, which, with the lessons of experience, is 'restrained'. Yet since in learning one's mother tongue one thereby learns to understand not just a particular language but language as such, believing what others say cannot quite be instinctive. What might be said, more appropriately of the principle of credulity than the principle of veracity, is that, to adapt Reid's words, belief comes 'forth spontaneously, if not held back'.[29] Belief is not subject to the will; but withholding belief is.

One need not be driven to Hume's avowedly or Reid's implicitly deterministic view of belief to appreciate that one cannot believe whatever one chooses. Evidence or argument sometimes compels belief. Yet if people were not at all responsible for their beliefs there could be no ethics of belief. One ought to be guided by reasons at least in acquiring one's beliefs. Now, while one cannot make oneself believe something, one can nevertheless refuse to believe it. Where evidence or argument is entirely compelling refusing to believe is unreasonable, or at best a pretence of sceptical philosophers, an abdication rather than an affirmation of responsibility. Where evidence or argument is less than conclusive one has to weigh up whatever is available or offered and judge on the basis of such reasons whether to — not believe — but rather withhold one's belief. Withholding belief covers different types of case: one might find reasons to doubt rather than believe one way or the other, or to suspend judgment until further evidence or a better argument is forthcoming, or to believe the very contrary. One cannot at all choose to believe, then, but only choose not to believe — meaning, choose to withhold belief for any of the above reasons; and do so only reasonably where belief is not absolutely compelling.

Now, what others tell one when they offer testimony specifically is not presumed by them to be what one already has conclusive evidence or arguments for; since in offering testimony they purport to be informing one of and not merely telling one something. And even if one happens to know already and take as fully established what others offer as testimony, this circumstance is incidental to their presenting it as testimony. There is therefore always room in principle for the reasonable withholding of belief in the receiving of testimony; for the person who receives something as testimony has not already got conclusive reasons for believing it. Testimony can be corroborative only to the extent that what is already believed is capable of further support. But what is given in testimony is offered to the addressee to believe on the basis that it is known by the testifier; for in giving testimony one is presumed to tell one's addressee, not just what one believes to be so, as with assertion generally, but what one knows to be so. It is not up to the addressee, then, to strive to establish that what is testified to is in fact so; for the testifier has already implied that it is not only so but known to be so. Rather, the addressee can only try to resist believing.

Thus, in the receiving of testimony, reasons are required, not for believing, but for withholding belief. For being given the testimony is in itself some reason for believing it. That is, the burden of proof is on those who would dispute or disallow what is given in testimony, which is the import of Reid's principle of credulity. Admittedly, in some special situations when testimony is being tested, such as with courts of law, public enquiries and research pursued in history or social anthropology, the burden of proof is shifted, if not exactly reversed: objections must be rebutted as unfounded if what is testified to is to be accepted as established. But even here there is no requirement that what is testified to be independently established without any reliance at all on testimony,[30] still less that testimony as a source of knowledge be given some sort of transcendental deduction before any testimony at all can be admitted. Like memory, testimony is taken for granted in general to constitute knowledge, notwithstanding the frequent fallibility of memory and the prevalence of corrupted testimony.

If addressees believe the statements made to them, they will usually also believe the person making the statement. One can believe what another says merely in the sense that one also happens to share that opinion; but here one does not necessarily believe any person, one merely believes what the other person also believes. Believing a person is connected with having confidence or faith in, trusting, the person. Now, it is disbelieving, not believing, a person, which, as Austin would say, 'wears the trousers'.[31] To disbelieve speakers — that is, wilfully to refrain from believing them — is to impugn their honesty, to impute some abuse to them such as one among the sorts mentioned earlier. To believe a speaker, by contrast, is to be free from any such doubt. So one can be said, *pace* Welbourne, to believe people who tell one what one already knows when one does not suspect them of any abuse, such as passing off a guess as what they definitely know.[32] If one is receiving testimony which is purely corroborative, one will believe the testifier; not despite, but because, one already knows to be so what is testified to.

Believing what a person tells one and believing the person can come apart. One can refuse to believe what a person states without disbelieving the person, as when one knows or believes what one is told to be otherwise without suspecting the teller of an abuse: the teller may be honestly mistaken or a victim of deceit by some other teller. More complicatedly, I may believe what you tell me, perhaps because I know it to be so, but not believe you: I may suspect you of wrongly thinking that you know otherwise or of passing off as what is mere guesswork or opinion as if you knew it. Finally, I may, of course, neither believe what you tell me nor believe you, as when I suspect you of simply lying.

One reason why believing a person may seem to amount to believing what the person tells one is that people often protest when others show any reluctance to believe what they state: *You don't believe me, do you?* Yet the retort could be in order: 'No, I do believe you; only I find what you tell me incredible.' While the two may come apart, believing what a person states usually goes along with believing the person. So when one finds what one states meeting with incredulity, one is apt to take it as a slur on one's good faith, and to insist that one ought to be believed — that is, trusted. People sometimes add at the end of their testimony *Believe me*. The imperative here has to be understood as saying that the addressee should believe the speaker; for one can no more believe a person than believe that something is the case to order or on advise. But phrases such as *Believe you me, ...* or *Believe me when I tell you that ...* have degenerated into introductions to merely emphatic expressions of opinion.

One sort of abuse not so far mentioned involves the failure by the speaker to have the appropriate intention towards the addressee. If I suspect a double bluff I shall suspect that you intend to deceive me into believing that what you tell me is false when you actually know or believe it to be true. If I am right in my suspicions, I shall not believe you but I shall believe that what you tell me is true.[33] While such cases fall within the general class of believing what the speaker states without believing the speaker, they are distinctive: for here speakers intend, not that their addressees believe what they state, as with other cases within the general class; rather they intend that their addressees believe (mistakenly) the contrary instead. A similar sort of abuse would arise if the speaker did not care whether the addressee believed what was stated or not. Such abuses are quite distinct from what is ordinarily understood by lying, for liars intend that their victims mistakenly believe what they are told.

Notes

1 Ryle (1930), p. 33.
2 Collingwood (1924), p. 78.
3 Austin (1962), p. 95: third contrasting pairs; and pp. 95-8. Cf. Vendler (1972), pp. 25-6.
4 Varro (1951), VI 69, 72; ii, pp. 237, 239-41; and X 31; ii, p. 559.
5 Hausser (1983), p. 101; cf. (1980), p. 94, note 8.
6 Cf. Hare (1970), pp. 80-81.
7 Austin (1962), pp. 69-83.
8 Austin (1962), p. 161.
9 Vendler (1972), pp. 10-12. Austin (1962), p. 148.
10 Austin (1962), pp. 161, 88 and 138. Cf. Vendler (1972), pp. 15, 29-30.
11 Cf. Austin (1962), pp. 95 and 148-9.
12 Cf. Gandhi (1976), pp. 29-30.
13 Cf. Austin (1962), p. 95.
14 See Austin (1962), pp. 133-4 and pp. 70-72.
15 Cf. Dummett (1981), pp. 333-5.
16 *OED*, i, p. 687c: sense 4c.
17 Contrast Katz (1968), note 6, pp. 467-8.
18 Moore (1912), p. 78; (1968), p. 541. Cf. Ryle (1930), p. 33.
19 For example, Warnock (1973), pp. 80-89.

20 Ryle (1950), pp. 245-6.
21 Reid (1764), VI xxiv; p. 196. Cf. (1785), VI v 10; p. 450b. Contrast Welbourne (1989), pp. 177-9.
22 Reid (1785), VI i; p. 413b.
23 Cf. Welbourne (1979), p. 6; (1980), p. 319; (1986a), pp. 18, 19.
24 Bell (1975), pp. 207-8. Welbourne (1986a), pp. 19-20; cf. pp. 13, 91; contrast p. 12. Cf. also Welbourne (1979), p. 2; (1980), pp. 320-21; and Vendler (1979), p. 231.
25 Cf. Woozley (1953), pp. 161-2.
26 Cf. Welbourne (1979), p. 2; (1980), p. 321; (1986a), pp. 20 and 93; and Vendler (1979), pp. 231-2.
27 Hintikka (1974), p. 104. Cf. David and Stephanie Lewis (1975), pp. 49-50.
28 Welbourne (1986a), p. 19; cf. (1980), p. 319.
29 Hume (1978), Appendix, p. 624; cf. (1975), V ii; pp. 47-8. Reid (1764), VI xxiv; pp. 197a, 196b.
30 Cf. Reid (1785), VI v 3; p. 444b.
31 Austin (1956a), p. 192.
32 See Welbourne (1979), pp. 5-6; (1986a), pp. 24-5.
33 Cf. Welbourne (1979), p. 4; (1986a), pp. 12, 19; (1989), p. 178.

Chapter 6

Interrogation

The intention of a speaker who makes a statement to others, it was seen, is presumed to be, with respect to them, that they believe what the speaker states. The intention of a speaker who puts a question to potential respondents is presumed to be, with respect to them, that they tell, state to, their interrogator what the answer is to the question. Not to have the presumed intention with respect to addressees in either case constitutes an abuse — of statement-making or interrogation. Thus, to ask others a question with the intention of merely showing up their ignorance,[1] tricking them into lying, inducing them to refuse to answer, confusing them into answering incorrectly, or provoking a — perhaps initially reluctant — third party to answer instead, is each an abuse of interrogation.

None of these abuses of interrogation has any bearing on the asking of questions as such, let alone questions themselves. Nor on interrogative sentences which are not primarily used to put a question to another. For while some so-called rhetorical questions may be said to exploit interrogative form in that the answer to the literal question is too obvious to need to be expressly stated, posers of such questions are not seriously putting the question to others; even if, in some situations, the audience is expected to chant back ritually the answer learnt by rote. Expository questions aired publicly are likewise not put to anybody; though these, more clearly than rhetorical questions, are genuinely asked by the speaker, though not *qua* interrogator.

The Notion of a Response

Putting a question to another is unlike making a statement to another or telling another to do something in that one is presumed to intend that one's addressee respond literally; though exceptionally one may change one's mind after putting a question to another and try to stop the other from answering, perhaps because one decides to have a shot at coming up with or working out the answer for oneself.[2]

In a loose sense a response can be understood as some acknowledgment, by word or deed, of what others do — or even the evincing of mere awareness of one's surroundings, as when a comatose patient is said to show no response. One may respond reciprocally to kindness shown by others; peace-loving persons will not respond to provocation. More pertinent are words, or gestures doing duty for words, addressed in return to a speaker who has earlier addressed the person making the response. A response quite literally, however, is the answering of a question put to one.

Both the noun and the verb *answer* are often used in senses unrelated to any question being put to one to signify an acknowledgment. A cat is said to answer to a name when it shows recognition that it specifically is being called. Idiom is more restrictive with the verb: one is said to respond or reply to, or answer, letters or criticism; but not to respond or reply to the telephone, the door or a call — such as 'nature's'; only to answer them. Yet when the telephone or the knock on the door goes unanswered, it can be said that there is no reply or response, besides no answer. Noun and verb are also used in a more specific sense connected with their etymology, though again unrelated to any question put to one: namely, the meeting of a charge or a rebuttal of criticism; more generally, a defence perhaps also flowing over into a counterattack. A charge or an argument may thus be said to be unanswerable. Any irony attaching to the retort, *There's no answer to that!* lies in its ambiguity: is what was said unassailable or does it merely leave one speechless in amazement or contempt?

Literally and seriously to address words to another is to assume that one's addressee is capable of some response; which cannot, therefore, be ruled out — even when unexpected, as when a member of a lecturer's audience volunteers an answer to a purely expository question. The ability to respond to a speaker's words requires at a minimum that the addressee has heard them; more specific responses require in addition that the addressee has heard them right and understood them.

With non-human animals any understanding on their part will be limited to what can be conveyed to them when the words uttered are supported by what Reid calls 'a natural language' of tone of voice, gesture and facial expression.[3] I may with the aid of gesticulation succeed in telling the cat to get off the table or that a saucer of milk awaits it, the criterion of success in performing the speech-acts here being my managing to get the cat to understand to some degree what I intend to convey to it — understanding manifested by the cat's subsequent conduct. Significantly, I cannot ask a cat a question, even with the help of gestures; though I may make-believe that I am asking it a question. Any response from non-human animals will necessarily be non-verbal; but it may nevertheless be both expressive and communicative, taking the form of cries and bodily movements — barking and tail-wagging with a dog. With supposedly supernatural beings no problems about their hearing, or its range, or their degree of understanding are usually thought to crop up; a plea to hear a prayer being rather a plea to hear it out and consider it, to grant it a hearing. The type of response looked for will, barring alleged miracles, be indirect. Those who sincerely pray generally hope to get some sort of answer to their petitionary prayers; even if it is manifested only by what is entirely explicable naturally, such as a change of mood or in the weather.

Imaginary, figurative or mock addressing, where the speaker does not seriously believe that any purported addressee can actually hear and understand the words, should be distinguished from cases where the speaker believes so mistakenly, as when one mistakes one's reflection for a burglar. Besides imaginary addressing of another in thought and figurative addressing in poetic personifications, mock addressing would include instances where one was said to talk to plants, even to tell them to grow, when one does so playfully; or, as one vents one's frustration, to tell a car to get a move on when it only sluggishly responds — figuratively — to depression of the accelerator pedal. And pretending to tell a bluebottle to buzz off may help to alleviate exasperation. None of these instances constitute the genuine addressing of another. Any talking to spoken of is only in a degenerate sense: a talking doll does not really talk to its child owner, but neither does she do anything more than make-believe she talks to it. For there to be genuine talking to another the speaker must seriously believe that the ostensible addressee is capable of hearing and having some understanding of what is said and of responding accordingly.

Often the general aim in addressing words to others is to elicit some verbal response from them: one's addressee is to take the part one has just played of being the speaker, and one is to become in turn the new speaker's addressee. Thus, the aim in addressing words to others can simply be to engage them in conversation, even if only briefly. More formal situations are different: a drill sergeant does not intend soldiers to say anything on being ordered to present arms, just to do it; and a head teacher may make several announcements to the assembled school with no expectation of receiving any comments on them, that there will be any 'answering back'. Conversations will tend to terminate after business between the parties to them has been concluded: when reports have been made or instructions issued, when information sought has been received or permission asked for granted. More informal conversations are open-ended: there may be no reason why one of the parties breaks off other than the practical necessity to get on with other things. There is an analogous distinction between business and personal correspondence: the former ceases once the business is completed; but a correspondence between friends, though perhaps interrupted when they meet face to face, may continue up to the death of one of them.

What is distinctive about interrogation is that addressees may be reasonably expected, whether in the sense of merely anticipated or in addition required — by good manners, regulations, duty, in law and so forth — to tell the interrogator what they take to be the answer to the question put to them. The rising intonation in many languages at the end of some spoken interrogative sentences serves as a prompt for the respondent to take over when the interrogator stops speaking. Whereas it is entirely in order for the pupils or the soldiers to hear out the teacher's announcements or the sergeant's orders in silence, when a question is put to them they are always expected to say something.

By contrast, sometimes I may say nothing in response to your passing observations, or simply comply with what you tell me to do, without thereby showing any rudeness. It is, of course, generally advisable to make some acknowledgment, by word or gesture, of the statements or commands others make or issue to one; if only to forestall their repeating what they have said because they are thereby led to suppose that one has not heard or understood properly, a possibility that can often be discounted in more formal situations. But any requirement to say anything at all is founded on good manners, prudence and sociability.

A statement made or an opinion expressed to others can stand by itself without any comment, qualification, expression of agreement or denial by others. The addressee may be of the view there is no occasion to pick up the speaker's remark. Hume must have been fortunate in the company he kept, since he declares 'that no man ever met with any such absurd creature, or conversed with a man, who had no opinion or principle concerning any subject'.[4] Provided they make some acknowledgment, at least by gesture, of what is said to them, those who say little because they have little to say need not offend against good manners and prudence. Statements made in answer to questions put by an interrogator can equally stand alone without comment from the interrogator — although, again, some indication that one has heard and understood the answer, say, by repeating it, is generally advisable.

Rather differently, a command always looks beyond itself to the action commanded; but unless the command is to say something, there may be no need, either, for the addressee to say anything in response: just carrying out the action may sometimes be sufficient to show that one has understood the command and is willing to comply with it, especially if the action is to be done immediately. Often it is not sufficient; and, again, to avoid misunderstanding or doubt when it matters, especially if the action is to be done later, it is sometimes required of addressees to acknowledge, by word or signs doing duty for words, that a command has been issued to them — thus by saying, formally, *Aye, aye, sir* or informally, *All right.*[5]

Only when one declines to do what one has been told to, or demurs at doing so, does saying something in response become practically necessary. When a question is put to one, by contrast, saying something is always required. If one is not going to answer the question, some explanation is required; but then the requirement to say something in reply to the interrogator is no different in principle from the requirement to explain why one is not going to comply with what one has been told to do, as well as the requirement to acknowledge a command to do something later. It is the purely practical requirement that otherwise one may lead the other to suppose that one has not heard or understood, perhaps understood it as something other than a question. For to say nothing at all, not even by gesture, when a question is put to one, or not to say or do anything when told to do something — by contrast with another's remark or answer that gives rise to no comment — leaves the other little option of an alternative hypothesis. Since if one has indeed heard and understood, one is showing disrespect: ignoring what the speaker has said, treating it as if it had not been said or one had not heard it, even acting as if the speaker were not there at all.

So respect for others dictates that one explain why one is not going to, or cannot, do as one has been told or answer a question put to one. One may reply to an interrogator by saying that one is unable to give the answer to the question — because one does not know how to, or to do so would be to betray a confidence; or by challenging, often by asking a question in reply, the interrogator's right to ask one the question, or its coherence or intelligibility, or the truth or reasonableness of its presupposition. So long as what one says relates in some way to the question, social protocol will not have been breached — by contrast with telling you to go to blazes. To reply 'Go away' would not be to answer a question if one's intention was to brush aside the interrogator's question. Thus, Hare's assertion that 'only a command' can 'answer a question of the form "What shall I do?"' takes no account of the need an imperative sentence generally has for some interpretation. Answers to questions of the form Hare mentions, when put to somebody as distinct from occurring merely in thought, are supplied by the term filling the blank in sentences of the form *You will* (*shall*) ... , which happens to coincide with an imperative sentence. And questions of the type *What should I do?* asked when advice as distinct from a set of instructions is being sought are supplied by the term filling the blank in sentences of the form *You should* ... .[6]

In contrast with a general requirement founded on respect for others to say something in response to their words addressed to one, the specific requirement that one give what one takes to be the answer to a question put to one has its basis in the relationship between a question and what answers it. The compliant that what a respondent says fails to provide an answer to the question, it was noted in Chapter 2, shows that logic, not respondents solely, determine what is to count as an answer to a question. For although ignoring an interrogator's question or refusing to answer it is scarcely to commit a logical error, any expectation or presumption that one will give what one takes to be the answer to an interrogator's question, as also any requirement to do so founded on social factors — such as good manners, affability, duty, the demands of higher authority, the law — is ultimately founded on logic.

Since it says nothing, a question does not imply its answer. A question is incapable of being true or false, so it cannot imply anything in the relevant truth-functional sense. (What implies something in the sense Moore identified is rather a speaker's use of words, not what the words themselves say.) Besides, if a question could imply its answer, its answer would be inferable from the question alone; and so the question would not have the opaqueness of the interrogative form of thought. Yet a question, though complete in itself, does not stand alone, as a proposition or statement is capable of doing, without making any allusion to any other thought or utterance; instead, as was said, a question looks forward to its answer. The relationship of a question to what answers it should not to be confused with any propositional relationship like implication; still less, it will be emerge, with the relationship between a command and action in compliance with the command. The presumption, and requirement, that one state what one takes to be the answer to a question put to one rests on this unique interrogative relationship.

This requirement explains why asking others a question places an imposition on them.[7] The feeling of being imposed on is quite absent when a speaker merely airs doubts or queries or poses purely expository questions in one's presence. Hence what is required of respondents of interrogators must be distinct from what the question itself requires of its answer. Generally, if one is accosted by a bore, one will feel constrained to say something in reply if only to appear obliging rather than disregard the intrusion. But when a question specifically is put to one the compunction not to ignore it can be overcome only by the strong-minded. Just to resist it by countering with a question of one's own, such as *What has it to do with you?* is to depart from what, on the face of it, is reasonably to be expected.

Being quizzed by strangers or those with little imagination can be tiresome, especially when the presupposition of the question is false — something those who suppose research can be conducted by handing out standardised questionnaires should ponder. It is not pleasant, either, to be the subject of others' gratuitous and often unflattering assumptions that frequently underlie the questions they put in small talk — such as that greed or indolence govern one's courses of action or that one shares popular tastes, sentiments, prejudices or pastimes. Such assumptions have to be repudiated with as much grace as can be summoned if self-respect is to be retained; even though to do so inevitably puts one at a distance from one's interrogator through rejection of not just the question put but also any accompanying bid to find common ground.

The more sinister nuances of the term *interrogation* need not be dwelt on to appreciate that to put a question to another, no matter how gently, is to act a little imperiously; for it is to cause addressees to feel constrained to state what they take to be the answer to the question.[8] Accordingly, the feeling may sometimes be confronted and denied with the reply that the speaker has no right to ask the addressee such a question — or even to put any question to one: a cat may look at a king, but it is an impertinence to ask a king a question. Interrogation becomes the taking of liberties when attempts to protect one's privacy from the prying attention of others only arouse suspicion: one must have something to hide, is the inference, if one seeks to evade the question. Not wanting others to know some things about oneself need not imply guilt or shame. For knowledge is power, as Hobbes learnt from Bacon. Social control is exercised by officials, police and even — perhaps especially — neighbours through the gathering of intelligence. In seeking to protect one's privacy one is but seeking to protect one's liberty and independence. There is little one can do when others take advantage and ask one a straight question but to give a candid answer; and often only by submitting oneself to some such interrogation can one get from others what one needs from them: social co-operation is only possible within a system of social control.

Since questioning others can be a means of gaining power over them, interrogation can be hostile. Not owing simply to the burden of answering; rather, when the questioner aims for the addressee's submission. Victory lies in the interrogator's power to make the addressee admit to whatever is desired thus establishing control even over individual judgment and conscience.

An interrogator can also be seen sometimes, by contrast, as a supplicant, appealing to the goodness of heart of the potential respondent to be indulgent and state what the answer to the question is. If interrogators are not browbeating their addressees, they may be gently teasing out answers from them by coaxing them to open up. As Talmy Givón observes, as a general rule 'the question is an interaction type where the speaker is ... more deferential to the hearer. ... It gives the stage to the hearer and the consideration to the hearer'.[9] Viewed in such a light, interrogation looks more like an extension of an invitation to others to hold forth. Questions initiating conversations often have such a function.

A respondent obliges an interrogator, however regarded, by answering — which explains why the kindness may typically be rendered perfunctorily or lazily by gesture: nodding for *Yes*, shaking the head for *No*, sometimes by pointing doing duty for stating what the location of a thing is, and most conveniently of all, shrugging the shoulders for the reply *I don't know*.

It may not seem initially surprising that many philosophers have held that a question put to another must be a command of some sort — generally, to give the answer, or a conformable answer, to the question, or other formulations held to be equivalent to these. If, in addition, all questions are wrongly thought to be put to an addressee, what may be called the imperative theory of questions, whereby an attempt is made to reduce interrogative to imperative sentences, results. Since imperative sentences have a built-in requirement for an addressee, even if only figurative, whereas questions need not be put to anybody, the theory as an account of questions as such is broken-backed from the start. But quite apart from this crucial flaw, what is surprising on reflection is that such philosophers do not know better; for they are already familiar with the type of error involved in supposing that an interrogator is as such telling — or indeed inviting, it will be seen in Chapter 7 — any potential respondent to answer the question put. For they have encountered this type of error in connection with imperative sentences themselves — as will be seen on revisiting Reichenbach's notion of a cognitive correlate, which turns out to be what is presumed of speakers with respect to addressees they engage in a social intellectual operation.

What is Presumed of Interrogators Generally

Reichenbach's cognitive correlate for questions is: 'I wish to know the answer to this question.'[10] But as Lewis and Langford argue: 'We must distinguish between the logical import of a question and the fact that so-and-so asks it;' 'under ordinary circumstances' this fact will lead others to conclude 'that an answer is desired' by the speaker[11] — granting, that is, that there is a speaker and that the question is not asked merely in thought. Only asking a question, not a question itself, could have a cognitive correlate. Reichenbach's formulation is unsatisfactory even for asking another a question. In particular, both the terms *wish* and *know* give rise to objection.

First, talk of wishing and desiring is inappropriate for what should instead be an account of the intention serving the object of goal-directed acts and presumed of their agents. Whether interrogators have any desire to know, or even care about, the answers to the questions they put to others concerns their motives, as distinct from their intentions, in so doing. The job of some people is to ask others questions: police and customs officers, lawyers, personnel in social security offices or market researchers may sometimes have no ardent desire to hear the answers, or any particular answers, to the questions it is their duty to put to others.[12] There can also be a difference between the answer to a question and the answer an interrogator wants to hear from a respondent: in trying to extract a confession, an interrogator does not want to hear that the suspect did not commit the crime. As the refrain of the Fleetwood Mac number goes: 'But don't ask me what I think of you, I might not give you the answer that you want me to.' Occasionally the answers to some questions put to people are anticipated to be distressing or embarrassing, and so these questions are prefaced with such words as: *I hate to have to ask you this, but ...* — though the words have become a chat show cliché.

Supposedly polite questions loom large in awkward conversation among strangers in social gatherings, politeness being belied sometimes by the boredom unwittingly displayed by interrogators on being given the mundane answers to such questions. Those initiating the conversation genuinely intend those they seek to engage in it to answer, for they intend to get their addressees talking; but can only hope that what they hear will lead to something that interests them. An unsociable tactic would be to reply by asking: *Do you really want to know about that?* The motive people have for asking others questions is very often curiosity, or else an interest in their welfare; but that asking this question in reply would not be absurd — even although rude when not joking — shows that people can have other motives. A logical retort would be: 'No, I don't really want to know because you're probably quite boring; but I ask you the question, so intend that you give me the answer to it.' Thus the comment, *I don't want to hear, know, about that!* is illogical only when having put the question one stops the respondent from giving an answer, thus frustrating the object of interrogation: the putting of the question presumes the intention that one be given the answer to it; but the subsequent interruption manifests the contrary intention. So while the motives of interrogators for asking others questions cannot always be safely inferred, their intention in so doing can always be presumed; for not to have the appropriate intention with respect to one's addressee constitutes an abuse of a social intellectual act.

Secondly, what an interrogator may be doing may be related to some enquiry but unconcerned with the seeking of entirely new knowledge afforded by testimony generally. An interrogator may be going over again and checking with a witness testimony previously given. Thus, a question might be phrased *Where did you say she went?* rather than simply *Where did she go?* If there has been no lapse of memory, the interrogator will already know what the answer to the question is and be aiming merely to confirm it. Moreover, an interrogator may be seeking to corroborate, sometimes refute, other testimony previously given by either the respondent or other respondents. The aim of an interrogator here may be to strengthen the earlier testimony, especially if the interrogator has accepted it, by providing further evidence for it; otherwise, to undermine it, to throw up discrepancies or inconsistencies[13] — though since the object of interrogation is to elicit the answer to the question from one's addressee, to seek to catch out others in lies rather than intend that they tell one what they take to be the truth is strictly an abuse of interrogation.

In general, when one is testing previous or current testimony or both, putting a question to another does not imply that one does not know — or indeed, that one already knows — what the answer to it is, or has any beliefs or suspicions as to the answer. For what one is prepared to accept as knowledge, or to believe, is partly to be determined by the outcome of the test. Often the judgment or honesty of a previous or the current testifier is also being put to the test. And when one does already know what the answer to the question is, the aim is to test more the reliability of the testifier than the testimony. A candid interrogator will make plain to respondents that a test is being conducted, though the fact will usually be evident to all but the most ingenuous in some situations — such as interviews conducted by the police. But there is no abuse if such more remote intentions in putting the question have not been declared; for there is no presumption in putting a question to another that one is *per impossibile* entirely ignorant about the subject of the question, even if sometimes some ignorance can often safely be inferred.

The examining of testimony, it can thus be seen, may include the testing of people. Since those who testify imply that they know to be so what they testify to, when testimony is being examined part of what is being examined is whether the testifier does actually know what is being testified to. So quite apart from dishonest testimony, sometimes the issue to be tested is not — or not so much — whether some event, say, testified to actually took place but whether the witness was in a position to know that it took place rather than merely surmise or infer that it did. In some situations, such as in law suits or public enquiries, where it is important to establish according to agreed standards of proof what the facts are, which cannot therefore simply be readily granted, the interrogator may be concerned not so much with either the truth of what is testified to or the veracity of the witness as with whether the testimony actually bears out fully what it purports to. The enquiry here is not into the truth as such, but what evidence there is for some conclusion.

Trying to determine in general whether somebody knows something is different again and need not specifically involve the examining of testimony. Besides enquiries into the facts of a case there are also enquiries into the extent of others' knowledge of these facts. So if another's knowledge can be inferred from other available evidence, no testimony — or at least the testimony of the person whose knowledge is the subject of the investigation — need be involved. If the investigation is being conducted by putting questions to the person, the interrogator indeed already knows what the answer to the question put is, and takes it to be conclusively established, but aims to find out whether, as a matter of fact, the respondent too knows what the answer to it is. (Note that asking another a question in the course of such an enquiry is not the same as setting others test questions as an exercise in schooling: John R. Searle's schema for 'exam questions' is '*S* wants to know if *H* knows';[14] but the schema is clearly too broad.) In answering the respondent makes a statement, tells the interrogator something. Yet the statement made would count as testimony only if its truth could be regarded as serving to establish, or confirm at least, what the answer to the question is. But since the interrogator takes the answer to the question to be not only known but fully established, nothing the respondent says can be regarded as providing even confirmation. Talk of testifying is appropriate where the weight of evidence for some proposition is being considered; not where it is taken to be established beyond all question. If the respondent intends to deceive, however, such purported evidence as to respondent's state of knowledge or ignorance would count as the respondent's testimony, only false testimony.

Likewise, as was seen in the previous chapter, when contestants in a quiz or examination candidates have their knowledge of some subject tested their answers to questions do not count as testimony. Competitors in a quiz are trying to prove to others — as opposed to an examination where others are trying to determine — the extent of their general knowledge or their specialist knowledge of some area. The pervasive habit of some respondents who lack confidence when having their knowledge tested, as in quizzes or oral examinations, of beginning their answer with the question *Is it* (*the answer*) ... *?* shows that while their question may lamentably evince their desire to know what the answer to the interrogator's question is, the interrogator is presumed here to know it already. Since such respondents are expected to state what they take to be the answer to the question, not to guess or to offer a tentative opinion, the appropriate response of the interrogator is to ask in turn *Are you asking me or telling me?*

The temptation of philosophers being strong to suppose there must be some intrinsic connection between being given the answer to a question and the acquisition of knowledge, their mistake needs to be accounted for. In Chapter 3 it was argued that such philosophers have things in the reverse order: it is not that the notion of the answer to a question has anything essentially to do with knowledge; rather knowledge can sometimes be conceived by reference to what answers some question. Having considered in Chapter 5 the presumption underlying the making of statements, it can now be appreciated how the temptation has arisen: generally, in making a statement one is presumed to know, or at least to think that one knows, to be so what one tells others; but in giving others what one takes to be the answer to a question one normally thereby makes a statement to them, and thus is presumed to know it to be so — ruling out, accordingly, guesses and expressions of opinion. Furthermore, the presumption underlying statement-making explains how the reply *I don't know* — though not a conformable answer to a question generally, only to the particular question *Do you know?* — is yet a relevant reply to a question put to one. There is no link, therefore, between being given the answer to a question and acquiring knowledge; instead the link is between being told (in earnest) that things are so by others and the knowledge thereby presumed of the teller. The notion of the answer to a question comes in only because those giving what they take to be the answer to a question put to them are normally thereby telling others that something is so.

Thus, Reichenbach's cognitive correlate may be amended to: *I intend that you tell me the answer to this question: ...* , which will be dubbed the cognitive correlate of interrogation. The substitution of *intend* and *tell* for 'wish' and 'know' needs no further comment. But an interrogator is presumed also to intend that the addressee, or one among the addressees if there are several, state what the answer is to the question — something Reichenbach omits to mention, perhaps because he supposes that he is accounting for questions themselves, or the asking of questions, rather than interrogation specifically. What Hintikka calls 'this relativization to a person (respondent)' is clearly not 'integral a part ... of the concept of a question',[15] but has solely to do with interrogation. Testimony may be vitiated and a test will be invalidated if somebody else interrupts the intended respondent and volunteers an answer. When examining witnesses for the prosecution, counsel requires their testimony, not that of a witness for the defence; the teacher intends that the pupil who was staring out of the window answer her question, not the show-off in the desk in the front row.

Both the original and the amended version of the correlate conceal an interrogative clause, after *know* or *tell*: *the answer* is elliptical for *what the answer is*. Searle speaks of 'our intuition' that '"Tell me the name of the first President of the United States"' is 'equivalent in force to "What's the name of the first President of the United States"'.[16] The latter is, of course, contained elliptically in the former — which is all this 'intuition' amounts to; for although one can tell tales and fibs or, in a different sense, beads, one cannot tell names. Since *Tell me your name* actually conceals the question *What is your name?* it can sometimes be a way of putting that question to another. By contrast, *Give me your name*, where there is no concealed interrogative clause, serves to tell the addressee to do something rather than to ask the addressee a question.[17] Yet even here the action specified by the command implicitly alludes to a question, since the term *name* here expresses what would supply the answer to a question — such as, *What are you called?* — and so expresses what is relative to a parent interrogative concept. So even although there is no concealed interrogative clause after *give*, as with the interrogative clauses after *tell*, *state* and *say*, the name given must be correct, not just any name, if what is commanded is to be complied with. For there is an allusion to what answers a question in the concept of what somebody's name is.

Thus, attempts to reduce asking (another) a question to issuing a command inevitably smuggle in some allusion to the question it is aimed to analyse away, even when an assurance to the contrary is offered. Hare declares that *Who is at the door?* 'can be translated "Name the person who is at the door" (where "who" is of course a relative and not an indirect interrogative)'.[18] Hare's grammar is impeccable. But naming here is not to bestow on the person at the door a proper name in the way one might give a name to a stray cat that has decided to make its home with one. Instead, it is to name a person as falling under some description, as being at the door; in other words, to state who is at the door. Similarly, to name various politicians as the guilty ones is to identify who the guilty are; and to name one's price is to give one's answer to the question *How much is it going to cost? Identity* and *price* primarily express interrogative concepts. So to be told to name somebody as such-and-such or name one's price, as with being told to give one's address, is to be told implicitly to state what the answer is to the question alluded to by the interrogative concept that is the parent concept of the counterpart propositional concept governing the description of the action commanded — such as *giving the name of the first President of the United States*. A name by itself, even a list of names or items, does not say anything about anything. However, a name or list of items given in answer to a question (whether express or implicit) does say something: here the name or list is not to be taken by itself but in the context of the question. And in answering a question one is held to an assertion. So in correctly answering another's implicit *who* question one tells the other who somebody is. Thus, the distinction between relative and interrogative pronouns is of no help to Hare. Though he appears to avoid the obvious circularity of cruder accounts like Searle's, he succumbs to a deeper circularity.

Just as one cannot simply name something in the relevant sense but only name it as being such-and-such, so one cannot simply 'cite' or 'indicate'[19] something in any sense except to cite or indicate it as being such-and-such. Numbers listed in the telephone directory are not lists of mere numbers but are listed as being the telephone numbers of the subscribers listed. In naming, citing, indicating or listing a thing as being such-and-such when answering a question (whether express or implicit) there is always an allusion to the interrogative concept exercised in the question whose propositional counterpart ranges over the thing that is such-and-such named, cited, indicated or listed in answer to the question.

Since the concealed clause after *tell* in the cognitive correlate of interrogation, being interrogative, alludes to the answer to a question, interrogators are presumed to intend that their respondents tell them only what is correct. In presenting what they style 'an imperative-assertoric analysis' of questions, the Lewis's write that the word *correct* is not redundant in the schema *Let it be that you tell me the correct answer!* 'since incorrect answers, although they cannot be known, certainly can be told'. Attention to the difference between *telling that* ... and *tell* followed by an interrogative clause — what they dismiss as 'superficial grammatical flags' — would have saved them from this error.[20] Moreover, in telling another that something is so in earnest — that is, in making a statement to another — one is presumed to know to be so what one tells the other; and therefore presumed to tell others only correctly. Not only are interrogators presumed to intend that their respondents tell them only what is correct, but also makers of statements are presumed to tell others only what is correct. Hence the notion of correctness comes in twice when answering a question put by another: once as contained in the notion of the answer to a question, which an interrogator is presumed to intend to elicit from a respondent; and again as presumed in the notion of making a statement which the serious telling of another that something is so constitutes.

More Specific Intentions of Interrogators

A rejoinder to the second objection to Reichenbach is at hand: even if sometimes the intention of interrogators is not to obtain information previously unknown to them, it is always to seek knowledge of some sort: - about the reliability of testimony or the veracity of a witness, about how much the respondent knows or understands, even about what the respondent's opinions are. It was granted in Chapter 3 that since *ask* is a verb of enquiry when its subject is a person, asking questions always has some bearing on an enquiry of some sort. The same applies to asking questions put to others.

The fact remains that interrogators need not be ignorant of the answers to their questions in pursuit of such further enquiries, which add a dimension to interrogation in their service. Reichenbach's correlate, it was noted, omits the requirement that only the intended respondent should give the answer to the question. The examining of testimony, enquiries into the extent of people's knowledge or understanding, together with the testing of it, and the canvassing of others' opinions — these require in addition that any answer given be the respondent's own unprompted answer; that is, what the respondent takes to be the answer to the question unaided by other, potential respondents. In general, if I ask you what the capital of Peru is, I shall not be bothered if you obtain your answers from some reference work or your knowledgable uncle: I may be asking you in the hope that your looking up or tracking down the answer to the question will save me the trouble of doing so for myself. Only when testimony is being examined can there be fear that the testimony might become contaminated with that of others or be suborned; only when the extent of people's knowledge or understanding is subject to determination have interrogators to guard against giving away clues with their questions; only when people's knowledge or understanding is being tested — that is, in examinations — have precautions against cheating and plagiarism to be set in place; only when the intention is to elicit the authentic or sincere sentiments of others is insulation against alien influences or merely conventional views necessary.

In these situations interrogators have a more specific intention with respect to respondents: they intend to elicit from the respondent not just the answer to the question, but further, the respondent's own answer to the question. This more specific intention, however, supervenes on the first: one can only intend to elicit the respondent's own answer to the question by intending to elicit the answer to the question from the respondent; for respondents purport to be giving the answer to the question in purporting to give what they take the answer to it to be — that is, in purporting to give their own answer to it.

The respondent's answer, of course, may not be what it purports to be: neither in fact the answer to the question nor what the respondent takes unaided by other potential respondents to be the answer to the question. So, as well as simply erroneous or fraudulent, testimony may be suborned; a captured spy may feign ignorance in accordance with a cover story agreed in advance with his controllers; a student's answer may be wrong or off the point as well as the work of another student; an expression of opinion may be hypocritical or self-deceiving as well as dictated by what the respondent thinks the interrogator wants to hear. In each case the primary intention of the interrogator has been frustrated, besides the more specific intention. The primary intention of eliciting from the respondent the answer to the question may, however, be fulfilled yet the more specific intention of eliciting the respondent's own answer to the question frustrated. Testimony may correspond to the facts, yet the witness may have been led; the spy may let slip guilty knowledge, yet still refuse to acknowledge it; a student's essay may achieve a fair mark, though it was largely copied out from a reference work; an opinion may be sincerely held, but taken from a celebrity columnist.

Thus, in examining testimony an interrogator will hope to bring out the respondent's individual perspective on or interpretation of what is being testified to by comparing this testimony with other testimony or what is otherwise known of the affair.

Similarly, in soliciting your opinion I seek to draw out your individual point of view. If opinion pollsters were scrupulous, they would take care to prevent their questions or questionnaires from suggesting any answers at all; but then they might not be able to summarise opinions of whole groups of people so simply. A distinction has to be drawn here between hedged and unhedged questions and answers. Except where it is evident to all that the subject can only be a matter of opinion or judgment, if an interrogator puts a straightforward question to another — like *Who did it?* — respondents will be guilty of an abuse if they state without qualification what is merely their guess or opinion as distinct from what they know to be so. A respondent may, however, legitimately hedge any answer offered with words such as *I don't know but I have a suspicion, I think, that it was ...* . The interrogator can likewise hedge the question with a parenthesis making clear that it is only the opinion or judgment of the respondent that is being enquired about,[21] as in *Who, do you believe (in your opinion), did it?*

Expressing an opinion or making a judgment is not ordinarily regarded as testimony, which concerns rather what people purport to be in a position to know. But a statement — by contrast with an expression — of opinion can become testimony;

as when the opinion or judgment of an authority or expert on some matter, or in general of a very experienced, sagacious, famous, powerful or influential person is sought. For people value authoritative opinion or judgment as providing some indication of the truth where knowledge is thought not to be obtainable. Even so, giving one's opinion or passing judgment falls within the overall restriction of testimony to what is purportedly known; for here what testifiers testify to is that what they state is their true opinion or honest judgment, which they are presumed to know to be such.

In enquiring generally into the extent of others' knowledge or understanding of some matter, one seeks to determine the sources open and opportunities available to them in obtaining it, to build up a picture of their individual epistemic situation.

An enquiry into people's knowledge or understanding includes as a special case the testing of it. If knowledge only is being tested the answer to the question being elicited may simply articulate the knowledge to be tested. That is, in stating what purports to be the answer to the question respondents are thereby held to the statement *that* ... , which purports to articulate the respondent's knowledge *that* ... . If what is stated in answer to the question is not actually known by those whose knowledge is being tested but only a guess, there is no cheating exactly; though there is, to be very scrupulous, an attempt to deceive if the answer is presented unqualifiedly as being known by them when they think they do not know it to be the answer.[22] For if what candidates state happens by good luck to be correct, the examiners will have been 'hoodwinked'.[23]

An articulation of one's knowledge, the relating to others of what one knows, might appear to be a certain mark of knowledge; rather as a confession might appear to be certain evidence of guilty. But the ease of fraud casts suspicion on such straightforward presentations of what is to be determined by the test unless they are accompanied by corroborative evidence. Even if the probability of cheating in examinations can sometimes in practice be discounted, there is still the probability of inspired guessing or plausible bluffing. Besides, knowledge as such is frequently thought to be a poor thing without understanding — understanding comprising knowing *how* and *why*. Hence general knowledge tests past a certain age are thought to have limited educational value, and the accumulation of useless information, while useful exercise for the memory, is little indication of intelligence but rather a source of entertainment for others, as in quiz contests.

Knowledge, then, is better, and understanding of what is known can only be, tested by providing opportunities for people to apply their knowledge and understanding by completing set tasks or attempting to solve problems. And just as the intention of examiners in testing knowledge alone is to elicit only the candidates' own answers to the questions, so the intention of examiners in providing opportunities to demonstrate knowledge and understanding of a subject through answering questions on it is to test only the candidates' own knowledge and understanding, not anybody else's. Barring cheating, including through impersonation, this aim is fulfilled by setting a task to be executed only by the candidate.

Practical tests obviously test practical knowledge, besides abilities, aptitudes, skills and competences — in short, knowing *how*, *what*, *where*, *when*, *whether*, etc. to do something. They clearly proceed by setting (a series of) tasks. It would be odd to describe the setting of tasks as the putting of questions — though the tasks may well present problems, which are characterised interrogatively. While one might say that the driving examiner asked one to make a three-point turn, one might equally say 'told one to'. The notion of a task, not of a question, governs a practical test. Now, although there is a rough-and-ready contrast between a theoretical test of knowledge articulated and understanding revealed in answers stated to questions on the field of study being examined — *The Highway Code*, for instance — and a practical test like a driving test, the boundary between the theoretical and the practical becomes blurred when the practice is in intellectual skills and capacities as distinct from mainly physical ones; for exercises of knowledge and understanding in theoretical areas require the use of coherent and intelligible discourse. Accordingly, examination questions are not invariably, or even generally, confined to a purely theoretical domain. Questions occurring, say, in a French oral examination or in an interview conducted by a political party of potential election nominees, have the function of not so much eliciting the answers to them from respondents, as affording opportunities for respondents to display their proficiencies or talents when giving their answers. The questions serve primarily to set exercises, albeit mental and not largely physical.

The sort of account given by Searle, that the aim of examinations is to find out if those being examined know or understand something, would still be unilluminating even if it could differentiate between examinations and more general enquiries into the extent of others' knowledge or understanding. For as the Lewis's object to a similar account, the examination might be 'graded not by the examiner himself but by his human or mechanical assistant' — though these counter-examples stand equally against their own account.[24] Their objection might seem frivolous; but it helps to bring out a feature about examinations not captured by the sort of thing Searle says. The purpose of an examination is to elicit evidence rather of the knowledge or understanding of those being examined. In such a *quasi*-judicial situation if they furnish such evidence there may be no requirement that they tell any specific person anything; nor is it possible literally to tell a machine anything. True, in answering a question candidates relate something, thereby making use of the opportunity to furnish evidence of their abilities; but the reception of what they relate is, strictly, beyond the scope of the object of an examination. Clearly, in an oral test the presumption underlying the putting of questions to candidates by examiners is that they tell them what they take to be the answers to the questions; but examinations tend to become impersonal through institutionalisation thereby rendering them borderline cases of interrogation, where the telling of another something is always presumed to be intended. To say that the jury wanted to know if the accused was guilty would similarly be to fail to appreciate the evidential function of the enquiry.

Viewed as gatherers of evidence examiners can be judged by their success in obtaining it in the way investigators in general are. Tests of all sorts test not just what is or those to be tested, but also the testers — their ingenuity, resourcefulness and efficiency. The adage, *ask a silly question and get a silly answer* throws up the ambiguity about whose intelligence is being tested by intelligence tests — quite apart from recently unearthed scandals in the history of educational psychology about faked experiments. The lack of good sense and imagination betrayed by failures to notice that what seems to be the obvious answer to a question may not be the sole correct answer to it, or that the question is ambiguous or unclear, fostered in the heyday of intelligence testing mediocrity, not meritocracy, besides blighting the prospects of those of uncommon intelligence. While the results of multiple-choice tests may be obtainable sooner, unlike essay-type examinations they allow no means of letting testers know when it is they who are making a mistake.

Essay questions may not seem like practical tests. Yet they provide candidates with opportunities to exhibit their skills in gathering, marshalling and weighing evidence, presenting and arguing a case, and expounding material clearly and in a logical order; besides their good judgment and sense of relevance. The view of one external examiner (now deceased) was that essay questions having the form of yes-no questions should be avoided, since if the candidate answered simply *Yes* or *No* examiners would be constrained to award either full or no marks depending on whether they agreed with the given answer. As these were philosophy examinations, much was betrayed about this philosopher's conception of philosophy. Most would readily accept that there is no — or no one — correct answer to any essay question, whatever the subject; or rather that what one takes the answer to be is more a matter of (informed, reasoned and balanced) opinion than simply knowledge — though to be able to express a reasonable opinion requires understanding, which consists in knowledge *how*, *why*, *what* and so forth. While guessing can, with strictness, always be regarded as an abuse in an examination, expressions of opinion as to the answer to a question are, when candidly offered as such and not passed off as if known to be established fact, allowable where more than simple knowledge of a subject is being put to the test. Examiners seek evidence, not concurrence with their personal opinions.

An essay question, though often a genuine question, such as Bell's example, *Was Kant an idealist?*[25] — which might, indeed, also occur in a general knowledge test or even be put to another not as a test question — is never merely a question. For it also sets candidates a task. Here the etymology of the term *essay* should be recalled. Candidates are required to show at least, if not explain, their reasons for producing their answers — as is also sometimes expressly stated in the rubrics to mathematics and logic examinations. Thus neither *Yes* nor *No* to Bell's question presents the stark choice of staking all on a mark of a hundred percent or risking a mark of zero; either would only ensure the mark of zero. There is therefore some basis for instructing examination candidates to 'attempt' rather than answer the questions set — though strictly, questions cannot be attempted since what is attempted is always a task. The requirement to demonstrate one's knowledge shows further the inadequacy of Searle's type of account. For if an examination question were really equivalent to a question of the form *Do you know if ... ?* one could sail through simply by answering *Yes* to all questions.[26]

In general examination questions do not merely ask something but also set intellectual tasks, including problems to be solved. Indeed, every examination question can be said quite trivially to set the task of answering it in that to set the question is thereby to set this minimal task. But other tasks described more complexly are often entailed in the enterprise of undertaking the minimal task of answering the question. Thus, essay questions sometimes begin *Examine why*, *Discuss whether*, *Explain how ...* ; which, being imperative sentences, expressly set tasks even although they also allude to questions signalled by the following interrogative clause. Some, however, of what are by convention called 'questions' in examinations, including those of the essay type, are not actually questions at all but simply set tasks: *Compare and contrast ...* , *Give an outline of ...* , *Prove the following theorem ...* . Yet to set a task can often present a problem to those who are to undertake it; and a problem is just a task expressed interrogatively. So the setting of a task can often implicitly raise a question.

Dummett takes the way a choice between essay questions is sometimes offered as illustrating a disjunction between acts of asking questions. Obviously, elements within a question can be disjoined, as when a single yes-no question has as its subject a disjunction between states of affairs (*Is it the case that either he is captured or he is dead?*); and two or more yes-no questions are disjoined in an alternative question. But can the askings of questions, as distinct from the questions asked, be disjoined as the askings of questions can readily be conjoined when somebody asks one question and then conjoins it with the asking of another question? I can be reported as first asking one question and then asking another question. But if I am reported as having either asked one question or asked another, given the truth of the report, I must in fact have asked either one of the questions or both. So, while the states of affairs of people's asking questions can be disjoined, acts of asking cannot. Dummett, also evidently not entirely happy with the notion of disjunctive askings, thinks that the

> disjunction comes in, not in the report of the linguistic act, but in that of the response to the question: if an addressee is to respond as the speaker prompts him to, then what he has to do is either to answer whether A or to answer whether B.

The disjunction, then, turns out to be between tasks which have been set; that is, it provides the addressee with a choice of what has to be done — 'either to answer [the question,] whether A or to answer [the question,] whether B'. It is not a disjunction between the askings of different questions.[27]

It is unsurprising that the example Dummett comes up with is from essay questions; for these do not merely ask questions but also set tasks. Even so, in a general knowledge quiz competitors are customarily given a choice of subject — Frege or cookery — before any questions are put to them. So boasting that I know a lot about both Frege and cookery, I might challenge you to ask me any question you choose about either. Even with examination questions choice is usually provided for by listing the questions separately under a rubric specifying a number of questions to be answered less than the number of questions listed. Only when examiners seek to prevent candidates from answering both of two questions, usually because they judge the subjects to be too closely connected, do they resort to the singular device of disjoining them under one numbered item on the list.

The setting of exercises often associated with genuine questions set in examinations seems to lend support to the imperative theory that putting questions to others falls within the overall class of telling them to do things. For it has been seen that all examination questions can be regarded — at least nominally — as setting the task of answering the question.[28] And it is clear that since they set at least this task, they must, unlike didactic questions generally, always be put to somebody who is being assigned the task. But setting people examination questions is not typical of the putting of questions to others, any more than is the formal examination of the testimony of witnesses in a judicial setting. Those who are to answer the questions put to them in such situations are also expressly subject to the formal authority of the interrogator — or implicitly so when, as it is reported, one is helping the police with their enquiries. Hence talk of telling as distinct from asking becomes appropriate. So, a presiding judge may have to tell an uncooperative witness to answer counsel's question, a driving examiner can be fairly reported as having told candidates to perform various manoeuvres, and the rubric at the top of a printed examination paper can be said to tell candidates to answer six questions.

Confusions of Imperative Theorists

The cognitive correlate of words addressed by speakers to others is in effect the notion of what is presumed to be true of speakers who engage their addressees in a social intellectual operation. It cannot be taken to be equivalent to, or any part of, the meaning of the words the speaker utters. An interrogator does not actually say in addressing in earnest an interrogative sentence to another *I intend that you tell me what the answer is to this question: ...* — though this second utterance might be issued to a potential respondent immediately after the question had been put. Similarly, Moore did not in fact teach, notwithstanding much misconceived commentary on his 'argument from a particular case', that saying *This pencil exists* is the same as saying *I do know that this pencil exists*, though the truth of the second proposition is presumed of a speaker who states the first proposition.[29]

One obvious reason for the non-equivalence between the meaning of the speaker's words and what is presumed of the speaker is that what is presumed of the speaker may in fact be false owing to an abuse. Another is that the words a speaker utters in performing the phatic act may constitute an interrogative or imperative sentence, and so the product of the rhetic act may be what is incapable of being either true or false. Indeed, the notion of a cognitive correlate was introduced solely in order to try to connect up in some way what is not itself capable of being either true or false with what is. Thus, while a cognitive correlate is necessarily a proposition, the actual words the speaker utters need not themselves express any proposition; for they may express a question — or a command, if imperative sentences prove resistant to any propositional analysis. As the term *correlate* suggests, what the speaker utters must not be confused with anything held to be its correlate.

Nevertheless, many philosophers and linguistic theorists have supposed that even although what a speaker utters may not express a proposition, the explicit performative for what the speaker utters does yield a proposition. They may concede that a question is not a proposition, but they argue that the sentence beginning *I ask you* followed by an interrogative clause does express a proposition; and the words *I ask you* can then be reduced to the cognitive correlate for interrogation. The mistake here can be seen by reflecting that although a question might belong to the right kind of category to be assimilated to a proposition, so that it would just be false, not nonsense, to identify the two, it would be to commit a category mistake to equate asking somebody a question, which is an act, with a proposition, which is instead an abstraction, at most what results from an act (of judging or stating). Neither the notion of a cognitive correlate nor of an explicit performative can apply to a question itself as distinct from the asking of another a question.

Confusion also results from a failure to see that a cognitive correlate is quite distinct from an explicit performative. Unlike a cognitive correlate, a performative utterance has no truth-value. Now, the words constituting an explicit performative need not be said, need not be made explicit; and so they, somewhat like a cognitive correlate, might be described as being merely implied by the words the speaker actually utters. But an explicit performative is implied by the words the speaker utters in the sense that the speaker's act of uttering these words can be taken to amount to the performance of the speech-act named by the explicit performative; not in Moore's sense that the speaker's act of uttering these words gives rise to a presumption that something is true of the speaker, a presumption which may turn out to be false.

In saying (now and in earnest) *I ask you* ... I thereby *I ask you* ... because my uttering the words amounts in that situation to performing the speech-act. Suppose I subsequently report my performance of this speech-act by saying that I asked you ... . While the report is true, the speech-act previously performed by me is incapable of being either true or false. And I cannot myself report my performing of an act in my performing it, for any act of reporting an act is a different act from the act reported on — even if the act reported on was itself an act of reporting. So, to try to replace the explicit performative, *I ask you* ... with the cognitive correlate of interrogation, *I intend that you tell me what the answer is to this question:* ...

would be to confuse a performative utterance, a speech-act incapable of being either true or false, with what is presumed to be true of the speaker in the issuing of it, something that is indeed either true or false. Furthermore, to say *I intend that you tell me what the answer is to this question: ...* but to mean by these words *I ask you ...* would itself in effect amount to the issuing of a performative utterance, having 'the force', as Austin would say, of asking another a question;[30] so uttering the words in this situation would not then be to say anything either true or false: the longer utterance would simply function as a way of asking another a question.

The argument just presented is essentially the same as Hare's against reducing an imperative sentence to its cognitive correlate. Few would see merit in equating the imperative sentence *Shut the door* with its cognitive correlate *I intend that you shut the door* — even though the non-propositional character of the imperatival is far from incontestable. Yet the typical reductive account of questions generalises to questions as such from an equating of a question put to others with what is expressed by an imperative sentence beginning *Tell me (what) the answer (is) to this question: ...* , which might be dubbed the imperatival correlate of interrogation. For the cognitive correlate of the above imperative sentence is *I intend that you tell me what the answer is to this question: ...* , which, as was seen, is just the cognitive correlate of interrogation.

The imperative theory thus attempts to reduce interrogation to its imperatival correlate, whose cognitive correlate in turn is just the cognitive correlate of interrogation. But if such an initial reduction is in order, why not reduce interrogation straightaway to its cognitive correlate, or reduce the imperatival correlate to its cognitive correlate? That you are to tell me what the answer is to the question put, which is how the imperatival correlate is to be understood, is no part of what a question put to others — still less, a question as such — means. Instead, it is what is presumed to be intended by an interrogator with respect to hoped-for respondents in putting the question to them. Not only would replacement of either the interrogative or imperative utterance by their cognitive correlates in effect turn these cognitive correlates into performative utterances, but as Hare also sees, the reductions are at best unenlightening, at worst circular — as is obvious with questions, since the question asked reappears in both imperatival and cognitive correlates and since an interrogative clause has also to follow *tell*. The charge of circularity is not to be taken as a spur to greater efforts at procuring non-circular reductions; rather, it ought to promote recognition that in being an irreducible form of thought, the interrogative serves more to explain than stands itself in need of explanation.

Hare argues that the attempt to reduce an imperative sentence to its cognitive correlate is similarly circular, since the same words (*shut the door*) occur in both. The likes of Hare, therefore, in their attempts to translate questions 'without loss of meaning into commands' are guilty of the same sort of confusion they themselves rightly condemn in the analysis of imperative sentences.[31] It is more plausible, however, to think that when the words *shut the door* occur after verbs like *intend* or *want* they do not normally serve any imperatival function — not unless they are being used performatively — but serve merely to specify the action concerned.

After a question has been put, if prevarication or evasion is suspected, or if the intended respondent appears to hesitate or has failed so far to answer and kept them waiting for an answer, interrogators will tend to tell the person to answer, saying *Answer me* or *(Just) Answer the question.* That such a command is sometimes necessary shows that it can be no part of the meaning of the previous interrogative sentence addressed to the other. It also shows that in asking another a question one is not thereby telling the other to answer it, as Bell for one supposes when he writes: 'If an act of questioning is generically a command, it is specifically a command to answer a question.'[32] If the imperative theory were sound interrogators would have already told their intended respondents to answer the question in asking them the question, in uttering the interrogative sentence expressing it. If there were no distinction between asking another a question, or the question itself, and telling the other to answer it, the imperative of the verb *answer* would be redundant and its job done instead by interrogative sentences being addressed to others. Again, there could never be any cases of indolent interrogators who do not take the trouble to press their addressees for answers. What might seem an attractive view for such theorists, that refusing to answer a question is refusing to do what one has been told, must be wrong; for one can refuse to answer a question without (yet) having been told to answer it.

To insist on the distinction between asking another a question and telling the person to answer it, as also the distinction between both and the question itself, is not to deny that it is normally paradoxical to ask a person a question but then to add *Don't answer that!* — the parallel to the paradox named after Moore of asserting something but adding *I don't believe it*. People do sometimes say *Don't answer that!* — and not just lawyers intervening to protect their clients from incriminating themselves. Typically people say the words when they suddenly realise that the interrogative sentence they have just uttered could be taken the wrong way: say, as a genuine question put to another as opposed to a rhetorical question; or, in patter between a comedian and his straight man, where there is an obvious *double entendre*.[33]

Bell argues that a respondent to a yes-no question, in order to comply with the command asking the question is being equated with on Hare's account, need not, as Hare states, strike out the inapplicable contradictory and so subscribe to something that is taken as true; for if the account were right, Bell argues, a respondent who 'asserted what is false' would not have complied with the command, 'would not have answered the question'.[34] Answering a question — that is, giving an answer to a question — is indeed not the same as stating what the answer to the question is, though in answering another's question one is presumed to state what one takes to be the answer to it. But Bell's objection simply assumes his own analysis of asking a question as the telling of potential respondents to assert the proposition they are held to when giving a conformable answer to the question —

the analysis in effect being the commanding of the giving of any conformable answer, as distinct from the answer, to the question.

Crucially, Bell has failed to see that the imperatival correlate of interrogation is that the respondent tell the interrogator what the answer is to the question, not just give a conformable answer to it; for the interrogative clause after *tell* conveys telling correctly. Besides, the presumption in making a statement to another, which is what answering another's question normally constitutes, is that one knows, or thinks one knows, it to be so. In answering another's question one at least purports to give the answer to it, not just a conformable answer to it. Thus even when told, subsequently and expressly, to answer a question previously put to one, the speaker in issuing such a command is presumed to intend that one state what one takes to be the answer to the question; for stating it is normally what answering another's question amounts to.

Not even a politician would have the gall to protest when accused of not answering a question 'But I did answer it, albeit what I said was false (incorrect).' Others, besides politicians, may have occasion to bargain, *Ask me no questions and I'll tell you no lies*. A lawyer might advise a client interviewed by police to answer the question but to lie. Lying, however, is an abuse of statement-making, and hence of answering another's question. To lie in answering an interrogator's question is not to do what the interrogator is presumed to intend that one do. Bell's view does not simply betray a unsure grasp of what is presumed in telling (or informing) another (of) something; more significantly, it reveals an inability to appreciate that interrogative characterisations of saying something preclude saying incorrectly.

Preliminary notice can be taken of the strangeness of telling an addressee to assert or state *that* ... ; which, while not the complete analysis, is an essential component of the standard imperative analysis of interrogation. A full diagnosis of the error at the root of the analysis will be given in Chapter 8.

There is no difficulty with the interrogative clauses following verbs like *inform*, *say*, *state* and *tell*, which are all usable in the imperative, since these clauses preclude doing so incorrectly. Indeed, *say* more readily governs an interrogative clause in the imperative, besides in questions and in the negative generally, than in an affirmative declarative sentence.[35] The imperative of *answer* takes as its direct object the phrase *the question*; and in answering a question one purports to be stating what one takes to be the answer to it, which, again, rules out knowingly doing so incorrectly as being in compliance with the command. All these imperative uses are tantamount to the putting — or re-putting — of a question to another. There is no difficulty, either, in my telling you to tell me, say to me, *that* ... when wanting it to be true, I crave for evidence or confirmation of it from you — as in the hackneyed *Tell me* (*Say*) *that you love me*. But here you are to tell me or say to me this only if it is true. A different set of cases arises where the truth is no object. I can tell you to state or say to, tell or inform, a third party *that* ... , to testify to something, whether it be true, false or misleading. Or, not wanting to hear the truth from you because I would rather not have the responsibility to act on what you tell me, or if the truth is too painful to hear or indeed bear, I might even tell you to lie to me. But such cases constitute abuses.

There is something gravely amiss with telling another to assert or make the statement *that* ... . For those who assert things are presumed to believe them to be so, and those who state things are presumed at least to think they know them to be so. These presumptions preclude the commissioning of assertions and statements to order or on advice; for one cannot believe or think one knows something at will — or indeed, come to know something by commission, which also puts paid to Hintikka's 'make me know ... ' account, besides accounts along the lines of telling others to inform one *that* ... .

Thus, the sort of commands interrogators on imperative analyses are supposed to issue to potential respondents are either intrinsically absurd or constitute abuses of assertion or statement-making. Moreover, one cannot sensibly tell another to assert sincerely, state truly, *that* ... ; though interrogative constructions after the imperative of *state* or *tell* qualified by *sincerely*, *honestly*, or *truly* are quite in order. Hare notes, albeit inconsistently, that 'the answerer has to consider which' assertion 'he is willing to make, which will, if he is a truthful person, depend on which is true', by contrast with making 'assertions at will'.[36] If Hare is to ensure exclusion of assertion at will, he will have to reintroduce the interrogative clauses taken by *state*, *tell* and *inform* with their exclusion of doing so incorrectly, clauses he had evidently hoped to analyse away along with questions.

The transparency of *that* propositional, in contrast with the opaqueness of interrogative, constructions produces a paradox. In telling you to assert or state, inform or tell me, sincerely, honestly or truly, that, say, Hitler was born in 1889, I thereby tell you what to assert or state, what to inform me of or tell me, since the *that* clause says what you are to say. Not only that, since you are to say it sincerely, honestly or truly, if compliance with the command is to be possible, my saying of it must have equally been sincere, honest and true.[37] Quite apart from the oddity of my telling you to inform me of or tell me what I am in effect now telling you or informing you of, if you cannot accept what I have just asserted or stated, informed you of or told you, you will be unable to comply with the command. For you cannot assert sincerely or state, inform me of or tell me, honestly or truly what you do not believe or think you know — such as that Hitler died in his sleep. Nor can you believe or think you know something to order or on advice.

What the Lewis's call their 'imperative-assertoric analysis' explicitly incorporates this absurdity of saying to another *Tell me truly that* ... in their 'assertoric operator "You tell me truly that ... "'. Even without this 'operator', their commitment to the absurdity can be seen as they make the obvious point against the much cruder account — but constantly repeated down the years as if it represented 'a new approach' — that an interrogator aims to come to know, to be informed of, something from a potential respondent, what the Lewis's dub the 'imperative-epistemic analysis'. The obvious objection to the cruder account is that sometimes an interrogator already knows what the answer is to the question. The Lewis's take a police detective who asks a 'suspect "Are you the one who did it?" although he already knows the correct answer, knows the suspect knows it too, ... '. The detective 'already has all the knowledge he needs; what he wants now is a confession'.[38]

What the Lewis's might have in mind is an interrogator who is trying to obtain corroboration through the testimony of the respondent of what there is already some other evidence for — though the phrase, 'all the knowledge he needs' will hardly fit. As was seen, interrogators can sometimes without abuse pursue more specific enquiries than those delineated by the subject of their questions — here into the reliability of the other evidence. According to the imperative-assertoric analysis, the detective is telling the suspect *Tell me truly that you are the one who did it* when he puts his question. If the *that* is replaced by *if* or *whether* what is said makes perfect sense, only the replacements reintroduce the interrogative words it is hoped to analyse away as 'superficial grammatical flags'. What also makes sense is a situation the Lewis's do not seem to have in mind: both the detective and the suspect know who did it, or at least know that the suspect did not do it, but the detective needs a confession if he is ever to make detective sergeant; so he tells the suspect *(Just) Tell me that you are the one who did it*, knowing it to be false that the suspect did it. Likewise, one can put a question to another with the intention of inducing the respondent to lie or say just anything. But such cases constitute only abuses.

Idiomatic Phrases

The presumptions underlying interrogation and statement-making, together with the imperatival correlate of interrogation, explain why questions put to others are frequently introduced by phrases that are virtually discounted and are not to be taken literally. One can always baldly ask another a third-person question like *What happened?* unaccompanied by any introductory phrase. But sometimes it is felt to be more polite to phrase the question as *Can you tell* (*inform*) *me what happened?* One can also politely phrase the question as *Do you know* (*remember*) *what happened?* Now, whereas *No* would be quite sufficient as an answer to either type of prefaced question — though to add an expression of regret would be more polite — *Yes* by itself would not be sufficient: if you can tell me or do know or remember what happened, in accordance with the cognitive correlate of interrogation I intend that you tell me what happened or what you know or remember about what happened.

What is presumed in interrogation thus explains the inclination not to take such prefaced questions literally and answer with only *(Yes,) I can* or *(Yes,) I do*. The addition of *but I'm not going to tell you* (*what happened* or *what I know, remember*) would show what is expected of the respondent. So such prefaced questions put to others are taken not at face value as yes-no questions but rather as roundabout ways of putting the unadorned question — but with *I can't tell (inform) you* or *I don't know, remember* as an additional conformable answer. They might accordingly be interpreted as: *If you can tell (inform) me what happened, what happened?* and *If you know (remember) what happened, what happened?*[39] But when the subject of the interrogative sentence is not the addressee, the answer to be elicited can only be the answer to the main question, not the question alluded to in the dependent interrogative clause. *Can he tell (inform) you what happened?* and *Do we know, does she remember, what happened?* are clearly not roundabout ways of asking somebody *What happened?*

Similarly, while *Tell (inform) me, just say, where she went* is an imperative sentence, it can sometimes serve as a way — insistent or coaxing — of putting the question *Where did she go?* As has been seen, *Tell me your name* is elliptical for *Tell me what your name is*; which in turn can be a way of asking somebody the question *What is your name? Tell me* can also be used parenthetically before a question in a direct construction: *Tell me, have you ever been to Mexico?* or even, *Tell me, would you like a drink?* There are no translations of questions into commands here. On the contrary, unlike the *Can you tell (inform) me* ... preamble, the supposed 'command' *Tell me* ... would not be used in general to put a question to another; only in some informal situations or where the interrogator is trying to ease the respondent into the question, as when conducting a test.[40]

The use of the imperative *tell* is explained by the cognitive correlate of interrogation being *I intend that you tell me what the answer is to this question:* ... . But it is not used actually to tell — or ask — one's addressee to answer a question one has previously put, since it precedes, not follows, the question. Thus, no support is lent by this idiom to the imperative theory. *Tell (inform) me where she went* is not a way of saying either *Answer the question 'Where did she go?'* or *Tell me (what) the answer (is) to the question 'Where did she go?'* Instead, it is simply a colloquial way of asking another the unadorned question *Where did she go?*

Something similar to the cognitive correlate of interrogation may, when addressed to another, lose its propositional character and become a performative utterance serving merely to put a question to the other. To say to another *What I want to know is, what happened* may occasionally be to confide in the other; but more often saying these words is simply an emphatic way of putting the question *What happened?* which is the primary utterance as distinct from a more explicit performative.[41] To respond with *Do you? How interesting!* would be either to misunderstand or, knowing that the words were not to be taken literally, simply to jest or be rude. The use of *know* is explained by the presumption that those who tell others things in answer to their questions know these things to be so, and thus impart knowledge to them.

Except for the last mentioned, where *want* implies the speaker's ignorance, there are no implications in any of these usages about the state of knowledge or ignorance of either speaker or addressee.[42]

Notes

1 See Rundle (1990), p. 91.
2 Cf. Rundle (1990), p. 91.
3 Reid (1764), IV ii; p. 118a. Cf. (1788), V vi; p. 665b.
4 Hume (1975), XII i; p. 149.
5 Cf. Bolinger (1977), p. 156.
6 Hare (1952), p. 46.
7 Cf. Parret (1988), p. 298.
8 Cf. David and Stephanie Lewis (1975), p. 47.
9 Talmy Givón in Chisholm *et al.* (1984), p. 265.
10 Reichenbach (1947), p. 340. Cf. Carnap (1937), p. 296.
11 Lewis and Langford (1932), p. 334.
12 Cf. Dummett (1981), p. 356; cf. p. 331.
13 Cf. Harrah (1963), pp. 70-71.
14 Searle (1969), p. 66.
15 Hintikka (1974), p. 105.
16 Searle (1969), p. 69.
17 Cf. Bolinger (1977), p. 182, note 15.
18 Hare (1949), pp. 4-5; cf. Belnap (1963), p. 32; Brown (1990), pp. 72, 79, 83.
19 Tichy (1978), p. 278.
20 David and Stephanie Lewis (1975), pp. 50 and 47.
21 Cf. Welbourne (1979), p. 2; (1980), p. 319; (1986a), p. 9.
22 See Welbourne (1979), p. 6.
23 Woozley (1953), p. 155.
24 David and Stephanie Lewis (1975), p. 51; cf. Åqvist (1969), pp. 119-20.
25 Bell (1975), p. 209; cf. p. 210.
26 Cf. Åqvist (1969), p. 120.
27 Dummett (1981), p. 338.
28 Cf. Sigwart (1895), i, p. 177; Ajdukiewcz (1974), p. 93 and (1978), p. 163; Field (1950), p. 232; Wittgenstein (1981), § 695.
29 Moore (1953), p. 125; cf. Ryle (1930), p. 33. Cf. also Hamblin (1958), pp. 160-61.
30 Cf. Austin (1962), p. 99.
31 See Hare (1952), pp. 5-7; cf. (1949), p. 4. Cf. also Reichenbach (1947), p. 342 but contrast pp. 19-20.
32 Bell (1975), p. 206; cf. pp. 207-9.
33 Cf. Rundle (1990), p. 91.
34 Bell (1975), p. 207; but contrast p. 196.
35 Cf. Vendler (1972), pp. 99, 109, 111, 113; (1979), p. 228.
36 Hare (1970), p. 81.
37 Cf. Woozley (1953), pp. 161-2; and Welbourne (1986b), pp. 229-30.
38 David and Stephanie Lewis (1975), pp. 50-51.
39 Cf. Mary and Arthur Prior (1955), pp. 52-5; Johnson (1976), p. 151, note 3; Kiefer (1980), pp. 113-14, 118, note 9.
40 Contrast Sadock (1970), p. 227; cf. Welbourne (1989), p. 182.
41 Cf. Rundle (1990), p. 89.
42 Cf. Woozley (1953), pp. 162 and 166.

Chapter 7

Requesting

Imperative theorists frequently hold not just that asking another a question is telling the other to answer it, issuing a command in the generic sense, but that it is specifically making a request — or, as is occasionally said or added, proffering an invitation[1] — usually to answer the question, or something supposed to be equivalent. Often it is held that questions are commands because questions are requests, it being assumed that requests are commands.[2] Such accounts have no explanatory value, since, as is clear from the derivation of the word *request*, a request is a type of question — as is also an invitation. But further, their advocates misconceive a request or an invitation as something other than a question: to wit, a command in the generic sense, a telling of somebody to do something. There are thus at least two confusions in such accounts: first, between questions as such and the specific types of question a request and an invitation belong to; and second, between asking and telling.[3]

Bell supposes that *ask* 'also doubles as merely one of the family of command verbs'.[4] Searle says that 'asking questions is really a special case of requesting', which 'partly explains', he supposes, 'why the verb "ask" covers both requests and questions'.[5] Instead, requesting is a special case of asking a question; and the use for requests and invitations of *ask*, by contrast with the use for commanding of *tell*, shows that requests and invitations are questions, not commands. Additional confusion, to be diagnosed in this chapter, is involved in attempts to specify the sort of request or invitation questions as such are being equated with. Notice the typical philosophical queerness of such accounts in implying some distinction between questions as such and requests while they are being assimilated to requests. The official line is that questions constitute a special kind of request, 'requests for information'; but leaving aside until the last section the difficulties with that formulation, advocates of such accounts continue to write as if questions as such were nevertheless different from requests, which they are. Thus, theorists covertly acknowledge that not all questions are the special sort of question requests are.

The Function of Requests

A request constitutes a yes-no question addressed to another which asks if a person — often, but not necessarily, the addressee — will do some action simply because the person is asked if he or she will do it. *Will* here is a modal auxiliary, not an auxiliary of tense. The question does not concern what action will in fact be performed by the person in the future. It is not even about whether the person is going to — meaning, is intending to — do the action requested; but whether the person wills it. The modal auxiliary has thus to be explicated by reference to the finite verb *to will*; for the actions of persons are presumed to be normally subject to their wills so that their willing an action is necessary for their performance of it.

Near synonyms of the modal auxiliary do not quite fit requests. Somebody making a request is in part enquiring if the person requested to do the action intends to or is willing to do it; for *ask* is, after all, a verb of enquiry when its subject is a person. But requesting is not simply enquiring. If intelligence were received that the person did at the time intend to do the action, making the request would be superfluous because the person would have intended to do it anyway. Only when the intentions of the person are unknown, or when the person did not originally have any intention to do it, would making the request serve a purpose. And if after taking discreet soundings from your confidants I learn that you would indeed be willing to do what I have in mind to propose to you, my subsequent proposing to you of the action might not actually constitute a request but rather a piece of advice or a suggestion; for you could have your own reasons for taking up my proposal and have no thought for those interests that concern me. Still, if you are unwilling to accept my proposal simply as a proposal, you might nonetheless be agreeable to do the action for me when I request you to do it. Hence the auxiliary *will* cannot be taken to mean want or desire to, either; since you might not want or desire to do the action but be willing to do it only because I had requested you to do it.

Making a request, then, has the object of creating an intention to do an action in the person requested to do it; of causing — not in the sense of bringing about but in the somewhat neglected sense of providing a reason for — the person to be willing to do it, the reason being simply that the person has been asked if he or she will do it. The intention in the person requested to do the action is created not by dropping hints, persuasion or compulsion, nor by telling the person to do the action, but by asking if the person will do the action. That is, the making of a request itself serves, if the request is acceded to, to produce the intention of doing an action in the person requested to do it precisely for the reason that the person has been requested to do it.

When requested to do some action, a person might riposte *Why should I?* The only honest and reasonable reply is that since the action has been requested there need be no reason why the person should do it other than having been asked if he or she will do it; that is, that appeals to self-interest are beside the point when a request is being made. Underlying requesting, therefore, is the presumption that people are generally disposed to help others when asked if they will do so in the absence of overriding reasons for doing otherwise. Requesting is thus founded on the presumption of a shared end of social co-operation and appeals to the better nature of others. It reveals something about the social relations between human beings; and accordingly does not fall within the province of logic as the notion of a question as such does.

A request has to be made to somebody; and so the question constituting it has to be put to somebody. Frege's view that an interrogative sentence contains a request[6] cannot be right: a question itself is an abstraction from people's askings of it. The most that could be argued is that putting a question to another is requesting an action like answering the question; though this account will not do either, it can be anticipated from the argument in the previous chapter about telling people to answer questions.

Requesting a thing — more strictly, some action in connection with a thing — is distinct from seeking the thing; since one can seek (for) or search after a thing, strive to get it, without requesting anybody for it. Since a request has to be made to somebody, it cannot be left unexpressed as a wish can; just as a complaint has to be made to, lodged with, somebody by contrast with grumbles one mutters to oneself. An expression of a wish is not a request, because no question is asked of anybody; it can at most be a hint to others to do some action. *I wish you would, I should like you to, be quiet* is not as such a request; though doubtless its utterance in many situations can often function performatively as a way of making a request. If I say in your presence *I've never tasted Southern Comfort*, logic is on your side if you do not take the hint. In that case I shall have to make a request to you expressly. But if my hinting works, you will extend an invitation to me.

A manipulator of others succeeds in getting them to do things they might not otherwise do by persuading them that the actions are in their interests. But an action requested is unashamedly for the benefit of somebody other than the person requested to do it. In asking if another will do some action for one, there is no room for any pretence that the action is for the benefit of the person requested to do it, consequently no need to disguise a request as a piece of advice. Despite what many who align requesting with imperatival uses of language sometimes suppose, requesting others to do something is not the same as trying to persuade them to do it — let alone force, make, them do it; for as more judicious authors appreciate, these are not even the same as telling others to do something.[7] But neither is requesting telling others to do things; whether, specifically, advising or suggesting, ordering or instructing; still less does it constitute a threat or warning. In particular, advice purports to have in view the interests of the person it is offered to; whereas a request has in view the interests of somebody other than the person requested to do the action.

Essential for requesting is that the person requested to do the action has an option of refusing to accede to the request without penalty, which rules out threats and warnings. If literal sense could be given to making a request to oneself, then some sense would also need to be given to declining to do what one has requested oneself to do; but since one cannot literally address any question to oneself, one cannot make a request to oneself that one, still less somebody else, do an action.

Orders and instructions usually preclude any option of refusal except in prescribed circumstances, such as conscientious objection. By contrast, in asking if others will do some action for one, one is paying regard to their desires, needs, feelings and attitudes by allowing them an option of refusal, thereby showing a civilised consideration for them.

It is especially inept, therefore, to suppose that requesting others to do something is trying to get them to do it, since performance of the action is specified as subject to the person requested to do it being willing to do it. A person making a request is showing respect for the autonomy of the will of the person requested to do the action. Here people cannot say, as when ordered to do some action, 'I had to do it, I had no choice'; for they are free to refuse to do an action that is merely requested. Instead, they are in a position to cite as the — possibly sole — reason for doing an action, 'Because I was asked if I would do it;' which, unlike 'Because I was told to do it,' or even 'Because I was advised to do it,' testifies to the autonomous decision of the agent, notwithstanding that the action might never have been performed had it not been requested.

The issuing of orders and instructions generally presumes authority over those receiving them — perhaps only the authority of those who know better or have more experience. A request, however, has as such no implications about the standing of either the person making the request or the person requested, nor about the relationship between them: one can request a person to do something for one simply as one human being to another; for requesting appeals to the autonomy of a free agent. There is some affinity with advice here. As Basil Mitchell observes: 'The person who gives advice places himself, as it were, on a level with the person whom he advises' — though advisers may also often have expertise or be more experienced. And: 'We give orders to young children and animals, we do not offer them advice.'[8] A further resemblance with requests is that it is left up to the advisee whether to take advice.[9] Both advising and requesting are founded on a general presumption of equality among persons. Petitions, prayers and supplications, however, are requests made specifically to a superior, usually endowed with the power to grant them which those of lesser status lack. Hare takes praying for, say rain, to be 'a species of telling to'. He actually says '*praying to*', which he juxtaposes with '*ordering to*, *requesting to*, *advising to*, *instructing to*', thereby confusing the dative *to* with the *to* of the infinitive. Whether telling, as distinct from asking, God to bring about something would count as blasphemous can best be determined by theists.[10]

Colleagues offer advice and make requests; heads of department issue instructions and hand out warnings. Asking somebody to do something is not, as Bell supposes, 'to command the performance of' it.[11] Asking people to do things is ordinarily contrasted with telling them to do them. If you thought that I was making a request to you which you might, if you cared, decline to meet instead of issuing you with an order, I might disabuse you of your mistake by saying *I'm telling you, not asking you*. Requesting or inviting somebody to do something is no more telling the person to do it than, as was seen in the previous chapter, asking another a question in general is telling the hoped-for respondent to do something: to wit, to answer the question. The confusion involved in supposing otherwise is the same: the person making the request or extending the invitation is presumed to intend that the other do the requested or invited action, just as an interrogator generally is presumed to intend that the addressee answer the question put. But a specification of what action is presumed to be intended by speakers to be done by others is not equivalent to the telling of others to do that action — though speakers can subsequent to their asking expressly tell others to do the action they are presumed to intend them to do.

This possibility of subsequently telling others to do an action previously requested gives rise to some perhaps excusable confusion. Politeness usually dictates that those in a position to give orders or issue instructions phrase them, at least initially, informally as requests; as if made, according to a polite fiction, by one equal to another. When powerful people make what is nominally a request to those they have authority over, it is prudent to take it as a directive or an instruction, a case of an iron fist in a velvet glove.[12] Rather as according to the fictions afforded by an unwritten constitution, the British monarch is deemed to be obliged to follow what is notionally described as the 'advice' of ministers; for talk of the government telling the monarch to do what it says would sound undignified. Even so, orders or instructions are never dressed up as requests where authority is formally, if not nakedly, on show — such as in the disciplined services and courts of law. Bolinger suggests that there is a further factor at work in more informal situations: a question — and a request, of course, is a question — initiates a conversation more smoothly than a command, which can only start things off abruptly, whether or not expressed by an imperative sentence.[13] The scope for any option of refusal determines whether something is really a request or instead a disguised order. Thus, if a subordinate demurs at an instruction initially phrased as a request, the superior can then expressly tell the subordinate to do the action.

The Wording of Requests and Invitations

The question constituting a request takes the form *Will you* (*he*) ... *?* Since the action is not necessarily what the person requested to do it wants to do, a *please* frequently accompanies a request. A *please*, indeed, serves as a mark of a request; for it is short for *if you please* — that is, *will*. So even imperative sentences, which are generally employed only in informal speech, when followed by a *please* are to be understood, at least nominally, as requests. *Don't shut the door* tells the addressee not to do something; an added *please* indicates that the speaker is merely asking if the addressee will refrain from doing it. Addition of the tag question *will you?* also removes any doubt that the speaker is asking, not telling, the addressee to refrain from doing the action: *Don't shut the door, will you?*

It is not that requests are politely worded commands, as imperative theorists often suppose; though one can always tell another, politely, to do something by phrasing the command one is issuing as if it were a request. Rather, one can sometimes make a request by addressing an imperative sentence to another.[14] For in an imperative sentence the verb is truncated by the omission of the auxiliary — whether the auxiliary is *is to* or *should*, as in telling or *will*, as in requesting. Politeness is not just a superimposed layer on the wording of a request as it can be on the wording of a command; it is intrinsic to requests since they leave room for the person to refuse to do the action; though occasionally what is conventionally worded as a request may be used to tell people to do an action in a manner that shows scant regard to politeness or respect for others.

Even a question in general put to another when accompanied by a *please* signals an implied request: A speaker who asks, *Where is the station, please?* implicitly requests to be told where the station is. Often the circumstances of the utterance indicate that the speaker is requesting to be given directions to the station,[15] so that the question might rather have been *How does one get to the station from here, please?* But the answer to the original question may enable an inference to be drawn to the answer to the more explicit question: *Just off the market square* will allow those who know how to get to the market square to infer how to get to the station. The ability to draw such inferences explains in general why people do not always ask the question they logically ought to ask. A question put to another is also an implicit request when it is prefaced with a *Tell me* ... and a *Do you know ... ?* Hence the confusion by philosophers of such implicit requests to be told what the answer is to a question put by another with the putting itself of the question, or even the question put. (Yet a parenthetical *Tell me, ...* cannot serve as a preamble to an explicit request such as *Will you shut the door?* since requesting is not simply enquiring about the intention of another but has the more specific object of producing that intention.)

Only where the interrogator's interests are seen to be served by the putting of the question is a *please* in order: typically, when accosting a stranger to request help or in pursuing some enquiry;[16] but also when one is acquainted with the addressee yet anticipates some reluctance to answer or encounters hesitation. So although to put any question to another is to place an imposition, however slight, on the addressee to give at least some reply, a *please* is not in order as an accompaniment to a question put to others in small talk. For while such questions are sometimes far more burdensome than the simple enquiries of a passer-by, the putting of questions to others in such ice-breaking situations is thought to show concern for the addressee and not simply to serve the interests of the interrogator.

Where the person requested to do the action is not the addressee, an imperative sentence cannot be used to make the request. But even though the imperative mood is essentially vocative, what it expresses is capable of being conveyed to a third party. Thus, when Mary makes a request to John that Alice shut the door, she asks, *John, will Alice shut the door?* Here Mary cannot make her request with an imperative sentence. Hence the imperative account of requests is mistaken. Moreover, Alice is being requested, but not asked, by Mary to shut the door. For since Mary's request is being made to John, who is the addressee of the question, Mary, though requesting Alice to shut the door, is not asking Alice to shut the door. John can then convey Mary's request to Alice by reporting the question he was asked by Mary when she made her request to him: *Alice, Mary asks if you will shut the door.* Only if John is also requested to do the action besides having the request made to him — besides being the addressee of the question — can he also be said to have been asked to do the action. Even an implicit request to be told what the answer is to a question can be conveyed to a third party by reporting the question originally asked: *Alice, Mary asks where the station is, please* or *Alice, Mary asks if you will tell her, if you know, where the station is, please.*

A polite way of making requests with *would* instead of *will* was originally accompanied by an *if* clause: *Would you ... , if you please?* — that is, *if you are willing to do it.* A request can also be phrased politely by being prefaced with a *Do* (*Would*) *you mind ... ?* And the tags, *if you don't, wouldn't, mind* added to imperative sentences in informal speech make clear that they are to be taken as requests, not as telling the addressee to do the action. Minding is understood as minding so much as to be unwilling to do the action.

Could is the corresponding polite form for *can*; which in turn is a more polite form for *will.* Thus, *Can, Could, you* (*he*) *shut the door?* are more polite ways of making the request. If people are unable to do actions, the question whether they will do them obviously does not arise. But *can* here does not mean *to be able to,* which cannot be substituted for it. People may sometimes be perfectly able to do an action but be of the view that they cannot for some reason, such as prior commitments, moral ideals, religious scruples and so forth, do it; and so they will be unwilling to do it. The use of *can* or *could,* therefore, seeks to establish that the person has no such reasons for being unwilling to do the action; it being presumed that if somebody requested to do an action can do it — in the relevant sense of having no objection in principle to doing it — then by default the person will do it. For the object of asking the question constituting a request is to create the intention to do the action in the person requested to do it.

One kind of request is where the action requested is for the person making the request to be allowed or granted permission to do or omit doing something — say, to take leave of absence, be exempted from bar examinations, marry one's cousin. Only where the request is specifically for the person's permission can the person be said to agree or consent to the other's action, as distinct from grant or accede to the request.[17] Often, though, one is perfectly capable of acting on one's own authority but deems it politic to ask permission before going ahead. *May I switch on the light, close the door?* and *May I come in, sit down, for a moment?* ask if the addressee will agree or consent to the speaker doing the action. Only ill-bred visitors proceed in one's presence to turn on the light or shut the door without so much as a by-your-leave. Politeness, being a regard for the feelings of others, also determines the form of what are strictly offers of help, not requests for permission to help: *(Will you) Let, Allow, Permit, me to help you(?)* serves more to advise, or warn, the addressee — such as a blind person at a crossing — that the speaker is about to intervene than ask permission to do so; but in being nominally a request it leaves the addressee with the option of refusing help and thus shows consideration for others and accordingly politeness.

An invitation constitutes a yes-no or an alternative question addressed to another which enquires if the other would like to do some action or other, or have it done, the action being for the person's benefit. Offers and invitations are sometimes politely phrased as requests, the polite fiction being that the acceptance by the other of some good is doing a favour rather to the benefactor. Printed invitations 'request', as it is said, the pleasure of one's company. Yet requests concern actions to be done usually for the person making the request, not for the person doing the action. Invitations, by contrast, concern actions the person proffering the invitation is presumed to suppose the person being invited might like to do or have done. There is a parallel with the contrast Hobbes draws between 'Command' (in the specific sense) and 'Counsell': that is, 'Command is directed to a mans own benefit,' but 'Counsell to the benefit of another man.'[18]

Thus, while *will* or *won't* can occur in invitations politely phrased as requests, as in *Will you sit down?* and *Won't you stay for dinner?* — which can even be accompanied by a *please* — such utterances are not to be understood as asking if the person will do the action. The proper way of extending an invitation to another is by asking *Would you like to ... ?* In informal situations imperative sentences accompanied by tag questions often function to extend invitations, even although the wording is appropriate to making requests: *Sit down, will you? Have a sandwich, won't you?* By contrast, *Sit down, will you?* when addressed to an irritating child functions as a request since the action is not primarily for benefit of the child. *May I help you?* however, is really an invitation, an offer of help, not a request to be given permission to help. Since the welfare of the addressee is being regarded, it is to be understood as asking if the addressee would like the speaker to help, not if the addressee will agree or consent to being helped.

Like requests, invitations can be passed on from the addressee to a third party: the speaker is asking the addressee even though the question concerns a third party; rather as any question in the third person generally, say about the capital of Peru, can always be put to an addressee. In order to answer the question the addressee will have to put the question, whether request or invitation, in turn to the third party it concerns — unless the addressee already knows what the third party's response will be, or simply presumes it. So John may report to Alice: *Mary asks if you would like a drink.* But since what primarily needs to be conveyed to the third party is what action the third party is being requested or invited to do, not a report of the question constituting the request or invitation the addressee was asked, the verbs *request* and *invite*, by contrast with *ask*, do not report a question but instead specify an action. Accordingly, they are not followed by an interrogative clause.

So, the addressee may say to the third party: *Mary requests you to shut the door, invites you to have a drink.*

Thus, the general job of *request* and *invite*, by contrast with *ask*, is to specify an action, not to report the question constituting the request or invitation. The same is true of imperative sentences when they can be used to express requests or invitations.[19] In the case of *request* sometimes no person in particular is mentioned as being requested to do the action, as in *Mary requests that the door be shut.* And use of the passive or an impersonal construction also allows the person making the request to go unmentioned, as in *You are requested to leave* or *It is requested that you leave*. *Invite* is less flexible: while the notion of an invitation can be abstracted from that of the person invited, as in the title *Invitation to the Dance*, a *that* construction is not available with *invite*, which instead is always a transitive verb. So while the passive can be used, as in *You are invited to dinner*, no impersonal construction is available. In the passive *ask* can do duty for both *request* and *invite*: *You are asked to leave* and *I was asked to dine with the captain.*

Infinitive and *that* constructions remove any need to report the question asked by the person making a request or extending an invitation. These constructions are traditionally classified by grammarians as 'indirect commands'. But rather than functioning imperatively so as to tell people to do actions, they serve merely to specify the action the request or invitation concerns. Even if saying *You are requested, invited, to* ... is sometimes itself to make a request or give out an invitation, rather than explicitly report what the speaker is doing, saying the words still has no imperatival function but serves merely to specify the action. For to request or invite is to ask, not tell.

The Oxford English Dictionary omits to take note of a *that* besides an infinitive construction with *ask*.[20] Certainly, the construction *ask somebody that* he or she (should) do something, parallel to the *that* construction following *tell* with a direct object, seems suspect. And the construction even with *request* is awkward, though a *that* construction without a direct object is quite standard. So perhaps people who write 'ask that ... ' mean *request that* ... . If there is indeed no legitimate construction *ask that* ... an explanation is readily at hand. For talk of asking somebody to do something is to be construed as asking if the person either will (a request) or would like to (an invitation) do it. There is room for an infinitive but no place for a *that* clause, just as with *invite*. So any putative construction *ask that* ... could be understood only as making a request, not as extending an invitation. But while *ask* may often seem a suitable substitute for *request*, it cannot be in general if it does not, while *request* does, permit a *that* clause to follow. Since *that* clauses are propositional in form, it would be only appropriate if *ask*, the verb that above all others invokes the interrogative form of thought, should resist them.

Differences in the constructions taken by *request* and *invite* are due to their taking different direct objects: actions are requested — though they are always requested of people, even when who the people are is not mentioned; but it is rather people themselves who are invited to do actions or have actions done for them. It is tempting to think that with *ask*, since questions are asked of people, the direct object is different again. Whether *ask* can be said to take a direct object at all will be touched on in the next chapter. In any case, since the person asked the question when a request is made need not be the person requested to do the action, *ask* and *request* are clearly not interchangeable: Mary can request Alice to shut the door without asking her to do so; she may instead have asked John, not to do anything, but if Alice would. The construction *ask somebody to* thus does a double job: it specifies the action a request or an invitation concerns; but it also indicates that the question constituting the request or invitation was put directly to the person requested or invited to do the action. The same, it would seem, would have to apply to any putative *ask that* ... construction. But it could not be said, when her addressee is John rather than Alice, that Mary asks that Alice shut the door. An impersonal construction *It is asked that* ... seems even more suspect; though use of the passive in specifying the action, as in *He asked that the cat be fed no more than twice daily*, in making no mention of either the addressee of the question or the person requested to do the action, is perhaps less jarring. Even so, the job of *ask* is to report a question, not to specify an action.

The Interrogative Character of Requests

Philosophers commonly suppose that requests are not really questions at all because they exclusively serve the practical function of bringing about actions. It has to be conceded that in spoken English interrogative intonation is often barely noticeable in direct speech when a yes-no question makes a request or extends an invitation. Waismann talks of a request being 'dressed up as a question'. Austin Duncan-Jones refers to questions beginning *Will you ... ?* as 'polite formulae' for imperative sentences, holding that they are only 'ostensibly questions'.[21] J. M. O. Wheatley asserts that they are 'thinly, but politely, disguised imperatives', denying that as such they 'call for linguistic responses'.[22] Winston Nesbitt supposes that they are 'degenerate cases of questions … and … must be construed as a species of imperative'.[23] Even Austin hints at a similar view when he distinguishes 'asking to' from 'asking whether and asking "Yes or no?"', the former being 'a response or sequel' which is '"one-way"', the latter '"two-way"'.[24] But as has been seen, the construction *asking somebody to* should be taken as a truncated form of *asking somebody if he or she will* (*would like to*) ... . But Reid sets *ask* along side *refuse* thereby suggesting, correctly, that a refusal is an answer.[25]

Any disguise is rather the other way round: requests and invitations, being questions, masquerade as commands (in the generic sense) when they are expressed by an imperative sentence; for the sentence here does not tell, it rather asks, somebody to do something. If the genus of imperative is to be circumscribed by the telling of people to do things, how can the option of denying a request or declining an invitation be accommodated within an imperative sentence? Though orders can sometimes be disobeyed on conscientious grounds and advice can always be rejected, only asking, as distinct from telling, can allow for the option of refusal through the answer given to a question put. Only asking makes performance of the action conditional on the will or preferences of the other. Contrary to what Wheatley and Llewelyn suppose, when a request is made or an invitation extended, an answer to the question constituting the request or invitation is required to determine whether the condition involved has been met.

Admittedly, one may occasionally without rudeness accede to a request, or even take up an invitation, simply by doing (or refraining from) the action without saying anything; though Nesbitt inconsistently concedes that requests 'retain a vestigial question-like character, in that *mere* action … is not an adequate response to them'.[26] His concession is unnecessary because one's action shows that one is answering the question affirmatively. Thus, it is possible to answer the sorts of question requests and invitations are 'in act if not in word' — to adopt a phrase of Hare's used for another purpose.[27] The person has not simply left the question unanswered. But then not to say anything at all, even though one is granting the request or accepting the invitation, is verging on rudeness. And while silence can sometimes be an expression of defiance and so indicative of a negative answer, it can be a sign of deafness too. So, action and silence can at most only do duty for the answer, which is indispensable in that it must always be understood when not explicitly given.

It will be objected that in making requests and extending invitations people are not concerned with any answer to a literal question but are interested only in the action specified. If one had answered affirmatively but failed to carry out the requested action or take up the invitation, then barring any unannounced change of mind, it would have to be inferred that one had not understood the utterance as a request or an invitation. It might further be pointed out that requests and invitations are not themselves said to be answered, as distinct from granted or denied, accepted or declined.

The unsuitability of the term *answer* is due to the denial of a request or the non-acceptance of an invitation being equally an answer — by contrast with a prayer, which when said to be 'answered' is granted, the only alternative being that it is ignored. While it is undeniable that requests and invitations essentially have to do with actions, it does not follow that an answer to the questions constituting them, whether given explicitly or merely understood, is not required. After all, printed invitations often have the letters *R.S.V.P.* embossed on them. Requests and invitations are obviously not merely questions, for the object in making or extending them is to produce the action specified. If their concern for action makes them 'imperatival', then it is in a sense that involves only asking people if they will or would like to do things, not telling them to do them. Their concern for action does not make requests and invitations any less questions, questions about a person's will or preferences in regard to a specified action. For the speaker is presumed to intend that performance of the action is conditional on an affirmative answer to the question;[28] which rules out the tempting suggestion of Duncan-Jones that questions constituting requests express 'a mixture of ... command and question'.[29] One cannot at the same time both tell and ask people to do a thing, intend that they do the action both regardless of how they feel about it and only if they are willing or would like to do it. Any difference that Llewelyn detects between questions beginning *Would you mind ... ?* and simply *Would you ... ?* turns, not on the latter precluding, as it stands, any answer at all — such as *(No,) I will not*; but on what are conventionally worded as requests sometimes having the function of orders.[30]

Tone of voice, besides the situation, helps to determine whether what is worded as one type of speech-act actually functions as another. *I wish you would be still*, though nominally an expression of a wish, when said to a fidgety child functions as a request; and *Be still, won't you?* while nominally a request, may be said so curtly as to leave no doubt that it has the function of a command. *I should like you to finish your work before you leave* most likely is not a mere expression of a preference but functions as an order; *I should like you to leave your address with the secretary*, a request; *I should like to know where you've been all this time*, an insistent question. Wording and tone of voice may pull in opposite directions: what is conventionally worded as a request, and hence nominally polite, may be said in such a manner as to be calculated to cause offence: the art of insult lies in the discourteous utilisation of civilities. An order conventionally phrased as a request is no more to be taken as a model to base one's account on than is the sarcastic proffering of an invitation: for the speaker does not really intend that the person concerned should, in the one case, be allowed any option of refusal or, in the other, should seriously take up the offer.

Noting that 'the *generic* act of commanding has many varieties' and that there is 'a whole family of what we may call *command verbs*', Bell is initially embarrassed that '*ask* does not appear to belong to an extended family of question verbs', which 'makes questioning look to be a rather impoverished kind of act, in contrast, say, with commanding'. His solution to the supposed difficulty is that acts of questioning 'may also have a force which could be made explicit by other verbs in the family, such as *order* or *command*, as in peremptory questions, or *beg*, as in pleading questions'.[31]

It is always possible to convey along with a report of the words spoken by a speaker something of the way they were spoken. A novice on a creative writing course might ring the changes on such 'quotatives' as *mused*, *demurred*, *remonstrated*, *opined*, *confided*, *cried*, and so forth, fearing repetition of the plain *said*. Such colourings introduce an element of interpretation into the report, but one founded ultimately on the tone of voice of the speaker. *Murder, she croaked* not only reports her dying words but in conveying the manner of their delivery glosses them as an accusation. Questions put to others can likewise be asked in a variety of tones. So the trainee creative writer thumbing through a thesaurus might come up with *demanded*, *implored*, *importuned*, *canvassed*, *probed*, *snapped*, and so forth. While imperative sentences can always be reported by the minimally interpretative *said* or *tell*, unlike declarative and interrogative sentences they usually demand some gloss: *ordered*, *urged*, *begged*, *warned*, *advised*, and so forth. Here tone of voice alone is insufficient — to decide between, say, an ordering and advising.

Thus, through a false analogy with commanding, Bell conflates the manner of asking a question, such as the various tones of voice it may be asked in — imperious, say, or deferential — with a notion that there might be distinct kinds of asking. (It is not in doubt that there are distinct kinds of questions asked, as opposed to distinct kinds of askings.) The supposed poverty of kinds of asking compared to the riches of kinds of telling, far from being a deficiency, reflects the logical basis of asking in a fundamental form of thought, the interrogative, as distinct from the primarily social and institutional bases of the kinds of telling others to do things. Logical import attaches to what words one utters, not how one utters them. A peremptory or pleading question is logically still a question, no matter how boorish or affecting it may be from a social perspective. Significantly, where specific types of asking questions are indeed distinguishable, as with requesting and inviting, the asking has an additional, social dimension. That is, requests are not just questions about the future performance of actions by others but are founded on a presumed equality of status among persons; and invitations are not just questions about the actual preferences or tastes of others but are founded on the ability or opportunity given to one person to do a favour to another.

The beauty for imperative theorists of taking the various tones of voice employed in asking questions to be classifications of speech-acts is that the distinction between a report of a question and a specification of an action can readily be smothered. Take *demand*. A question may be asked of another so abruptly or pressingly as to be described as a demand; yet in English, as opposed to French, *demand* does not mean to ask a question but to insist that some action be done. *Ask* need not be followed by an infinitive construction specifying an action; it is in fact more usually followed by an interrogative clause. Indeed, the infinitive construction *ask somebody to* should be understood, it has been seen, as concealing an interrogative clause: *ask somebody if* (*whether*) *he or she will* (*would like to*) ... . But *demand* demands, appropriately, a construction that specifies an action: if no action has been specified in a question characterised as a demand, some action to complement *demand* has to be understood. Thus, if a speaker is reported as having demanded *Who are you?* the tone of voice is being glossed as demanding to be given the addressee's name, even although the speaker has not actually said *Give me your name*. Likewise with *begged*, *implored*, *pleaded*.

The Requesting Account of Questions

Questions as such are not requests; but it is misleading to oppose questions to requests as if requests themselves were somehow not exactly questions but something else.[32] Admittedly, requests are not simply questions.

The assimilation of questions as such to requests or invitations of some sort might be countered with Wittgenstein's diagnosis of 'philosophical disease — a one-sided diet: one nourishes one's thinking with only one kind of example'.[33] Requests and invitations are not even typical questions, as is evidenced by the tendency of theorists to mistake them for commands. There is a whole variety of questions, it might accordingly be urged, even if one confines oneself to questions asked of others and ignores questions not put to anybody, such as expository and some didactic questions or questions occurring in silent soliloquy. Thus, besides requests and invitations, there are greetings: *How do you do?* questions just to get the other person talking, conversational ice-breakers: *Do you come here often?* questions seeking advice or counselling: *What shall, should, I do?* riddles and jokes: *What is the difference between ... ? What do you call a ... ?* puns: *What did Della wear?* challenges: *How many sales have you clinched today?* guessing games; then there are questions asked in special situations of interrogation mentioned in the previous chapter: namely, questions designed to test or corroborate testimony, to discover how much somebody knows or understands, questions canvassing opinion and quiz or examination questions. Some cases do not involve the serious asking of questions, such as joke questions; others need not make use of a question, such as greetings, the conversational ice-breakers, riddles, challenges and jokes again. More objectionably, in some of the examples questions themselves are being characterised according to the motives people may have in asking them of others. While the Wittgensteinian position that questions form a family provides a corrective to sweeping generalisations about questions, it nevertheless fails to lay bare the confusion of taking questions as such to be requests or invitations.

It was noted that to add a *please* to a question put to another — such as *Where is the station?* — is implicitly to request to be told where the station is; in general, that one's addressee tell one what the answer is to the question one has put. It was also noted, at the end of the last chapter, that one may put a question to another by prefacing it with a *Can you tell (inform) me ... ?* It should now be evident that when such phrases as *Tell me ... (won't you, please)?* and *Can, Could, Will, Would you tell me ... (please)?* introduce a question asked of another — such as *Where is the station?* — they indicate, in general, requests to be told what the answer is to the question put. But it is equally evident that since such requests are questions about a question, the question *Where is the station?* cannot itself be a request of any sort.

For if an infinite regress is to be avoided, not all questions can be requests. That is, the request to be told where the station is itself alludes to a question — namely, *Where is the station?* But if questions as such were requests, that request would be a request concerning a request; but what action the second request — or the request at the end of a series — concerned would be left quite unspecified. A similar argument goes for invitations: *Would you like to tell me what's troubling you?* extends an invitation to tell the speaker what the answer is to the embedded question, which cannot itself therefore be construed as an invitation to tell the speaker what the answer is to a question unless some further question is alluded to. And in the light of the argument presented in Chapter 6, it is fruitless to maintain that a request or an invitation to answer a question previously put is the same as putting that question, any more than is telling another to answer it. Still less can requesting, inviting or telling somebody to answer a question be identified with the question itself.

Hare's view that a question is 'an invitation or request' to respondents 'to make just one out of a number of suggested assertions' they are willing to make comes unstuck here. He expressly, and correctly, denies that answers (to yes-no questions) are 'statements that the answerer was willing to make the affirmative or negative assertions'.[34] The assertions respondents are held to in giving a conformable answer to a question like *Are you married?* are, indeed, quite distinct from those they are held to in giving a conformable answer to the question *Are you willing to state whether you are married?* — or even *Are you willing either to assert that you are married or to assert that you are not married?* Since invitations and requests concern what people are willing to do, the question *Are you married?* cannot itself, then, on Hare's own showing be an invitation or a request to make an assertion.

The notion of requesting or inviting another to assert or state *that* ... runs up against the same difficulty with the transparency of *that* clauses as the notion of telling another to assert or state *that* ... noted in the last chapter. Assertion and statement-making are no more possible by request or invitation than to order or on advice; for neither can be done honestly at will. Nor, for the same reason, can one request that one come to know *that* something is so, as distinct from requesting to be informed of something. The notion of 'an *epistemic request*',[35] if it is not an obtuse way of thinking and talking about a request to be informed, presumes that another can exercise one's mental powers. Moreover, one can request only to be informed *if*, *who*, *how*, *when*, and so forth, not to be informed *that* ... ; for the description of such a request itself informs one *that* ... owing to the transparency of propositional constructions. No doubt to request a second drink is greedy; but not even greed could lead one to request the drink that one had already been given, though a lapse of memory could.

Yet *state*, unlike *assert*, can take interrogative constructions; so people can be asked quite sensibly if they will or would like to state *if*, *who*, *how*, *when*, and so forth. The question people are usually asked, though, is not if they will or would like to but if they can state that something is so. The *can* here is not a polite form for *will* as in requests, but has to be understood to be asking if respondents are in a position, given their knowledge and the facts or the truth, to state the thing — which precludes lying.

It is not absurd, however, to ask others if they will confirm *that* ... . For interrogators can ask if their respondents will confirm or corroborate testimony already accepted from another source. To give a negative answer to this question is to refuse to co-operate in the interrogator's enquiry. By contrast, both a negative and an affirmative answer honestly given to the different question *Can you confirm that ... ?* will further an investigation; for the negative answer signals not a refusal to give evidence but simply that the respondent has no evidence.

As the inclination to suppose that requesting is a kind of telling another to do something stems from the hasty assimilation of the construction *ask somebody to* with *tell somebody to*, so the assumption that questions as such are requests results from a further, unnoticed sliding between *ask* (tout court) and *ask for*. In general, requesting can be not only asking a person to do some action but also asking a person for a thing. Theorists are accustomed to say that questions not only 'request',[36] in accordance with the requesting account, but also 'ask for',[37] 'call for'[38] or 'demand'[39] things such as 'information' or 'linguistic responses', quite oblivious to the potential for confusion involved in these ways of speaking.

Only people and, in a derivative sense, requests themselves can make requests. Again, people primarily are said to ask others for things (as distinct from actions), to call for them, besides to demand them of others or require them from others; but in a derivative sense the words people utter can be said to ask for, call for, demand or require things — though hardly to request them. *Ask for* and *request* always, and *call for*, *demand* and *require* often, imply some action to be done for the person by another. Hence a request itself may be said in a derivative sense to ask for, call for — even demand or require, if it is equivalent to a demand or a requirement — besides request, some action, at least implicitly; even when the thing requested, asked for, called for, demanded or required is not itself an action. And since a person who is requested for a thing is always, at least implicitly, requested to do some action, and so can be asked or called upon to do it, the request itself may likewise be said in a derivative sense to request, ask, or call on somebody to do the action. But questions as such do not ask for, call for, or request anything unless they happen themselves to be requests.

A noun phrase following *ask for* and *request* always implies some action to be done by somebody, and *call for*, *demand* and *require* often do so. To request, ask for, call for, demand or require, say, a porter, a drink, a record or an explanation is to request, ask, call on or require somebody to do some implied action — such as fetch a porter, pour a drink, play a record or offer an explanation; or request, demand or require that the implied action be done — such as, that a porter be sent up, a drink served, a record played on the radio or an explanation supplied. To ask for somebody's name is to request to be given the person's name; the request often being conveyed implicitly in putting the question *What is your* (*his*) *name, please?* to another rather than explicitly as *Will you give me your* (*his*) *name?*

The distinction between asking another a question generally and asking the question constituting a request is marked by the contrast between *asking after* or *about* and *asking for*. If I ask somebody you know how you are, I am fairly reported as having asked, enquired, after or about your health; but if I am reported as having asked for you, being a request, some action is implied, such as asking if I may be allowed to see you or asking for arrangements to be made for us to meet. Frege is mistranslated as asking, 'And are we not really asking for something in this [interrogative] sentence?' when he actually wrote *Und wird nicht in der Tat in ihm nach etwas gefragt?*[40] While sometimes a request is inferred from a question in general put to another, the distinction between asking another a question as such and making a request remains. Thus, if a trader asks an assistant in one of his shops *Where is the manager?* he can be reported strictly as only having asked after or about the manager of the shop, but it can often be safely inferred that he wants the manager to be summoned; if so, then he can be reported, not inaccurately, as having asked for, requested, the manager — as having requested to see his manager.

An interrogator, or a third party, may request, ask for, call for, demand of or require from a respondent the answer to a question previously put, and so may request, ask, call on, require the respondent to answer the question; that is, may request, demand or require that the question be answered. From what has been argued it should be apparent that the original question could not itself be a request to answer itself; at most it could only be a request to answer a still earlier question that had been put. The same goes for an invitation to answer a question. In any case, a question itself cannot request or ask for its answer; nor request, ask, call on or require anybody to answer it; nor request, demand of anybody or require from anybody that it be answered. A question always asks something; but unless it happens also to be a request it never asks for something, and even then not for its answer: if any answer is asked for, it must be to some other question put earlier. By contrast, people not only ask questions, they also sometimes ask for or invite questions. When speakers at the end of meetings ask *Any questions?* they may simply be asking if — that is, enquiring whether — any members of the audience have any questions to put to them; but often speakers are understood to be asking — that is, inviting or requesting — members of the audience to put questions to them. Finally, actions are never asked, only asked for.

If asking were no different from asking for, a question on the requesting account of questions as such would be asking what on this account it is supposedly asking for — namely, its answer; but it is ridiculous to say that what is asked *tout court* is the answer to a question and not the question itself. This confusion between *asking* and *asking for*, together with the confusion between *asking somebody to* and *telling somebody to*, underlies Bell's view that 'asking, when we mean asking questions, is a special kind of commanding'. If one ponders what other sort of asking he must have in mind, and then comes on his remark that *ask* 'can be used to command the performance of any kind of act' it emerges that he is assimilating asking *tout court* with asking somebody to do something or asking somebody for something.[41] But even although requests both ask a question and ask for an action to be done, a person making a request does not thereby ask for the answer to the question constituting the request but rather for the action requested.

What can be said — but only figuratively — is that a question calls for, demands or requires an answer of a certain form; since the notion of a requirement, when abstracted from people's demands and what they require of others, is the notion of a specification to be met. Similarly, regulations can be said, figuratively, to call for, demand or require things; as well as, derivatively, to tell one to do things.[42] The type of answer, or the answer, called for, demanded or required, not literally by any interrogator but figuratively by the question itself, is what meets the specification, set out in interrogative form, in the question of a conformable answer; or, again set out in interrogative form, what answers the question — what achieves the standard for answering the question. In short, the slipping between *asking* and *asking for* mistakes the specification in interrogative form within a question for the specification of an action.[43]

This mistake is at the root of the assumption that a question must always request somebody to do some action; as well as in the imperative theory generally, that a question always tells somebody to do something such as answer the question. A question can only ask (*tout court*); it cannot ask or tell somebody to do something or ask for anything. True, the question's interrogative specification of its conformable answers provides guidance to potential respondents on how to answer it; but as an abstraction, the question does not itself constitute a set of instructions directed to potential respondents on how to come up with its answer, which is an abstraction too and not an action to be performed by respondents.

The confusion between a requirement in the sense of what is required by a person, an institution, a set of regulations and so forth — namely, some action — and a requirement in the much broader sense of a specification to be met or a condition to be fulfilled, which need not be an action at all,[44] insinuates itself even into accounts of questions not overtly imperativist. Rundle notes 'a likeness to commands', which aim 'at eliciting action' and questions, which aim 'at eliciting something more specific, an answer'. Any suspicion of the imperativist doctrine that an answer to a question is a kind of action — such as making 'a linguistic response' — is not allayed by his talk of eliciting 'words of a certain form'.[45] As an abstraction from people's acts of answering questions, a conformable answer to a question cannot be taken to be an action.

Besides, the contrast between issuing a command and asking a question is false. Whereas a command has to be issued to somebody, a question can be asked without being asked of anybody. Rundle's contrast misleadingly suggests that eliciting an answer to a question must be eliciting it from an addressee; and further, must be the eliciting of a kind of action — namely, answering. But not only is an answer to — as distinct from answering — a question not an action, but the eliciting talked of here takes two distinct forms. One attempts to elicit an action from another by either asking or telling the person to do the action; that is, by either asking for (requesting) or commanding the action. Often simply asking or telling the person to do the action is sufficient for the action to be done. By contrast with eliciting actions, one could scarcely in general attempt to elicit an answer to a question simply by asking the question without then engaging (or having engaged) in some enquiry. True, with interrogation an answer to a question can be elicited from others; but then it is elicited rather from their action of answering the question. So what one can be said to aim to elicit specifically in interrogation, as distinct from asking questions as such, is not as such an answer but rather the respondent's action of giving an answer.

Requesting Information

The preferred candidate of imperative theorists for what a question itself supposedly requests, and what a person requests in asking (another) a question, is information. The expression, 'a request for information' has the air of the circumlocutions writers of dictionary definitions are compelled to adopt to avoid tautology; where the aim is to fix on some form of words which, though only approximately equivalent in meaning to what is being defined, can serve to convey something of its meaning. As such asking a question can in no way be said to be requesting information, and only weary familiarity with the jargon of theorists could lead anybody to forget what a request for information actually is.

The situations where talk of requesting information occurs naturally are somewhat special, such as making an application for official information under a Freedom of Information Act. By contrast, talk of requesting to be informed about some subject — as well as to be told about it, formally or officially, when one already fully knows about it — is more frequent. Part of the trouble here is the increasingly sloppy use of the term *information*, which is only to be expected from science journalists but not from philosophers, who should know better. Information is the intelligence derived from what people tell others, and thus is evidential in character. Since what people tell others may be mistaken or calculated to deceive or mislead, information includes misinformation and disinformation. And since what people tell others, or intend to inform them of, may be what others already know, information can also be quite uninformative to those already acquainted with its contents.

Requests are always made to somebody — always involve putting a question, explicitly or implicitly, to others. But requesting information need not be seeking or searching after information — even from potential respondents, rather than in secret files or forgotten archives. When, for the record, one asks for information whose contents one has already got wind of, one need not be conducting any enquiry: one may simply seek oral evidence or documentation.

Requesting information, then, is not necessarily requesting to be informed, or even told. All requests for things, it was seen, imply some action to be done by another, even when the action is not expressly mentioned. Contrasts between 'requests for information' questions as such are being misidentified with and 'requests for actions',[46] only betray confusion between asking a question and asking for something. A request for information can only be construed as a request to be supplied with information, which can include having related to one a story, being given an oral account, or the provision of documentation of some sort —

whether in the form of manuscripts, printed matter, audio tapes, photographs, film, video tapes, computer disks or the like. So a request for information is a request for something to be done too; namely, to supply the information. But while being supplied with information can also include actually being informed or told (orally or in writing), it might instead consist in being handed a bulky file. If I ask you what your telephone number is, I have grounds for complaint that you have not answered my question if you simply throw the telephone directory over to me;[47] but it would be untrue to say that you had not given me the information if your number is listed there. The request-for-information account of questions thus fails to accommodate the presumption of interrogation that the respondent actually tell the interrogator what the answer is to the question.

The difference between supplying information and answering a question put to one, and hence the difference between requesting to be supplied with information and a request, specifically, to be informed or just told about some matter, can be captured by considering a difficulty arising from a remark of Hintikka's: 'Once it is specified what information a questioner wants, all that remains is for him to ask for it.'[48] Whereas information requested to be supplied need not be specified interrogatively, one can sensibly request specifically to be informed or just told about a subject only if it is specified interrogatively.

Information can often be specified simply by specifying what it is about; so one can sensibly request information not only when, prior to its being supplied to one, one already knows what its contents are, but also when one is totally ignorant of its contents apart from the knowledge that it concerns some subject, such as a person, an organisation, a country, a period of history. An employer may be requested to supply an employee's file or a hospital a patient's medical records, the information being specified by reference to the individual employee or patient. All that is presumed in making such a request, and so all that has to be known prior to being supplied with the information in order to specify it, is that there exist some file or record for that individual. But now, the only question-like character of a request for information specified as being about somebody or something derives from requests themselves constituting a type of question. In requesting information specified merely as *information about so-and-so*, no question, other than the question constituting the request, has been asked by anybody: there is no 'questioner' who 'wants' anything — who asks some specific question on some subject, and so is presumed to intend that another inform or just tell him or her what the other takes to be the answer to it; there is only somebody making a request. Information specified merely as about such-and-such can hardly serve as analysis of a question on some specific subject, for no question has yet emerged to be analysed.

If the information is to be further specified, a question-like character may indeed emerge, but in the form of a dependent interrogative clause, rendering the account circular as an analysis of questions. The information I request may be, say, my consultant's prognosis; but the term *prognosis* alludes covertly to an interrogative clause, such as whether my condition is going to improve or deteriorate.

Perhaps, though, it is being maintained that what is requested is information *that* ... . There is no difficulty in requesting information *that* ... in the ordinary sense of requesting to be supplied with information *that* ... ; for one can request documentation — though one cannot, it was seen, sensibly request to be informed *that* ... owing to the transparency of propositional constructions. But again, no question emerges for analysis in such specifications of information.

In short, advocates of the request-for-information account of asking others questions as such face a dilemma: the information to be supplied has to be characterised interrogatively if it is to be specified other than as being either about somebody or something or information *that* ... , neither of which yields a question to be analysed; but if the information is characterised interrogatively, the analysis is circular, for the question to be analysed cannot be analysed as concerning a piece of information capable of being specified independently of the question.

Cohen pointed out long ago the circularity involved in the account that questions are 'requests for information': -

> ... the idea that a question is a request for information does not in the least explain the nature of questions. If I ask who discovered America, I am none the wiser as to what I have done when told that I have requested information. What information? Why, of course, information as to *who discovered America.*[49]

The insistence of Alf Ross that 'a genuine question is ... a request to give information', despite his admission, and here he refers to Cohen, that the 'description ... is hardly sufficient',[50] is surprising. For how could the account be refined so as to avoid circularity?

In smothering the distinction between requesting to be supplied with information and requesting to be informed or told, the account also smothers the distinction between non-interrogative and interrogative specifications of information. One may already know what the contents are of information one requests to be supplied with. So one can sensibly request to be supplied with information about such-and-such, or information *that* ... , whether or not already acquainted with its contents; as well as request information specified interrogatively. What the misleading talk of 'requesting' information is actually trying to fix on, of course, is not the supplying of information — a rather specialised notion having to do with corroborative evidence afforded by testimony or documentation — but simply informing. So if, by contrast, one requests to be informed of or just told some matter, one either does not yet know what one is going to be informed of or one already knows it and simply requests the other to tell one it. But then one cannot sensibly request to be informed or told *that* ... .[51] And to request to be informed or told about such-and-such is just to request to be supplied with information about such-and-such: *Tell me about John* does not specify what you are to tell me other than that it should be (some) information about John. If one is to specify what the other is to inform one of or tell one, as distinct from supplying (some, any) information about the subject, the specification has to be interrogative, the indispensable type of specification which the request-for-information account hoped to analyse away.

Instead of attempting to define questions by reference to information, pieces of information are most conveniently specified by reference to a question; that is, through an interrogative concept exercised in an interrogative clause.

Notes

1 See, for example, Reichenbach (1947), p. 340 and Hare (1970), pp. 80-81.
2 See, for example, Ross (1968), p. 77, note 1.
3 But contrast Hamblin (1987), pp. 6-7.
4 Bell (1975), p. 206.
5 Searle (1969), p. 69.
6 Frege (1918), p. 346/355 and (1919), p. 362/373.
7 Cf. Hare (1951), pp. 206-10; Austin (1962), pp. 101-3, 116-18, 120-31; Urmson (1968), pp. 27-8.
8 Mitchell (1957), pp. 185 and 186.
9 Cf. Williams (1963), p. 153, note 1; Rundle (1990), pp. 95-6, 141.
10 Hare (1971), p. 111.
11 Bell (1975), p. 206.
12 Cf. Mitchell (1957), pp. 183-4.
13 See Bolinger (1977), p. 185.
14 Cf. Rundle (1990), p. 95.
15 Cf. Kiefer (1988), pp. 258, 276-7.
16 Cf. Johnson (1976), pp. 147 and 150.
17 Contrast Mitchell (1957), p. 188.
18 Hobbes (1991), xxv; pp. 176-7.
19 Cf. Rundle (1990), p. 97; contrast pp. 142-4.
20 See *OED*, i, pp. 687b-8c; especially III, senses 9-16. Contrast, for instance, Vendler (1967), p. 61; Prior (1971), p. 75.
21 Waismann (1965), p. 407; Duncan-Jones (1952), p. 192.
22 Wheatley (1955), p. 55 and note 1. Cf. also Llewelyn (1964), p. 79; Bell (1975), pp. 206-8, 211; Kiefer (1980), p. 97.
23 Nesbitt (1973), p. 256.
24 Austin (1962), p. 116.
25 Reid (1764), IV ii; p. 118a; (1785), VI v; pp. 448b, 450a; cf. I viii; p. 244b; (1788), V vi; p. 664b; cf. p. 664a.
26 Nesbitt (1973), p. 256.
27 Hare (1952), p. 158.
28 Cf. Rundle (1990), p. 89.
29 Duncan-Jones (1952), p. 192.
30 See Llewelyn (1964), pp. 78-9.
31 Bell (1975), pp. 205 and 207.
32 Cf. Johnson (1976), pp. 145-51.
33 Wittgenstein (1958), I, § 593; p. 155[e].
34 Hare (1970), pp. 80-81.

35 Belnap (1969), pp. 122-3.
36 For instance: Carnap (1937), p. 296; Belnap (1969), pp. 125-7.
37 For instance: Bambrough (1951), p. 96; Wheatley (1955), p. 50; Belnap (1963), pp. 15, 17, 42-3, note 20, 48-9, 82, 86, 93; cf. p. 59; Åqvist (1965), p. 106; Belnap (1969), pp. 125-7; Belnap and Steel (1976), pp. 4, 48, 61.
38 For instance: Wheatley (1955), pp. 50-58; Mayo (1956), pp. 58, 63; Belnap (1963), p. 83; Åqvist (1965), pp. 48, 70; Belnap (1969), pp. 124-7; Belnap and Steel (1976), pp. 13, 15, 48-50, 63, 70, 101-6; Dummett (1981), pp. 338, 357; Harrah (1984), pp. 715-16.
39 For instance: Carnap (1937), p. 296; Gasking (1946), p. 4; Belnap (1963), p. 16; Belnap (1969), pp. 125-7.
40 Frege (1919), p. 363/374; translation by Peter Geach.
41 Bell (1975), p. 206.
42 Contrast Mayo (1957), p. 168.
43 See, for instance, Waismann (1965), p. 411.
44 Contrast Prior (1971), p. 78.
45 Rundle (1979), p. 422.
46 Cf. Llewelyn (1964), p. 78; Nesbitt (1973), p. 256.
47 Cf. David and Stephanie Lewis (1975), pp. 49-50.
48 Hintikka (1974), p. 104; cf. (1976), p. 23.
49 Cohen (1929), p. 352.
50 Ross (1968), p. 77, note 1.
51 Cf. Welbourne (1986b), p. 230; Tichy (1978), pp. 276-7.

Chapter 8

Interrogative Form

Both questions and answers to them, it has been argued, are abstractions — from, respectively, people asking questions and their answering them. What pertains to situations where people ask questions or ask others questions, answer others' questions or answer their own questions, tell or ask — request — others to answer questions is irrelevant to the logical study, besides the significance for epistemology, of questions and their answers. Insistence on the distinction between asking a question and the question asked prevents considerations relevant only to the asking of a question — such as the motives, desires, purposes, reasons, needs and state of knowledge or ignorance of the questioner — getting entangled with the logical character of the question asked. But the distinction does not leave room for any notion of an 'unasked' question — if something different is meant from merely an unspoken question kept to oneself and neither uttered out loud, if one is asking oneself, nor put to anybody else. A question always asks something, even in abstraction, as it is when conceived logically, from people's acts of asking it. Therein lies the utilisation by questions of their interrogative form. The utilisation of interrogative form by interrogative clauses following *know* and kindred verbs, however, is in answering a question but without saying what it is that answers the question.

Misconceptions of Interrogative Form

Remarkably, interrogative form has hitherto gone unrecognised by philosophers and logicians, as also by linguistic theorists, though it is familiar to all who have the use of language. The interrogative has been misconceived as exhibiting either supposed 'semantic mood', a notion that assimilates the distinctiveness of interrogative form to differences marked by verbal mood — between indicative and imperative, besides conditional — which arguably fall entirely within propositional forms of thought; or '(illocutionary) force', part of the baggage of the speech-act fallacy, which confines the interrogative to an end served, instead of a form of thought expressed, by language.

Most philosophers taking notice of the field have subscribed without much thought to the speech-act fallacy. But even some of these — as also others, especially the logicians among them — have sometimes granted the distinction between the asking of a question and the question asked. Thus, Frege writes that 'the request to judge' (*die Aufforderung zu urteilen*) — whatever that may mean — can be distinguished from 'the special content of the question', which he identifies with 'the sense of the corresponding interrogative sentence'.[1] Cohen distinguishes 'the act of questioning' from 'the content of the thought'; and Lewis and Langford, following Cohen, the 'act of asking the question' from 'the logical import of a question'. They then identify a question with a propositional function.[2] And Bell, rightly stressing that 'in logic by *a question* we do not mean an act of asking a question but rather what is asked', distinguishes between what a question is 'from a logical point of view' and 'the act of questioning'. He concludes that 'questions are, logically, sets of propositions'.[3] So as was seen at the end of Chapter 3, even when the status of questions as abstractions is granted, their interrogative form is still at risk of being misconstrued propositionally. The distinctive, non-propositional character of interrogative form needs to be grasped if not just questions but also the interrogative clauses governed by *know* and kindred verbs are to be adequately accounted for.

Other accounts appear to identify what is supposedly requested when a question as such is being asked with the presupposition of the question, which is then taken to be matched by an answer.[4] While imperative-epistemic theorists identify it with knowledge *that* ... to be 'brought about' in an interrogator. Citing Lewis and Langford, besides Carnap, whose account, by contrast, invokes the notion of asking others to make assertions, Ryle speaks of interrogative sentences as being 'sentences-frames' 'when considered in abstraction from their practical role as petitions or commands'.[5] Thus, such accounts attempt to accommodate interrogative form within something propositional held to remain for logic to study after abstraction from the asking of the question.

Abstracting from people's acts of commanding, petitioning, requesting, inviting and so forth, however, yields a kind of action, not the object of an action; so that the practical has not yet been abstracted from. It would be odd to think of a receipt itself rather than the giving of a receipt as an abstraction from my request to be given a receipt. As was seen, imperativist accounts confuse a requirement — that is, a specification — to be met, whereby the interrogative form of a question determines the form of any conformable answer to it, with the notion that somebody is to perform some action — making an assertion being a favoured candidate, though imperative-epistemic theorists champion 'bringing about' knowledge *that* ... . While what is required or specified may incidentally be the performing of some action, requirements or specifications are not as such concerned with people acting in some way.

If an object of an action is scarcely to be thought of as an abstraction from somebody's acting, if a stone is not to be conceived as an abstraction from acts of kicking, can a question be conceived as an abstraction from an act of asking it? Ordinary talk of asking a question carries no risk of being misleading, and has never been challenged by philosophers. Yet it parallels talk of asserting or believing a proposition. The term *a question* is just as much, or as little, the object of the verb *ask* as the term *a proposition* is of the verb *believe*. But there is only a deceptive similarity between talk of asking and talk of answering a question. Whereas *a question* is grammatically the direct object of *answer*, what complements *ask* and is represented by the proxy term *a question*, which can also stand in apposition, is instead either an interrogative clause introduced by *if*, *what*, *where*, *why*, and so forth or a complete interrogative sentence in direct quotation. Thus, talk of a question that is asked is just an abbreviated way of referring to a variety of linguistic constructions. The question asked is not something over and above the *if*, *what*, *how*, *why*, and so forth asked — what can be expressed by either an interrogative clause or a complete interrogative sentence in direct speech.

The overscrupulous may protest that one can only believe or disbelieve persons, not propositions.[6] To submit to such a ruling would be tantamount to licensing a parallel ruling that one can only ask people, not questions. But not only is talk of asking questions perfectly clear besides convenient, the argument behind the prohibition is also incoherent. For although one can ask without thereby asking any person, one could not ask persons without thereby asking them some question. It might be equally argued, too, that although one can hold a belief without believing or disbelieving any person, believing or disbelieving persons is properly to be construed as believing or disbelieving persons *that* ... .[7]

Thus, just as the complement of verbs such as *assert* and *believe* is a propositional clause introduced by *that*, so the complement of *ask* is an interrogative clause. What is abstracted from people's acts of asking, then, is not the object of some action requested by them, such as making an assertion or 'bringing about' knowledge *that* ... ; instead it is thought having interrogative form expressed by interrogative clauses and sentences.

The distinction between interrogative and propositional forms of thought, marked by the contrast between interrogative clauses and those clauses introduced by *that*, shows that there can be no interrogative counterpart in an 'unasked question', as Bell supposes, to an unasserted proposition occurring as a component in an asserted compound proposition; still less are questions 'from a logical point of view' to be assimilated to sets of unasserted propositions.[8] The notion of the unasserted invokes a technical, logician's sense of *assert* more specific than the ordinary sense of publicly declare that something is or is not so. It gives rise to technical talk of asserting propositions, which, like talk of 'believing propositions', is open to objection that a proposition is not an appropriate object of assertion or belief. But there need be no suggestion that a proposition must be something over and above what is asserted or believed — namely, *that* ... . And one need not confuse simply asserting that the cat is dead with asserting that the proposition, *the cat is dead* is true. Here logicians' symbolism may confuse by not differentiating *p* from '*p*'; for *p* is to be taken as *that* ... .

An unasserted proposition is merely considered; what it says is so is merely supposed, as distinct from judged, to be so. Assertion in the logical sense need be no more the product of a linguistic act than supposal is; for both only require acts of thinking, even although propositions are essentially linguistic. The inclination to think the contrary is just the speech-act fallacy in logic.[9] When in the presence of others I make assertions in the ordinary sense, others can cite my authority for and hold me to them — even although they do not constitute statements in that my giving voice to them need not imply that I am in a position to know what I say to be so as distinct from an expression of opinion. But I am not accountable to others for the judgments and opinions I keep to myself.

The antecedent of an *if ... then* sentence or one of the propositional disjuncts of a disjunctive proposition are unasserted propositions — even although the whole proposition expressed by the *if ... then* sentence or the whole disjunctive proposition is asserted. There can be no interrogative counterpart to propositions in such contexts. Questions cannot be asserted; because, whether in the ordinary or in the logical sense, an assertion always says that something is or is not so, is an affirmation or a denial. But questions do not saying anything. Equally, neither can questions be unasserted; for the unasserted, in the logical sense, occurs only within an asserted whole, being part of a whole which asserts that something is or is not so. As Bell concedes, the unasserted has to be understood as what, but only when standing alone, might be asserted — what is assertable.[10] Thus, the unasserted, just as much as the asserted, is propositional, not interrogative, in form. Besides, questions, being incapable of being either true or false, cannot combine with each other into truth-functional wholes as propositions can. It does not follow, then, from the correct denial that questions assert anything that 'logically' they are unasserted. As questions do not say anything, they cannot occur as either asserted or unasserted.

Bell's further talk of considering a question 'as it were, in quotation'[11] might suggest some interrogative counterpart to an unasserted proposition. The difference between direct and reported speech, though, gives rise to the contrast between the asserted and the non-asserted, not the asserted and the unasserted. In reported speech statements are not asserted, nor questions asked, by the reporter; but they are allegedly asserted or asked by the speaker whose words are being reported. So the speaker's words are not being conceived as unasserted or unasked as such. Moreover, the analogy with quotation fails to bring out the difference between questions and propositions: that whereas questions ask something, propositions say that something is or is not so.

There is a limited parallelism, however. Just as one can merely think of, conceive or consider propositions without judging that what they say is or is not the case, so questions can sometimes be merely thought of, conceived or considered without actually being asked by the thinker. The question is, as it were, held at some distance, 'bracketed' or 'put within quotation marks'; it is mentioned but not used — that is, asked. One attends to it, as Gandhi says.[12] Propositions asserted or questions asked by others can be considered by a thinker — as well as those asserted or asked by pretence in works of fiction and those featuring as examples in logic textbooks, which are not actually asserted or asked by anybody at all. In general, to understand an interrogative sentence or clause is to be able to consider its meaning without necessarily oneself asking the question it expresses or alludes to. This ability, indeed, is exercised when the sense of an interrogative clause following verbs like *know* is grasped; for although a question is alluded to, it is not asked but instead answered interrogatively.

Yet the parallelism holds only so far. For *not asked* is not the same as *unasked.* While a question can be thought of as not asked but rather as answered, as when alluded to by an interrogative clause following verbs like *know*, it cannot be thought of as unasked in a way that would make it a counterpart to a proposition occurring unasserted.

Ryle confesses that for a long time he assumed 'that entertaining a proposition is a more elementary or naïve performance than affirming that something is the case'. He had previously believed, in 1930, that 'there is a sort of "thinking that" which is completely neutral and attitudeless, and that this must be an ingredient in all varieties of "thinking that"'. He later came to think that 'affirming that something is the case' is not equivalent to 'entertaining a proposition' plus some element of belief or judgment. Rather, supposal is curbing the inclination to judge that something is the case; it is considering the proposition while purposefully refraining from judging and asserting it — as Ryle says, a higher-order, more sophisticated operation.[13]

A parallel account fits questions. When a question is made the subject of logical study it is considered in a detached fashion without actually being asked by the thinker; but it is always conceived, in so far as it is intelligible and coherent, as something that might be asked by somebody or other — never as unasked as such. For questions occur in thought initially only as asked and the inclination to ask them has to be curbed if the question is to be simply considered. By contrast, propositions can occur in thought as mere suppositions or possibilities; that is, one can think hypothetically. Such suppositions or possibilities can come up for subsequent judgment, lending plausibility rather to Ryle's previous view. Since a supposition or hypothesis is what is capable of being either true or false, something a question can never be, hypothetical thoughts can only be propositional in form. Suppositions still say something, about possibilities, even if they do not assert that something actually is or is not so; whereas questions rather ask something.

It might be argued, however, that questions could be conceived in a way parallel to Ryle's previous view of 'entertaining a proposition' — namely, as initially unasked. Now, questions are ordinarily said to arise in some situation, to be prompted or raised by some factor, to occur to one in thought. Such words convey receptivity on the part of the thinker or speaker. But while a question often just occurs to one in thought, as a supposition or possibility may also, a question never occurs initially as simply conceived or entertained as a supposition or possibility may. Merely to consider a question without asking it is to engage in higher-order, reflective thought about it, which is to respond actively to it: to distance oneself from the question. There is a tendency to take the questions occurring in thought at face value, without refraining from also asking them in thought; and without pondering their import and examining their presuppositions. Thus, there is a potential for people not to realise the silliness or inappropriateness of some of the questions initially occurring to them.

The traditional philosophical view that a question can be identified with a supposition or unasserted proposition because both are not asserted rests, it can now be seen, on an equivocation between *not asserted* and *unasserted*. But such a view can also be seen to be mistaken by noting that while the occurrence in thought of suppositions or possibilities is quite separate from one's subsequently judging them to be true or false, questions occurring to one in thought are at the same time conceived as asked in thought so that one has deliberately to detach oneself from them if one's object is not to ask them but merely to consider them.

The attempt to conceive a question as occurring unasked presupposes that the question could be thought of, or expressed in language, by somebody without anybody — even a person whose question is quoted — asking anything. In short, it would be an attempt to strip the interrogative character from a question by conceiving it as not thereby enabling people to ask something by means of its interrogative character. Questions themselves can be said to ask things, of course, only because people can ask questions. Conceiving the question itself as asking something reflects the intimate connection between thinking of a question, or expressing it in words, and asking the question — a connection only to be broken by suspending one's asking of it, by 'bracketing' the question. So to suppose that a question could occur unasked would be to conceive it as not enabling people to ask something by means of it, and hence as not itself asking anything — that is, to conceive it as deprived of its interrogative form.

Bell's view that what he supposes are questions occurring 'unasked' — in interrogative clauses following verbs like *know* or in abstraction from acts of questioning others — are really sets of unasserted propositions derives from a position adumbrated by Frege; only Bell is rather more explicit, yet not forthright enough. When such accounts are distilled they amount to an old-fashioned view of questions as hypotheses or suppositions; that is, unasserted propositions. In the words of Hiz, previously quoted, a question does not 'express thought, because it is an expression of suspended thought, of lack of judgement'.[14] The assimilation of questions to unasserted propositions is only implicit in accounts indebted to Frege, probably owing partly to some awareness of the difficulties such a position encounters plus delusive vanity that a logically more rigorous line is being taken than traditional philosophers were capable of.

Word Questions

If his stray remarks could be regarded as amounting to an account, Frege is unable to give a unified account of questions — something, it will be seen in the next chapter, that casts doubt on the adequacy of his approach. While in his earlier survey of dependent clauses he had not explicitly distinguished between types of indirect question, he subsequently declines to consider word questions, because in them 'we utter an incomplete sentence, which is meant to be given a true sense just by means of the completion for which we are asking'.[15]

Frege's expositor, Dummett appears to be not quite faithful to the master when he remarks 'complete utterances will include, for example, what Frege calls "word-questions" … whose sense neither Frege nor anyone else would take as being a thought'.[16] The German *Satz* blurs the distinction between a proposition and a sentence, thus making it difficult to say that in expressing a question an interrogative sentence expresses something non-propositional. Perhaps Frege meant by his seemingly unequivocal remark that 'we utter an incomplete sentence', not that the interrogative sentence itself expressing a word question is incomplete, but that what the interrogative sentence expresses — namely, the word question — contains as one of its elements an incomplete proposition, the other element being a request. And so it would become possible to give Frege the credit that Dummett denies him and everybody else, of recognising that word questions express thoughts — though on this interpretation they would be incomplete thoughts. In connection with yes-no questions Frege speaks of 'the thought that was already completely contained in the interrogative sentence', which might imply a contrast with incomplete thoughts. But as he had a moment before put aside sentences expressing commands, wishes and pleas as not having senses that are thoughts, besides 'exclamations in which one vents one's feelings, groans, sighs, laughs',[17] Dummett may well be right at least in holding that Frege denied that the senses of word questions are thoughts at all.

In any case, the notion of an incomplete thought is suspect; because the distinction between thinking a thought and merely thinking of — that is, having a concept of — something turns on the completeness given to a thought in thinking it. By contrast, a fragmentary sentence is what is capable of being completed so as to give expression to a proposition or question, or something else such as an exclamation. Whether he is right about Frege, Dummett is certainly right that the interrogative sentences expressing word questions are complete; for they can be contrasted with fragmentary sentences: *Who is at the door?* does not contain a gap as *Who is —— ?* does.

Frege may be taken as holding that a complete interrogative sentence expressing a word question expresses an incomplete proposition together with a request to complete the proposition so as to yield a thought. This interpretation accords with some accounts offered immediately afterwards. Hiz relates: 'In 1928 Ajdukiewicz described questions as consisting of a sentential matrix (a sentence with one or more of its components replaced by variables) preceded by an interrogative operator.'[18] The general pattern of analysis here is extended beyond word questions; but it also introduces in place of Frege's talk of requesting — what Ryle takes to be the 'practical associations' of questions[19] — the notion of an interrogative operator, which is more explicit than what Ajdukiewicz himself says about 'interrogative particles' and 'question marks'.[20] But not to be preferred; since it signals the general doctrine, which has now become standard: that in a question an operation is performed on something with propositional content; that there is therefore something, the propositional content, shared in common by what has propositional and interrogative form; and that in thus containing a propositional element, the interrogative is explicable by the propositional.

Carnap also talks of 'a question-operator'; but as he talks of asking 'someone to make an assertion' and applies the analysis only to word questions, his account is closer to Frege's.[21] To the extent that Frege and Carnap attempt to capture interrogative form within the notion of requesting, they acknowledge, like Ajdukiewicz, some difference between a word question and an incomplete proposition. Not so Cohen, whom Lewis and Langford follow. Like Ajdukiewicz, they give the same uniform analysis to all questions; only they identify them with propositional functions, thus failing to give any recognition to interrogative form; though they rightly reject the usual stuff said about requesting. Given that a propositional function is just a technical name for a proposition with a gap or gaps to be filled by one or more of its terms, such a doctrine comes down to the view initially suggested by Frege's talk of uttering incomplete sentences, that interrogative sentences (or rather for Frege, those expressing word questions) are incomplete.

There is nothing incomplete about a word question, for the thought taking interrogative form it formulates is not incomplete; and to equate its interrogative form with an incomplete proposition is to mistake the interrogative for the propositional. Neither is a conformable answer to a word question, which supposedly completes the incomplete proposition, incomplete; though a dying man in striving to give his answer may not survive long enough to utter more than one syllable of it. What gives rise, then, to the idea of incompleteness in such analyses? Underlying them is the assumption that answers to questions are essentially propositions. It has been seen that a conformable answer to a word question is supplied by a term whose form is determined by the question it is in answer to. The term has to be understood in the context of the question, and within that context can be expanded into a proposition that contains the term. If the term is then deleted from the proposition, what remains is an incomplete proposition.[22] Now, what is the justification for identifying such a remainder with the question or part of its content? Only, it would seem, because, since any question is distinct from any answer to it, the question does not contain the term supplying an answer to it. But though true, it does not follow that the question, or part of its content, is to be identified with the incomplete proposition resulting from deleting the term supplying a conformable answer to it contained in the proposition the term can be expanded into in the light of the question.

The convolutions required to state the conclusion of the analysis reflect the circuitous route its adherents have taken. First, they work back in the usual fashion from a given answer, a term, to the word question it is in answer to, so as to secure an understanding of what that answer is, or rather, says. They thus expand the term in the light of the question into a proposition, thereby yielding the assertion a respondent would be held to in giving a conformable answer to the question by the term. Next, they delete the answer at hand, the term, from the proposition resulting from the expansion of the term in the light of the question, thereby obtaining an incomplete proposition. Finally, they identify this incomplete proposition with the question, or part of its content; even although both the incomplete proposition, and the complete proposition it is obtained from through deletion of the term supplying the answer at hand, are arrived at only by understanding the term in the light of the question.

In short, the analysis is circular. Only the assumption that all thought is exclusively propositional could induce its adherents to proceed round this circle rather than take the usual direct route from a term at hand to the word question it is in answer to and back again from the question to the term at hand, thereby bypassing the assertion respondents are held to. For when a conformable answer is subtracted from the pair *question* and *answer*, what is left is not something propositional in form that is incomplete but instead something interrogative in form that is complete: namely, the question. Only on the assumption that word questions contain within themselves some propositional element is there room for any idea of incompleteness; but since there is no incompleteness about either word questions or their conformable answers, the inference must be that word questions do not contain any propositional element within themselves but instead have a distinctive interrogative and non-propositional form.

It might be pointed out that sometimes people do ask others word questions by uttering incomplete sentences. Thus an official filling in a form for somebody might ask the person the questions on the form by uttering the words, say, *And your occupation is ... ?* the trailing off being an indication that the addressee should complete the sentence thereby giving the answer to the implied question. But all that this manner of putting a question to another shows is that questions put to others are not always expressed by interrogative sentences but can sometimes be expressed by incomplete declarative sentences. In being used to put a question to another the words are complete. The trailing off itself signifies, paradoxically, the completeness of the question; that is, the point where the interrogator has stopped speaking marks the end of the question. The passage from interrogator leaving off and respondent taking over marks the transition from question to answer. To take another instance, declarative sentences and interrogative sentences expressing yes-no questions always differ in English syntactically as well as in intonation, though in other languages the interrogative sentence expressing a yes-no question can sometimes in the spoken language differ from a counterpart declarative sentence only in intonation; yet even in English occasionally a declarative sentence given interrogative intonation may be used to put a yes-no question to others, but only when speakers are seeking confirmation from them for what is already gathered. In neither case do these singular ways of putting word or yes-no questions to others show that the question so expressed is identifiable with what is propositional in form; for here the function the utterance serves overrides its anomalous syntax. Note that such idiomatic uses are not ways of asking questions generally but only of putting a question to another.

If truth will out, so might interrogative form, which is incapable of giving expression to what is true. The talk of incompleteness, it will emerge, signals a failed attempt to capture the logical peculiarities of interrogative form within the propositional. Likewise, question marks signifying supposed interrogative operators front the *ad hoc* symbolism logicians devise, engagingly described by Belnap and Steel as 'henscratches'; who are also responsible for the coinage 'queriables', 'queried variables ... which are "erotetically bound", neither bound to an ordinary assertoric quantifier, nor free, but bound to the interrogative itself'.[23] The suggestion here that interrogative words are to be distinguished from 'ordinary assertoric quantifiers' has to be counterbalanced against the talk of bound and free variables.

The logician's notion of a quantifier invokes the interrogative concept of quantity. Interrogative concepts, it was seen, have propositional counterparts exercised in stating what can be construed, according to the Aristotelian approach, as an answer to a question. Notwithstanding the name, quantification serves principally as an analysis of predication, which pertains exclusively to the propositional and cannot occur in questions. To predicate something of a subject is to say that the something is true of it. But since a question cannot say anything at all but only asks something about its subject, there can be no predication in a question. In other words, since to say that something is true of a thing is to say that the thing is ... is so, something which is either true or false, and since a question cannot be either true or false, a question cannot say that anything is true of a thing, cannot predicate anything of it. But to classify a variable as bound or free is to make it the subject of a predication: actual if bound, potential if free.

A predicate is a term; but a term of a proposition. The same term may occur in a question as in a proposition; but it cannot be assumed that it has the same function regardless of its context. The words *at the door* predicate something of a subject in the proposition *John is at the door* but are used only in asking something in the question *Who is at the door?* They do not, together with the other words in the sentence they occur in, exhaust the meaning of the sentence; for the logical form of the sentence, declarative or interrogative, contributes to the meaning of the sentence over and above the meaning of the individual words that go to make up the sentence.

'Ordinary assertoric quantifiers' can be read as ordinary indefinite pronouns — that is, non-interrogative indefinite pronouns. But again, there is a difference in function between interrogative words, such as *who*, *what*, *where*, *how* and their propositional counterparts, *somebody*, *something*, *somewhere*, *somehow*. The two types of words are equally indefinite; but interrogative form will elude philosophers' accounts of word questions if the distinction between them is not respected. The distinction as such is marked, not by the words themselves; for in some languages the same word may serve both functions — or differ only in the intonation used, as in Greek.[24] The interrogative indefinites occur only in what (a clause or whole sentence) exhibits interrogative form. *The cat is somewhere* is propositional in form, by contrast with *Where is the cat?* The two are related, since the indefinite proposition is the presupposition of the word question; but if a question were the same as its presupposition, there would be no job for the question and hence none for the answer to it to do — that is, the answer would not, as it is meant to, resolve anything; would not remove the indefiniteness presupposed in the question.

Imperative-epistemic theorists, indeed, suppose that the questioner knows that the cat is somewhere but not where the cat is. Yet recognition of the distinction between knowing where the cat is and merely knowing that the cat is somewhere does not amount in their case to a recognition of interrogative form as exhibited in interrogative characterisations of knowledge; for they then attempt to reduce knowing where the cat is to knowing, with respect to some place, that the cat is at that place.[25] The opaqueness of interrogative characterisations of knowledge is thus lost besides the distinction between interrogative and propositional form. The truth-conditions of the two different attributions of knowledge are the same, but the manner of conception of the knowledge is not; for the knowledge that, with respect to some place, the cat is at it is only presupposed by the proposition *You know where the cat is*, not part of what that proposition itself says.

Although quantifiers serve in the logical analysis of sentences containing such words as *all*, *each*, *every*, *no*, *some* and *a*, their primary function is to bind free variables; something manifested in logicians' symbolism, the brackets enclosing the quantifier. These brackets serve to connect the quantifier to the expressions that follow — unlike any brackets enclosing these expressions, which merely determine scope. Quantification can therefore be explained informally as a way of casting predications into the form of a relative clause whose antecedent is indefinite. *The cat is black* is construed as 'There is something that is both a cat and is black.'

Relative clauses are at the interface between the propositional and the interrogative. The catalogue by the Fowlers of differences in usage between the *which* and the *that* versions of the relative pronoun was not quite a *which* hunt conducted by the devotees of *that*. The fundamental difference can be summarised as the contrast between an implicit looking back to a notional question which can be regarded as having been answered — a relative which, in Bolinger's words, 'can be seen as basically interrogative' — and an implicit looking forward to that which is to be said in the clause that follows.[26] The affinity of some relative to interrogative pronouns does not, nevertheless, make relative clauses, and thus the quantification analysis of predication that utilises them, any less propositional in form. Again, what is decisive is not any particular word but rather the logical form of the clause or whole sentence it occurs in.

The quantification analysis of word questions, therefore, is incapable of doing justice to their interrogative form. To suppose that interrogative words (*who*, *what*, *where*) serve the same function as their propositional counterparts (*somebody*, *something*, *somewhere*) because they share the same indefiniteness is simply to ignore the interrogative form of the clause or whole sentence these interrogative words occur in, a logical form which cannot then be explained away by any supposed requesting. Nor are interrogative words interrogative counterparts to quantifiers;[27] for predication is essential to quantification but impossible in either direct word questions or interrogative clauses alluding to word questions. Saying contrasts with, and has no parallel in, asking or alluding to.

Frege on Yes-No Questions

Frege confines himself to what he calls *Satzfragen* — his unfortunate term for yes-no questions — when he speaks without qualification of a question and of an interrogative sentence (*Fragesatz*).[28] His restricted usage will be followed during the exposition of his view of yes-no questions. His term *Satzfrage* reflects his doctrine that a yes-no question contains a complete proposition, grasped in an act of thinking, but as yet not judged to be true and therefore not asserted. Once again, the too general term *Satz* causes difficulty. In German as also in English, unlike in many other languages, the interrogative sentence standardly used to express a yes-no question quite clearly does not 'contain' a declarative sentence, since the two are explicitly marked off from each other by word order. Nevertheless, Frege proclaims: -

> An interrogative sentence and an assertoric one contain the same thought; but the assertoric sentence contains something else as well, namely, assertion. The interrogative sentence contains something more too, namely a request. Therefore two things must be distinguished in an assertoric sentence: the content, which it has in common with the corresponding propositional question; and assertion.

Hence a yes-no question also contains a request 'that we should either acknowledge the truth of a thought, or reject it as false'. So there are two elements to the question: a request 'to judge' — *tout court* as Frege has it but to judge *whether*, it must be; and 'the special content of the question, ... or the sense of the corresponding interrogative sentence'. The answer to a question, he says, 'is an assertion based upon a judgement; this is so equally whether the answer is affirmative or negative'.[29]

Frege evidently takes *Yes* and *No* to be what are sometimes described by linguists as 'coded' answers for propositions: 'The answer "yes" means the same as an assertoric sentence, for in saying "yes" the speaker presents as true the thought that was already completely contained in the interrogative sentence.'[30]

Dummett, it will be recalled, supposes that it is 'more logical' to answer the negative question *Have you no bananas?* with *Yes, we have no bananas*, and that the joke in the song turns on only 'a quirk of Indo-European languages'; since one 'would expect that' the answer would be '"Yes" if the thought expressed by the corresponding assertoric sentence were true, "No" if it were false'. Dummett is right at least about usage being involved: if unnamed 'West African languages' have a different usage, then these languages (also other non-Indo-European languages such as Japanese) have not exactly equivalent terms for *Yes* and *No*.[31] But why should one expect *Yes* to go with a true, *No* with a false, assertion? Only because Dummett has additionally assumed, with Frege, that a yes-no question has within it the same thought as the 'corresponding' assertoric sentence, so that when the question is positive, *Yes* signals acknowledgment that the thought is true, *No* rejection of it as false; and so when the conducive negative version of the question is employed, *Yes* must signal acknowledgment that the negative thought is true. But while usage in other languages may not tell against Frege's theory, the incongruity of *Yes* with denial does: in answering a yes-no question one must be doing more than simply acknowledging or rejecting a thought already presented by the question, such as reaching a decision as to the answer. Moreover, it was seen that the standard way in English to seek mere acknowledgment from another of a judgment is to give interrogative intonation to a declarative sentence, which being confined to the putting of questions to others, is not the standard way of asking a yes-no question generally.

The direction of Frege's argument is not at first clear: he appears to be labouring the obvious, that an interrogative sentence has a sense, which is a thought. But as he himself points out: 'It is a matter of what we take the word "thought" to mean;' and on his understanding of what a thought is, it is by no means obvious that an interrogative sentence contains a thought.[32] He is not committed to holding that only what is capable of being either true or false has a sense — is intelligible, as it might be more generally said. He allows that an imperative sentence (*Befehlsatz*) has a sense; but its sense does not expresses a thought, for 'this sense is not such that the question of truth could arise for it'.[33] Now, an interrogative sentence can be intelligible even although the question it expresses is incapable of being either true or false; and further reflection on questions brings recognition that thoughts need not be confined to what is capable of being either true or false. Frege instead insists that an interrogative sentence contains a sense which is a thought, and 'a thought is something which must be either true or false, *tertium non datur*',[34] while apparently recognising that no question can be true: 'Truth cannot go along with the sense of an interrogative sentence; that would contradict the very nature of a question.'[35] It seems, then, that either an interrogative sentence cannot after all contain a thought; or else that a question must after all be capable of being true.

There is a way out of the dilemma Frege appears to be trapped in. His remarks are within the context of a specific argument that a thought need not be true to have a sense, that a false thought still has a sense. Such an argument suggests a more general argument: that something — a question, for instance — need not be capable of being either true or false to be intelligible; that *true*, *false* or *nonsense* is a bogus trichotomy. Frege is not concerned with any such conclusion. He urges instead that the content of an interrogative sentence, its sense, cannot always be identified with a true thought; that the 'true' answer to a question may be negative. But the conclusion he draws is not that the sense of an interrogative sentence is incapable of being either true or false; on the contrary, his conclusion is that the sense of an interrogative sentence is to be either true or false, which it is being left unresolved until the question is given a 'true' answer. Thus he writes: 'in an interrogative sentence neither the truth nor the falsity of the sense may be asserted'.[36]

The difference for Frege between an interrogative sentence and the 'corresponding' assertoric sentence — what he takes to constitute an answer to the question — turns on the difference between grasping the thought contained in the interrogative sentence without judging whether it is true or false, and, by means of an assertoric sentence, either acknowledging the truth of the thought or rejecting it as false: 'The very nature of a question demands a separation between the acts of grasping a sense and of judging.' He adds that 'since the sense of an interrogative sentence is always inherent in the assertoric sentence that gives an answer to a question, this separation must be carried out for assertoric sentences too'.[37]

The puzzle here is that if the 'separation' between grasping the sense and judging whether it is true or false is to be made for both interrogative and assertoric sentences, how then do they differ? One might argue instead that since there is an evident difference between the two types of sentence, Frege's premise that 'the sense of an interrogative sentence is always inherent in the assertoric sentence that gives an answer to a question' must be denied; that the sense of an interrogative sentence cannot be contained as part of the sense of an assertoric sentence but must be distinctively interrogative.

His talk of 'separation' is equivocal. There is indeed a distinction between grasping the sense of an assertoric sentence and judging the proposition it expresses to be true, and thus asserting the proposition. But the general interrogative counterpart to such a distinction is between grasping the sense of an interrogative sentence and asking the question it expresses. There is scope for judging with an assertoric but none with an interrogative sentence. For seeing that what an interrogative sentence expresses is incapable of being either true or false, it cannot be judged to be true or false. Only in this sense is it right to say that the essence of a question requires a divorce from judgment. Frege might have said that whereas the sense of an assertoric sentence may be not only grasped but also judged to be true, with an interrogative sentence there is only a sense to be grasped. Yet had he done so the doctrine that the sense of an interrogative sentence was capable of judgment would still be implied.

It becomes impossible on this doctrine to mark the distinction between a yes-no question and a proposition. Although Frege is entirely right to argue that it must be possible to grasp the sense of an interrogative sentence expressing a yes-no question without judging whether an affirmative or a negative answer to the question is correct,[38] it is due to the opaqueness of interrogative form; not because the question somehow contains its conformable answers construed as propositions waiting to be asserted. The upshot is that the content of an interrogative sentence expressing a yes-no question is a sense consisting of a thought grasped as being either true or false without being judged to be either; in short, the thought expressed by the disjunction of a proposition and its contradictory. But while neither disjunct is asserted in the disjunction *Either it is raining or it is not raining* the whole disjunction, in standing alone, is asserted. So is a yes-no question to be identified with an asserted disjunction? That would equate a yes-no question with its presupposition; and presumably Frege himself would deny that a question contains any assertion.[39]

Whatever his view, there is further confusion in Frege's notion of assertion, since it is opposed to an ambiguous notion of grasping a sense, of both an unasserted proposition and a yes-no question, brought to light by his mention of non-serious uses of language, as in playacting. The distinction between serious and non-serious utterances can be seen not to coincide with the distinction between the assertoric and the non-assertoric by noting that an actor may utter not just, as Frege notes, assertoric sentences but also non-assertoric ones: in a stage performance possibilities can be 'conceived' and questions 'asked'; Since both are non-serious, the difference between them must lie in something other than the absence of serious assertion.[40]

Dummett writes that Frege 'thinks that a sentential interrogative expresses the same thought as the corresponding assertoric sentence, and differs from it only in the force attached to it'. The wording of second point is faithful in letter to Frege's doctrine, just as the first point is; but Dummett means that the same thought may have different forces attached to it, something that the references he cites do not bear out.[41] Dummett might have cited another passage, which has been mistranslated. The translation, first published in 1963, runs: 'uttered with neither assertoric nor interrogative force'. But Frege says nothing about a supposed 'interrogative force'; his words are: *ohne behauptende Kraft und nicht als Frage ausgesprochen*.[42] There is no reason to suppose that Frege thought that there was any other sort of force than assertoric force so that what lacked assertoric might have instead some other sort of force. His metaphor, redolent of his dour scientism, would surely have been elaborated had he imagined there were other, potentially countervailing, forces.

Austin's doctrine of 'illocutionary forces', whose foremost illustration is the asking of a question, opposes force to 'meaning in the sense in which meaning is equivalent to sense and reference'. It is expressly presented as a refinement to the general notion of meaning modelled on the precedent of Frege's distinction between 'sense and reference'.[43] But Austin's subject is language, or rather speech, not logic; and so his doctrine of illocutionary forces concerns speech-acts. Frege, by contrast with his expositor, Dummett, commendably betrays no inclination towards the speech-act fallacy in logic. Instead, he employs the notion of the form of an assertoric sentence, present even when assertoric force is lacking, as in actors' lines.[44]

The notion of form here invites a contrast with a different sort of form to that of an assertoric sentence: namely, that of an interrogative sentence. Regrettably, Frege does not take up the notion of a distinctive interrogative form which might contribute to the difference in sense an interrogative sentence expressing a yes-no question has to that of the 'corresponding' assertoric sentence — that is, what Frege takes to be a conformable answer to the question. On the contrary, the implication of what he says is that the interrogative sentence has the form of an assertoric sentence, only it lacks assertoric force. For he writes: 'Assertoric force can most easily be eliminated by changing the whole into a question; for one can express the same thought in a question as in an assertoric sentence, only without asserting it.'[45] Again, there is no suggestion here that another sort of force, interrogative force, takes over once assertoric force is eliminated.

Noteworthy in Frege's remarks are stock comparisons of traditional accounts of questions. Besides playacting, the use of language in poetry gets a mention. Then the divorce in a question between grasping its sense and judging whether it is true or false leads to a discussion of the status of the antecedents of *if ... then* sentences. Finally, grasping a sense, which is said to be done when a yes-no question is framed, is assigned a part in scientific investigation.[46] Similar points are made by the early Collingwood, who, by contrast with the late nineteenth-century consensus he was following on the subject, attempted to work out in more detail the doctrine that asking questions is a case of supposal.[47]

Sham assertion is not assertion; yet sham assertion is not simply the absence of assertion.[48] In a roughly similar way, asking questions does not involve assertion; yet when a question is asked assertion is not simply absent. In short, the non-asserted must not be confused with the unasserted, which, as was seen, is rather what is assertable but not actually asserted. It is beyond dispute that to ask a question is not to assert anything; but it does not follow that there must be something unasserted in a yes-no question — something that might be asserted, say, when an answer is given to the question so that the question contains its conformable answers unasserted within itself.

Frege's view gains some plausibility from a practice, one might almost say abuse, that speakers sometimes adopt to evade responsibility for what they say: by asking a yes-no question or an alternative question one can insinuate what answer one would give to the question without actually stating what that answer is, and so without expressly committing oneself to asserting anything. The final sentence of a book review might have originally run: 'This is the author's worse book to date.' The editor might coax the reviewer to amend it to 'Could this be the author's worse book to date?' — not for fear of any libel action but for the reason that by merely asking a question the point is made more tellingly; for doubt might be suggested, not about the original assertion, but whether previous books of the author might not be better contenders for the appellation. Wording an expression of opinion as a yes-no or an alternative question so as to engender an air of doubt and contention, or simply to shock, is a device of television journalists who prize a reputation for cynicism; but owing to overuse it no longer has its intended effect. The longer established custom of putting across an opinion by asking a yes-no or an alternative question whose answer is suggested by the phrasing of the question flourishes in authoritarian climates, whether the author has the arrogant tones afforded by power or the more diffident voice of dissent. Berkeley uses such a device in *The Querist* to vent his opinion of the effect of the English on the Irish economy, at one point asking, ironically as if there could be any doubt, 'Whether he who only asks asserts?' adding, 'and whether any man can fairly confute the querist?'.[49] The expression *rhetorical question*, however, is best reserved for when the opinion being insinuated is not presumed to be contentious.

That *if* (as also *si* in French) is used both to specify conditions and report yes-no and alternative questions testifies to some vague analogy felt to hold between the two uses. The antecedent of an *if ... then* sentence, being unasserted, could be seen as parallel to a question, which being only asked cannot be asserted; the consequent in turn could be seen as a parallel to an answer given to the question. But the logical differences are more important than any neatness of the analogy. Both antecedent and consequent are contained within the same speaker's utterance, whereas question and answer may, though need not, be distributed between two different speakers. A speaker is committed to asserting what the whole *if ... then* sentence expresses; whereas a questioner as such is committed to only what the question asked presupposes. Moreover, while both antecedent and consequent and question and answer are related to one another, the relationship is different: the consequent need have no logical connection with the antecedent — unless it happens to be a logical truth; but an answer to be a conformable answer to the question must be of the appropriate form. A dramatic way of representing antecedent and consequent of an *if ... then* sentence as discrete utterances turns the sentence more into a piece of dialogue, where a reply is made rather than where conformable answers are given to a question.[50]

The answer to a yes-no or an alternative question can be alluded to by an antecedent and followed by the consequent, which can even be a further question. Thus, *If so*, *if not*, *if the red one*, *then* ... (*?*). Were there really no difference between supposal and asking a question, between the antecedent of an *if ... then* sentence and a simple question, hypothetical questions would come out as two antecedents mysteriously linked with no consequent to resolve them. In short, there are different *ifs*, which was the point Austin was making when he spoke of the non-conditional *if* in *I can if I choose* having the function of '*the raising of the question* whether I choose to'; not, as Belnap reads Austin, that the clause 'expresses a question'.[51]

The expression *the question* deserves notice. Sometimes, as in the Austin passage, it refers to any question that is being raised, thus is akin to *issue*. But it has a more restricted use, where 'the question' has no correlative in 'the answer', as in the English phrase *begging the question* used as a translation of *petitio principii.* The use of the definite article signals that it is unnecessary to specify what or which question. The question in question, as one might put it, is the yes-no question of the truth or falsity of a proposition (or principle) being debated. Whately defines the term *Question* as 'That which is to be established as a Conclusion, stated in an interrogative form.' While his definition suffices for syllogistic logic, 'the question' can concern the truth or falsity of any proposition under consideration; so the question of the truth or falsity of the premises of a deductive argument is only one type of case where one may speak of 'the question'.[52] *The issue* is not an equivalent term since issues are sometimes to be stated by word questions, such as the Eastern Question of nineteenth-century Europe. In the restricted sense 'the question' is always statable as a yes-no question about the truth or falsity of some proposition.

When, as Hume says, 'we dissent from' a proposition another advances, 'we conceive both sides of the question'. To understand what a proposition says is to conceive both what it would be for it to be true and what it would be for it to be false. In logical space 'the question' is a Möbius strip. 'The question', then, is not simply a question *whether* or — Hume lists the variant as a Scotticism — *if*.[53] For 'the question' always concerns truth or falsity. It would be hypercritical to object that Hamlet ought rather to have declared 'That is the decision (to be taken);' for his question did not concern the truth or falsity of a proposition. The uneducated use by journalists of the idiom *begging the question* when they mean giving rise to a question not only mistakes the sense of *beg* but also confuses the restricted with the unrestricted sense of the term *the question.*

This special sense of the term *the question* takes the paradoxical edge off Frege's view that since the question of truth arises for a thought an interrogative sentence expressing a yes-no question contains the same thought as the 'corresponding' assertoric sentence. For every proposition, seeing that it is either true or false with no third possibility, can give rise to — rather than contains — the question of its truth or falsity. Grasping the sense of a proposition requires conceiving both sides of 'the question' in the special sense: conceiving, namely, that the proposition might be true, and that it might be false. But conceiving the possible truth or falsity of a proposition is not the same as asking — or even considering — whether it is true or false. For the question whether a proposition is actually true or false presupposes that it is possible for the proposition to be true; but it can be further asked whether this presupposition is true, since what one conceives to be possible may not in reality be possible — which was one of Reid's objections to one of Hume's main methods of arguing.[54]

A question is not to be identified with the mere conception of a possibility; rather, a question presupposes that what is conceived is possible. It might not in reality be possible, and so the conception can give rise to the new question whether what is conceived is in reality possible. Investigators can ask not only if some possibility actually obtains, as investigators in natural history or history might; but also if something is a possibility, the finding of the answer to such a question being more in keeping with the advances in science Frege speaks of. When investigators ask the sort of question Frege cites, 'whether bovine tuberculosis is communicable to men', they seek to determine or rule out a possibility; they are not merely conceiving that it is a possibility, for that would take for granted what they aim to find out.[55]

The error in Frege's view can now be more precisely diagnosed. Presuming that conformable answers to yes-no questions are propositions, he argues that these propositions are contained in yes-no questions, thus assimilating yes-no questions as such with questions about the truth of a proposition.[56] Wittgenstein likens Frege's doctrine 'that every assertion contains an assumption, which is the thing asserted' to what one 'might (using the language of chemistry) call ... a propositional-radical'.[57] According to this doctrine one always asserts that a proposition is true whenever one asserts *that* ... ; namely, the proposition formulated by *that* ... . But just as there is a difference between *The cat is dead* and *It is true that the cat is dead*, so asking if B.S.E. can cross species boundaries is different from asking if it is true that B.S.E. can cross species boundaries. The first question concerns a condition, a disease; the second a proposition being debated. The subjects of yes-no questions usually constitute states of affairs, events, actions, and the like; only occasionally propositions.

Hare's analysis of imperative sentences as containing an element shared with their counterpart indicative sentences, 'the *phrastic*', provides a corrective contrast.[58] A phrastic does not express a proposition but instead alludes to some state of affairs, event or, indeed, action — the carrying out of the enjoined action. Hare's analysis is thus more appropriate than patently circular analyses along the lines of a command disguised as 'an operator' such as *See to it*, *Make it true*, *Bring about that* ... .[59]

Frege's treatment of yes-no questions furnishes a model for more general views that all questions have some propositional content. Questions are analysed as consisting in an operator prefixed to this propositional content. Yes-no questions are taken simply as asking *Is it the case that ... ?* with a parallel analysis given for word questions.[60] Quite apart from the feeling that no analysis has actually been provided because the *analysans* is itself a question, such accounts mistake states of affairs for propositions.

As yes-no and alternative questions are non-propositional in form, they cannot contain any propositions. Instead, they concern states of affairs. They are about something's being the case, not saying that something is the case. Even questions about the truth or falsity of propositions concern the state of affairs of its being true or its being false *that* ... . Admittedly, statements that states of affairs do or do not obtain contain propositions; yet the states of affairs these propositions are about cannot themselves constitute propositions, at most only the states of affairs of the truth or falsity of propositions. When these states of affairs are made the subject of a yes-no or an alternative question there is even less reason for supposing they constitute propositions; for then nothing is said about what does or does not obtain, there is only something asked.

The Principle of Interrogative Opaqueness

Accounts assimilating asking questions as such to requests must have it that what is requested is some action relating to something propositional, which is supposed to constitute what the question is 'logically'. What is asked when a question is asked, of course, is a question — or more precisely, the thought taking interrogative form expressible by the particular interrogative clause governed by the verb *ask*. But in attempting to expound such accounts — in trying to present clearly what in fact is a tissue of confusion — the pretence has to be gone along with that what is asked when a question is asked is somehow something other than a question. Now, those accounts of what is asked when a question is asked that equate it with something propositional fail to capture interrogative form simply because the propositional lacks the peculiar opaqueness of interrogative form.

The opaqueness of interrogative form can be summed up in the inability of what exhibits interrogative form to say anything in itself, thereby marking it off from the propositional. Since a question merely asks something and says nothing, it cannot be identified with anything propositional; in particular, with any of its conformable answers, either in combination or singularly. *Question* and *answer* being correlatives, one might argue, though flippantly, that saying that a question is (the set of) its conformable answers is rather like saying that a husband is (the set of) the several wives he might marry in the course of a lifetime. A question cannot specify what its answer is, or even what a possible answer (in the ordinary sense) to it is. The answer to a question is not inferable from the question, though a question can sometimes, as grammarians say, expect some particular answer, and not just any conformable answer in general.

Thus, the wording of a question may be suggestive of a particular answer or even the answer to it. Yes-no and alternative questions may be conducive, virtually prompting respondents to give a particular answer. Counsel may lead the witness by failing to establish first the truth of the presuppositions of the questions put, which then become 'leading questions'. Then there are rhetorical questions, which succeed in saying things through suggestion even although literally they merely ask things. Besides those already mentioned — namely, those rhetorical yes-no and alternative questions that insinuate a particular conformable answer — there are rhetorical word questions, which instead suggest repudiation of the presupposition of the question, thus giving rise to the common but too general description of rhetorical questions as those not expecting any answer. Now, as all these instances are confined to cases where questions are actually — or, in the case of rhetorical questions, figuratively — put to others, none of them are relevant to the logical consideration of questions. Considered logically, the question asked is opaque with respect to its actual and any possible answer to it, though the manner of phrasing it may sometimes be quite revealing.

Propositional misconceptions of interrogative form stem chiefly from the error of supposing that conformable answers to questions are as such propositions, and that these propositions — or, in the case of word questions and alternative questions, the material for constructing these propositions — are covertly contained within the question. Yet even with recognition that conformable answers to questions are not as such propositions, it would still be an error to suppose that these conformable answers were contained in the question; for although not themselves propositions, they are nevertheless propositional, conformable answers to word and alternative questions, for instance, being terms of propositions.

It might seem obvious that at least alternative questions contain within themselves their conformable answers, even if it is conceded, as it generally is not, that other questions — namely, *what* questions — do not.[61] Indeed, the commonly urged argument that yes-no questions are really a species of alternative questions starts from the observation that only one of the two contradictories is actually mentioned in a yes-no question and concludes that the other must be implicitly contained within the question. Add to which, the possible answers (in the ordinary sense) to a *which* question may also be explicitly presented within the question, so that it might seem that even some word questions contain their conformable answers within themselves. For a quiz question may be set out as *When (in which year) did Napoleon die: 1815, 1821 or 1828?*[62] The parallel with the implicit containment supposedly exemplified by yes-no questions would be when possibilities are not expressly listed but nevertheless implied by a term or terms of the question. *Which of the Cambridge Apostles was a traitor?* implies some selection from a complete list of members of that society since its inception. So Belnap declares: 'We are to think of a question as presenting a set of alternatives.'[63] Abstracting from the supposed request element, such a view incorporates the conclusion Frege shrunk from: namely, that a yes-no question is simply the tautological disjunction of contradictories. For to present a set of alternatives is in effect to assert a disjunctive proposition, that there is either this or that or this third or … thing; but if the content of a question were a disjunctive proposition, it would assert rather than merely ask something.

Thus, the conformable answers to yes-no, alternative and *which* questions cannot be presented in the question itself. Belnap's account suffers from a one-sided diet: he generalises to questions as such from alternative questions by way of assimilating the possibilities presupposed in *which* questions to alternatives — thereby ignoring *what* questions, which are not amenable to his set-of-alternatives treatment.

When Belnap's *present* is amended, as it needs to be, to *presuppose* — and he allows that '"explicitly contained" in' may be understood as '"effectively constructible"'[64] — the contrast between the explicit and the implicit dissolves. That is, between, on the one hand, the explicit listing of alternatives in an alternative question or the way possibilities presupposed by *which* questions can be explicitly set out after a colon; and on the other, the supposedly implicit presentation of one of the contradictory alternatives by yes-no questions or the way a term in a *which* question can imply the possibilities presupposed, as in the example of the Cambridge Apostles. Logically, though not conversationally, it is unimportant whether one recasts the yes-no question *Did she go?* or *Didn't she go?* as *Did she, or did she not, go?* or even *Did she go: yes or no?* For all the different versions of the question equally presuppose the same tautological disjunction. What matters logically is not what is explicitly itemised in, but what is presupposed by, the question. So alternative questions as such and yes-no questions are clearly different — even when a yes-no question is recast as an alternative question — because the presuppositions of the two types of question differ in their logical status. The presuppositions of yes-no questions, being disjunctions of contradictories, have no stringency at all; but the presupposition of an alternative question may be challenged as being dubious or false.

Likewise, a *which* question as such has a less stringent presupposition than any alternative question that can be recast as a *which* question. Unlike the usually plural as distinct from dual implication of *which*, the conjunctions *whether* and *either* are dual in number; so that the occurrence of more than two disjuncts is a result of co-ordination making for alternatives as distinct from possibilities: either the first or the second, or either the first or the third, or either the second or the third, and so on. Since an alternative question is a series of yes-no questions co-ordinated and disjoined, if one of the alternative obtains, none of the remainder does. Thus, if the series of yes-no questions were asked separately in sequence, a *Yes* to the first, or any other, in the series would obviate any need to ask the others; but if all the answers were so far *Noes*, one would have to go on asking the questions in the series until one got a *Yes* answer that resolved the matter. By contrast, a *which* question as such presupposes merely that at least one of the possibilities obtains and it is left open by *which* whether more than one of them obtains, though the subject of the question and logic generally, besides the facts, may preclude more than one possibility obtaining, as in the case of the date of the demise of the diminutive defeated Corsican despot as distinct from the (possible) plurality of traitors among the Cambridge Apostles. There is thus a clear distinction between alternative questions and *which* questions as such — even if there is a some affinity between them in that alternative questions can always be recast as *which* questions, though not the other way round.

And even if alternatives were presented within rather than presupposed by alternative questions, the presentation of these alternatives would not amount to conformable answers presented by the question, since the overall indefiniteness of the disjunction remains to be resolved. Sometimes what appears to say more can actually say less. To add *or* ... to what one has said is not merely to qualify but to cast doubt on it. If a witness says, 'It was a red car' but then adds 'or a blue one', there is a loss of credibility. As Wittgenstein remarks, I know nothing about the weather 'when I know that it is either raining or not raining'.[65] Even though the presuppositions of alternative and *which* questions are not as totally uninformative as those of yes-no questions, they too leave something to be resolved, and so neither can be regarded as actually containing within themselves their conformable answers. For to reply *either this or that* or *one of these* is not in fact to give a conformable answer to an alternative question or to a *which* question, though it might furnish an indirect answer to those word questions that do not as such presuppose a given set of alternatives or possibilities — namely, *what* questions.

Since the very description *conformable answer* conveys that such an answer has a form determined by the question it is an answer to, are not the conformable answers to a question in some way contained within the question? No; for conformable answers to a question are determinable rather by the presupposition of the question;[66] and the presupposition of a question, unlike a question itself, is a proposition. And although the presupposition of a question is derivable from the question, it is certainly not contained in the question; otherwise, being a proposition, there would be something contained in the question which asserted rather than merely presupposed something, and so a question would after all say and not merely ask something, contrary to its nature. A question must therefore specify its conformable answers not propositionally as when such answers are given by respondents but interrogatively — and hence opaquely.

An opaque specification sounds like a contradiction in terms; for is not to specify to spell out, say, what something is? Well, a question specifies only what the form of any conformable answer to it must take; it does not specify what the (actual) answer to it is, if there is any answer to it. A question points to what Reid calls 'the notion of a correlate'; and the notion of the correlate here, what answers the question, is a relative notion, which, Reid says, 'is strictly speaking, no notion of the thing itself at all, but only of some relation which it bears to something else'[67] — here, the question. The peculiarity of interrogative specification lies in the way a question is able to specify the form of what answers it: by the specification being presupposed by, not stated in, the question. A question obviously contains terms; but it does not use its terms to predicate anything of, as distinct from ask something about, its subject. Instead, it borrows its terms, other than its peculiar interrogative words, from its presupposition.

A better description, it might seem, is an incomplete specification.[68] But there is nothing incomplete about a question. For this reason, talk of filling gaps can also be misleading. The required notion is rather of indefiniteness: the specification presupposed by a question is yet left unspecified in some way. Not incidentally, as I might specify the make of a car but not its colour. Instead, the question purposefully leaves room for further specification to be provided for by its answer, which then fulfils the function of resolving the indefiniteness presupposed by the question, to make definite what was indefinite. The presupposition of a question is indefinite in that it says something about something without saying exactly what (or which) or about precisely what (or which); or that either this or that obtains, each of which is in itself indeed definite, but without saying which one obtains.

Unlike its presupposition, a question cannot say anything. Instead, it offers the indefiniteness of its presupposition for resolution by its answer. There are thus two elements to the opaqueness of interrogative form: first, the presupposing rather than the actually saying of something — about either what is merely presupposed or any conformable answer to the question being expressed or alluded to; second, the indefiniteness of what is presupposed, which is resolvable by the answer to the question being expressed or alluded to.

The lesson to be drawn from the difficulty Meno raised is somewhat trite: the subject of a question must be specified in some way. A further generalisation, beyond questions, can be drawn: the subject of any discourse must be specifiable. Whether saying or asking something, one has to know what one is talking about. The second horn of the eristic dilemma derives what plausibility it has from the denial supposedly required by enquiry of this truism; for enquiry by its nature is into what one does not know about. It was seen that the argument of the first horn can be reconstructed to furnish the argument that one cannot enquire into what one has already found out. Thus reconstructed, it is ineffective, it was also seen, against the possibility of asking questions whose answers one already knows. Abstracting, however, from the asking of questions to questions themselves, the argument of the first horn can be extended further so as to make a logical point about questions only a little less fundamental than the truism Meno's difficulty serves to emphasise.

If the answer to a question were already contained within the question, the question would cease to have a function — as rhetorical questions cease to function, at least fully, as questions. The function of a question is to specify what requires to be resolved by the answer to the question — though there is no requirement for any person to do anything as the confusion underlying imperativist theories has it. But if the answer to the question were already contained within the question, then the function of specifying what requires to be resolved would become redundant since there would then be nothing further to resolve. So the argument now is that a question could not ask what was already being answered by itself. Since a question quite evidently does ask something, it cannot therefore contain any propositional element of the sort provided by the answer to it; otherwise the question would in principle be capable of answering itself, would lose the opaqueness of its interrogative form, and would not therefore ask anything. The subject of a question must be specified in some way, is the obvious point arising from Meno's difficulty; but not specified too much is the point to be extracted when the reconstructed first horn of the eristic dilemma is likewise applied to questions themselves.

The requirement that what is required to resolve the indefiniteness presupposed in a question be specified but without thereby specifying its actual answer may be called the principle of interrogative opaqueness. Interrogative form meets this requirement. As Welbourne points out, an enquirer

> can identify what he wants to know. He does it with the interrogative sentence he uses to pose his question and thus does it, as he must, without spelling out the knowledge which, as yet he lacks.[69]

Interrogative characterisations of knowledge enable one to specify knowledge even when one has not got it; so one can come to know what one does not yet know — the *what* here being not a relative but an interrogative pronoun. A saying of the Academic Sceptics was that Socratic ignorance was sheer dogmatism: how could one claim to know even that one did not know something? But if the knowledge Socrates sought to obtain — namely, what he was ignorant of — is characterised interrogatively rather than propositionally, then Socratic ignorance can be seen as not simply specifying — namely, interrogatively — what remains to be discovered, useful enough in empirical enquiries, but more profoundly as knowing what the right questions are to ask about a subject, something required equally in philosophical investigations. Now, the argument of the preceding paragraph was that the principle of interrogative opaqueness applies beyond enquiry to questions themselves considered logically: since a question is opaque, its answer cannot be contained within itself.

The indefinite can specify the unspecified; for it conveys what remains to be said. Not, obviously, by saying it but by leaving it unsaid. Silence can proverbially speak volumes; but here only if something is said to begin with, just as a rest in music would have no significance if no notes had yet been, or were yet to be, played. In this way the indefinite prompts questions: *a man called* or *she was either drunk or ill*, a report runs; *who?* and *which of the two?* one immediately thinks, questions that presuppose the indefinite things said. Interrogative form incorporates the unspecified designedly within the specification it presupposes. Thus, the thought suggested by pondering specifically on enquiry, that there is both something one knows about and also something one is ignorant about the subject of an enquiry, both of which one is nevertheless able to specify,[70] appropriately reflects the logical form of the interrogative generally: there is something one can specify as requiring further specification to be supplied by the answer to a question. Such is the interrogative kind of specification supplied by interrogative form.

It would be ungracious not to acknowledge that occasionally the peculiarity of interrogative form, with its distinction between what has already been and what remains to be specified, has not been dimly glimpsed. Hobbes, for instance, distinguishes 'one name expressed, and another desired and expected from him of whom we ask the same'. Less illuminatingly, Reichenbach writes that a question 'must indicate' the 'knowledge desired ... to be formulated in a statement' 'by making the statement in an incomplete form; the listener is then invited to make it complete'.[71] Philosophy being a descriptive enterprise, however, a misdescription is a miss by as good as a mile.

The principle of interrogative opaqueness provides a test of adequacy for accounts of questions. Those that identify asking a question with a command, or a request or an invitation, to assert or state to questioners, to tell or inform them, *that* ... are attempting the unachievable, to replicate the opaqueness of interrogative form by means of the transparency of the propositional. They half succeed, which explains the air of both empty circularity and grave misconception in imperativist accounts. For if what is to be told had been characterised interrogatively, the account would have passed the opaqueness test, but on pain of trivial circularity.

If, however, what is to be told is to be characterised propositionally, then it can hardly be expressed by the proposition contained in the assertion respondents are held to when they answer the question correctly. Somebody who is supposed to request *Tell me (truly), Inform me, 'Make me know', that Stalin died in 1953* is not asking *When did Stalin die?* — quite apart from the absurdity, noted in Chapter 6, of telling another to tell (inform) one (of) what one is thereby telling (informing) the other (of). For whatever else is being done in this unreal situation, since the analysis contains a statement of what the answer is to the question, it is certainly not asking but more like stating something.[72] No theorist, it may be protested, has ever proposed anything quite so ridiculous. But attempts to refine the analysis fair only worse. For any attempt to insert into the propositional the indefiniteness necessary to capture interrogative form — by disjunction or by variables to be read as indefinite pronouns — results in gratuitous assertion or telling; that is, fails to allow for the standard of correctness aimed for in answering and built into the concept of the answer to a question. Both *Either tell me that Stalin died in 1953 or tell me that Stalin died in some other year* and *Tell me that with respect to some year that year is the year of Stalin's death* clearly need to be repaired; but they cannot be repaired by inserting a *truly* after the *Tell me* without succumbing to the absurdities previously detailed arising from the transparency of propositional constructions.

The propositional serves to accommodate error besides the truth, and in an analogous way the interrogative serves to accommodate ignorance besides knowledge; though it no more follows that one can ask only when ignorant, than it does that one can say only what is erroneous. Now, if one is to be told the truth and not error, one cannot in particular cases specify this proviso propositionally; only an interrogative specification, which is equally compatible with ignorance as with knowledge of what the thing fulfilling it happens in fact to be, will do the trick.[73] The inevitability here results from the function the answer to a question has in resolving the indefiniteness presupposed in the question, with the consequence that any conformable answer to a question cannot be as indefinite as (or more indefinite than) what is presupposed in the question. So if one is to have indefiniteness in propositional form, one cannot also have the standard of correctness invoked by the answer to the question; the two features can be combined only in interrogative form.

Welbourne argues that the form of a question cannot be '"Tell me something or other"'; it has rather to be along the lines '"Tell me this, namely ... "'[74] if there is to be any specification of what is needed to resolve the question. But what follows the 'namely' can only be an interrogative clause if a return to cruder accounts theorists must aim to refine is to be avoided. In fairness, it should be noted that the supposed request is of the forms *Either tell me that ... or tell me that ...* and *Tell me with respect to something that ...* ; not *Tell me either that ... or that ...* and *Tell me that something ...* . However, the difference in scope does not affect the overall point of the objection, which is that the indefiniteness presupposed by interrogative form has to reappear in any attempted propositional analysis if the analysis is even to appear adequate; but then only what is required of a conformable answer, not what is required of the answer, to the question can be specified propositionally independently of being given the answer to the question. That is, it can be specified that with respect to some year that it is the year of Stalin's death, which in turn presupposes that Stalin died in some year; but such an indefinite specification is distinct from a specification of the actual year of Stalin's death. The requisite specification of the answer to a question, however, is readily attainable through interrogative form, notwithstanding the indefiniteness it presupposes, as in *When* (*What year*) *did Stalin die* (*in*)*?* For the answer to a question when specified interrogatively is just the relative notion of what answers a question.

There is a notable contrast with commands and requests. Since commands and requests specify actions to be performed, the specifications cannot be entirely indefinite, for what one does can only be definite — though one can grant permission to others to do whatever they please. *Do something* or *Say something* have to be understood in the context of a *Don't just sit there* or a *Don't gawp*. Admittedly, commands and requests can also, like permissions, present a choice of actions, as when one is told or asked either to do one thing or another. Here the action enjoined or requested is specified disjunctively, the disjunction to be resolved by the choice made. But the presentation of a choice of action, far from showing that questions are really commands or requests, only reveals the interrogative form involved in the notion of choice: one chooses *what* or *which* to do or *whether* to do one thing or another. The interrogative has significance not only for epistemology.

Clauses Answering Questions

The principle of interrogative opaqueness was derived from a reconstruction of the first horn of the eristic dilemma generalised to questions as objects of logical consideration. It renders the asking of a question by a sentence or a clause incompatible with its answering the question. It thus explains how if a clause answers a question that clause cannot at the same time ask the question. Interrogative clauses after some verbs, especially *know* and other verbs implying knowledge, as also some phrases, it was seen, convey that the question they allude to is not being asked but answered, though without saying what it is that answers the question. Since such clauses allude to what answers the question they allude to, they cannot also, according to the principle of interrogative opaqueness, ask the question.

The asking or answering spoken of here is being done by clauses. What is being exercised in an interrogative clause is an interrogative concept, which utilises the interrogative form of the clause so as either to ask a question or else to answer it but without saying what it is that answers it; not to do both at once. People, of course, can answer the questions they themselves have just asked, and also, as in expository discourse, ask the questions they have answered in their previous enquiries; but even so, people cannot in asking a question thereby answer it, nor in answering a question thereby ask it.

Bell's notion of unasked questions appears to derive from a construction he places on interrogative clauses governed by *know*: he sees that they do not express a question actually asked by anybody but seems to infer that therefore the question must occur unasked in them. As was argued, such clauses allude to a question conceived as neither asked nor unasked but as answered by the clause: what is known is conceived in such clauses interrogatively as what answers a question, not as what asks a question. By contrast, the error of imperative-epistemic accounts lies in taking the asking done by an interrogative sentence expressing a question as an answering done by a clause following the verb *know* — as if somehow answering were logically prior to asking instead of the other way round; for the specification of a conformable answer is presupposed in, not determined independently of, the question.

What determines whether an interrogative clause is asking or instead answering the question alluded to includes the sense of the verb or phrase governing it.[75] But the overall sense will have to be gathered from the wider context. A reference, whether explicit or implicit, to the future as distinct from the present or the past will indicate that since what answers the question has yet be resolved, the clause can only be understood as asking the question alluded to. The sentences *They decided whom to consult*, *What he did depended on where he was* and *It matters to her who her neighbours are* all convey that what answers the question alluded to has been determined, though what it is may not always be known. Whereas the sentences *They have yet to decide whom to consult*, *What he does depends on when he gets there* and *Who moves in next door troubles her* convey that the question alluded to is still open, so the clauses merely raise questions without answering them. In this way not only the same words making up the clause but even the same verb or phrase governing it can flip according to the context from conveying the asking of the question to the answering of it.

Since interrogative clauses following *know* convey that what answers the question they allude to is settled and no longer open — regardless of whether the whole sentence is declarative, and whether in turn affirmative or negative, or is itself interrogative — clauses that simply ask questions cannot be analysed by reference to clauses following *know* — whether interrogative or *that* clauses — along the lines proposed by the imperative-epistemic theory. The reconstructed argument of the first horn of the eristic dilemma turns on the logical impossibility of doing what has already been done. If a clause merely asks a question there is scope still for answering the question — to be conveyed by another clause in some other context, obviously. But if a clause answers a question there can no longer be any room for it to ask the question since its answering the question forecloses its asking of it.

It is a mistake, then, to suppose that interrogative clauses following *know* and kindred verbs ask a question. Since they answer a question, they cannot then ask it; and conversely, if they were merely to ask the question, they could not then also answer it. But — and herein lies the significance of interrogative form for epistemology — while the whole sentence containing these clauses may happen to say something, if it is a declarative sentence, the clauses themselves do not say anything. Nor, it has just been argued, do they ask a question. Instead, they answer a question but without saying anything. That is, what they convey is conceived interrogatively — and hence, opaquely — as answering a question; and so although specifying the general form of what answers the question they allude to, they do not specify what specifically answers the question they allude to. But in alluding to what answers the question they allude to, such clauses allude to the answer to the question and not just any conformable answer to it.

Notes

1 Frege (1919), p. 363/373.
2 Cohen (1929), p. 353; Lewis and Langford (1932), p. 334. Cf. Hamblin (1958), pp. 160-61, 163; Prior (1971), p. 72.
3 Bell (1975), pp. 198-200, 211; cf. p. 203. See also Stahl (1969), p. 211 and cf. Harrah (1963), p. 52; Belnap (1963), p. 105; Belnap and Steel (1976), p. 121.
4 See Harrah (1961), pp. 40-43 and (1963), pp. 28-9. Cf. Prior (1971), pp. 73, 77.
5 Ryle (1938), p. 174; cf. p. 172. Carnap (1937), p. 295.
6 See White (1972), pp. 69-71, 73-4; cf. Rundle (1979), pp. 293-8 and Ryle (1979), pp. 98-9. Contrast Hume (1978), I iii 7; p. 95.
7 See Welbourne (1986a), p. 47.
8 See Bell (1975), pp. 198-200, 201-4, 209, 211. Cf. Prior (1971), p. 78.
9 *Pace* Dummett (1981), pp. 308-9, 312-14, 328; contrast pp. 353, 357, 362-3.
10 See Bell (1975), p. 199.
11 Bell (1975), p. 209.
12 Gandhi (1976), p. 31.
13 Ryle (1963), VIII (5) pp. 249-50. Ryle (1930), p. 28.
14 Hiz (1978a), p. IX.
15 Frege (1892), p. 153/167; (1918), p. 346/355; cf. (1919), p. 362/373, note.
16 Dummett (1981), pp. 364-5; cf. p. 328.

17 Frege (1918), p. 346/355; cf. (1892), p. 153/167. Cf. also Ajdukiewicz (1978), p. 157.
18 Hiz (1978a), p. IX; cf. (1962), pp. 255-6.
19 Ryle (1938), p. 172.
20 See Ajdukiewicz (1978), pp. 156-7; cf. (1974), pp. 85-7.
21 Carnap (1937), p. 296.
22 See Hiz (1978b), pp. 213, 218-19, 225, note 9.
23 Belnap and Steel (1976), pp. 201 and 25.
24 See Kahn (1978), p. 267, note 1.
25 See Hintikka (1974), pp. 110-11 and (1976), pp. 33-4, 114-15.
26 H. W. and F. G. Fowler (1930), pp. 88-93. Bolinger (1977), p. 12.
27 Cf. Åqvist (1965), pp. 12, 82-128.
28 Frege (1919), p. 362/373, note; (1918), p. 346/355.
29 Frege (1918), p. 346/355; (1919), pp. 362-3/373.
30 Frege (1918), p. 346/355.
31 Dummett (1981), pp. 306-7. Cf. Kiefer (1983a), pp. 34 and Wunderlich (1981), pp. 138-9.
32 Frege (1919) p. 364/374.
33 Frege (1918), p. 346/355; cf. (1892), p. 153/167.
34 Frege (1923), p. 380/392.
35 Frege (1919), p. 363/374.
36 Frege (1919), p. 364/374.
37 Frege (1919), p. 364/374. Cf. (1918), pp. 346-7/355-6 and note; (1919), pp. 336/376-7; 370-71/381-2; 372/383; (1923), p. 379/391 and note.
38 See Frege (1919), p. 364/374.
39 Cf. Hamblin (1963), p. 63.
40 See Frege (1918), p. 347/356; cf. (1892), p. 150/164. See also Dummett (1981), pp. 310-11, 312.
41 Dummett (1981), p. 308; cf. pp. 364-5.
42 Stoothof (1963), p. 4; Frege (1923), p. 381/393.
43 Austin (1962), pp. 99 and 100.
44 See Frege (1892), p. 150/164; (1918), pp. 346-7/356 and note; (1919), p. 372/383. Cf. Sloman (1965), p. 172, note.
45 Frege (1923), p. 379/391.
46 See Frege (1918), pp. 346-7/355-6; (1919), pp. 364-6/374-7.
47 See Collingwood (1924), pp. 78-9, 183, 186, 188. For commentary see Somerville (1989), pp. 527-31, 534-5.
48 Cf. Dummett (1981), pp. 310-11, 312.
49 Berkeley (1953), I, no. 316 (first edition only), p. 161; cf. p. 90.
50 See the example in Bolinger (1978), p. 101; cf. also p. 102 and pp. 104-5, notes 7 and 8.
51 See Austin (1956b), p. 212 but cf. p. 213, note 1. Belnap (1990), p. 29, note 17.
52 Whately (1913), Index, p. 268b; cf. II iii § 1; p. 51; § 2; p. 54 and IV iii § 1; p. 174. Cf. also Arnauld and Nicole (1996), III i , pp. 135, 136; and Walton (1988), pp. 204-5, 211.
53 Hume (1978), I iii 7; p. 95; (1875), ii, p. 462.
54 See Reid (1785), IV iii; pp. 377-9.
55 Frege (1918), pp. 346-7/356 and (1919), p. 365/376. Cf. Llewelyn (1965), pp. 306-7.
56 See Dummett (1981), p. 368, who is more explicit than Frege is himself.
57 Wittgenstein (1958), I § 22, p. 10[e]; p. 11[e].
58 See Hare (1952), pp. 17-18. Contrast Prior (1971), p. 70.

59 See Prior (1971), pp. 70-71. Cf. Rundle (1990), p. 136.
60 See Prior (1971), pp. 74, 76-7.
61 Cf. Belnap (1963), pp. 6, 14, 37-8, 40, 60; cf. Belnap and Steel (1976), p. 11.
62 Cf. Belnap (1963), pp. 39, 48, 50, 87-9, 93; Åqvist (1965), pp. 65, 117; Belnap and Steel (1976), pp. 58-9, 117-18.
63 Belnap (1963), p. 15; cf. p. 13. Cf. also Belnap and Steel (1976), pp. 34, 17-19.
64 Belnap (1963), p. 38.
65 Wittgenstein (1961), 4.461; p. 34.
66 Contrast Belnap (1963), p. 11.
67 Reid (1785), VI i; p. 421a and II xvii; p. 314a.
68 Cf. Reichenbach (1947), p. 340.
69 Welbourne (1986b), p. 230. Cf. Waismann (1965), pp. 391, 394.
70 Cf. Welbourne (1989), pp. 180-81. See also passages in Cook Wilson cited in Chapter 3 above.
71 Hobbes (1656), I iii 1; p. 25. Reichenbach (1947), p. 340. Cf. Prior (1971), pp. 77-8.
72 Cf. Belnap and Steel (1976), p. 104.
73 Cf. Welbourne (1989), pp. 177-81.
74 Welbourne (1986b), p. 230.
75 Cf. Kiefer (1981), pp. 165-72.

Chapter 9

Logic and the Different Types of Question

Logical differences between yes-no, alternative and word questions are determined, it has been seen, solely by the presupposition of the question. But it has also been noted how a question of one of these types can be recast as a question of a different type: occasionally a yes-no question can be worded as an alternative question — in everyday life, not merely at the behest of some theory; and an alternative question can readily be rephrased as a *which* question. It follows that a yes-no question can be recast as a *which* question. The converse of each of these points does not hold. Tritely, if an alternative question is reduced to one of its alternatives so as to become a yes-no question, it ceases to be an alternative question. And if a *which* question as such is recast as an alternative question, the presupposition of the question thereby becomes more restrictive and may no longer be acceptable. More significantly, the tempting proposal to construe a *which* question as a series of conjoined yes-no questions will be seen to be a misconstruction.

Now, some explanation is required how a question can be phrased in a way at variance with its logical type as determined by its presupposition. How can a yes-no question sometimes masquerade as an alternative question and both types of question take on the garb of a *which* question?

There is a different though similar puzzle. Asking a yes-no question can sometimes serve as a way of asking a word question generally, not just a *which* question. The question in effect, though not expressly, is a hybrid. But the question can also be expressly worded as a hybrid. Setting aside alternative questions as merely co-ordinate yes-no questions, the two fundamental types of question — yes-no and word questions — far from being totally alien to one another can thus exhibit an unsuspected association. What accounts for the apparent anomaly whereby asking a question of one type can be tantamount to asking a question of another type? As before, formal differences between types of question as determined by the presupposition of the question appear to have been bypassed.

In both cases the explanation lies in the way the question is conceived, which may sometimes differ from its express form and so from its logical type. The Aristotelian approach whereby a proposition is conceived as answering some question can be developed, it was seen, into a doctrine of interrogative concepts whereby objects of logical attention are conceived interrogatively. Questions themselves, it will be argued, can, in accordance with the Aristotelian approach, be subsumed under interrogative concepts other than the specific one they exercise. In general this conceptual approach to logic contrasts with formal and symbolic methods.

Multiple-Choice Reformulations of Questions

Hare, the Priors remark, has 'put his finger on two irreducibly different types of question — the type where we fill something in, and the type where we strike something out'.[1] These descriptions apply figuratively to the difference between questions where only the form of a conformable answer to the question is presupposed in the question, as with *what* questions, and those where in addition a set of alternatives or possibilities is also presupposed, conformable answers being drawn from the set, as with yes-no, alternative and *which* questions. Now, yes-no questions presuppose contradictory alternatives, even though the pair of contradictories is not usually expressly itemised in the question itself; and as determined by their presupposition, *which* questions as such differ logically from both alternative and yes-no questions in having to do with possibilities as distinct from alternatives. But the overall division here abstracts from such logical differences. Even so, it reflects a more general logical difference. Hare, however, takes talk of filling in or striking out literally: 'The simplest explanation ... of interrogative sentence form that I have been able to think of is that typified by many questionnaires and by multiple-choice examinations.'[2] On the contrary, multiple-choice reformulations of questions ignore logical differences between types of question.

Both *what* and *which* are pronouns besides adjectives; but since the pronouns can be understood as meaning 'what one' and 'which one', *what* and *which* are primarily adjectival. Accordingly, the remaining interrogative pronouns and adverbs can be given a reading with either *what* or *which* governing the relevant category. Since the use of *which* is special, the *which* reading is rarer. Thus, *who* and its cases can occasionally be read as *which* or *which sort* (*kind*) *of person*(*s*); *where* as *which* (*kind of*) *place*(*s*); *when* as *which* (*kind of*) *time*(*s*), *year*(*s*) or *time*(*s*) *of day* and so forth; and more seldom, *how* as *which* (*kind of*) *way*(*s*) and *why* as *which* (*kind of*) *reason*(*s*) or *cause*(*s*). All these interrogative pronouns and adverbs can also be read, much oftener, as having their category governed rather by the interrogative adjective *what*; and this is the commonest reading to be given *how* and *why*. The economy of ordinary language in making the same word serve to require identifications of both individuals and kinds should not be mistaken for logical sloppiness.

What questions do not presuppose a definite set of possibilities, merely the general form of any answer to the question. The subject or context, however, may impose limits on the range of possible answers — that is, in the ordinary sense of what is possibly the answer to the question by contrast with a merely conformable answer. But in principle the range of possible answers can be infinite and the extent of the range is often in fact unknown. Hence *what* questions are more opaque, more characteristic of interrogative form, than *which* questions, which instead presuppose some expressly listed or implied set of conformable answers while yet preserving their interrogative opaqueness in not revealing the actual answer (or answers) to the question. *Who* understood as *what person* restricts the range of conformable answers to persons; but understood as *which person* narrows the range down further to a definite set of persons.[3] For *which* is used only where a specific set of conformable answers is either expressly listed, as after a colon; or has been previously mentioned in or implied by the context; or indeed is implicitly listed as when an alternative or a yes-no question is subsequently rephrased as a *which* question.

Somewhat as alternative and yes-no questions always presuppose alternatives, *which* questions as such always presuppose a definite set of, in their case, possibilities. Membership of the set is not simply gathered from the subject as such. Thus questions about history are always in principle implicitly restricted to periods within recorded history — though future dates would logically constitute conformable answers. Yet some further restriction to a specific set of dates must be presupposed if the question is not to be *What year?* but *Which year?* Again, the range of possible answers to *What is your age?* is known to be limited in fact: *989* would possibly be the answer to it only if the respondent were an Old Testament prophet. By contrast, *Which is your age?* is a question that arises only in peculiar circumstances, such as when different newspaper reports give different ages for you. Likewise, *Which sex are you?* would only appropriately be asked if the issue of your being male or your being female had been expressly canvassed. Somewhat as Hobbes distinguishes 'hunting or tracing', where one is guided by a train of thoughts, from 'ranging', where 'we take a beginning arbitrarily',[4] the attempt to answer a *which* question is guided by an explicit or implicit list; whereas a *what* question can present a leap in the dark for those not in the know, who, from the question itself, are left clueless.

The difference between *what* and *which* points to a distinct, epistemological distinction between those subjects where the limits to the range of possible answers to the question are known and those where it is unknown. (The range of conformable answers to a question, by contrast, is a matter of logic, determined by the form of the question.) Everybody knows what in fact is the range of possible answers to *What sex are you?* and that numerals over a hundred form the very upper limit to the range of possible answers to *What is your age?* If, though, I ask you what your address is, the chances are that the answer will be new to me — though by chance you might happen to live where my cousin, say, lived years ago. But a mailing company may have all the postal addresses in the country listed in a database, so that it is merely a matter of matching your name with one of the millions of addresses on a very long but fully specifiable list. Here the answer to the question would in fact, though not in logic, be restricted to the items on the list — provided the mailing company can keep abreast of the voracious appetite of house-builders for greenfield sites. The question *Which is your address?* would be in order logically in the context of an implied list, such as in a database; that is, the answer will say which item on the list gives your address.

Any tempting proposal of theorists that asking questions be explained on the model of retrieving information somehow previously acquired and stored just for the contingency that it might be sought is flawed because it leaves out many *what* questions. It is as inapplicable to questions as such as the Platonic counterpart in the doctrine of recollection is inapplicable to learning and enquiry. Sometimes, indeed, life might be said to set a multiple-choice test in that the truth or the facts limits what is possibly the answer, even to a *what* question, to a few options and it is also known that these only are available. But things are not in general so favourably disposed towards potential respondents. Instead of having possible answers handed to one, so to speak, on a plate as in multiple-choice reformations of questions, one has more frequently to employ imagination, ingenuity and effort in endeavouring to unearth the answers to many *what* questions. Thus, theorists provide no room for genuine discovery, just as Plato denies the possibility of genuine learning and teaching; for they presume that all the discoveries to be made have somehow already been made in compiling the list containing the answer (or answers) to a question. But often the problem is not how to select from such a list, but whether compiling a list is possible at all.

Confusion of the logical distinction between *which* and *what* with the epistemological distinction — that is, between where there are known limits to the range of possible answers to the question and where it is unknown whether there are any limits and if so what they are — can foster further confusion. David Harrah declares: 'whether questions ask about a small or at least finite set of possibilities, whereas which questions ask about an infinite or indefinite or relatively large set of possibilities'.[5] There is no mention of *what* questions, where no possibilities are listed or even implied by the terms. And should the number of possibilities become unmanageably large for human contemplation, listing by a machine in a *which* question is not in principle precluded; but is quite distinct from being indefinitely large, and hence of unknown range; or infinite, and so incapable of being listed.

The further confusion here is between alternative questions and *which* questions as such.[6] Alternative questions are co-ordinate yes-no questions, only unlike a simple yes-no question they do not have a tautological presupposition. But both alternative and yes-no questions presuppose alternatives; that is, that only one item in the set presupposed provides the answer to the question. By contrast, *which* questions as such presuppose a set of possibilities in that the form of the question leaves open whether more than one item in the set may supply equally correct answers to the question. Even if more than one possibility is admissible by an alternative question through its having as a distinct alternative *Both* or *All of these* listed in its own right, the question remains an alternative question and does not become as such a *which* question; since more than one alternative is still inadmissible as an answer: *For pleasure* and *Both* would together be out of order in answer to *Is your trip for business, for pleasure or both?*

Now, this distinction between *which* questions as such, on the one hand, and alternative and yes-no questions, on the other, is not easily accommodated by the convention of striking something out. It is too simple-minded, in any case, to suppose that rephrasing a question normally expressed by an interrogative sentence so that it accords with some standardised format, whether on a form or, as Hare proposes, in a questionnaire or a multiple-choice test, by itself provides an analysis of questions, let alone a reduction of questions to something else. Far from being the 'simplest explanation' of 'interrogative sentence form', these reformulations constitute no explanation at all — only a different way of framing the question, reminiscent of Wittgenstein's imaginary examples of alternative ways of asking questions in alien languages.[7]

In general it is logically insignificant whether forms and questionnaires have interrogative sentences followed by spaces to be filled by respondents' answers, or boxes to be ticked or marked with a cross; whether they merely have headings, such as *age*, *occupation*, *address*, with blanks left for the answers; or whether they have statements to be deleted when inapplicable, or followed by boxes to be ticked or crossed. For whatever the format, logically questions are being asked even if the words do not actually go to make up interrogative sentences with question marks at the end. All such formats are simply ways of (implicitly) asking questions. Formats that explicitly employ interrogative sentences tend to be more user-friendly; but forms or questionnaires with simple headings or boxes, once completed, are more easily read by officials or machines. Those completing the forms or questionnaires will take it that they are being asked questions, whereas those who are reading the completed versions will take it that they are being given statements; and those who are undergoing a multiple-choice test will take it that they are being set questions to answer, whereas those conducting the test will take it that they are being given answers to their set questions.

Besides, talk of 'striking out' should not be taken literally. In addition to oral answers and written transcripts of them, written answers to questions can just as well be indicated by ticking (or marking with a cross) boxes — labelled, say, *Yes*, *over 65*, *council tenant* and so forth — as they can by deleting what is inapplicable. And talk of 'filling in' may especially mislead. Much of a form is indeed to be filled in, since most of the questions are *what* questions and thus do not presuppose a definite set of possible answers; just as examination candidates when answering an essay question fill in (or rather, fill up) an answer book. But questionnaires and tests in multiple-choice formats are largely not, in the relevant sense, filled in; though sometimes questionnaires leave room, usually at the end, for any comments those completing them may care to make. If respondents are also asked their name — as examination candidates usually are on the front page of the answer book — or their address, these questions cannot be answered by ticking boxes. Clearly, 'filling in' cannot amount to just ticking boxes if the distinction from 'striking out' (which can be indicated by ticking boxes) is to be maintained.

The description 'multiple-choice' is Orwellian; for questionnaires and tests in such formats instead curtail choice to a predetermined range. As will emerge, in not being able to accommodate *what* questions, these formats are at best confined to yes-no, alternative and *which* questions. Accordingly, multiple-choice formats specifically, as distinct from formats used in forms generally, smother formal differences between questions.

Hare's example, *Are you married?* seems curious in the context of his talk of 'an invitation or request ... to make just one out of a number of suggested assertions', since a yes-no question provides only a dual, not a multiple, choice.[8] Social changes, indeed, have long rendered (even in 1949) such a question anachronistic for an official form, it having been superseded by *What is your marital status?* If it is a matter, not of filling in a space provided for the answer, but of ticking boxes marked *Single, Married, Separated, Divorced, Widowed,* say, under a heading *Marital Status* — or, indeed, deleting all but one of the terms listed — then it might seem that the question ought to be *Which is your marital status?* which sounds unnatural. What is contrived, evidently, is the use of multiple-choice formats for *what* questions. For here the multiple-choice format apparently sets out a *what* question as if it were a *which* question thereby misrepresenting the logical character of the question. In effect, respondents are being prompted, or at least reminded, of possible answers — a feature that will be seen to crop up again in mixtures of word and yes-no questions. Accordingly, multiple-choice formats compromise the efficiency of examinations. But they also fall foul of the requirement that the answer given be the candidate's own answer; for any given will have been at the suggestion of the examiners — unless candidates become bolshie and repudiate all the options on offer.

By contrast with alternative questions, *which* questions as such must allow that more than one box may be ticked. In Hare's example it seems at first that what is set out in multiple-choice format were a *which* question, even although more than one choice is obviously precluded — though if one ticked both the *Divorced* and *Widowed* boxes it might indicate what used to be known as divorce Italian style. So the question has to be understood at least, even if it is not expressly framed as such, as the alternative question *Are you single, married, separated, divorced or widowed?* Since alternative questions are just co-ordinate yes-no questions, there is no need for two boxes labelled *Yes* and *No* after each alternative; one box for each alternative listed is sufficient. And as both yes-no and alternative questions presuppose only alternatives, striking out the other items listed will leave no doubt as to the answer given, unlike ticking boxes which will lead only to confusion if more than one box is ticked.

Thus, far from clarifying the logic of questions, multiple-choice formats tend to obfuscate since they can make it unclear whether the question is meant to be an alternative or a *which* question as such — which might, indeed, be more naturally expressed by *what*; but then *what* questions cannot be put into multiple-choice formats at all. Sometimes it is stated that more than one box under some of the questions may be ticked, sometimes that only one of the boxes should be ticked, at other times it is unclear which. Most questionnaires are such a mess logically — in that they also do not in their design and ordering of questions allow that the presuppositions of some of them may be false — as to prohibit the scrupulous to attempt in good conscience to complete them. A consumer survey that asks which — *what* is meant, but a multiple-choice question is unable to ask that — brands of cat food the customer buys but omits to ask if she keeps a cat is going to fail to pick up evidence about cat food bought by those who do not have a cat. And it will not suffice to have a box marked *None*; for besides failing to pick up those who have a cat but leave it to fend for itself, the boundary between alternative question and *which* question as such is again blurred since *None* can only be an alternative as distinct from a possibility. Besides, to have a box marked *None* (or *Neither*, if there are only two other boxes) is illogical since such a reply repudiates the presupposition of the question. By contrast, a box marked *Other* is logically in order.

Thus multiple-choice formats force all questions into the mould of alternative questions. It is unsurprising that Hare should look kindly on these formats, since alternative questions are far easier for imperativists to cope with. It should also be recalled that Belnap's whole account of questions is based on the model of alternative questions. *What* questions, perhaps the commonest asked, cannot be accommodated at all by multiple-choice formats: at best they are treated, mistakenly, as if they were *which* questions. Then *which* questions as such are treated as if they were alternative questions, so that the difference in the presupposition of the two types of question is either ignored or blurred. Often it is unclear whether when put into multiple-choice format a question was originally the alternative question the format indicates it to be or was intended to be a *which* question as such thus opening up the possibility that more than one answer may be correct — that more than one box may be ticked, for striking out less readily captures such a possibility. Finally, yes-no questions are treated as if they were alternative questions, in accordance with most theorists' predilections, which explains Hare's odd inclusion of a dual choice within the category of multiple choice. Again, the term *multiple choice* is misleading: not only is choice restricted; neither is there multiplicity as such, only the duality of alternatives.

The logical distortions inherent in multiple-choice reformulations of questions do not seem as glaring as they actually are because alternative questions can easily be rephrased as *which* questions and yes-no questions can occasionally be recast as alternative questions. If ordinary language were sometimes to fail to respect the formal differences between *which*, alternative and yes-no questions, then licence might be given to multiple-choice reformulations of questions to do so too. But they are not at all disregarded by ordinary language: they remain intact even when an alternative question is conceived as a *which* question, or when a yes-no question is conceived as an alternative question, and so also when a yes-no question is conceived as a *which* question.

In rephrasing an alternative question previously asked — even sometimes about to be asked — as a *which* question there is no intention to relax the presupposition of the question by making the alternatives possibilities thus allowing that there may be more than one correct answer to the question and so changing the question itself. The alternatives do not become possibilities. Rather, they are now conceived under the interrogative concept of which one ('whichness'). The singular shows that only one of the items previously mentioned or implied — or about to be mentioned — supplies the answer to the question; so that they are alternatives, not possibilities. Contrariwise, to frame a *which* question as if it were an alternative question, as multiple-choice reformulations of questions do, is indeed to change the presupposition of the question, and so the question, turning it into another of a different logical type.

When one asks *Which is it?* after having asked — or just before asking — an alternative or a yes-no question, the *which* governs alternatives; or, in the case of the yes-no question, alternatives that are contradictories. As the presupposition of a yes-no question is a tautology, its presupposition cannot be relaxed any further. It follows that when a yes-no question is conceived as a *which* question — *Which is it: Yes or No?* — there can be no intention to change the presupposition of the question, which must remain as it is. The concept of an alternative or of a contradictory rules out there being more than one correct answer. But the tacitly understood list of alternatives or the tacitly understood pair of contradictories are subsumed under the interrogative concept of whichness — economically too, for to repeat an alternative question with more than three alternatives is cumbersome. So while differing logically from one another, alternative questions have some affinity to *which* questions: *which* can sometimes in effect be which of two, or *whether*.

Again, it is evident that when a yes-no question is conceived as an alternative question there can be no intention to loosen up the presupposition of the question so as to make the contradictories become contraries — still less pairs that are logically, if not in fact, compatible. Often the alternatives are not verbally but logically contradictory, as in *Is she dead or alive?* This is nominally an alternative question; but since the alternatives are logically exclusive they come down to a yes-no or *if* (by contrast with *whether*) question. In conceiving a yes-no question as an alternative question, one is thinking of the pair of contradictories as if they were merely alternatives — in the example, as if somehow being alive were not the negation of being dead. In wording a yes-no question as an alternative question one expressly conceives each of the pair of contradictory alternatives in turn, by contrast with the merely implicit conception in a standardly framed yes-no or *if* question of one of the pair, the pair itself only being presupposed in the question. Not the same as, but similar to, Hume's conceiving both sides of the question; for Hume is concerned with the conceiving in turn specifically of propositions as being true or false, as distinct from states of affairs generally as obtaining or not obtaining.

Philosophers have their own motives for subsuming yes-no under *which* questions. An alternative question does not expressly mention any category the alternatives fall under; but it is usually clear from the alternatives presupposed what category is involved. Questions about red, blue or green shirts are obviously about the colour of shirts, so that it is usually of little interest to make the subject of the question more explicit by phrasing it as the *which* question beginning *Which colour of shirt ... ?* Philosophers, curious about what category the subjects of yes-no questions belong to — in other words, what interrogative concept is as such exercised in yes-no questions — have a motive to word them as *which* questions thereby yielding a more unified account of questions. In *Which is it: yes or no?* the *which* governs the category of conformable answer. Moreover, it in effect means *which of two*, so is equivalent to *whether*. What category, though, do these answers fall under? Simply what states the truth or the facts. One would not usually have occasion, though, to ask *Which is the truth?* or *Which are the facts?* — unless one had two (or more) versions of the truth or the facts before one. Instead, one would ask *What is the truth?* or *What are the facts?* and seek the answer to these general questions by asking specific questions, including yes-no questions. Thus, while the category concerned is the truth, the facts or what states of affairs in general obtain, yes-no questions cannot as such be taken as *which* questions. Yet philosophers, gliding over the distinction between asking if something is so and asking specifically if a proposition is true, have mistakenly thought that a yes-no question is essentially a question about which truth-value a proposition has.[9] But the (interrogative) concepts of the truth and of truth-value are distinct: while the truth is multifarious, there are but two truth-values.

It would be wrong to take all such attempts to relate yes-no questions to *which* questions to be reductive in spirit. Though the Priors read Whately correctly as subsuming the one type of question under the other, the subsumption in itself need not involve any denial of the logical differences between the two;[10] it may simply be a way of conceiving the one type after the manner of the other. It is one thing to conceive the alternatives or contradictories presupposed by alternative and yes-no questions under the interrogative concept of whichness; quite another to argue that alternative and yes-no questions are simply species of *which* questions as such. Indeed, Whately's assertion 'that all questions may be considered as falling under two classes' hardly supports any reading that he aimed to reduce all questions to one logical type.[11] And even if there were no formal differences between alternative, yes-no and *which* questions, such a reductive programme would still leave out *what* questions.

Yes-no questions cannot as such be reduced to *which* questions; but perhaps *which* — even some *what* — questions can be reduced to yes-no questions. One might imagine detectives seeking the answers to the question *What bars does the suspect frequent?* compiling a list of bars in the vicinity, and having interrogated staff, marking each item on the list with either a tick or a cross. Arguably taking a *which* question as a series of yes-no questions is even more plausible, because unlike a *what* question it in addition presupposes a set of possibilities. There would still be a distinction between *which* questions as such and alternative questions, since alternative questions are a series of disjoined yes-no questions, each disjunction being exclusive: that is, either yes or no for the first, or yes or no for the second, or yes or no for the third, and so on; so that while there may be several *Noes*, one *Yes* clinches things in that all the other answers must then be *No* and there cannot be another *Yes*. The proposal rather is that *which* questions are a series of conjoined but discrete yes-no questions: that is, the question *Item one, yes or no?* followed by the question *Item two, yes or no?* and so on. In this way *which* questions as such would still admit more than one correct answer, more than one *Yes*, by contrast with alternative questions: the suspect's use of bars may be promiscuous. The objection to the reduction is that *which* questions do not clearly require the *No* answers to any of these yes-no questions — what are conformable answers rather to *Which of these bars does the suspect not frequent?* Of course, if it is understood that the complete set of *Yes* answers is required, and not just a sample from the complete set, then all the *No* answers are inferable; but still, to come up with the answers to the negative *which* question when the positive *which* question was asked is to go beyond what the question required. By enquiring into matters they need not pursue, the police would arguably be wasting public money.[12]

Here multiple-choice formats can, exceptionally, help to illustrate — but only so far — the formal difference between a *which* question and a series of yes-no questions asked successively. A yes-no or an alternative question requires, obviously enough, that only one box be ticked. But further, one does not tick one box and mark the other box or boxes with a different, 'negative' mark; any more than voters in an election, as distinct from a debate, are allowed the opportunity to show their disapproval of candidates by some mark that could be taken to mean voting against, for express provision is made only for voting for in an election. Now, when a *which* question as such is forced into multiple-choice format, no allowance is made similarly for 'negative' answers: a box ticked or crossed can definitely be taken to say *Yes* to the item on the list; but an unmarked box can be taken as saying *No* to the item only if it is made explicit that all the correct answers to the question are required. If this requirement is not made explicit, it cannot be inferred that an unmarked box indicates saying *No* to the item: it may merely indicate that the item is not a salient example in the respondent's mind — that, say, it is not the customer's regular brand of cat food, not that she never buys it. Where a test is being set, an unmarked box may, of course, betray lack of recognition that the item provides a correct answer to the question; but again, the inference can safely be drawn only if the complete set of correct answers is required. As failure to recognise is different from ignorance, more attention is usually paid to successful recognition, indicated by the marked boxes; and so usually the requirement is only that some correct answers be given, not the complete set.

Cook Wilson's Examples

Cook Wilson distinguishes the statement, 'That building is the Bodleian', taken by him as being an answer to *What building is that?* from the statement, '*That* building is the Bodleian', taken by him as being an answer to *Which building is the Bodleian?* — 'in the same words as before, but with a different stress-accent'; what he later, as amended by his editor, calls 'the predicative stress'.[13] He remarks: 'Thus the same form of words should be analysed differently according as the words are the answer to one question or another.'[14] Although the difference he wishes to draw attention to concerns statements, his example suggests some distinctions between different kinds of question, none of which exactly coincides with the two contrasted in the example.

Collingwood cites the example as showing how 'in our writing and printing there is no notation for' some differences in speech, such as in 'the tone and tempo of ... voice'; that 'even the logical structure of a proposition is not always clear from its written or printed form'. The moral he draws is that 'the written sentence "That building is the Bodleian" represents two quite different propositions'. Logicians, he continues, who ignore the tone of voice words are spoken in only 'discuss the import of "propositions"'; but such a notion of a proposition 'understood as a form of words expressing thought and not emotion ... is a fictitious entity'. As abstractions propositions are merely notional. But is written language in any way logically — as distinct, say, from poetically or dramatically — more impoverished than speech? Collingwood wisely makes the qualification 'not always'; since he himself manages to bring out tolerably well with the use of italics the differences in interpretation that Cook Wilson's sentence admits.[15] And linguists, in accordance with the precedence set by musical notation, have devised means of marking intonation of speech. Moreover, a cleft construction, which can occur in writing just as much as in speech, can reinforce emphasis placed in speech on one of the terms: *It is the Bodleian which is that building* as against *It is that building which is the Bodleian*; though as Cook Wilson notes, there may also be emphasis placed on different words in such a construction — depending, he holds, on what question the statement can be conceived as answering — and so he concludes that the stress is indispensable.[16]

While italics or underlining can indicate in writing emphasis in speech, Collingwood is on to something in his complaint that logicians are unable to capture with their 'typographical jargon'[17] the significance of emphasis in speech — or, indeed, of cleft constructions. Written language is not impoverished; only logical notation. But it is not quite right to say, as does Cook Wilson, that the differences being alluded to are not captured by 'the grammatical form as such'[18] of the sentence, whether spoken or written; for even if emphasis and intonation are not thought to be grammatical devices, a cleft construction is.

Hence in addition to italics, resort is made by Cook Wilson to the Aristotelian method of conceiving the words as answering different questions to bring out differences underlying uses of the same words. As was noted, the method assumes that conformable answers to questions constitute propositions as such. The statements taken as being made in answer to various questions are not actually conformable answers to these questions, though the propositions abstractable from these statements contain conformable answers to them. Regarded as a way of invoking interrogative concepts so as to clarify the thought expressed, the approach is sound in principle. But Cook Wilson's account, it will emerge, is vitiated by the assumption that the statements he cites are themselves conformable answers to questions.

In his section entitled 'Drift of Propositions', Whately counsels: 'We should consider in each case what *Question* it is that is proposed, and what answer to it would, in the instance before us, be the most *opposite* or *contrasted* to the one to be examined.' What determines for Whately the differences in the 'drift and force' of propositions, however, seems initially to be only the notion of what is implicitly contrasted with a particular term. He shows how the sentence "The Organon of Bacon was not designed to supersede the Organon of Aristotle" can give rise to six (at least) separate contrasts as six each of the terms in the sentence are emphasised in turn. In his example '"this man is a *murderer*"', the term *murderer* contrasts with 'one who has slain another *accidentally*, or in *self-defence*'; while '"this man *is* a murderer"' contrasts simply with '"he is *not* a murderer"'. The bit about 'what answer' to a question proposed is being contrasted with other answers to it has to be understood as referring to conformable answers — not to propositions, as seems to be Whately's own view.[19] But how does the notion of different questions being proposed come in at all?

The significance of emphasis and cleft constructions, which formal logic fails to capture in symbolism, lies in ranges of contrasts only implied by, not expressly stated in, an assertion. One has, then, to go beyond the assertion and have regard to what else has been thought or expressed in words — whether by the person making the assertion or by others. In short, in giving an interpretation to a sentence one has to have regard to 'its context', as Cook Wilson expressly notes.[20] Symbolic logic, by contrast with the conceptual approach, is unable to accommodate the allusion to a question provided by context because the context of an assertion necessarily lies outside it.

But people may imply, hint at or insinuate many different sorts of things by their words, tone of voice or gestures. The conceiving of differences in people's assertions as lying in differences in the questions they would be, supposedly, answering by making these assertions thus provides some way of lending precision to the notion that the context of the assertion implies a range of contrasts. For if the assertion is conceived as though it stood in relation to a previously asked question, then the range of the implied contrasts, and its extent, can be fixed by the question through the question's determination (through in turn its presupposition) of its conformable answers. In other words, the assertion is being conceived according to the interrogative concept governing the subject of the notional question, which may not be expressly mentioned by any of the terms of the assertion.[21] This Aristotelian method of conceiving assertions testifies to the unsuspected way interrogative concepts order thought and the import of what people say.

The type of question that presupposes a range of contrasts, thereby excluding overlapping or conjunction of terms, is the alternative question. In *Was the killing murder, accidental, in self-defence or suicide?* the items listed are alternatives: it could not have been both murder and an accident. The yes-no question *Was it murder?* also presupposes alternatives, contradictory alternatives: that it was murder or that it was something other than murder. As was seen, a yes-no question can be conceived as an alternative question, notwithstanding the formal difference between the two types of question. And both alternative and yes-no questions, it was also seen, can be conceived, by means of the interrogative concept of whichness, as *which* questions — even although neither are as such *which* questions, which are logically different in that they have a less stringent presupposition.

The advantage in conceiving alternative and yes-no questions as *which* questions is that the subject is thereby made explicit. The subject of the question is made explicit in *Which sort of homicide was it: murder, accidental, in self-defence or suicide?* By contrast, the notion of homicide is only implicit in *Was it murder?* Apparently likewise, in Cook Wilson's other example '*glass* is elastic', supposing that 'the matter of inquiry was elasticity', he says that 'there is no word in the sentence to denote it'.[22] His examples, however, generally illustrate rather different features from Whately's examples, it will be seen.

Now, *which* questions as such need not provide any contrasts, since they deal with possibilities, not alternatives. Only those *which* questions that are logically alternative or yes-no questions conceived as *which* questions presuppose alternatives. If *which* questions as such need provide no contrasts, then neither need *what* questions: *Leipzig* and *Saxony* are not rival contenders to be the answer to the question *Where* (*In what place*) *was he born?* as either *Moscow* or *Patagonia* would be to either of them.

Cook Wilson was familiar with Whately's *Logic*; but it is not clear, as his editor believes, that he was thinking of the contrastive use of terms discussed by Whately.[23] The notion of the predicative stress is instead related to 'the part of the sentence which conveys the new information'.[24] It is thus only too obvious how questions are supposed to come in: what he takes to be 'the new information' is supplied by the answer to a question — a thoroughly threadbare theme. Not only can the answer to a question be perfectly familiar to those who ask it, neither need statements be made in response to previous questions; so that the notion of informing, and hence the distinction between new and old information, is not essential to the making of statements: what is said may be wholly new or all old.

Even if there was a previously asked question, there is a greater difficulty for Cook Wilson: conformable answers to word questions are supplied by a term, not a proposition as such; so one simply mentions the term without any marked emphasis, for there are no other terms to be said without emphasis. Only if others are having trouble in hearing what one is saying would one make a full statement in answer to a word question; and then the term that furnishes one's answer to the question would be marked out by emphasis from the other words in one's sentence simply because it was the one term necessary to give one's answer.

It begins to look doubtful whether there is any such thing as 'predicative stress', and Cook Wilson's editor worries about the notion in insisting on the distinction between 'stress' and 'intonation'.[25] Initially, the first of the two statements is presented as 'That building is the Bodleian', which is said to be the 'reply'; and while no italics are employed, it is said that 'there is a peculiar stress accent upon the word "Bodleian", which is absent from "that building"'. A couple of sections later the sentence becomes 'that building is the *Bodleian*'.[26] The version without the italics would constitute the assertion a respondent would be held to in giving a conformable answer to *What building is that?* As also to *Which building is that?* — a question that would be asked in situations where familiarity with at least the names of public buildings in Oxford was assumed. The statement might also have been made just as a passing remark with no previous question having been asked; so that the addressee would be told not only that the building is the Bodleian but also that the Bodleian is that building, thus collapsing any distinction between new and old information. The version with the italics would be appropriate if the question had rather been, say, *Is that building the Sheldonian?* (whether or not the term *the Sheldonian* receives emphasis) and the conformable answer given had been *No* with the explanation added by way of a reply as distinct from a conformable answer, 'That building is the *Bodleian*', the emphasis serving to contrast the two buildings. Or the question might have been the hybrid question, *What* (or *Which*) *building is that? (Is it) The Sheldonian?*

The second statement, '*That* building is the Bodleian' would readily be taken too as implying a contrast with other buildings in the vicinity; and accordingly Cook Wilson has as the associated question an alternative question phrased as a *which* question, *Which building is the Bodleian?* not a *what* question.[27] Again, emphasis, and so an implied range of contrasts, is not essential to the example. Admittedly, Oxford is a built-up area. But suppose I point to an isolated ruin on the moors and remark with no particular emphasis on any word 'That building was the inspiration for *Wuthering Heights*;' there can be no contrast here with other buildings, for there are no others in sight.

In the other example, '*glass* is elastic' the emphasis does not imply a contrast with materials other than glass but a contrast rather with the more usual 'glass is elastic' said without any particular emphasis on any word; for the question the assertion with the emphasis could be conceived as containing a conformable answer to might be a *what* besides a *which* question. Cook Wilson himself says that the question might be 'what substances possessed the property of elasticity' and here 'the kind of stress which fell upon "elastic" when glass was the subject, would now be transferred to "glass"'. But it is doubtful if there is any peculiar emphasis, the supposed predicative stress, on the predicate term in the first of the pair. In a third example, 'Smith is a good *skater*' is opposed to 'Smith is a *good* skater'.

In the glass and skating examples there is genuine emphasis in at least one of the pair of statements; but unlike the second statement in the Bodleian example, emphasis does not mark a contrastive use of a term. Nor is the emphasis that does occur in the two examples to be explained by the statements answering different questions. For conformable answers to the relevant questions — namely, *What is one of the properties of glass?* and *What (is an example of a) material (which) possesses the property of elasticity?* or *What sort of skater is Smith?* and *What can Smith do well?* — would simply be *Elastic* and *Glass* or *A good one* and *Skate.*[28] There can be little room for emphasis when just one word or phrase is spoken.

Although there is no contrast of terms implied in these examples, different subjects governed by the interrogative concepts exercised in the questions Cook Wilson associates with the opposed statements are contrasted. The contrast is between when glass is the subject of discourse and when elasticity is; between Smith's skating in particular and Smith's talents in general. The bit about answering questions is therefore irrelevant to the function of emphasis in these examples. The reference to questions comes in rather through the interrogative concept governing the subject of discourse. In a different way, Whately's reference to a question is explained by an interrogative concept defining the range and extent of the contrasts implied in the contrastive use of terms.

A major logical objection to taking a proposition as such as being a conformable answer to a question is that it would result in yes-no and some word questions having the same conformable answers, which they patently do not.[29] Unsurprisingly, then, Cook Wilson seems uncertain at times whether he is discussing word or yes-no questions. He says that

> in a sentence of the form 'A is B', the stress may fall upon either A, or B, or on the verb 'is', according as the statement answers the question 'what is it that is B?', or 'what is A?', or 'Is A really B?'[30]

Using the example given, the first case seems to be associated by him with not only 'Who is rowing badly?' but also 'Is (it) *Jones* (who) is rowing badly?' both, he supposes, being answered by '(It is) *Jones* (who) is rowing badly'. Emphasis in the statement implies a contrast with other rowers. The second case seems to be aligned to 'Is Jones rowing badly?' where emphasis in the statement would imply a contrast with other things Jones might be up to. But while emphasis in the associated question might instead be brought out by the cleft construction 'Is rowing badly the thing that Jones is doing?' in asking 'What is Jones doing?' one need not employ any emphasis. The third case is linked to '*Is* it Jones who is rowing badly?' answered supposedly by 'It *is* Jones who is rowing badly.'

These three cases resemble the threefold distinction drawn by D. A. T. Gasking between 'scientific', 'logical' and 'philosophical' questions, illustrated by the shifting emphasis in the three questions 'Is *this* cupag?,' 'Is this *cupag*?' and '*Is* this cupag?'. The first is about 'what properties "this" actually has'; the second 'about the conventional meaning of "cupag"'; the third 'protests at classifying this with other things called by the name'. Each of these, though a yes-no question, could also be given an interpretation as a word question. The 'scientific' question could be thought of as asking what (or which) this sample in fact is; the 'logical' question as asking what (or which) cupag is — that is, what (or which) cupag is by convention defined as — given that the sample has in fact such-and-such properties; and the 'philosophical' question as asking what (or which) standards ought to be applied, again, given the actual properties of the sample.[31] Emphasis here serves to contrast different subjects of discourse, just as in the glass and skating examples.

The last two questions in the rowing example might be embellished along such lines. One might ask whether Jones's rowing is in fact bad enough for him to be dropped from the team; or whether it is actually bad at all rather than innovative. If the embellishment of the second case is unconvincing, it only shows that the supposed 'predicative' stress is distinct from genuine emphasis. Cook Wilson is thus unable to distinguish the 'scientific' question, 'Is Jones rowing badly?' — in the sense of 'Is rowing badly what Jones is as a matter of fact up to now?' — from the 'logical' question, 'Is Jones rowing *badly*?' — that is, whether his rowing falls below recognised standards. And since it is a question, there can be no predicate in any case.

Indeed, it seems to have escaped Cook Wilson's notice that in the rowing example emphasis is occurring not only in statements — where he comes closest to Whately's discussion of contrastive terms — but now also in questions. No resort can be made to explaining the emphasis here by conceiving the words as in answer to a question, since the words themselves constitute a question, so in accordance with the principle of interrogative opaqueness cannot also be conceived as the answer to a question. Instead, the capacity for interrogative concepts to order thought by specifying the subject of discourse explains the emphasis.

Cook Wilson accordingly fails to notice the difference between the use of emphasis in questions and in statements. In questions emphasis primarily serves to contrast different subjects of discourse, as it does also in the glass and skating examples; further, the question could be either a yes-no question or a word question generally — that is, a *what* or a *which* question. But in the statements supposed as given in answer to questions emphasis instead marks the contrastive use of terms, where any conformable answer contained in the statements would be restricted to conformable answers to *which* questions. Thus, emphasis in questions seems to draw yes-no questions closer to word questions generally, notwithstanding the formal differences between the two. Hybrid questions were also encountered when discussing the Bodleian example.

While neither the Bodleian nor glass examples actually illustrate the contrastive use of terms, Whately's construing of the different contrasts marked by emphasis on different terms of a declarative sentence as 'several different Propositions ... each having a distinct Predicate' may have misled Cook Wilson into not only thinking that contrastive emphasis is related to predication, but also regarding predication itself as essentially involving contrastive emphasis.[32] The first thesis is clearly false, since emphasis in a question implies a contrast between different subjects of discourse; but a question predicates nothing of its subject. Admittedly, Whately's example with its six contrasts can nominally be made to work as six distinct predications if his sentence is recast as six distinct cleft constructions: 'It was not the *Organon* of Bacon that ... ', 'It was not *Bacon's* Organon that ... ', 'It was not the *design* of the Organon of Bacon to supersede ... ' and so on. But the Bodleian example involves identification as opposed to predication; so the distinction between subject and predicate will not illuminate any difference Cook Wilson hoped to bring out there — still less any distinction between types of question, since the distinction between subject and predicate is inapplicable to questions.

Four Distinctions Arising

The first distinction between types of question arising from the Bodleian example, between *what* and *which* questions, operates independently of whatever difference Cook Wilson had in mind between his two statements. Differences owing to contrastive uses of terms discussed by Whately do not coincide with the distinction because, as was seen, only assertions containing conformable answers to *which* questions imply a range of contrasts and so use emphasis or a cleft construction to do so; even then, not *which* questions as such but only alternative and yes-no questions worded as *which* questions. The second statement, '*That* building is the Bodleian' implies a contrast of a building in view with others and so can be conceived as containing a conformable answer to *Which building is the Bodleian?* But the first statement, 'That building is the Bodleian' (with no marked emphasis) implies no range of contrasts, yet could be conceived as containing a conformable answer to either *What building is that?* or *Which building is that?* Hence even statements containing conformable answers to a *which* question need not imply a range of contrasts. Furthermore, besides *Which building is the Bodleian?* one can ask *What building is the Bodleian?* — whose answer is *The University Library*. Generally, statements containing conformable answers to *what* questions need not signal any contrast. Several mutually compatible answers are possible to *What is that?* It might be wood, oak, a piece of furniture, a work of art, a retirement gift and so forth. Nor would emphasis normally be used; certainly not to imply any contrast, though it might if one was having difficulty in making oneself heard.

The Bodleian example suggests a second distinction, more to the fore in Cook Wilson's account. His use of the demonstrative adjective and pronoun *that*, together with his talk of the building being 'pointed out', invokes a distinction between terms used ostensively, on the one hand, and purely descriptive terms or proper names, on the other — as does Collingwood's version of the second question, 'Which of these is the Bodleian?'[33] As applied to questions, the distinction is between those whose subject is (at least in part) defined ostensively and those whose subject is specified exclusively by a description or is the bearer of a proper name. The first of the questions, *What building is that?* concerns 'that'; the second has the Bodleian as its subject. Conformable answers to the first sort of question are supplied by a descriptive term or a proper name; whereas conformable answers to the second are supplied by a demonstrative word, though there may also be a descriptive element.

Hintikka has observed a

> curious duality ... in our use of questions. Someone can walk into a room full of people, point to a man, ask, 'Who is that man over there?', and draw the reply, 'Why, he is John Jones'. Someone else can walk into the same room, ask, 'Who is John Jones?', and prompt the response, 'Why, that man over there' (pointing to him).[34]

Confusingly, Hintikka calls the first question with the demonstrative the 'descriptive' as opposed to the 'ostensive' question.[35] Admittedly, descriptive terms can sometimes replace demonstratives. Returning from Oxford one could offer a description of the building: *What* (or *Which*) *was the circular building?* The subject of the question then ceases to be specified with the aid of demonstratives but is described. By the same token, with the second sort of question, the ostensive element can be refined into a description in giving a conformable answer: *Which is the Radcliffe Camera? — The circular building (over there)*. Yet one is still inclined to understand the *the* in either case as a *that*, since these cases contrast with others where subjects of questions are specified, or conformable answers to questions are given, solely by descriptive terms or proper names. For what was originally conceived ostensively by use of demonstratives (and perhaps also some descriptive words) is now given some (more) description. Thus, *What* (or *Which*) *building is that?* — even when the *that* is replaced by a description beginning *the* ... — is a different type of question from, say, *What* (or *Which*) *building did Austin use for his Saturday morning meetings?* which is purely descriptive. When a pure description or a proper name is employed in either question or answer, such as *What* (or *Which*) *is the building faced by Hertford College? — The Bodleian (is the building faced by Hertford College)*, or a grid reference is cited, no ostensive element is contained in either question or answer. Questions employing an ostensive word with a description or a proper name — such as *Which building here is the Bodleian?* — can only, of course, have an answer at least partly reliant on a demonstrative.

An answer employing a demonstrative, such as *That is (the Bodleian)*, differs from an answer given by purely descriptive terms or a proper name — such as the answer *The Indian Institute* to the question about Austin — in being conformable only to a *which* question. Accordingly, *What building is the Bodleian?* can only have a description as a conformable answer, such as *The University Library*; whereas the corresponding *which* question, *Which building is the Bodleian?* could have as a conformable answer not only a description, *The University Library* — drawn from a (perhaps implied) set (of university buildings) presupposed by the question — but also a demonstrative whose reference is contained in the set, usually given by points in a visual field, though means of indicating buildings through other senses are possible.

Again, the distinction Hintikka draws attention to, between questions that contain a demonstrative and those whose conformable answers contain a demonstrative, does not coincide with the two opposed questions in the Bodleian example. For while a question with a demonstrative can only have a description or a proper name as a conformable answer — *Which Bodleian is that?* can only be answered with something like *The old one* or *The New Bodleian* — a conformable answer to *Which building is the Bodleian?* could equally be descriptive (*The University Library*) as demonstrative (Cook Wilson's '*That* building'). This observation is not a criticism: Cook Wilson was concerned to distinguish different statements sharing the same form of words, not to consider a variety of distinctions between different sorts of question.

The distinction between the two sorts of question arising from the use of demonstratives does not coincide, either, with the distinction between *what* and *which*. For while saying which of two or more things a thing is can often be done with a demonstrative accompanied by pointing, it can also be done, as has just been seen, by giving a pure description or mentioning a proper name — these not being later substitutes for what were originally ostensively conceived. A question beginning *Which of the six wives of Henry VIII ... ?* cannot today be answered with a demonstrative — unless one is discussing only portraits. But the possibility of a demonstrative answer, of answering more by showing than by saying, is brought out by Austin's distinction of 'a bill-filling' from 'a cap-fitting' sense of *identify*. Austin allows that one might 'christen' 'cap-fitting' 'what-identifying' and 'bill-filling' 'which-identifying'.[36] His two senses of *identify*, therefore, coincide with the distinction between the different sorts of identification required by *what* and *which* questions respectively.

In picking a suspect out from an identity parade a witness may simply point to which individual it is. I can answer your question which of two or more things a thing is by bringing you the thing that it is, leaving the others that are not behind. Here answering by deed does duty for demonstratives. But in order for me to answer your question what a thing is I have to provide you with some description or a proper name. Whereas mere pointing and showing are possible ways of giving the answer to a *which* question, they would not be at all appropriate in responding to a *what* question. Pointing to or leading you to the Bodleian would not by itself answer *What is the Bodleian?* but instead effectively answer *Which is the Bodleian?*

Because a *which* question can be answered demonstratively, saying which is which is generally much easier than saying what is what. For a set of possibilities (or alternatives) is given by the possible referents of the demonstratives. Thus, multiple-choice tests, which are unable to accommodate *what* questions, are poor at excluding lucky guessing: one may know (or think one knows) which of the suggested answers is correct without knowing what about the difference between it and the others makes it correct — in other words, why it is correct. A *what* question is simpler than a *which* question because it presupposes less, rendering it more opaque.

Demonstrative answers given to *which* questions, when correct, can settle the issue of the identity of (sorts of) things; whereas not being demonstrative, answers to *what* questions, even when correct, may give rise to further questions requiring further identification. Sometimes, indeed, there may be doubt about what it is (or which it is) one is showing another or pointing to. *Which is the Bodleian?* you ask; *That building*, I answer; *What* (or *Which*) *building?* you rejoin. Or you ask *What* (or *Which*) *is that building?* and I echo your question in return *What* (or *Which*) *is what* (or *which*) *building?* In the one case I could just repeat *That building*; and in the other you could also just repeat *That building*. Repetition may secure uptake of the reference by the other. But even if resort has to be made to some description of what (or which) thing is being shown the other or pointed to, uptake of the reference will be secured once the other perceives what (or which) thing the first was trying to draw attention to. That is, the reference is ultimately established demonstratively.

By contrast, when another identifies things (in either sense of *identify*) by giving pure descriptions or citing proper names, one can ask for a further identification of the things already to some extent identified by asking a (or another) *what* or *which* question. The Bodleian example thus suggests a third distinction: between questions requiring identifications that can be finally established demonstratively and questions requiring identifications that can always in principle admit of further identification through descriptions or proper names. Again, the distinction does not coincide with Cook Wilson's two opposed questions.

Dennis W. Stampe seems partly to have in mind this third distinction when he contrasts what he calls a 'subject-wanting' question, which supplies a predicate and requires a subject for its conformable answer, and a 'predicate-wanting' question, which supplies a subject and requires a predicate for its conformable answer.[37] He is not applying the distinction between subject and predicate to questions but to statements containing conformable answers to questions. Of course, the interrogative word need not be the subject, in the grammatical sense, of an interrogative sentence expressing a word question: *what* and *which* can be in the accusative case — a distinction made explicit by the difference between *who* and *whom*; or by the genitive *whose* and the adverbs *when*, *where*, *how* and *why*. But this grammatical distinction is not what concerns Stampe. His terminology is unfortunate because he is actually concerned with identification, not at all with predication — as he himself sees at one point when he observes that 'a name cannot serve as a predicate'.[38]

Taking over the specimen sentence 'Who is the man who murdered Smith?' Stampe distinguishes the 'subject-wanting' sense where only some identification of the murderer of Smith is required from a more complicated sense indicated by emphasis, 'Who *is* the man who murdered Smith?' where further identification is required than the identification already made by the phrase *the man who murdered Smith*. The case as described is that the murderer is caught in the act but the identity of the agent has yet to be revealed. Murder is a judicial concept; so while the killing of a human being by another can indeed be observed, some legal rigmarole has also to be gone through before a person can properly be pronounced a murderer. While a past tense version of the first question might be asked after judicial proceedings had been completed, say, in a general knowledge quiz, the second question could be asked after the trial only if one had doubts about the purported identity of the convicted person. The case as presented is not that any further identification made might be incorrect but that as yet no further identification has been made of — as it has to be said — the killer identified so far only as the killer. The man might be unknown to bystanders and not be carrying any documents revealing his identity. So the question arises who exactly, in the sense of what (sort of) man, is the killer. What the question requires is, Stampe says, 'what may be predicated of him'.[39] Or the killer might be wearing a mask, and it might also be presumed, as in the unreal world of drawing-room murder mysteries, that the killer is one on a list of suspects; so the question arises who exactly, in the sense of which of these suspects, is the killer.

In answering a *what* or *which* question, one makes an identification of the subject of the question through the assertion one is held to in answering: one is held to be asserting that what one says in answer gives the identity of the subject of the question. To answer *What building is that?* with *The Bodleian* is to be held to the assertion that the Bodleian is the same as *that*, the building pointed to; and to answer *Which building is the Bodleian?* with *That building* is to be held to the assertion that the building pointed to is the same as the Bodleian. Thus, an answer to a *which* question furnishes an identification of the subject of the question if a demonstrative picks out an item from others — say, in a visual field — which constitutes the subject of the question. An answer to a *what* question, sometimes also to a *which* question, furnishes an identification of the subject of the question when a description given is intended to apply only to the subject of the question or a proper name is cited. So if the *who* is understood as *which person*, one could answer *Who is the man who murdered Smith?* by *That man over there* (as he is led away after the trial). Or, whether the *who* is taken as *what* or *which person*, by *The richest man in Armenia* or *John Jones*. By contrast, *An old tramp* or *Somebody who is left-handed* constitute predications, since these descriptions are not intended to apply only to the subject of the question but can be used to apply generally.

(Even a proper name may in fact have many bearers; but is used with the intention of speaking of only one individual.)

By contrast with demonstratives, identifications made by descriptions or proper names can always in principle prompt *what* or *which* questions requiring further identifications. *Who* (*What* or *Which person*) *is the man who murdered Smith? — The richest man in Armenia — But who* (*what* or *which person*) *is the richest man in Armenia?* Equally, on being given the answer *John Jones* one may then ask *But who* (*what* or *which person*) *is John Jones?* Supercilious wordings make allowance for a proper name not providing sufficient identification: 'One John Jones' or 'A certain John Jones',[40] thus pre-empting the question, *But who is John Jones?* On being informed that the building pointed to is the Bodleian, you might ask *But what* (or *which*) *is the Bodleian?* The answer, *The University Library* tells you what building or which among university buildings the Bodleian is.

Whether identifications by descriptions or proper names are sufficient to make the identity of things known to others evidently depends on their state of knowledge. Accordingly, theorists who suppose that asking questions has to do with wanting to know things suppose a problem is presented about 'answerhood', what is to count as an answer to the question.[41] What is to count as an answer to a question, however, is decided logically by the form of the question: an answer to a question conforms to the form of the question. Proper names, and descriptions intended to apply only to the subject of the question, supply conformable answers to *what* and *which* questions regardless of whether others are thereby able to identify the subject of the question. Answers like *Gustav Mahler* or *The man who composed 'The Skater's Waltz'* are conformable answers to *what* or *which* questions notwithstanding much abysmal ignorance — itself an argument against theories attempting to link questions conceptually to knowledge.

The Aristotelian approach being applied here to questions themselves originally had regard to the context a proposition is asserted or considered in. It took the context to be determined by a notional question imagined to have been previously asked. Now, context has to be understood in the strict sense of the relationships of the words under consideration, and the thoughts expressed by them, to other words and the thoughts expressed by them: 'context' should not be taken as the conversational situation the words are uttered in — one of Austin's speech situations; or the overall circumstances of their utterance, such as the purposes or the states of knowledge of speakers and their addressees. In being concerned with a manner of conceiving objects of logical consideration, the Aristotelian approach has not deserted logic for the philosophy of language, still less for epistemological or metaphysical issues about identity. Besides, context here is purely notional. For instance, only the notion of different questions being answered is being appealed to in the explanation of contrastive emphasis.

Cook Wilson's first question is a *what* question thus requiring 'cap-fitting' identification of its subject. It also contains a demonstrative. From these two features it follows that a description or a proper name is required as a conformable answer, which can in principle prompt further questions requiring further identification (in either sense of *identify*) of its subject. But the question might have been a *which* question, so requiring 'bill-filling' identification of the subject. Now, a *which* question can have a demonstrative conformable answer; but since there is a demonstrative in the question here, the question requires a description or a proper name as a conformable answer. The other features just mentioned, then, would be unchanged. Cook Wilson's second question is a *which* question thus requiring 'bill-filling' identification of its subject. Since it contains no demonstrative, a conformable answer to it can be demonstrative, besides supplied by a description or a proper name. Had it been supplied by a description or a proper name, it could in principle have prompted further questions requiring further identification (in either sense of *identify*) of its subject. Indeed, the question might have from the start been a *what* instead of a *which* question. But given the demonstrative answer, the question could not have been a *what* question; more importantly, the identification of its subject can, given time, be settled so that no further questions (*which* or *what*) requiring further identification of the subject are in order.

Stampe also applies his distinction in a way inapplicable to the Bodleian example. On either interpretation of Cook Wilson's sentence an identification is made; but Stampe contrasts what might be thought of as an identification in an extended sense with what he mistakes, again, for a predication, thus giving rise to a fourth distinction between types of questions. When explanations of notions are given in answer to the *What is ... ?* questions typical of children and philosophers, the subjects of the questions may be viewed, somewhat artificially, as being identified. Here a perfectly satisfactory explanation will likely fall short of what the question literally requires. One usually does better by citing instances.

Stampe takes the rather different case of an explanation of a technical term. *What is the GNP?* can be answered by 'The total value of all goods and services purchased nationally in a given year.' Such an answer may be said to be timeless by contrast with the way the answer to the question expressed by the same words may vary over time as the economy improves or deteriorates. With this latter type of question, noticed in Chapter 2, the *is* cannot at all be taken as an *is* of identity: it either stands proxy for another verb or alludes to a different question to the *what* or *which* question requiring an explanation of a concept. So, *What is the GNP?* can also be read as asking *What* (or *Which*) *does the GNP (currently) amount to?* or *How big is the GNP?* Likewise, asking what or which is your weight is asking *What* (or *Which*) *do you weigh?* or *How heavy are you?* These *What is ... ?* questions are not, even in an artificial sense, concerned with the identity of their subjects; but neither do their answers predicate anything of them, as Stampe supposes.[42] *47* predicated of the years you have lived so far gives your age, which is the subject of the question *What is your age?* But *47* is predicated neither of *your age* nor *you*; instead what is predicated of you is that you have lived forty-seven years so far. What would be predicated of your age would be that it is a mature or dangerous age, not that it is 47. And your age, still less you, can hardly be the same as 47; since your age is 47 for one year only. Likewise, *I am six foot tall* predicates something of my body, not of my height. Instead *six foot* gives, though it is not the same as, my height.[43]

The Overall Unity of Questions

Philosophers labouring under propositional misconceptions of interrogative form claim sovereignty of the propositional over yes-no and alternative questions immediately and either put word questions aside permanently, as did Frege, or view their annexation by the propositional as an aspiration.[44] Had *which* questions been reducible to conjoined yes-no questions, it would have brought comfort to those who see yes-no questions as a propositional Trojan horse within the interrogative camp. Instead, the ready conception of yes-no and alternative questions as *which* questions indicates that the concept of a word question regulates even yes-no questions, alternative questions being co-ordinate yes-no questions.

Interrogative form will prove resistant to reduction to the propositional if an intimate association is found between the two main types of question. A yes-no question, it will be seen, may sometimes approach a word question generally, not just a *which* question — be much closer than to any supposedly 'corresponding' proposition. Rather than yes-no questions belonging to the propositional camp it is hoped word questions too might be dragged to, their dalliance with word questions is further proof that they are as question-like as word questions. Indeed, if yes-no and word questions have an affinity, Frege's tactics render him vulnerable: for to concede defeat before any contest with word questions casts doubt on his capacity to subdue even yes-no questions.

Emphasis or a cleft construction in questions, it was seen, serves to imply contrasts between different subjects of discourse governed by an interrogative concept. Thus, differing emphasis in a yes-no question gives rise to different interpretations of the question, which could also be understood as either a *what* or a *which* question. 'Is (it) *Jones* (who is) rowing badly?' has as its subject either what person in general or specifically which rower in the boat, and so can be understood as in effect asking either what person or which rower is rowing badly. By contrast, '*Is* Jones rowing badly?' has as its subject the performance of Jones and badness in rowing — a complex subject, as Cook Wilson observes, even although he is concerned rather with the subjects of statements.[45] The question can be understood as in effect asking what is to count as bad rowing — or which, if the performances of other rowers is being implicitly compared to that of Jones.

Kiefer has pointed out that whereas such yes-no questions — what he calls 'focussed yes-no questions' — can be answered simply by *Yes*, a *No* without further explanation would not suffice as an answer. The reason is that what is being asked is tantamount to a word question; so while *Yes* confirms that the answer to this word question is what emphasis or a cleft construction in a yes-no question serves to suggest is the answer, *No* provides no indication at all of what the answer to the word question is. *No* would be insufficient as an answer to 'Are you leaving *tomorrow*?' because what in effect is being asked is *When are you leaving?* The emphasis serves to imply a range of contrasts governed by the interrogative concept expressed by *what* (or *which*) *day*; so that to answer *No* would not merely be a denial but also imply that it was some day other than tomorrow, and so prompt the question *What* (or *Which*) *day?* Thus, while the answer *Yes* merely confirms that you are leaving tomorrow, if the answer to the nominal yes-no question is *No*, then the answer to the implied word question remains to be given. All this might have been made explicit: 'Are you leaving *tomorrow*? If not, when (are you leaving)?'[46] Answering *Yes* would make giving the answer to the second (word) question superfluous; but in the event of a *No* answer being given, the word question is then expressly asked.

It might be wondered why people do not always ask what they mean: why the word question is not simply asked without either being disguised as or introduced by the yes-no question. Perhaps on some occasions putting a straight question to another is thought to reveal a too magisterial attitude, and so some attempt is made to conceal the bluntness of the question by also suggesting an answer and offering it humbly to one's addressee for confirmation or rejection. Be that as it may, such considerations bear on etiquette and idiom. They are irrelevant to how a yes-no question can be conceived to be related to a word question.

The word question alone is clearly not equivalent to what is asked because it provides no clue to its answer. Instead, what is being asked is in effect a hybrid between yes-no and word question — something that can also be made explicit by asking a word question and then suggesting the answer to it using either emphasis or a cleft construction: '*When* (is it that) are you leaving? (Is it) *Tomorrow* (that you are leaving)?' The subject of discourse is when (on what or which day) you are leaving, which is the interrogative concept being exercised in the word question; not whether you are leaving tomorrow, which would be the interrogative concept exercised in a straight yes-no question. The word question in the hybrid introduces the subject of discourse, when you are leaving; then an answer to the word question is suggested by an implied yes-no question. Admittedly, one could answer such a hybrid with *Yes*; but if one rejected the suggested answer, one's answer would have to be a conformable answer to the word question. So, one could answer *(No,) On Sunday*. The hybrid is thus logically just one question, despite the pause in the middle and the two question marks; since it requires only one answer — unlike the 'If not, when?' formulation, which in the event of a *No* answer to the yes-no question requires a distinct answer to the word question. Besides being less economical, the 'If not, when?' formulation also disguises the subject of discourse as whether you are leaving tomorrow, though it is actually when you are leaving.

It is a mistake to think that differing interpretations of what is asked or said afforded by emphasis point to ambiguity. Specifically, emphasis in a question serves to indicate the subject of discourse. But absence of emphasis likewise indicates a difference in the subject of discourse from the subjects of discourse concerned when the question occurs with emphasis on different terms. Dieter Wunderlich thinks that *Are you Dr Livingstone?* is 'ambiguous between' 'Are *you* Dr Livingstone?' and 'Are you *Dr Livingstone*?' As he observes, the first focused question is similar to the hybrid, *Who is Dr Livingstone? (Are) You?* and the second to *Who are you? (Are you) Dr Livingstone?* The subject of both first focused and mixed questions is Dr Livingstone; that of the second two, your identity.[47] But an unemphasised question also has a subject. A change of example is less likely to mislead: in the unemphasised yes-no question, *Are you feeling well?* the subject is the complex one of whether you are well. It is a straight yes-no question.

The way the hybrids suggest an answer recalls multiple-choice reformulations of questions; but the resemblance is only superficial. Logically the multiple-choice format forces a question into the form of an alternative question (if it was not an alternative question already). True, a hybrid can suggest as answers a 'multiple' choice (falsely so called) between alternatives, as in *When are you leaving? (Are you leaving) Today, tomorrow or on Thursday?* but whereas it is in order to reject all the suggested answers to the hybrid by answering *None of these, but on Friday*, multiple-choice reformulations make no allowance for repudiation of all the suggested answers — except where a box marked 'Other' is provided. Even then, the subsidiary question *Please specify* — that is, *what* or *which* — has to be added clumsily to make amends for the logical deficiencies of the reformulation, the 'If not the others, then what or which?' formulation being less economical.

When focused, a yes-no question is conceived atypically as a word question. Likewise, a hybrid question is obviously not a typical word question. Thus it may be thought that a gulf threatening the overall unity of questions remains between straight yes-no and straight word questions. It might be argued that the two fundamental types of question must remain aloof from each other when not conceived atypically because they have distinct functions.

Whately declares that 'all questions may be considered as falling under two classes; *viz.* "*What* shall be *predicated* of a certain Subject;" and, "*Which Copula*, affirmative or negative, shall connect a certain Subject and Predicate".' He assigns the first class of question to 'the *Philosopher*' or, as the marginal heading has it, 'Investigator', who, he implies, 'brings to light truths *unknown* or *unthought-of*'; the second — that is, yes-no questions — to 'the *Advocate*', whose business is 'to *prove*', often 'an *unwelcome* truth'. The business of the first is to come up with ('*infer*') answers where previously there were none; in the second profession one aims to determine the truth or falsity of propositions 'put before' one.[48] Two objections can be noted before further criticism: discoveries are not typically made through inference, let alone deductive inference; and asking if something is so is distinct from asking if some proposition is true — though if some proposition is true, then what is so in that case is that the proposition is true.

Whately is distinguishing between the two main types of questions by reference to the purposes people may have in asking them. But do the different aims of the investigator and of the advocate line up with the distinction between word and yes-no questions? Obtaining the answer to a yes-no question — *Is there life on Mars?* — can constitute a discovery; and eliciting the answer to a word question (*How did you know what she said?*) can contribute to the building up or destroying of a case. And are their aims wholly distinct? Certainly, a barrister seeks to avoid getting to hear only in court of some nasty surprises from a witness, but simply because such discovery (and significantly, the term also has a legal sense) is required before attempting to make a case. Investigators aim likewise to establish the truth, otherwise the truth has only been conjectured; and so corroboration and confirmation of the truth, besides refutation of erroneous accounts or explanations, are among their aims too — especially if there is any reliance on inference. In short, the advocate has to engage in some preliminary investigations, while the seeker after truth has to be something of a debater. In Chapter 6 it was seen that enquiries can be conducted specifically into the extent of others' knowledge, the strength and reliability of their testimony, the authenticity of their opinions, their degree of knowledge and understanding of some subject. All these are the proper concern of the investigator besides the advocate.

Not only does the distinction between the aims of the investigator and the advocate not correspond to the distinction between word and yes-no questions; neither does Whately's contrast between bringing to light truths unknown or unthought of and proving an unwelcome truth — but one already brought to light, is the implication. The answer to a question in his second class can still be news — whether welcome or unwelcome; so the state of people's knowledge or ignorance is not relevant to any distinctions between questions themselves. Abstracting from the epistemic position of both questioner and answerer — if they are distinct persons, that is — Whately's division comes down to the distinction between a question that requires its answer (or answers) be found entirely out of the blue, so to speak, and one that requires only that it (or them) be selected from a predetermined set. Such a distinction is just the distinction set out at the beginning of the first section of this chapter — namely, between *what* questions, which presuppose only the form of their conformable answers, and those questions that presuppose in addition a set of alternatives or possibilities from which their conformable answers are to be drawn, as with yes-no, alternative and *which* questions. While a question in the second class reveals the set containing its answer (or answers), and so to that extent does not require it (or them) to be entirely unthought of, since the question still requires to be answered — that is, the remaining element of indefiniteness in the question has to be resolved — the question is not wholly transparent. And so how it is to be answered is, from the form of the question alone, unknown — albeit not unthought of. In that way its answer (or answers) can still be news.

All purely formal distinctions between types of question are founded on differences in the presupposition of the question. Any attempt to conceive straight yes-no questions more broadly results in either introducing considerations irrelevant to logic or including some word questions too. For even a pure yes-no question can be conceived as a *which* question; and focused yes-no questions are to be conceived as either *what* or *which* questions. Thus yes-no questions in general cannot be conceived in total isolation from word questions.

Notes

1 Mary and Arthur Prior (1955), p. 48.
2 Hare (1970), p. 80.
3 Contrast Hintikka (1976), p. 86.
4 Hobbes (1889), I iv 3-4; p. 14; cf. (1991), iv; pp. 21-2.
5 Harrah (1963), p. 32. Cf. Belnap (1963), p. 37.
6 See Harrah (1963), p. 32 and Belnap (1963), pp. 39, 48.
7 Hare (1970), p. 80; cf. (1949), p. 5. Wittgenstein (1956), I, Appendix I; p. 49[e].
8 Hare (1970), pp. 80-81.
9 See Whately (1913), II iv § 1; p. 66 note 37; Cohen (1929), pp. 355-6; Mary and Arthur Prior (1955), p. 49. Cf. Åqvist (1965), p. 118.
10 See Mary and Arthur Prior (1955), pp. 45, 46, 48-9.
11 Whately (1913), IV iii § 2; p. 174.
12 Cf. Hintikka (1976), pp. 79-82; Karttunen (1978), pp. 182-3, p. 208, note 14. Contrast Kiefer (1980), p. 104.
13 Cook Wilson (1926), i, §§ 56, 57, 58; pp. 117, 119, 123. Cf. p. 119, note a.
14 Cook Wilson (1926), i, § 57; p. 120.
15 Collingwood (1938), pp. 265 and 266; see also p. 265, note 1.
16 Cook Wilson (1926), i, § 59; pp. 124-5.
17 Collingwood (1939), pp. 35-6, note 1.
18 Cook Wilson (1926), i, § 59; p. 124 and cf. p. 126.
19 Whately (1913), II iv § 1; pp. 65-6. Cf. Ryle (1929), pp. 4-7.
20 Cook Wilson (1926), i, § 59; p. 126.
21 Cf. Cook Wilson (1926), i, §§ 57, 58; pp. 121, 123.
22 Cook Wilson (1926), i, § 57; pp. 119, 121.
23 See Cook Wilson (1926), i, § 8; p. 32 and cf. § 56; p. 119, note a.
24 Cook Wilson (1926), i, § 56; p. 118 and cf. § 58; p. 123.
25 See Cook Wilson (1926), i, §§ 57, 59; pp. 119, note a and 125, note a.
26 Cook Wilson (1926), i, § 56; p. 118 and § 58; p. 123. Cf. Collingwood (1938), p. 265, note 1.
27 Cook Wilson (1926), i, § 57; p. 119.
28 Cook Wilson (1926), i, §§ 56, 57, 59; pp. 117-18, 119, 125.
29 Cf. Tichy (1978), p. 279; contrast Kiefer (1988), pp. 270-71.
30 Cook Wilson (1926), i, § 59; p. 126.
31 Gasking (1946), p. 4.
32 Whately (1913), II iv § 1; p. 66.
33 Cook Wilson (1926), i, § 56; p. 118. Collingwood (1938), p. 265, note 1.
34 Hintikka (1974), p. 153; cf. (1976), p. 56.
35 Hintikka (1983), pp. 188-9.
36 Austin (1953), p. 143, note 1.
37 Stampe (1974), p. 166.

38 Stampe (1974), p. 168.
39 Stampe (1974), p. 166.
40 See Rundle (1979), p. 76.
41 See, for example, Hintikka (1974), pp. 132-43; (1976), pp. 29-31, 41-54; (1983), pp. 180-83 and Kiefer (1988), pp. 257-8, 264-9, 275-7.
42 See Stampe (1974), pp. 166-7.
43 See Rundle (1979), pp. 66-7, 241-4, 378; (1990), pp. 171-2.
44 Cf. for instance Segal (1991), pp. 104, 112.
45 See Cook Wilson (1926), i, § 59; pp. 125-6.
46 See Kiefer (1980), pp. 103, 105, 106, 108; and p. 117, note 5. Cf. (1988), pp. 259, 273-4.
47 See Wunderlich (1981), pp. 139-41.
48 Whately (1913), IV iii § 2; pp. 174-5.

Appendix

The Logic of Questions

The opaqueness of interrogative form — the inability of questions to say anything — severely constrains any enterprise going under the description, 'the logic of questions'. Its conception has to be broached through a radical divestment of preconceptions of what a logic, as distinct from logic, should constitute.

The (or a) logic of questions clearly cannot be an alethic logic. So both predication and inference are excluded. Also any relations conceived truth-functionally either between questions themselves or questions and propositions. Although a question can be related to an antecedent proposition — a conditional *if* — as in a hypothetical question, it cannot be related to a consequential proposition: nothing follows from a question, and so a question itself does not imply (in the truth-functional sense) anything.[1] A question only presupposes something, which indeed is a proposition. Thus, the antecedent proposition to a hypothetical question can be regarded as simply making explicit a more complex presupposition of a question than that accommodated by the standard forms of the main types of question.

Negation can occur within yes-no and word questions; but not within alternative questions, since they co-ordinate only the positives of two or more yes-no questions. External negation cannot be used in alternative or word questions. While it is applicable to yes-no questions, *Is it not the case that you hit him?* is only the negative version of the yes-no question whose subject concerns a state of affairs expressly conceived as such, as distinct from the implicit conception of the same state of affairs constituting the subject of the negative version of the unadorned yes-no question — namely, *Did you not hit him?*

Questions do have subjects, even if they do not have predicates. And questions as such can be disjoined, since alternative questions are just co-ordinations of two or more exclusively disjoined yes-no questions. In Chapter 6 Dummett's idea that acts of asking questions, as distinct from questions themselves, could be disjoined was rejected. With questions themselves, it was argued, disjunction occurs only when either two or more yes-no questions are disjoined, as with alternative questions, or a single yes-no question itself concerns a disjunctive state of affairs. But word questions cannot be disjoined — though the category interrogative words govern can be disjunctive, as in the (single) question *Who or what caused the damage?*

Can questions be conjoined? There is nothing absurd in a person asking a question and then immediately asking another; and this common occurrence may obscure the issue whether questions themselves can be conjoined. Part of the issue is whether, as Frege puts it, 'two questions are involved here, or only one'.[2] When an *and* links word questions there are two questions; but since there are also two askings, the questions themselves are not conjoined: to ask *Where did you go and what did you do?* is merely to ask another question immediately after having asked the first question. Sometimes an *and* only serves to make a single compound word question less cumbersome: *What did she do and when?* would not be worded *What did she do when?* though *Who did what when?* is quite in order.[3] The issue concerns rather yes-no questions — hence Frege's interest.

The notion that there could be single yes-no questions formed from the conjunction of constituent yes-no questions meets resistance from a suspicion that some abuse must be involved.[4] Is it not the deplorable practice of authoritarian rulers like de Gaulle to put to their people in a plebiscite a conjunction of two or more questions? There are two confusions underlying this objection.

First, having two or more questions in a plebiscite would not be to conjoin the questions themselves but instead to ask a single yes-no question which conjoined elements within it — elements, which when taken by themselves might well be yes-no questions. But whether these elements when they occur within a yes-no question are each themselves yes-no questions is the point at issue. The subject of a yes-no question generally is some state of affairs; so what can be conjoined in a yes-no question can at most be descriptions of states of affairs. Though the term is not being used in its strict logical sense, it may be recalled that 'propositions' are spoken of in connection with plebiscites: proposals to be put to the people. By contrast, the question at stake here is whether one gives one's assent or consent to what may actually amount to more than one 'proposition' or proposal. So while there may be more than one 'proposition', there can, strictly, be only one question.

In general, a yes-no question containing conjoined elements, each concerning distinct states of affairs, is the conjunctive parallel to a yes-no question about a disjunctive state of affairs. A question about a disjoined state of affairs certainly does not disjoin constituent yes-no questions, otherwise it would be no different from an alternative question. So both conjunctive and disjunctive states of affairs can be made subjects of single yes-no questions. Such questions are most easily framed with the prefatory *Is it the case that ... ?* However, what is implied by what Frege says — namely, *Is it true that ... ?* — would be a different question. Thus, there are single yes-no questions (introduced by *Is it the case that ... ?*) about both conjoined and disjoined states of affairs — and about hypothetical states of affairs and the negations of states of affairs, for that matter.

The remaining situation with conjunction is the reverse of that with disjunction: yes-no questions, unlike word questions, cannot be conjoined to make a compound question, though the askings of either type of question can be conjoined; in contrast, yes-no questions, unlike word questions, can be disjoined so as to form alternative questions, but the askings of either type of question cannot be disjoined.

A single question about a conjoined or disjoined state of affairs, then, is distinct from two or more discrete questions about each component going to make up the conjoined or disjoined state of affairs. As Frege points out, a single yes-no question containing a conjunction has only the two admissible answers, *Yes* or *No*; whereas two discrete yes-no questions taken successively each admit the answers *Yes* or *No*, thus allowing one to give four permutations of answer.[5] Thus, logic requires that one rejects the entire package offered in a plebiscite (as a significant number of the French did in 1969) if one has any misgivings about any of the parts of it, though good sense and discretion may counsel compromise.

Secondly, a single yes-no question about a conjoined or disjoined state of affairs has no logical defect as such; no more than single yes-no questions without conjoined or disjoined elements. The objection that a respondent may not accept the presupposition of such a question would apply equally to alternative questions, which presuppose that just one of the alternatives obtains, and that they are the only alternatives. In principle it is no objection to a question itself, as distinct from the asking of it, that it has an unacceptable, even a patently false, presupposition. Such considerations lie outside the logical study of questions themselves, though they are pertinent to the logic of the asking of questions, what can be called by contrast, erotetic logic. To ask a question — it can but need not be of another — one has no right, given one's epistemic position, to ask is to commit a logical fault: the asking of it is unreasonable, also fallacious if the question is put to another. Thus, the logic of questions should be distinguished from erotetic logic — part of the logic of debate (with others) or argument (sometimes by oneself) as also the logic of enquiry, both branches of applied logic.

Rightly primacy has traditionally been accorded to the asking of yes-no questions. Since this privileged status derives from their presuppositions being logical truths, it is not accorded to co-ordinated yes-no questions — that is, alternative questions — which are derivative. Theorists have supposed that yes-no questions constitute a species of alternative questions, whereas the truth is the other way round. But from the perspective of the logic of questions themselves there is no reason to think yes-no questions have more significance than word questions. As has been seen, the interrogative import of yes-no questions can be encapsulated by concepts exercised in word questions.

Aristotle called yes-no questions 'dialectical' or 'syllogistic' questions.[6] These epithets suggest that their function is restricted to debate and argument; but the criticism of Whately showed that obtaining the answers to yes-no questions can also further investigation. Since *Yes* signifies affirmation, *No* denial, to have another give one a conformable answer to a yes-no question is to have the other person committed to an affirmation or a denial. Yet somebody who answers a word question is likewise held to an affirmation — or, less commonly, a denial when the word question contains a negative. So the function served by obtaining an answer to a yes-no question is not simply the furnishing of premises for argument or debate — or even as a basis for inference while conducting an investigation; for obtaining answers to word questions would equally do so. Aristotle's talk of putting the question 'into a more definite form' and of the interrogator endeavouring 'to formulate propositions'[7] hints that what is special for argument and debate about a yes-no question, as distinct from a word question, is that what is possibly the answer to it has already been articulated in the question itself; so that the truth, whichever it may be, is not, in Whately's word, 'unthought-of' even though it may still be unknown. This characteristic makes the asking of yes-no questions especially suitable for obtaining confirmation, or repudiation, of hypotheses and conjectures; for only what has already been articulated can be confirmed or repudiated, by contrast with what is newly discovered or only now revealed to others.

Since obtaining a *Yes* answer to a yes-no question can serve to confirm, the asking of the question at all can sometimes have the effect of doing the contrary — that is, of raising a doubt, of suggesting that what is articulated in the question may not be so. Hence one of the senses of the verb *question* is to throw doubt on. The verb *doubt* does not take the full range of interrogative clauses but is limited to clauses introduced *if*, *whether* and *which*; that is, to allusion to a yes-no or an alternative question, which can also, it was seen, be conceived as *which* questions. Sometimes asking another a yes-no question has the effect of issuing a challenge, either to confirm what is articulated in the question or to contradict it.

It is amusing to watch the lengths politicians go to avoid giving a straight *Yes* or *No* to what appears to be quite innocuous questions. They are wise to do so: they know what trouble awaits them once they permit journalists to speak for them; for even the most innocent sounding question can be used to attempt to fasten some damaging admission on an unwary respondent. Often it is not just prudence that moves politicians to evasion but good sense: it is tiresome, not amusing, to watch a television interviewer insist on a straight *Yes* or *No* to a patently silly question.

Two factors conspire to give such power to interrogators over their respondents when answers to their yes-no questions have successfully been extracted from them. First, the articulation within the question itself of what is possibly the answer to the question enables interrogators to prompt respondents with answers not of their own devising, to attribute to them sentiments not expressed in their own words. This feature is not peculiar to yes-no questions: it applies, of course, to alternative questions, which are co-ordinate yes-no questions; but also to *which* questions and hybrid questions with their suggested answers, besides multiple-choice reformulations of questions. So the second factor of the unique logical status of the presuppositions of yes-no questions also contributes to the power interrogators can wield over respondents: to seek to evade, as politicians do, answering a yes-no question gives the appearance of being illogical. It is not always illogical to reject a yes-no question; for the terms of the question may be unclear, ambiguous or vague, so that a 'yes and no' or a 'yes in one sense, no in another sense' answer may be what the truth or the facts demand — in general, some qualified answer. *Is Prince Charles bald?* The eventual fate of his scalp is not in question; but at present neither *Yes* nor *No* will do as an answer: one can only explain that he is going bald.

Lack of clarity, ambiguity and vagueness are not confined to questions. It is rather the terms of a yes-no question that can be deficient in these respects; for the form of the question is in order — indeed, is logically basic. What offends against erotetic logic in particular, and fairness in debate generally, is the insistence by an interrogator on a yes or a no answer when the truth or the facts do not admit such unqualified answers. For it is a fault of argument with others to disallow them the opportunity to offer explanations why the truth or the facts are not as simple as what is presupposed in general by what one says.[8] The fundamental rule of erotetic logic, then, is that what are formally contradictories in the presupposition of the question be also, when taken by themselves, either true or false in content. If the state of the weather just now makes it neither true nor false to say that it is raining and neither true nor false to say that it is not raining, then the rule is violated if one insists that respondents give a conformable answer to the question *Is it raining?* Otherwise one will succeed in committing them to saying what is neither (wholly) true nor (wholly) false.

The next rule, which may excuse any initial violation of the fundamental rule, is that the questioner has reason to believe that the presupposition of the question asked is true; and further, that an interrogator has reason to believe that any potential respondent addressed also believes that the presupposition of the question asked is true. Since the presupposition of a yes-no question is formally true, the primacy in argument and debate of yes-no questions over other types of question is accordingly explained by this rule: formally, if not in content, a yes-no question can never, as Bolinger puts it, 'beg the question'.[9]

Word questions generally, by contrast, presuppose states of affairs specified only indefinitely. Accordingly, a word question should not be asked prior to establishing the truth of its presupposition — or at least gaining the acceptance of it from one's addressee — say, through obtaining the answer to the yes-no question whose subject is the presupposition of the word question. For to ask any question in earnest is to commit oneself to its presupposition: one's asking of the question implies (in Moore' sense) the truth of the presupposition of the question. But *how*, *where*, *when* and *why* questions presuppose in addition a definite state of affairs: *How* (or *where*) *did the burglar get in?* and *When* (or *why*) *did she go away?* presuppose not only some means or place of entry and some time or reason for departure but also that the burglar entered and that she went away.[10] Accordingly, *how*, *where*, *when* and *why* questions should not be asked until or unless the facts presupposed by them have been established, or at least accepted by the parties concerned.

Suppose you inform me that you once lived in a Scandinavian country. I then ask you *Was it Denmark, Sweden, Norway or Iceland?* I may reasonably do so since it is common knowledge that these four countries are the only Scandinavian countries. By contrast, a salesman who asks a middle-aged man answering the door, *Is the lady of the house in?* is not entitled to the presupposition of the question, even if statistics show that most middle-aged men are married; for the salesman has no reason to suppose that this particular man is.

There is a further reason why the asking of a yes-no question has primacy over the asking of a question of another type. If the presupposition of an alternative or a word question is false, a respondent can only indicate so to the interrogator by repudiating the question: *Was she wearing her red, green or blue hat? — She wasn't wearing a hat. Where did you go? — Nowhere.* But a yes-no question with a false presupposition can still admit the answer *No* if the denial is taken to involve external negation. Since *No* is a conformable answer, the question has not quite been repudiated even although its presupposition has not be accepted by the respondent. The answer *No* to *Is the lady of the house in?* is ambiguous: it may be to deny, using internal negation, that she is in; or, using external negation, that it is the case that she is in — or that she is not in, for that matter. The second denial rejects the presupposition of the question that the lady of the house is either in or is not in. Similarly, a yes-no question which presupposes contradictories neither true nor false in themselves admits of a *No* answer when external negation is meant: *It is not the case that Charles is bald*; but not the denial employing internal negation, *Charles is not bald* — for that would be to accept the presupposition of the question that Charles is either bald or not bald.

At this stage interrogative presupposition gives way to non-interrogative presupposition. The description (or term) *the lady of the house* presupposes that a woman presides over the house, and *bald* that whom it is true of has no hair (at all) on the head. If there are no good reasons for thinking such presuppositions true, then neither questions, whether asked of oneself or put to others, nor judgments, as well as statements made to others, will be in order when the terms occur in them.

In the course of enquiry the right questions to ask are generally those whose presuppositions one has reason to suppose are true. So the wrong questions to ask include those whose presuppositions one has no good reason to think are true. When mistakes about the burden of proof are made, the wrong question to ask is usually one with a different polarity to the question that ought to be asked instead. In other cases what is wrong is rather that the question has been asked in the wrong order — that is, before the answers to other questions have been obtained — even when there may be already good reason to think the presupposition of the question true.

Notes

1 Cf. Belnap and Steel (1976), p. 1. Contrast Wisniewski (1995), pp. 1-3, 26-7, 209-11.
2 Frege (1923), p. 380/392. Cf. Wisniewski (1995), pp. 2, 23, 24, 61, 74, 93-4.
3 Cf. Hintikka (1976), p. 103.

4 Cf. Aristotle (1928c), xvii; 176a6-13.
5 See Frege (1923), pp. 380-81/392-3.
6 Aristotle (1928a), 11; 20b22-31 and (1928b), I 12; 77a36.
7 Aristotle (1928a), 11; 20b29-31 and (1928c), VIII 2; 158a14-22.
8 Cf. Rundle (1990), p. 129-30.
9 Bolinger (1978), p. 99.
10 Cf. Ajdukiewicz (1978), p. 157.

Epilogue

The widespread conviction that questions essentially bear on knowledge misconceives questions, and accordingly the interrogative. Like many popular misconceptions, the error consists in oversimplification and overgeneralisation of a truth: knowledge can be acquired through being given the answer to a question; which is explained, not by questions being connected to the acquisition of knowledge, but by the notion of being given the answer to a question. For first, in giving another a conformable answer to a question, a respondent, when in earnest, makes a statement. In making a statement one purports to know to be so what one states to be so. Thus, in stating that something is the answer to a question one implies (in Moore's sense) that one knows that it is and so can communicate any knowledge one may have to others. Secondly, the notion of the answer to a question is an abstraction from the notion of people answering a question correctly. The notion of correctness in turn invokes that of measuring up to some standard. The standard appealed to is set by the question, what is required to answer it — a requirement specified interrogatively, captured by the artificial phrase *what answers the question*. This standard can also be appealed to in the attribution of knowledge when a piece of knowledge is characterised interrogatively. So, being given the answer to the question *Where is the cat?* is to come to know where the cat is. Likewise, in telling another where the cat is one tells only correctly, the standard here being that what one says is true.

It is not that questions essentially bear on knowledge; rather, knowledge can be conceived as related to the answer to a question. Conceiving knowledge thus forms part of the Aristotelian approach to thought; but one also grounded in quite ordinary ways of thinking as reflected by the ability of *know* to govern interrogative clauses. The existence of this linguistic facility dictates the approach to be taken to the interrogative. The crucial argument is that the occurrence of interrogative clauses after *know* requires that questions and the things that answer them be conceived in abstraction from any notion of people asking or answering; thereby indicating that questions and what interrogative clauses express exemplify a form of thought, not simply a social use of language. In taking the interrogative clauses following *know* as a starting point, insight into the more general notion of interrogative form questions specifically exhibit can be obtained, so avoiding the speech-act fallacy in logic.

Meno's difficulty shows that any subject of discourse must be specified somehow. So questions have subjects. But nothing is predicated of, is said to be true of, the subject in a question because questions only ask; they say nothing. The opaqueness of interrogative form consists in its complete inability to say anything.

Questions do not simply leave something unsaid which might have been said, as the merely indefinite does. While saying nothing, questions also specify what remains to be said until they receive their answers. Now, the first horn of the eristic dilemma can be reconstructed to yield a logical principle concerning time, that it is impossible for something to be done which has already been done. When applied to interrogative form, the principle becomes the principle of interrogative opaqueness: it is impossible for the same interrogative thought both to ask and to answer a question at the same time. The asking of questions by interrogative sentences or clauses precludes their answering them. And when an interrogative clause answers a question it cannot also ask the question. The principle explains how a question is able to specify what is required to answer it without specifying what the actual answer to it is; but also the logical incompatibility between the different utilisation of interrogative form in clauses following *ask* and *know* respectively.

Theorists of questions, failing to recognise the opaqueness of interrogative form, seek to replace it with the transparency of the propositional. Conformable answers to questions are not sets of propositions in isolation from the questions whose form they conform to; still less are the questions themselves to be identified with the sets of propositions their conformable answers are wrongly taken to comprise. *Qua* answers, answers are neither true nor false. To suppose otherwise is to attempt to treat the relative notion of an answer as if it were a direct notion. The direct notion of a question determines the relative notion of the presupposition of the question too. Proceeding in the opposite direction by deriving any number of propositions from others granted as true — namely, those supposed to be 'true' answers to a question — only conceals the distinctiveness of the interrogative version of presupposition, that a question has only one presupposition. The logical study of questions must start with questions, not propositions — albeit mistaken for conformable answers to questions.

The delineation of the logical characteristics of interrogative form establishes its general relevance to epistemology, because interrogative form is utilised by interrogative clauses following *know*. A more specific application to epistemology can begin to deliver the fresh start promised by Ryle's opposition of knowing *how* to knowing *that*. His and Austin's talk of 'knowing the answer to' a question has impeded the development of an interrogative conception of knowledge. For knowledge of what the answer is to a question is attainable only by those who can state that the answer is such-and-such, since answers are given by words or what does duty for words. Thus, it remains to be shown how an interrogative conception of knowledge fosters a more fruitful approach to epistemology without also harbouring the error of 'intellectualism' — though to be fair, Ryle has in fact done much to counter overintellectualised accounts of knowledge. The task may be embarked on with rather more confidence once the significance of the interrogative for epistemology, besides other subjects of philosophical concern, is begun to be appreciated. That goal has come within grasp now that the confusions underlying stock accounts of questions and the interrogative form they manifest have been diagnosed and exposed.

Bibliography

Ajdukiewicz, Kasimierz (1974), *Pragmatic Logic*, translated by Olgierd Wojtasiewicz, D. Reidel Publishing Company, Dordrecht.

Ajdukiewicz, Kasimierz (1978), 'Interrogative Sentences' (1934/1938) in *The Scientific World-Perspective and Other Essays*, edited by Jerzy Giedymin, D. Reidel Publishing Company, Dordrecht, pp. 155-64.

Åqvist, Lennart (1965), *A New Approach to the Logical Theory of Interrogatives* Part I Analysis, Almqvist and Wiksells, Uppsala.

Åqvist, Lennart (1969), 'Scattered Topics in Interrogative Logic' in Davis *et al.* (1969), pp. 114-21.

Aristotle (1924), *De Poetica*, translated by Ingram Bywater in Vol. 9 of *The Works of Aristotle, translated into English under the Editorship of W. D. Ross*, Oxford University Press, London.

Aristotle (1928a), *Categoriae* and *De Interpretatione*, translated by E. M. Edghill in Vol. 1 of *The Works of Aristotle, translated into English under the Editorship of W. D. Ross*, Oxford University Press, London, reprinted 1955.

Aristotle (1928b), *Analytica Posteriora*, translated by G. R. G. Mure in Vol. 1 of *The Works of Aristotle, translated into English under the Editorship of W. D. Ross*, Oxford University Press, London, reprinted 1955.

Aristotle (1928c), *Topica* and *De Sophisticis Elenchis*, translated by W. A. Pickard-Cambridge in Vol. 1 of *The Works of Aristotle, translated into English under the Editorship of W. D. Ross*, Oxford University Press, London, reprinted 1955.

Aristotle (1928d), *Metaphysica*, translated by W. D. Ross in Vol. 8 of *The Works of Aristotle, translated into English under the Editorship of W. D. Ross*, Oxford University Press, London.

Arnauld, Antoine and Nicole, Pierre (1996), *Logic or the Art of Thinking*, edited by Jill Vance Buroker, Cambridge University Press, Cambridge.

Austin, J. L. (1946), 'Other Minds', *Proceedings of the Aristotelian Society*, Supplementary Vol. 20, pp. 148-87; in Austin (1970), pp. 76-116.

Austin, J. L. (1950), 'Truth', *Proceedings of the Aristotelian Society*, Supplementary Vol. 24, pp. 111-28; in Austin (1970), pp. 117-33.

Austin, J. L. (1953), 'How To Talk', *Proceedings of the Aristotelian Society*, Vol. 53, 227-46; in Austin (1970), pp. 134-53.

Austin, J. L. (1956a), 'A Plea For Excuses', *Proceedings of the Aristotelian Society*, Vol. 57, 1-30; in Austin (1970), pp. 175-204.

Austin, J. L. (1956b), 'Ifs and Cans', *Proceedings of the British Academy*, Vol. 42, pp. 109-32; in Austin (1970), pp. 205-32.

Austin, J. L. (1962), *How To Do Things With Words*, The Clarendon Press, Oxford.

Austin, J. L. (1970), *Philosophical Papers*, second edition Oxford University Press, Oxford, reprinted 1976.

Bambrough, Renford (1951), 'Gods and Giants', *The Listener*, July 19th, Vol. 46, pp. 95-6.

Bambrough, Renford (1966), 'Unanswerable Questions', *Proceedings of the Aristotelian Society*, Supplementary Vol. 40, pp. 151-72.

Bell, Martin (1975), 'Questioning', *The Philosophical Quarterly*, Vol. 25, pp. 193-212.

Belnap, Nuel D. Jr (1963), *An Analysis of Questions: Preliminary Report*, Technical Memorandum TM 1287, System Development Corporation, Santa Monica, California.

Belnap, Nuel D. Jr (1969), 'Åqvist's Corrections-Accumulating Question-Sequences' in Davis *et al.* (1969), pp. 122-34.

Belnap, Nuel (1990), 'Declaratives are not Enough', *Philosophical Studies*, Vol. 59, pp. 1-30.

Belnap, Nuel D. Jr and Steel, Thomas B. (1976), *The Logic of Questions and Answers*, Yale University Press, New Haven and London.

Berkeley, George (1953), *The Querist* in Vol. 6 of *The Works of George Berkeley Bishop of Cloyne*, edited by A. A. Luce and T. E. Jessop, Thomas Nelson and Sons Ltd, London.

Bolinger, Dwight (1977), *Meaning and Form*, Longman, London.

Bolinger, Dwight (1978), 'Yes-no Questions are not Alternative Questions' in Hiz (1978c), pp. 87-105.

Bosanquet, Bernard (1911), *Logic of the Morphology of Knowledge*, second edition, The Clarendon Press, Oxford, two volumes.

Brown, D. G. (1971), 'Knowing How and Knowing That, What' in *Ryle*, edited by Oscar P. Wood and George Pitcher, Macmillan, London and Basingstoke, pp. 213-48.

Brown, Mark A. (1990), 'Questions and Quantifiers', *Theoria*, Vol. 56, pp. 62-84.

Campbell, George (1823), *The Philosophy of Rhetoric*, seventh edition, John Bumpus, London.

Carlson, Lauri (1988), 'Questions of Identity in Discourse' in Meyer (1988), pp. 144-81.

Carnap, Rudolf (1937), *Logical Syntax of Language*, translated by Amethe Smeaton, Kegan Paul, Trench, Trubner and Co. Ltd, London.

Carroll, Lewis (1970), *Through the Looking-Glass and What Alice Found There* in *The Annotated Alice*, edited by Martin Gardner, Penguin Books, Harmondsworth, Middlesex.

Chisholm, William S., Milic, Louis T., Greppin, John A. C. (1984), *Interrogativity: A Colloquium on the Grammar, Typology and Pragmatics of Questions in Seven Diverse Languages*, John Benjamins Publishing Company, Amsterdam/Philadelphia.

Chomsky, Noam (1957), *Syntactic Structures*, Mouton Publishers, The Hague; reprinted 1978.

Coady, C. A. J. (1992), *Testimony A Philosophical Study*, Clarendon Press, Oxford.

Cohen, Felix, S. (1929), 'What Is A Question?', *The Monist*, Vol. 39, pp. 350-64.

Cohen, Felix, S. (1959), *Ethical Systems and Legal Ideals, An Essay on the Foundations of Legal Criticism*, Great Seal Books, Ithaca, New York; first published 1933.

Collingwood, R. G. (1924), *Speculum Mentis or The Map of Knowledge*, The Clarendon Press, Oxford.

Collingwood, R. G. (1938), *The Principles of Art*, The Clarendon Press, Oxford, reprinted 1963.

Collingwood, R. G. (1939), *An Autobiography*, Clarendon Press, Oxford, reprinted 1989.

Collingwood, R. G. (1940), *An Essay on Metaphysics*, The Clarendon Press, Oxford.

Collingwood, R. G. (1946), *The Idea of History*, The Clarendon Press, Oxford.

Comrie, Bernard (1984), 'Russian' in Chisholm *et al.* (1984), pp. 7-46.

Cook Wilson, John (1926), *Statement and Inference with Other Philosophical Papers*, edited from the Mss., &c. by A. S. L. Farquharson, The Clarendon Press, Oxford, two volumes.

Davis, J. W., Hockney, D. J. and Wilson, W. K. (eds) (1969), *Philosophical Logic*, D. Reidel Publishing Company, Dordrecht.

Dummett, Michael (1981), *Frege: Philosophy of Language*, second edition, Duckworth, London, reprinted 1992.

Duncan-Jones, Austin (1952), 'Assertions and Commands', *Proceedings of the Aristotelian Society*, Vol. 52, pp. 189-206.

Field, G. C. (1950), 'Note on Imperatives', *Mind*, Vol. 59, pp. 230-32.

Fowler, H. W. and F. G. (1930), *The King's English*, third edition; reprinted 1993 by Wordsworth Editions Ltd, Ware, Hertfordshire.

Frege, Gottlob (1892), 'Über Sinn und Bedeutung' in Frege (1967), pp. 143-62; translated by Max Black in Frege (1984), pp. 157-77.

Frege, Gottlob (1918), 'Der Gedanke' in Frege (1967), pp. 342-62; translated by Peter Geach and R. H. Stoothof in Frege (1984), pp. 351-72.

Frege, Gottlob (1919), 'Die Verneinung' in Frege (1967), pp. 362-78; translated by Peter Geach and R. H. Stoothof in Frege (1984), pp. 373-89.

Frege, Gottlob (1923), 'Gedankengefüge' in Frege (1967), pp. 378-94; translated by Peter Geach and R. H. Stoothof in Frege (1984), pp. 390-406.

Frege, Gottlob (1967), *Kleine Schriften*, edited by Ignacio Angelelli, Georg Olms Verlagsbuchhandlung, Hildesheim.

Frege, Gottlob (1984), *Collected Papers on Mathematics Logic and Philosophy*, edited by Brian McGuinness, Basil Blackwell, Oxford.

Gandhi, Ramchandra (1976), *The Availability of Religious Ideas*, The Macmillan Press Ltd, London and Basingstoke.

Gasking, D. A. T. (1946), 'Types of Questions', *Melbourne University Magazine*, pp. 4-6.

Hamblin, C. L. (1958), 'Questions', *The Australasian Journal of Philosophy*, Vol. 36, pp. 159-68.

Hamblin, C. L. (1963), 'Questions Aren't Statements', *Philosophy of Science*, Vol. 30, pp. 62-3.

Hamblin, C. L. (1987), *Imperatives*, Basil Blackwell, Oxford.

Hare, R. M. (1949), 'Imperative Sentences', *Mind*, Vol. 58, pp. 21-39 in Hare (1971), pp. 1-21.

Hare, R. M. (1950), Extract from 'Practical Reason', an unpublished thesis; in Hare (1971), pp. 22-4.

Hare, R. M. (1951), 'The Freedom of the Will', *Proceedings of the Aristotelian Society*, Supplementary Vol. 25, pp. 201-16.

Hare, R. M. (1952), *The Language of Morals*, The Clarendon Press, Oxford, reprinted 1961.

Hare, R. M. (1963), *Freedom and Reason*, Oxford University Press, Oxford, reprinted 1977.

Hare, R. M. (1968), 'Wanting: Some Pitfalls' in Robert Binkley, Richard Bronaugh and Ausonio Marras (eds), *Agent, Action and Reason* (1971), Basil Blackwell, Oxford, pp. 81-97; reprinted in Hare (1971), pp. 44-58.

Hare, R. M. (1970), 'Meaning and Speech Acts', *The Philosophical Review*, Vol. 79, pp. 3-24 in Hare (1971), pp. 74-93.

Hare, R. M. (1971), *Practical Inferences*, Macmillan, London, reprinted 1972.

Hare, R. M. (1981), *Moral Thinking Its Levels, Method, and Point*, Clarendon Press, Oxford.

Hare, R. M. (1989), 'Some Sub-Atomic Particles of Logic', *Mind*, Vol. 98, pp. 23-37.

Harrah, David (1961), 'A Logic of Questions and Answers', *Philosophy of Science*, Vol. 28, pp. 40-46.

Harrah, David (1963), *Communication: A Logical Model*, The M.I.T. Press, Cambridge, Massachusetts.

Harrah, David (1984), 'The Logic of Questions' in D. Gabbay and F. Guenthner (eds) *Handbook of Philosophical Logic, Volume II: Extensions of Classical Logic*, D. Reidel Publishing Company, Dordrecht, pp. 715-64.

Hausser, Roland R. (1980), 'Surface Compositionality and the Semantics of Mood' in Searle *et al.* (1980), pp. 71-95.

Hausser, Roland R. (1983), 'The Syntax and Semantics of English Mood' in Kiefer (1983b), pp. 97-158.

Hinds, John (1984), 'Japanese' in Chisholm *et al.* (1984), pp. 145-88.

Hintikka, Jaakko (1974), 'Questions about Questions' in Munitz and Unger (1974), pp. 103-58.

Hintikka, Jaakko (1976), 'The Semantics of Questions and the Questions of Semantics: Case Studies in the Interrelations of Logic, Semantics, and Syntax', *Acta Philosophica Fennica*, Vol. 28, issue 4, North-Holland Publishing Company, Amsterdam.

Hintikka, Jaakko (1983), 'New Foundations for a Theory of Questions and Answers' in Kiefer (1983b), pp. 159-90.

Hiz, Henry (1962), 'Questions and Answers', *The Journal of Philosophy*, Vol. 59, pp. 253-65.

Hiz, Henry (1978a), Introduction to *Questions* in Hiz (1978c), pp. IX-XVII.

Hiz, Henry (1978b), 'Difficult Questions' in Hiz (1978c), pp. 211-26.

Hiz, Henry (ed.) (1978c), *Questions*, Synthese Language Library, D. Reidel Publishing Company, Dordrecht.

Hobbes, Thomas (1656), *Elements of Philosophy Concerning Body*, from *The English Works of Thomas Hobbes*, edited by W. Molesworth, Vol. 1, London, 1941; in *Hobbes Selections*, edited by Frederick J. E. Woodbridge, Charles Scribner's Sons, Chicago, 1930.

Hobbes, Thomas (1889), *The Elements of Law Natural and Politic*, edited by Ferdinand Tönnies, second edition, 1969, Frank Cass and Co. Ltd, London.

Hobbes, Thomas (1991), *Leviathan*, edited by Richard Tuck, Cambridge University Press, Cambridge.

Hoepelman, J. (1983), 'On Questions' in Kiefer (1983b), pp. 190-227.

Hookway, Christopher (1996), 'Questions of Context', *Proceedings of the Aristotelian Society*, Vol. 96, pp. 1-16.

Hudson, Richard A. (1975), 'The Meaning of Questions', *Language*, Vol. 51, pp. 1-31.

Hume, David (1875), *Essays Moral, Political, and Literary*, edited by T. H. Green and T. H. Grose, Longmans, Green, and Co., London, two volumes.

Hume, David (1975), *Enquiries concerning Human Understanding and concerning the Principles of Morals*, Reprinted from the 1777 edition, edited by L. A. Selby-Bigge and revised by P. H. Nidditch, The Clarendon Press, Oxford, reprinted 1979.

Hume, David (1978), *A Treatise of Human Nature*, edited by L. A. Selby-Bigge and revised by P. H. Nidditch, The Clarendon Press, Oxford, reprinted 1981.

Johnson, Marion R. (1976), 'Questions and Requests', *Ohio State University Working Papers in Linguistics*, Vol. 21, pp. 145-52.

Kahn, Charles H. (1978), 'Questions and Categories Aristotle's Doctrine of Categories in the Light of Modern Research' in Hiz (1978c), pp. 227-78.

Kames, Henry Home of, (1813), *Sketches of the History of Man*, Vol. 3, William Creech, and Bell and Bradfute, Edinburgh.

Karttunen, Lauri (1978), 'Syntax and Semantics of Questions' in Hiz (1978c), pp. 165-210.

Katz, J. J. (1968), 'The Logic of Questions' in B. van Rootselaar and J. F. Stall (eds) *Logic, Methodology and Philosophy of Science III*, North Holland Publishing Company, Amsterdam, pp. 463-93.

Kiefer, Ferenc (1980), 'Yes-No Questions as Wh-Questions' in Searle *et al.* (1980), pp. 97-119.

Kiefer, Ferenc (1981), 'Questions and Attitudes' in Klein and Levelt (1981), pp. 159-76.

Kiefer, Ferenc (1983a), Introduction to *Questions and Answers* in Kiefer (1983b), pp. 1-8.

Kiefer, Ferenc (ed.) (1983b), *Questions and Answers*, D. Reidel Publishing Company, Dordrecht.

Kiefer, Kerence (1988), 'On the Pragmatics of Answers' in Meyer (1988), pp. 255-79.

Klein, Wolfgang and Levelt, Willem (eds) (1981), *Crossing the Boundaries in Linguistics*, D. Reidel Publishing Company, Dordrecht.

Lewis, Clarence Irving and Langford, Cooper Harold (1932), *Symbolic Logic*, The Century Co., New York and London.

Lewis, David and Stephanie R. (1975), Review of *Contemporary Philosophy in Scandinavia*, edited by Raymond Olson and Anthony Paul, The John Hopkins Press, 1972, Baltimore; *Theoria*, Vol. 41, pp. 39-60.

Li, Charles N. and Thompson, Sandra A. (1984), 'Mandarin' in Chisholm *et al.* (1984), pp. 47-61.

Llewelyn, J. E. (1964), 'Propositions As Answers', *American Philosophical Quarterly*, Vol. 2, pp. 305-11.

Llewelyn, John E. (1964), 'What is a Question?', *Australasian Journal of Philosophy*, Vol. 42, pp. 69-85.

Locke, John (1975), *An Essay Concerning Human Understanding*, edited by Peter H. Nidditch, The Clarendon Press, reprinted 1979.

Mayo, Bernard (1956), 'Deliberative Questions: A Criticism', *Analysis*, Vol. 16, pp. 58-63.

Mayo, Bernard (1957), 'Varieties of Imperative', *Proceedings of the Aristotelian Society*, Supplementary Vol. 31, pp. 161-74.

Meyer, Michel (ed.) (1988), *Questions and Questioning*, Walter de Gruyter, Berlin.

Mitchell, Basil (1957), 'Varieties of Imperative', *Proceedings of the Aristotelian Society*, Supplementary Vol. 31, pp. 175-90.

Moore, G. E. (1903), *Principia Ethica*, Cambridge University Press, Cambridge, reprinted 1960.

Moore, G. E. (1912), *Ethics*, Oxford University Press, London; reprinted 1963.

Moore, G. E. (1953), *Some Main Problems of Philosophy*, George Allen and Unwin, London.

Moore, G. E. (1968), 'A Reply to my Critics' in Paul Arthur Schilpp (ed.), *The Philosophy of G. E. Moore*, third edition, Open Court, La Salle, Illinois.

Munitz, Milton K. and Unger, Peter K. (eds) (1974), *Semantics and Philosophy*, New York University Press, New York.

Nesbitt, Winston (1973), 'Value-Judgements, Prescriptive Language and Imperatives', *The Philosophical Quarterly*, Vol. 23, pp. 253-57.

Parret, Herman (1988), 'The Epistemics of the Question-Answer Sequence and Its Psycho-Pragmatic Limitations' in Meyer (1988), pp. 280-303.

Passmore, John (1957), *A Hundred Years of Philosophy*, Gerald Duckworth and Co. Ltd, London, reprinted 1959.

Passmore, John (1966), *A Hundred Years of Philosophy*, second edition, published in Penguin Books Ltd, Harmondsworth, Middlesex, 1968, reprinted 1978.

Pendlebury, Michael (1986), 'Against the Power of Force: Reflections on the Meaning of Mood', *Mind*, Vol. 95, pp. 361-72.

Plato (1892), *The Dialogues of Plato*, translated by B. Jowett, third edition, The Clarendon Press, Oxford, five volumes.

Presley, C. F. (1959), 'A Note on Questions', *The Australasian Journal of Philosophy*, Vol. 37, pp. 64-6.

Prichard, H. A. (1950), *Knowledge and Perception: Essays and Lectures*, The Clarendon Press, Oxford.

Prior, Arthur N. (1971), *Objects of Thought*, edited by P. T. Geach and A. J. Kenny, The Clarendon Press, Oxford.

Prior, Mary and Arthur (1955), 'Erotetic Logic', *The Philosophical Review*, Vol. 64, pp. 43-59.

Reichenbach, Hans (1947), *Elements of Symbolic Logic*, The Macmillan Company, New York.

Reid, Thomas (1764), *An Inquiry into the Human Mind, on the Principles of Common Sense* in Reid (1983).

Reid, Thomas (1774), *A Brief Account of Aristotle's Logic, with Remarks* in Kames (1813) and Reid (1983).

Reid, Thomas (1785), *Essays on the Intellectual Powers of Man* in Reid (1983).

Reid, Thomas (1788), *Essays on the Active Powers of Man* in Reid (1983).

Reid, Thomas (1983), *Philosophical Works With Notes and Supplementary Dissertations by Sir William Hamilton I/II with an introduction by Harry M. Bracken*, reprinted of eighth edition Edinburgh 1895, Georg Olms Verlag, Hildesheim.

Rhees, Rush (1966), 'Unanswerable Questions', *Proceedings of the Aristotelian Society*, Supplementary Vol. 40, pp. 173-86.

Ross, Alf (1968), *Directives and Norms*, Routledge and Kegan Paul, London.

Rundle, Bede (1972), *Perception, Sensation and Verification*, Clarendon Press, Oxford.

Rundle, Bede (1979), *Grammar in Philosophy*, Clarendon Press, Oxford.

Rundle, Bede (1990), *Wittgenstein and Contemporary Philosophy of Language*, Basil Blackwell, Oxford.

Ryle, Gilbert (1929), 'Negation', *Proceedings of the Aristotelian Society*, Supplementary Vol. 9, pp. 80-96; in Ryle (1971), pp. 1-11.

Ryle, Gilbert (1930), 'Are There Propositions?', *Proceedings of the Aristotelian Society*, Vol. 30, pp. 91-126; in Ryle (1971), pp. 12-38.

Ryle, Gilbert (1932), 'Systematically Misleading Expressions', *Proceedings of the Aristotelian Society*, Vol. 32, pp. 139-70; in Ryle (1971), pp. 39-62.

Ryle, Gilbert (1937), 'Taking Sides in Philosophy', *Philosophy*, Vol. 12, pp. 317-32; in Ryle (1971), pp. 153-69.

Ryle, Gilbert (1938), 'Categories', *Proceedings of the Aristotelian Society*, Vol. 38, pp. 189-206; in Ryle (1971), pp. 170-84.

Ryle, Gilbert (1945a), 'Philosophical Arguments' in Ryle (1971), pp. 194-211.

Ryle, Gilbert (1945b), 'Knowing How and Knowing That', *Proceedings of the Aristotelian Society*, Vol. 46, pp. 1-16; in Ryle (1971), pp. 212-25.

Ryle, Gilbert (1950), '"If", "So" and "Because"' in Max Black (ed.), *Philosophical Analysis: A Collection of Essays*, Cornell University Press, Ithaca, New York, pp. 323-40; reprinted in Ryle (1971), pp. 234-57.

Ryle, Gilbert (1951), 'Thinking and Language', *Proceedings of the Aristotelian Society*, Supplementary Vol. 25, pp. 65-82; in Ryle (1971), pp. 258-71.

Ryle, Gilbert (1958), 'A Puzzling Element in the Notion of Thinking', *Proceedings of the British Academy*, Vol. 44, pp. 129-44; in Ryle (1971), pp. 391-406.

Ryle, Gilbert (1963), *The Concept of Mind*, Penguin Books, Harmondsworth, Middlesex.

Ryle, Gilbert (1971), *Collected Papers*, vol. 2, Hutchinson, London.

Ryle, Gilbert (1979), *On Thinking*, Basil Blackwell, Oxford, reprinted 1982.

Sadock, Jerrold M. (1970), 'Whimperatives' in *Studies Presented to Robert B. Lees by his Students*, edited by Jerrold M. Sadock and Anthony L. Vanek, Linguistic Research, Inc., Edmonton, Alberta.

Sadock, Jerrold M. (1984), 'West Greenlandic' in Chisholm *et al.* (1984), pp. 189-214.

Schiffer, Stephen R. (1972), *Meaning*, The Clarendon Press, Oxford.

Schlick, Moritz (1931), 'The Future of Philosophy' in Schlick (1979), pp. 210-24.

Schlick, Moritz (1936), 'Meaning and Verification' in Schlick (1979), pp. 456-81.

Schlick, Moritz (1979), *Philosophical Papers*, edited by Henk L. Mulder and Barbara F. B. Van De Velde-Schlick, Vol. 2, D. Reidel Publishing Company, Dordrecht.

Searle, John R. (1968), 'Austin on Locutionary and Illocutionary Acts', *The Philosophical Review*, Vol. 77, pp. 405-24.

Searle, John R. (1969), *Speech Acts: An Essay in the Philosophy of Language*, Cambridge University Press, Cambridge, reprinted 1977.

Searle, John, Kiefer, Ferenc and Bierwisch, Manfred (eds) (1980), *Speech Act Theory and Pragmatics*, Synthese Language Library, D. Reidel Publishing Company, Dordrecht.

Segal, Gabriel (1991), 'In the Mood for a Semantic Theory', *Proceedings of the Aristotelian Society*, Vol. 91, pp. 103-18.

Sigwart, Christoph (1895), *Logic*, second edition, translated by Helen Dendy, Swan Sonnenschein and Co., London, two volumes.

Sloman, A. (1965), 'Functions and Rogators' in J. N. Crossley and M. A. E. Dummett (eds), *Formal Systems and Recursive Functions*, North-Holland Publishing Company, Amsterdam, pp. 156-75.

Somerville, James (1989), 'Collingwood's Logic of Question and Answer', *The Monist*, Vol. 72, pp. 526-41.

Stahl, Gerold (1969), 'The Effectivity of Questions', *Noûs*, Vol. 3, pp. 211-18.

Stampe, Dennis W. (1974), 'Attributives and Interrogatives' in Munitz and Unger (1974), pp. 159-96.

Stoothof, R. H. (1963), Translation of Frege: 'Compound Thoughts', *Mind*, Vol. 72, pp. 1-17.

Struyker Boudier, C. E. M. (1988), 'Towards a History of the Question' in Meyer (1988), pp. 9-35.

The Oxford English Dictionary Second Edition (1989, 1991), Prepared by J. A. Simpson and E. S. C. Weiner, Clarendon Press, Oxford, twenty volumes. Cited by '*OED*' together with volume, page and column.

Tichy, Pavel (1978), 'Questions, Answers, and Logic', *American Philosophical Quarterly*, Vol. 15, pp. 275-84.

Urmson, J. O. (1968), *The Emotive Theory of Ethics*, Hutchinson University Library, London, reprinted 1971.

Varro, Marcus Terentius (1951), *De Lingua Latina, On The Latin Language*, published 43 B.C.; English translation by Roland G. Kent; The Loeb Classical Library, William Heinemann Ltd, London and Harvard University Press, Cambridge, Massachusetts; two volumes.

Vendler, Zeno (1967), *Adjectives and Nominalizations*, Mouton, The Hague.

Vendler, Zeno (1972), *Res Cogitans: An Essay in Rational Psychology*, Cornell University Press, Ithaca and London.

Vendler, Zeno (1979), 'Telling the Facts' in Peter A. French, Theodore E. Uehling, Jr and Howard K. Wettstein (eds), *Contemporary Perspectives in the Philosophy of Language*, University of Minnesota Press, Minneapolis, pp. 220-32; also in Searle *et al.* (1980), 273-90.

Vesey, Godfrey (1991), *Inner and Outer: Essays on a Philosophical Myth*, St. Martin's Press, New York.

Waismann, Friedrich (1965), *The Principles of Linguistic Philosophy*, edited by R. Harré, The Macmillan Press Ltd, London and Basingstoke; reprinted 1971.

Walton, Douglas N. (1988), 'Question-Asking Fallacies' in Meyer (1988), pp. 195-221.

Warnock, G. J. (1973), 'Some Types of Performative Utterance' in *Essays on J. L. Austin*, Sir Isaiah Berlin and others, The Clarendon Press, Oxford.

Warnock, G. J. (1976), 'Imperatives and Meaning' in H. D. Lewis (ed.) *Contemporary British Philosophy*, Fourth Series, Allen and Unwin, London, pp. 292-305; reprinted in G. J. Warnock, *Morality and Language* (1983), Basil Blackwell, Oxford, pp. 126-37.

Welbourne, Michael (1979), 'The Transmission of Knowledge', *The Philosophical Quarterly*, Vol. 29, pp. 1-9.

Welbourne, Michael (1980), 'Knowing and Believing', *Philosophy*, Vol. 55, pp. 317-28.

Welbourne, Michael (1986a), *The Community of Knowledge*, Aberdeen University Press, Aberdeen.

Welbourne, Michael (1986b), 'Meno's Paradox', *Philosophy*, Vol. 61, pp. 229-43.

Welbourne, Michael (1989), 'A Puzzle About Telling', *Philosophy*, Vol. 64, pp. 175-85.

Whately, Richard (1913), *Elements of Logic*; reprinted from the ninth (octavo) edition, Longman, Green, and Co., London.

Wheatley, J. M. O. (1955), 'Deliberative Questions', *Analysis*, Vol. 15, pp. 49-60.

White, Alan R. (1972), 'What We Believe', *American Philosophical Quarterly*, Monograph Series No. 6, pp. 69-84.

White, Alan R. (1982), *The Nature of Knowledge*, Rowman and Littlefield, Totowa, New Jersey.

White, Nicholas P. (1974), 'Inquiry', *The Review of Metaphysics*, Vol. 28, pp. 289-310.

Williams, B. A. O. (1963), 'Imperative Inference', *Analysis*, Vol. 23, Supplement, pp. 30-36; reprinted in Williams (1973), pp. 152-59.

Williams, Bernard (1973), *Problems of the Self, Philosophical Papers 1956-1972*, Cambridge University Press, Cambridge; reprinted 1979.

Wilson, Deirdre and Sperber, Dan (1988), 'Mood and the Analysis of Non-declarative Sentences' in *Human Agency: Language, Duty, and Value*, edited by Jonathan Dancy, J. M. E. Moravcsik, and C. C. W. Taylor, Stanford University Press, Stanford, California.

Wisniewski, Andrzej (1995), *The Posing of Questions: Logical Foundations of Erotetic Inferences*, Kluwer Academic Publishers, Dordrecht.

Wittgenstein, Ludwig (1956), *Remarks on the Foundations of Mathematics*, translated by G. E. M. Anscombe, Basil Blackwell, Oxford.

Wittgenstein, Ludwig (1958), *Philosophical Investigations*, translated by G. E. M. Anscombe, second edition, Basil Blackwell, Oxford.

Wittgenstein, Ludwig (1961), *Tractatus Logico-Philosophicus*, translated by D. F. Pears and B. F. McGuinness, Routledge and Kegan Paul Ltd, London, reprinted 1974.

Wittgenstein, Ludwig (1981), *Zettel*, second edition; translated by G. E. M. Anscombe, Basil Blackwell, Oxford.

Woozley, A. D. (1953), 'Knowing and Not Knowing', *Proceedings of the Aristotelian Society*, Vol. 53, pp. 151-72.

Wunderlich, Dieter (1981), 'Questions about Questions' in Klein and Levelt (1981), pp. 131-58.

Index